26

Story & Art by
Taeko Watanabe

Contents

Story Thus Far

It is the end of the Bakufu era, the third year of Bunkyu (1863) in Kyoto. The Shinsengumi is a band of warriors formed to protect the shogun.

Tominaga Sei, the daughter of a former Bakufu *bushi*, joined the Shinsengumi disguised as a boy by the name of Kamiya Seizaburo to avenge her father and brother. She has continued her training under the only person in the Shinsengumi who knows her true identity, Okita Soji, and she aspires to become a true *bushi*.

The beloved Shinsengumi captain Kondo is sent on a journey to Hiroshima once again to keep an eye on Choshu-han's movements, only to witness the downfall of the Bakufu's authority. In order to welcome the disenchanted Kondo back to Kyoto, vice captain Hijikata redeems the prostitute Miyuki-Dayu for him, releasing her to live with him alongside the Shinsengumi.

It seems at first as if Kondo and Miyuki will begin a happy life together, but Hijikata orders Sei to keep an eye on Miyuki. On Kondo and Miyuki's second night together, Miyuki suddenly begins to cry and pleads for forgiveness. What does she mean by this…?

Characters

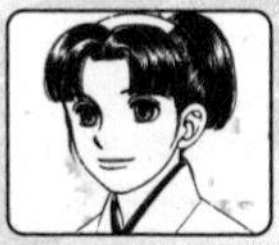

Tominaga Sei
She disguises herself as a boy to enter the Mibu-Roshi. She trains under Soji, aspiring to become a true *bushi*. But secretly, she is in love with Soji.

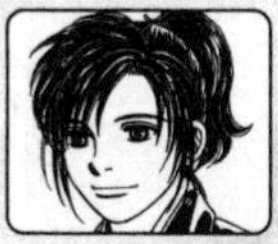

Okita Soji
Assistant vice captain of the Shinsengumi and licensed master of the Ten'nen Rishin-ryu. He supports the troop alongside Kondo and Hijikata and guides Seizaburo with a kind yet firm hand.

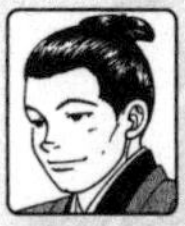

Kondo Isami
Captain of the Shinsengumi and fourth grandmaster of the Ten'nen Rishin-ryu. A passionate, warm and well-respected leader.

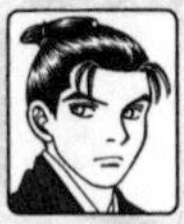

Hijikata Toshizo
Vice captain of the Shinsengumi. He commands both the group and himself with a rigid strictness. He is also known as the "Oni vice captain."

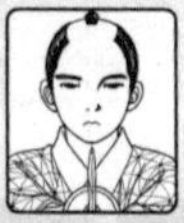

Saito Hajime
Assistant vice captain. He was a friend of Sei's older brother. Sei is attached to him in place of her lost brother.

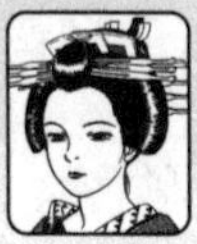

Miyuki-Dayu
A *yujo* (prostitute) Kondo met for the first time in Shinmachi, Osaka. There is a rumor that she is the daughter of a *bushi* from Kanazawa.

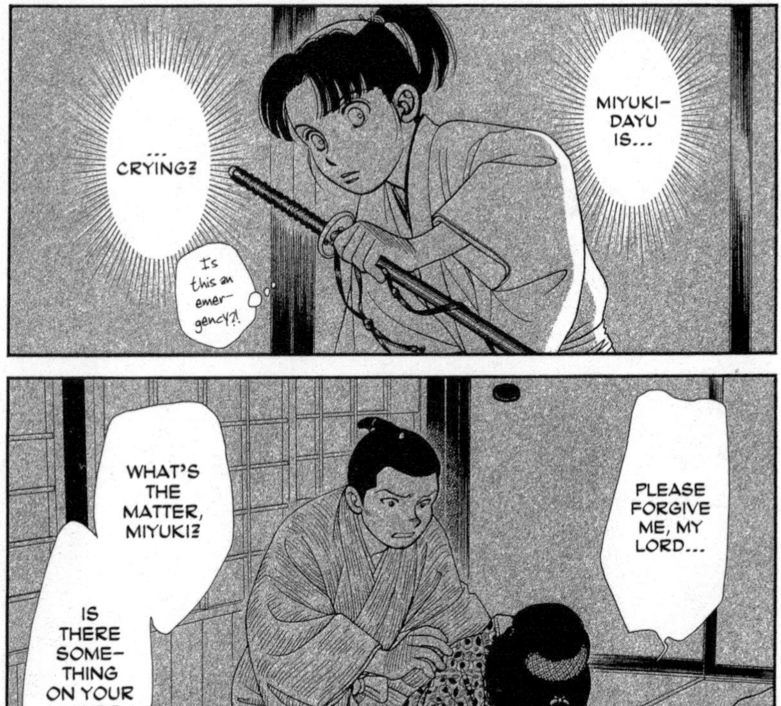
MIYUKI-DAYU IS...
...CRYING?
Is this an emergency?!
PLEASE FORGIVE ME, MY LORD...
WHAT'S THE MATTER, MIYUKI?
IS THERE SOMETHING ON YOUR MIND?

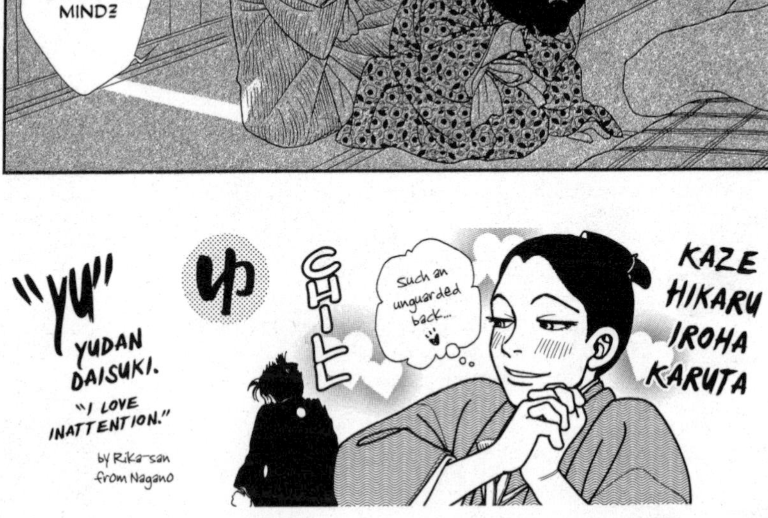
KAZE HIKARU IROHA KARUTA
Such an unguarded back...
ゆ
"YU"
YUDAN DAISUKI.
"I LOVE INATTENTION."
by Rika-san from Nagano

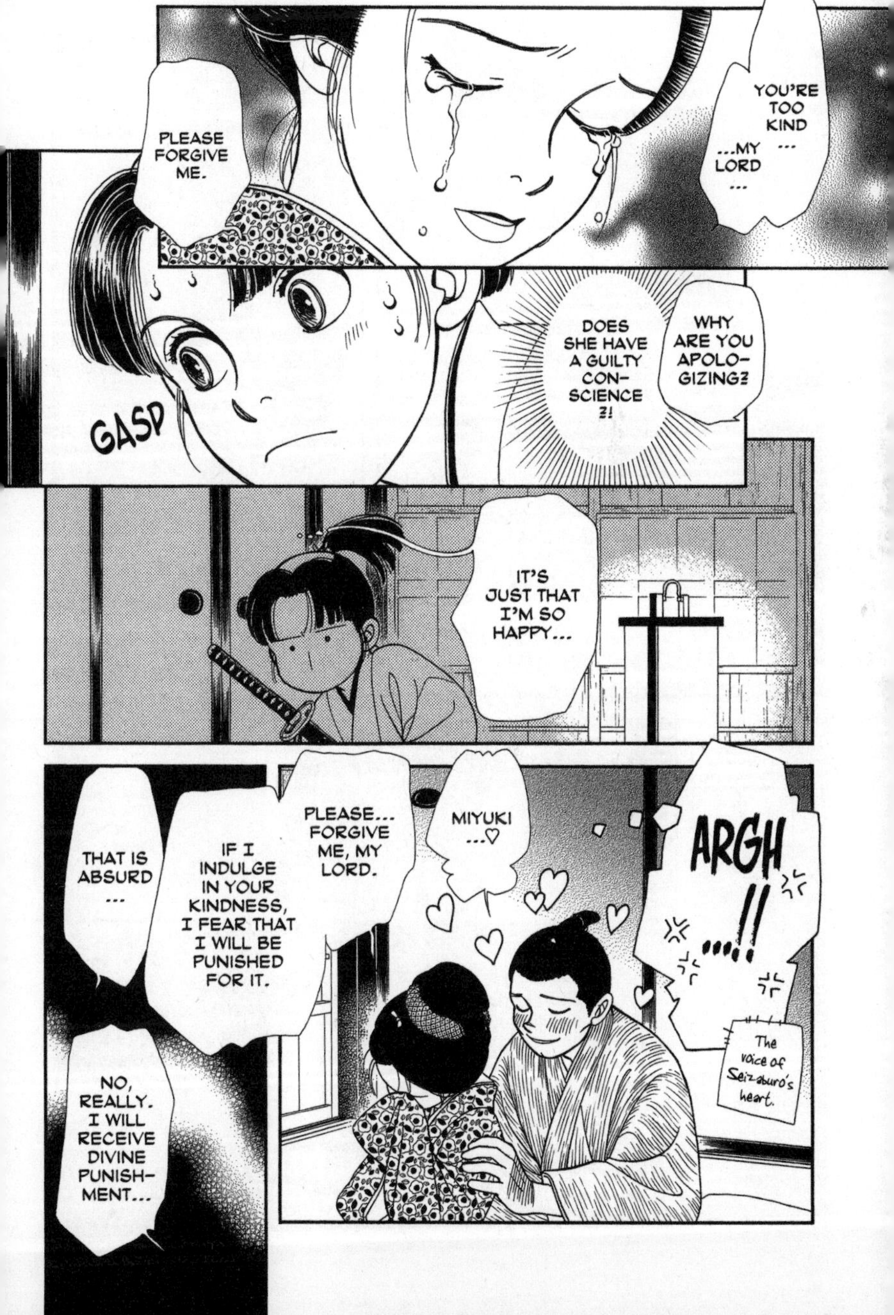
YOU'RE TOO KIND ... ...MY LORD ...
PLEASE FORGIVE ME.
WHY ARE YOU APOLOGIZING?
DOES SHE HAVE A GUILTY CON-SCIENCE ?!
GASP
IT'S JUST THAT I'M SO HAPPY...
ARGH ....!!
The voice of Seizaburo's heart.
MIYUKI ...♡
PLEASE... FORGIVE ME, MY LORD.
IF I INDULGE IN YOUR KINDNESS, I FEAR THAT I WILL BE PUNISHED FOR IT.
THAT IS ABSURD ...
NO, REALLY. I WILL RECEIVE DIVINE PUNISH-MENT...

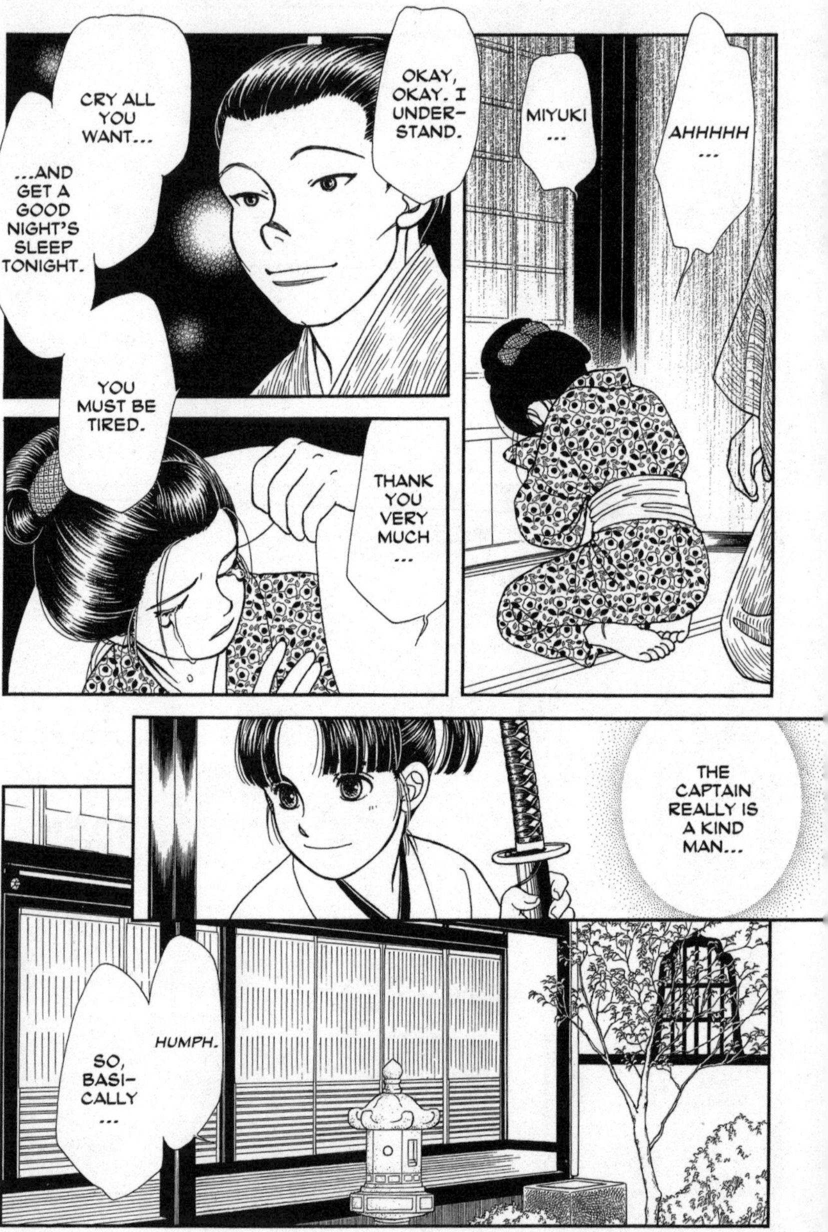
AHHHHH...
MIYUKI...
OKAY, OKAY. I UNDER-STAND.
CRY ALL YOU WANT...
...AND GET A GOOD NIGHT'S SLEEP TONIGHT.
YOU MUST BE TIRED.
THANK YOU VERY MUCH...
THE CAPTAIN REALLY IS A KIND MAN...
HUMPH.
SO, BASI-CALLY...

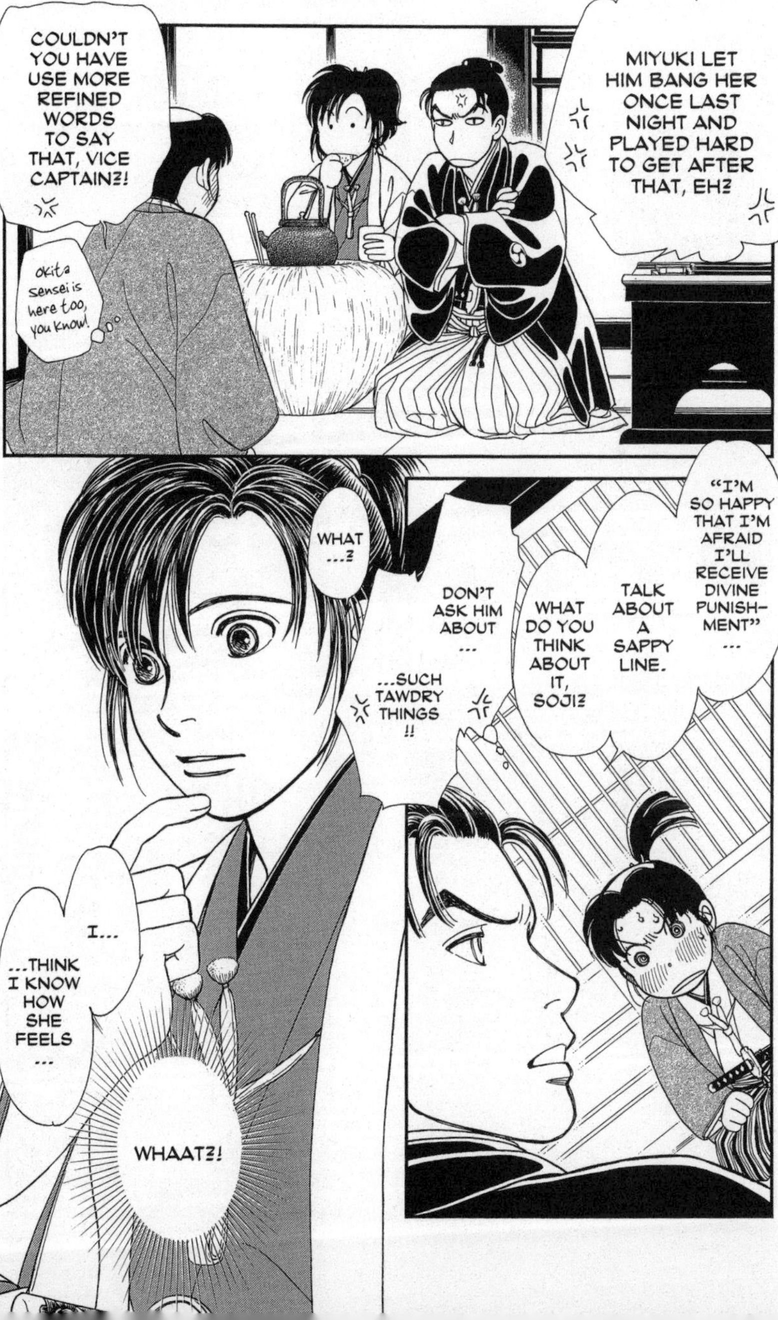
MIYUKI LET HIM BANG HER ONCE LAST NIGHT AND PLAYED HARD TO GET AFTER THAT, EH?
COULDN'T YOU HAVE USE MORE REFINED WORDS TO SAY THAT, VICE CAPTAIN?!
Okita sensei is here too, you know!
"I'M SO HAPPY THAT I'M AFRAID I'LL RECEIVE DIVINE PUNISHMENT"...
TALK ABOUT A SAPPY LINE.
WHAT DO YOU THINK ABOUT IT, SOJI?
DON'T ASK HIM ABOUT...
...SUCH TAWDRY THINGS!!
WHAT...?
I...
...THINK I KNOW HOW SHE FEELS...
WHAAT?!

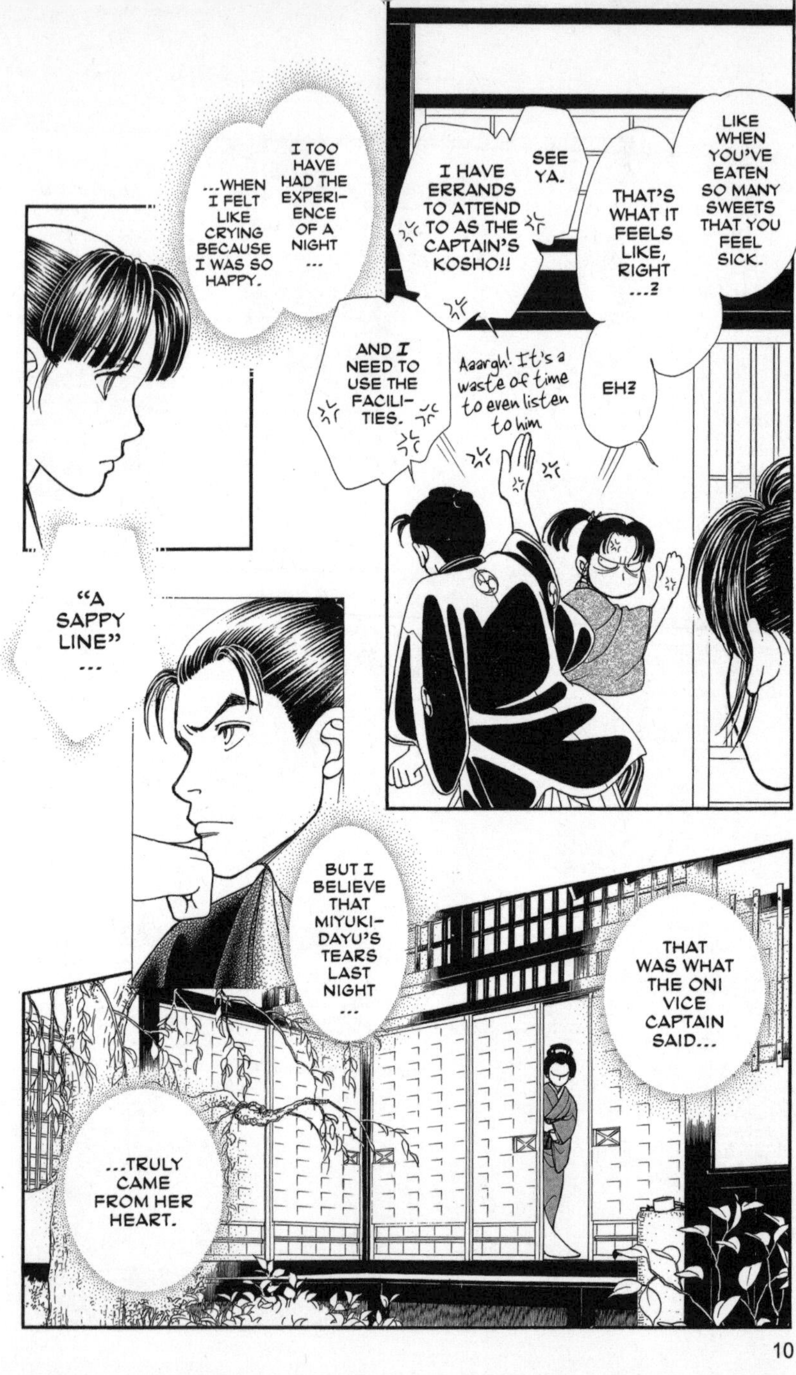
LIKE WHEN YOU'VE EATEN SO MANY SWEETS THAT YOU FEEL SICK.
THAT'S WHAT IT FEELS LIKE, RIGHT...?
SEE YA.
I HAVE ERRANDS TO ATTEND TO AS THE CAPTAIN'S KOSHO!!
EH?
Aaargh! It's a waste of time to even listen to him.
AND I NEED TO USE THE FACILITIES.
I TOO HAVE HAD THE EXPERIENCE OF A NIGHT...
...WHEN I FELT LIKE CRYING BECAUSE I WAS SO HAPPY.
"A SAPPY LINE"...
THAT WAS WHAT THE ONI VICE CAPTAIN SAID...
BUT I BELIEVE THAT MIYUKI-DAYU'S TEARS LAST NIGHT...
...TRULY CAME FROM HER HEART.

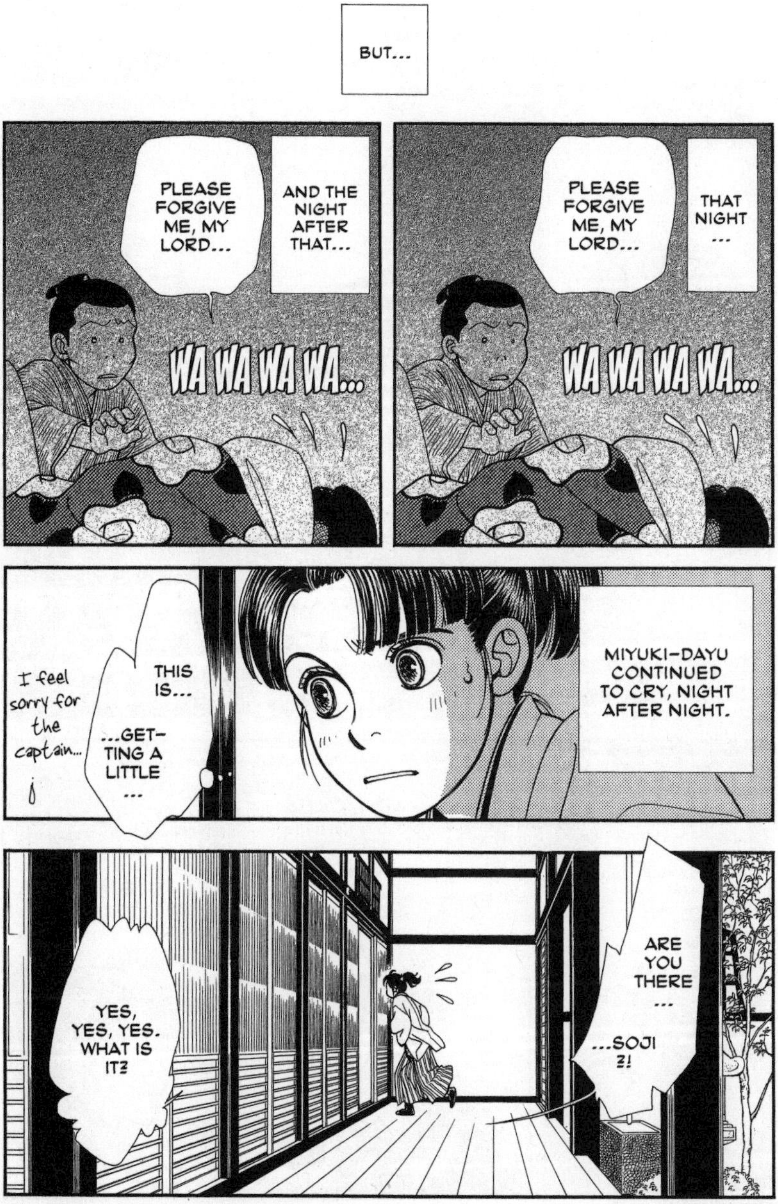
BUT...
THAT NIGHT ...
PLEASE FORGIVE ME, MY LORD...
WA WA WA WA...
AND THE NIGHT AFTER THAT...
PLEASE FORGIVE ME, MY LORD...
WA WA WA WA...
MIYUKI-DAYU CONTINUED TO CRY, NIGHT AFTER NIGHT.
THIS IS... ...GET-TING A LITTLE ...
I feel sorry for the captain...
ARE YOU THERE ... ...SOJI ?!
YES, YES, YES. WHAT IS IT?

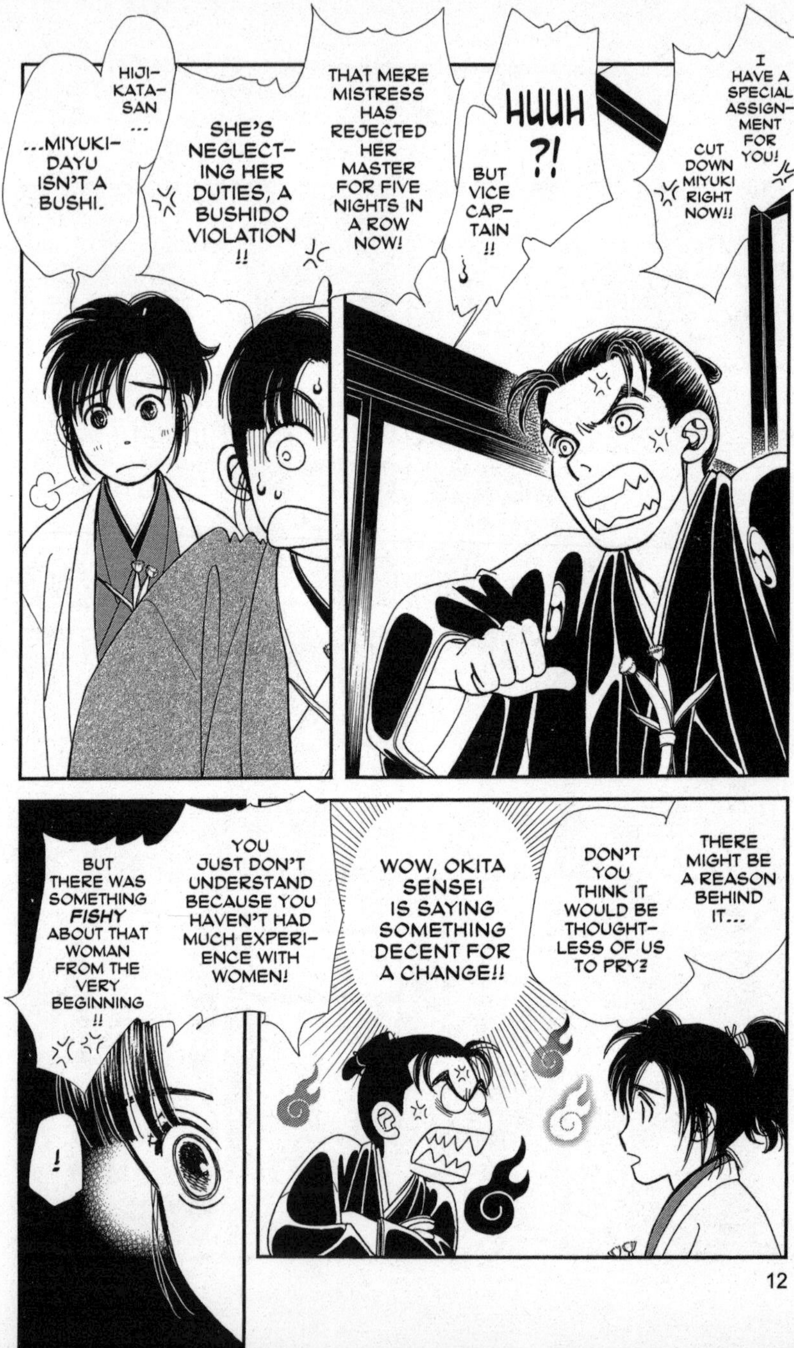

I HAVE A SPECIAL ASSIGNMENT FOR YOU!
CUT DOWN MIYUKI RIGHT NOW!!
HUUH ?!
BUT VICE CAPTAIN !!
THAT MERE MISTRESS HAS REJECTED HER MASTER FOR FIVE NIGHTS IN A ROW NOW!
SHE'S NEGLECTING HER DUTIES, A BUSHIDO VIOLATION !!
HIJIKATA-SAN ...
...MIYUKI-DAYU ISN'T A BUSHI.
THERE MIGHT BE A REASON BEHIND IT...
DON'T YOU THINK IT WOULD BE THOUGHTLESS OF US TO PRY?
WOW, OKITA SENSEI IS SAYING SOMETHING DECENT FOR A CHANGE!!
YOU JUST DON'T UNDERSTAND BECAUSE YOU HAVEN'T HAD MUCH EXPERIENCE WITH WOMEN!
BUT THERE WAS SOMETHING *FISHY* ABOUT THAT WOMAN FROM THE VERY BEGINNING !!
!

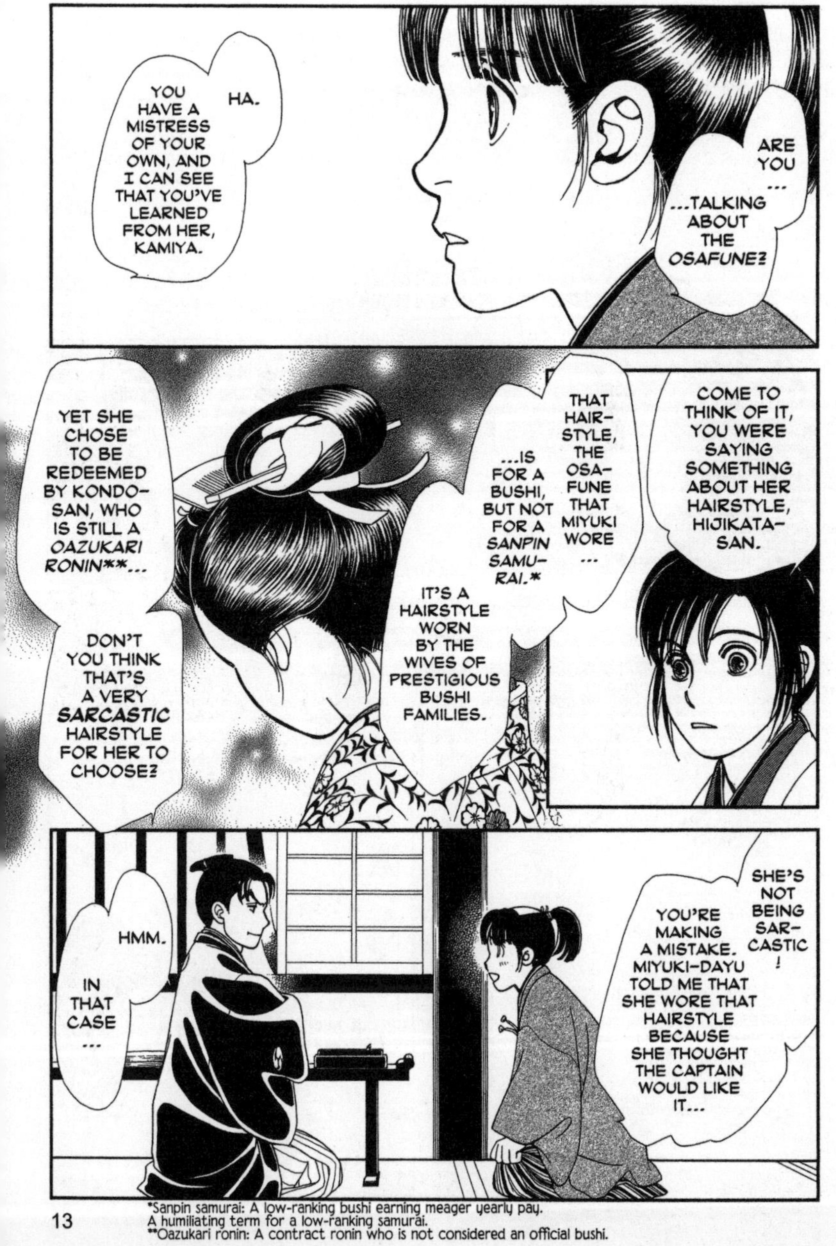
ARE YOU ... ...TALKING ABOUT THE OSAFUNE?
HA.
YOU HAVE A MISTRESS OF YOUR OWN, AND I CAN SEE THAT YOU'VE LEARNED FROM HER, KAMIYA.
COME TO THINK OF IT, YOU WERE SAYING SOMETHING ABOUT HER HAIRSTYLE, HIJIKATA-SAN.
THAT HAIRSTYLE, THE OSAFUNE THAT MIYUKI WORE ...
...IS FOR A BUSHI, BUT NOT FOR A SANPIN SAMURAI.*
IT'S A HAIRSTYLE WORN BY THE WIVES OF PRESTIGIOUS BUSHI FAMILIES.
YET SHE CHOSE TO BE REDEEMED BY KONDO-SAN, WHO IS STILL A OAZUKARI RONIN**...
DON'T YOU THINK THAT'S A VERY SARCASTIC HAIRSTYLE FOR HER TO CHOOSE?
SHE'S NOT BEING SARCASTIC!
YOU'RE MAKING A MISTAKE. MIYUKI-DAYU TOLD ME THAT SHE WORE THAT HAIRSTYLE BECAUSE SHE THOUGHT THE CAPTAIN WOULD LIKE IT...
HMM.
IN THAT CASE ...

*Sanpin samurai: A low-ranking bushi earning meager yearly pay. A humiliating term for a low-ranking samurai.
**Oazukari ronin: A contract ronin who is not considered an official bushi.

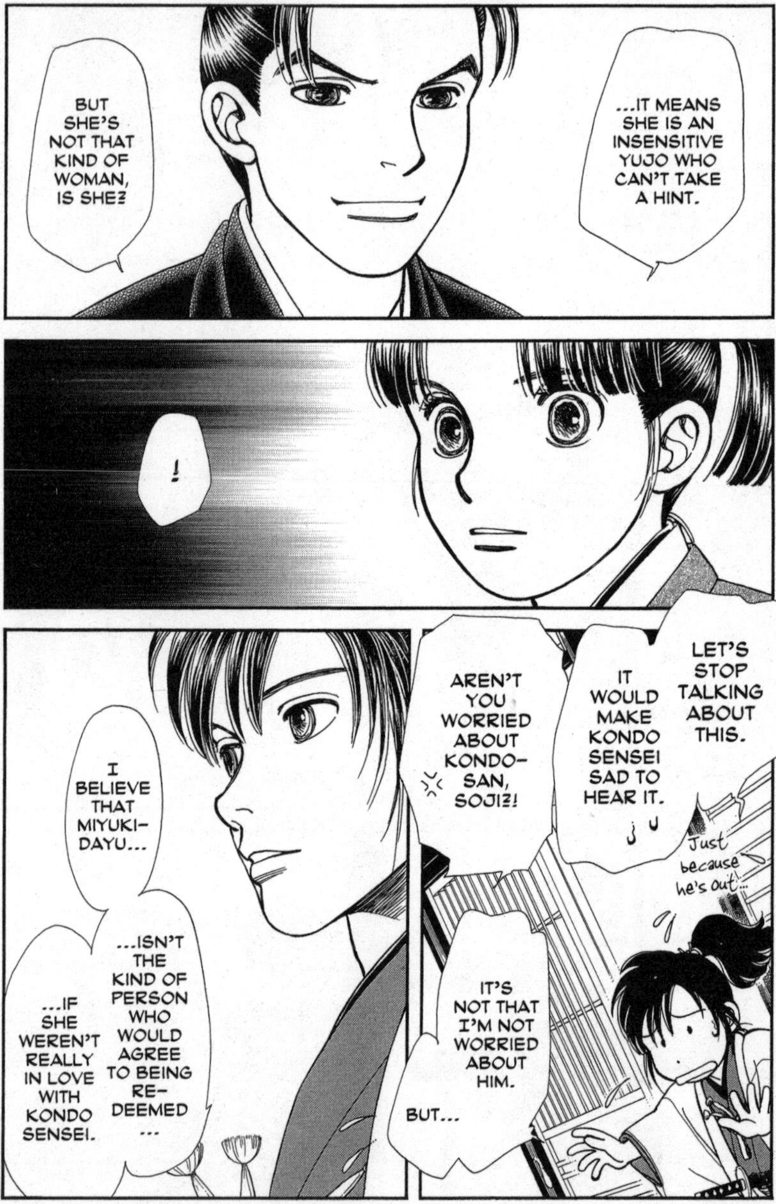
...IT MEANS SHE IS AN INSENSITIVE YUJO WHO CAN'T TAKE A HINT.
BUT SHE'S NOT THAT KIND OF WOMAN, IS SHE?
!
LET'S STOP TALKING ABOUT THIS.
IT WOULD MAKE KONDO SENSEI SAD TO HEAR IT.
AREN'T YOU WORRIED ABOUT KONDO-SAN, SOJI?!
Just because he's out...
IT'S NOT THAT I'M NOT WORRIED ABOUT HIM.
BUT...
I BELIEVE THAT MIYUKI-DAYU...
...ISN'T THE KIND OF PERSON WHO WOULD AGREE TO BEING RE-DEEMED...
...IF SHE WEREN'T REALLY IN LOVE WITH KONDO SENSEI.

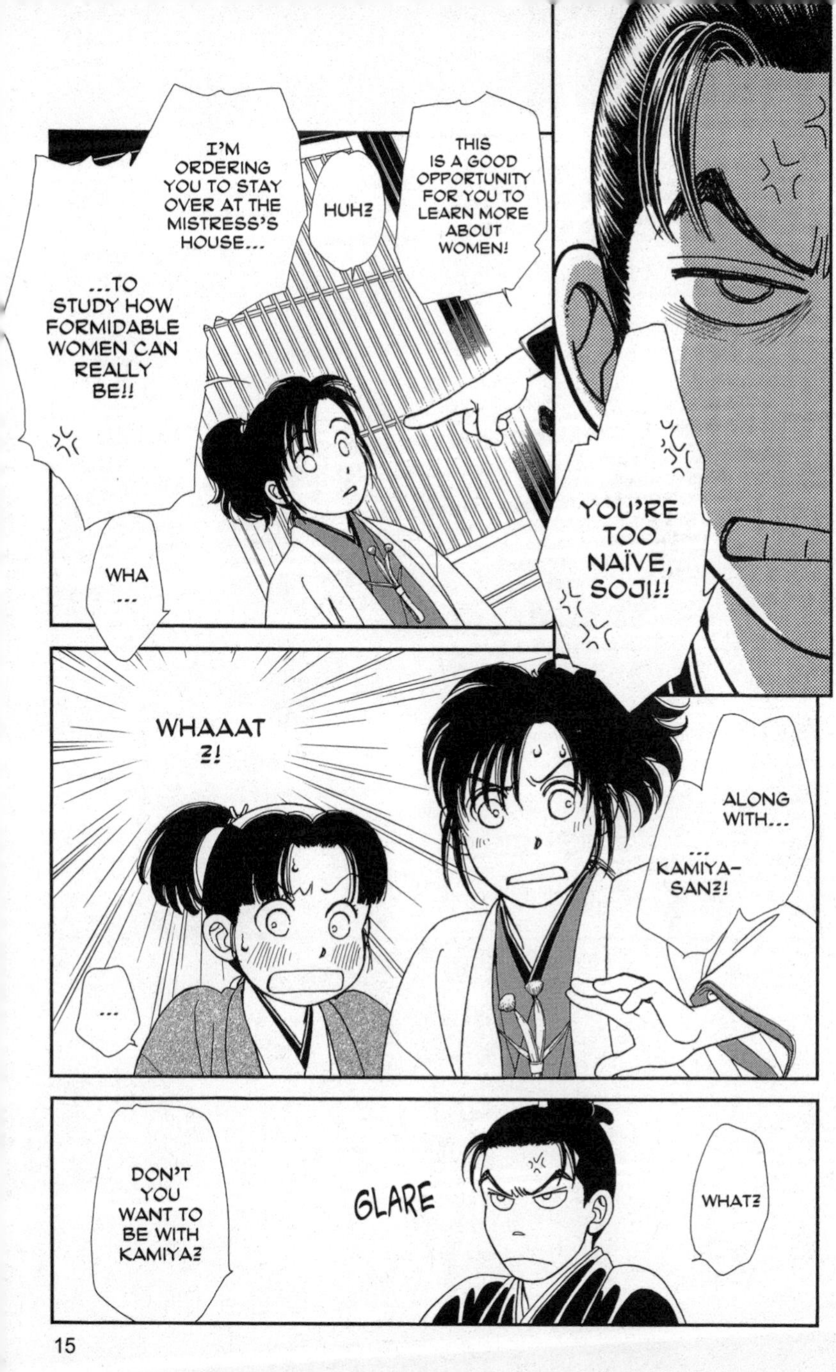
YOU'RE TOO NAÏVE, SOJI!!
THIS IS A GOOD OPPORTUNITY FOR YOU TO LEARN MORE ABOUT WOMEN!
HUH?
I'M ORDERING YOU TO STAY OVER AT THE MISTRESS'S HOUSE...
...TO STUDY HOW FORMIDABLE WOMEN CAN REALLY BE!!
WHA...
ALONG WITH...
...KAMIYA-SAN?!
WHAAAT?!
...
WHAT?
GLARE
DON'T YOU WANT TO BE WITH KAMIYA?

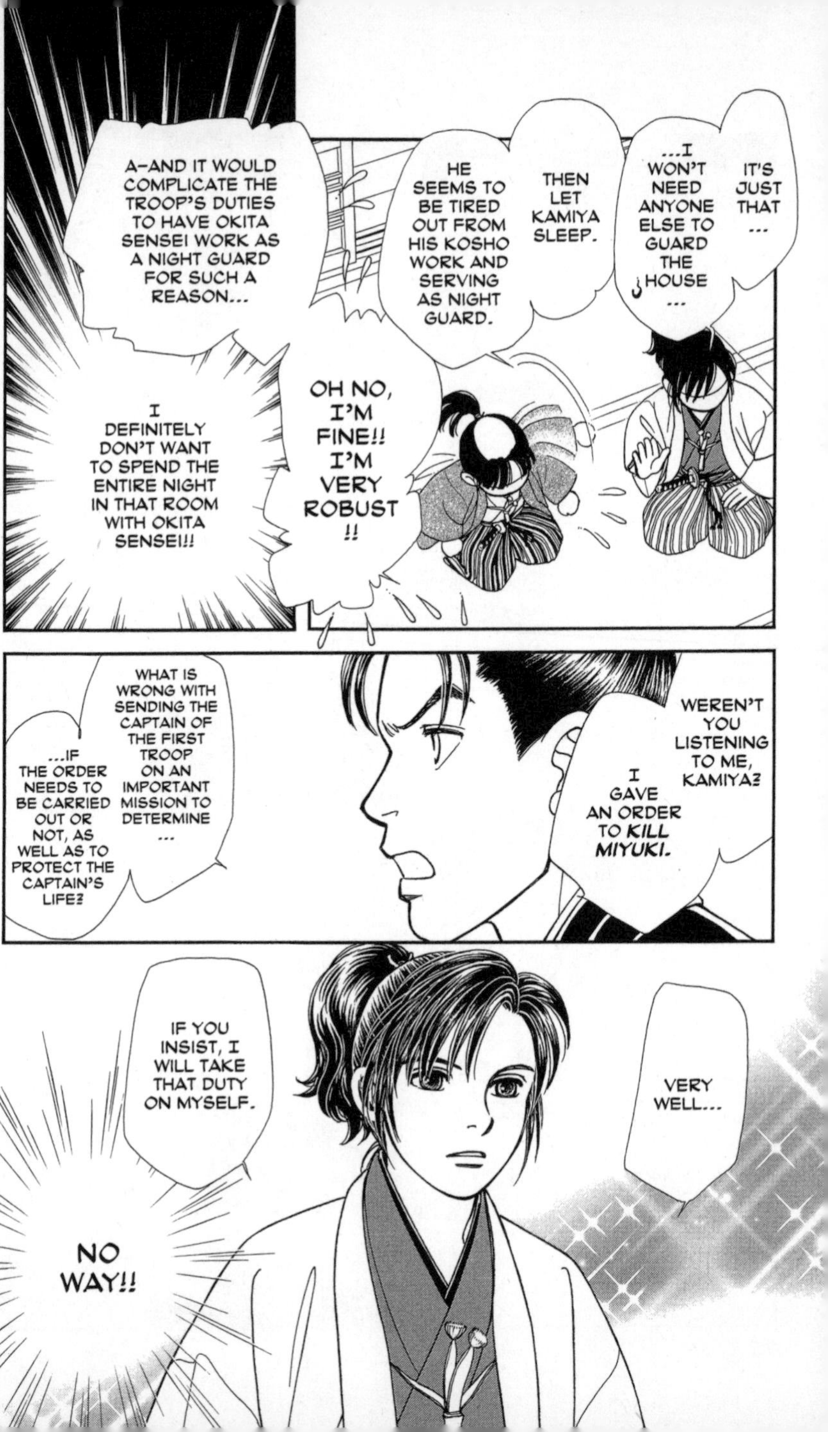
IT'S JUST THAT ...
...I WON'T NEED ANYONE ELSE TO GUARD THE HOUSE ...
THEN LET KAMIYA SLEEP.
HE SEEMS TO BE TIRED OUT FROM HIS KOSHO WORK AND SERVING AS NIGHT GUARD.
OH NO, I'M FINE!! I'M VERY ROBUST !!
A-AND IT WOULD COMPLICATE THE TROOP'S DUTIES TO HAVE OKITA SENSEI WORK AS A NIGHT GUARD FOR SUCH A REASON...
I DEFINITELY DON'T WANT TO SPEND THE ENTIRE NIGHT IN THAT ROOM WITH OKITA SENSEI!!!
WEREN'T YOU LISTENING TO ME, KAMIYA?
I GAVE AN ORDER TO KILL MIYUKI.
WHAT IS WRONG WITH SENDING THE CAPTAIN OF THE FIRST TROOP ON AN IMPORTANT MISSION TO DETERMINE ...
...IF THE ORDER NEEDS TO BE CARRIED OUT OR NOT, AS WELL AS TO PROTECT THE CAPTAIN'S LIFE?
VERY WELL...
IF YOU INSIST, I WILL TAKE THAT DUTY ON MYSELF.
NO WAY!!

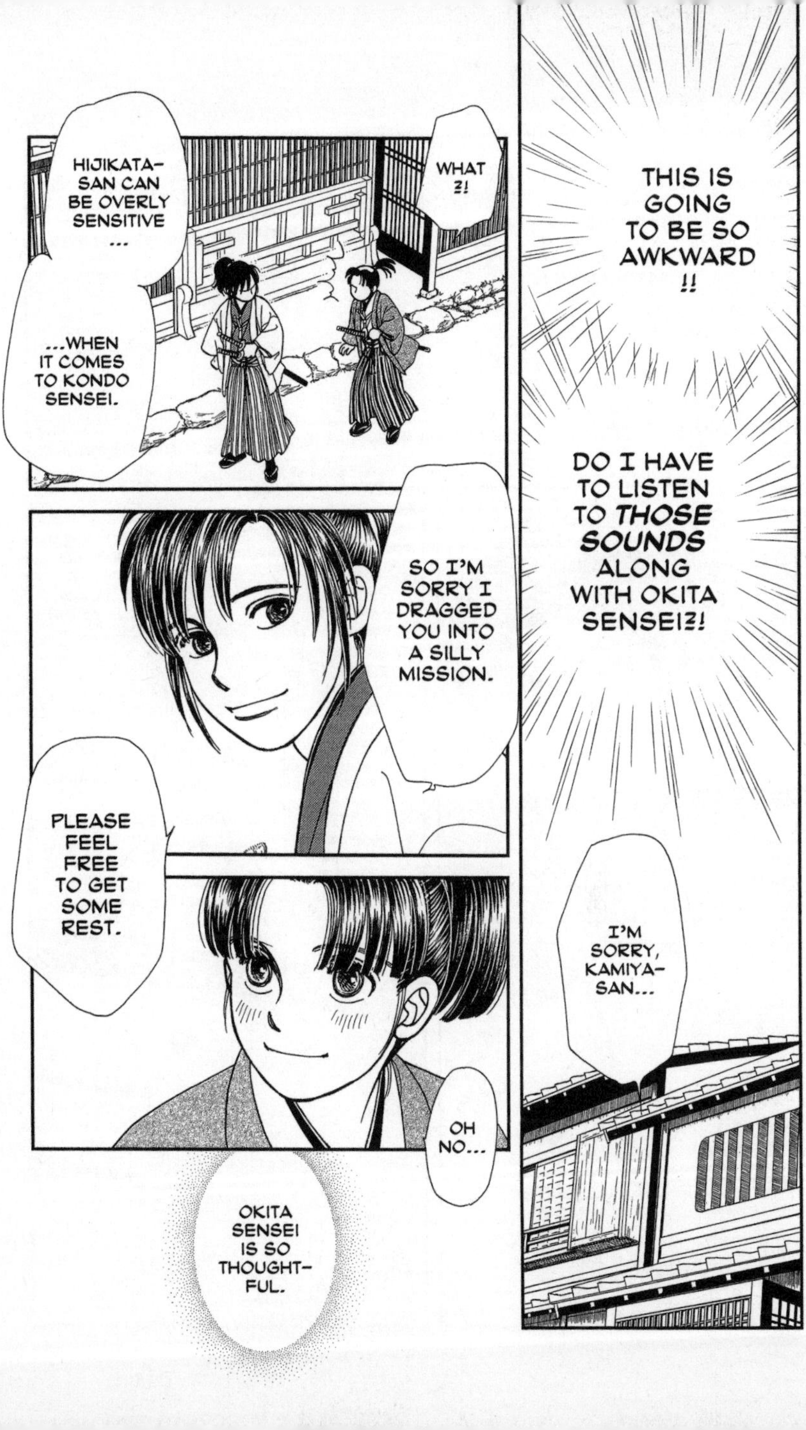
THIS IS GOING TO BE SO AWKWARD!!
DO I HAVE TO LISTEN TO *THOSE SOUNDS* ALONG WITH OKITA SENSEI?!
I'M SORRY, KAMIYA-SAN...
WHAT?!
HIJIKATA-SAN CAN BE OVERLY SENSITIVE...
...WHEN IT COMES TO KONDO SENSEI.
SO I'M SORRY I DRAGGED YOU INTO A SILLY MISSION.
PLEASE FEEL FREE TO GET SOME REST.
OH NO...
OKITA SENSEI IS SO THOUGHTFUL.

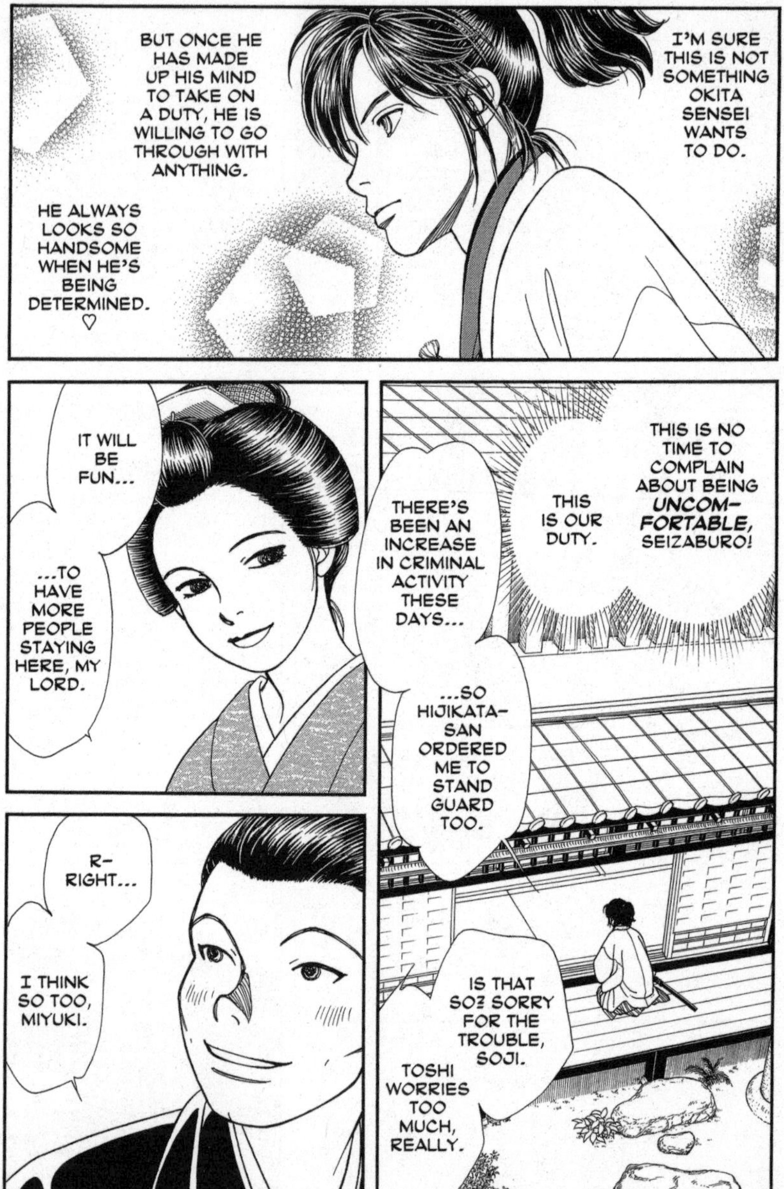
I'M SURE THIS IS NOT SOMETHING OKITA SENSEI WANTS TO DO.
BUT ONCE HE HAS MADE UP HIS MIND TO TAKE ON A DUTY, HE IS WILLING TO GO THROUGH WITH ANYTHING.
HE ALWAYS LOOKS SO HANDSOME WHEN HE'S BEING DETERMINED. ♡
THIS IS NO TIME TO COMPLAIN ABOUT BEING *UNCOMFORTABLE,* SEIZABURO!
THIS IS OUR DUTY.
THERE'S BEEN AN INCREASE IN CRIMINAL ACTIVITY THESE DAYS...
...SO HIJIKATA-SAN ORDERED ME TO STAND GUARD TOO.
IS THAT SO? SORRY FOR THE TROUBLE, SOJI.
TOSHI WORRIES TOO MUCH, REALLY.
IT WILL BE FUN...
...TO HAVE MORE PEOPLE STAYING HERE, MY LORD.
R-RIGHT...
I THINK SO TOO, MIYUKI.

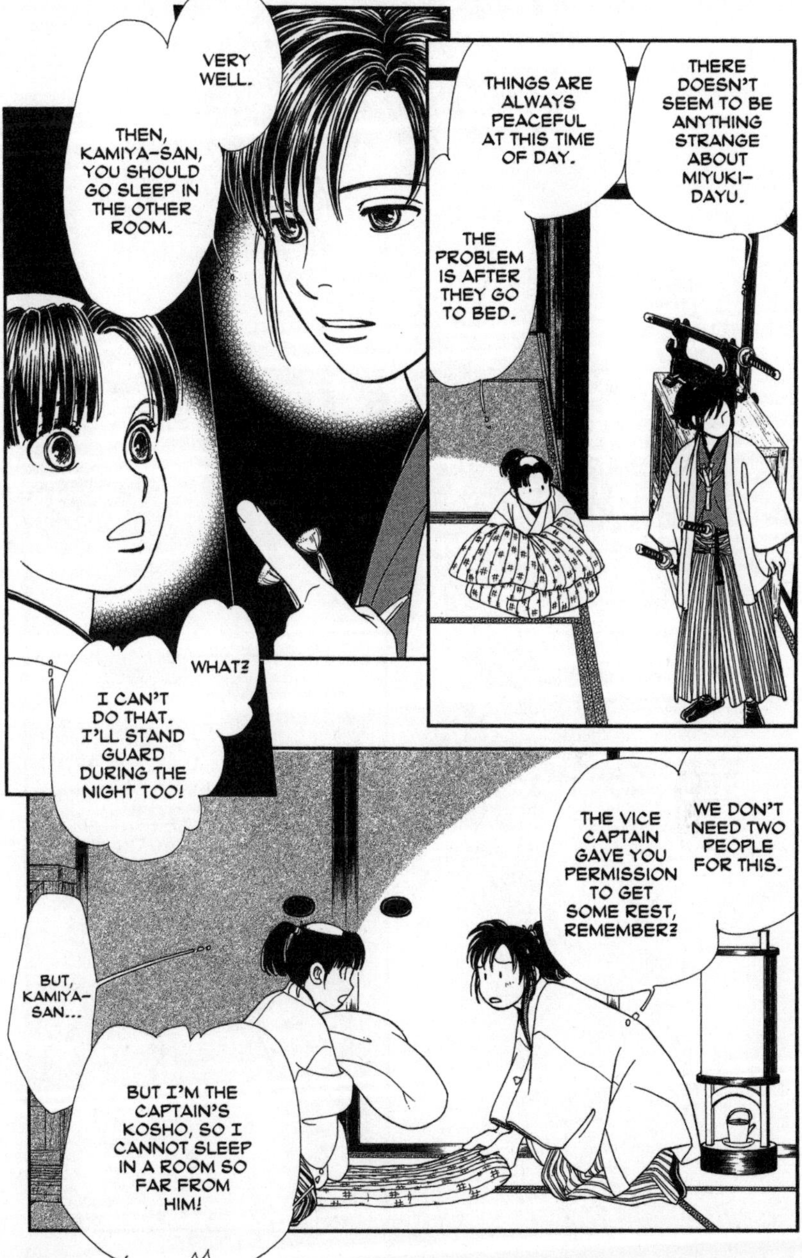
THERE DOESN'T SEEM TO BE ANYTHING STRANGE ABOUT MIYUKI-DAYU.
THINGS ARE ALWAYS PEACEFUL AT THIS TIME OF DAY.
THE PROBLEM IS AFTER THEY GO TO BED.
VERY WELL.
THEN, KAMIYA-SAN, YOU SHOULD GO SLEEP IN THE OTHER ROOM.
WHAT?
I CAN'T DO THAT. I'LL STAND GUARD DURING THE NIGHT TOO!
WE DON'T NEED TWO PEOPLE FOR THIS.
THE VICE CAPTAIN GAVE YOU PERMISSION TO GET SOME REST, REMEMBER?
BUT, KAMIYA-SAN...
BUT I'M THE CAPTAIN'S KOSHO, SO I CANNOT SLEEP IN A ROOM SO FAR FROM HIM!

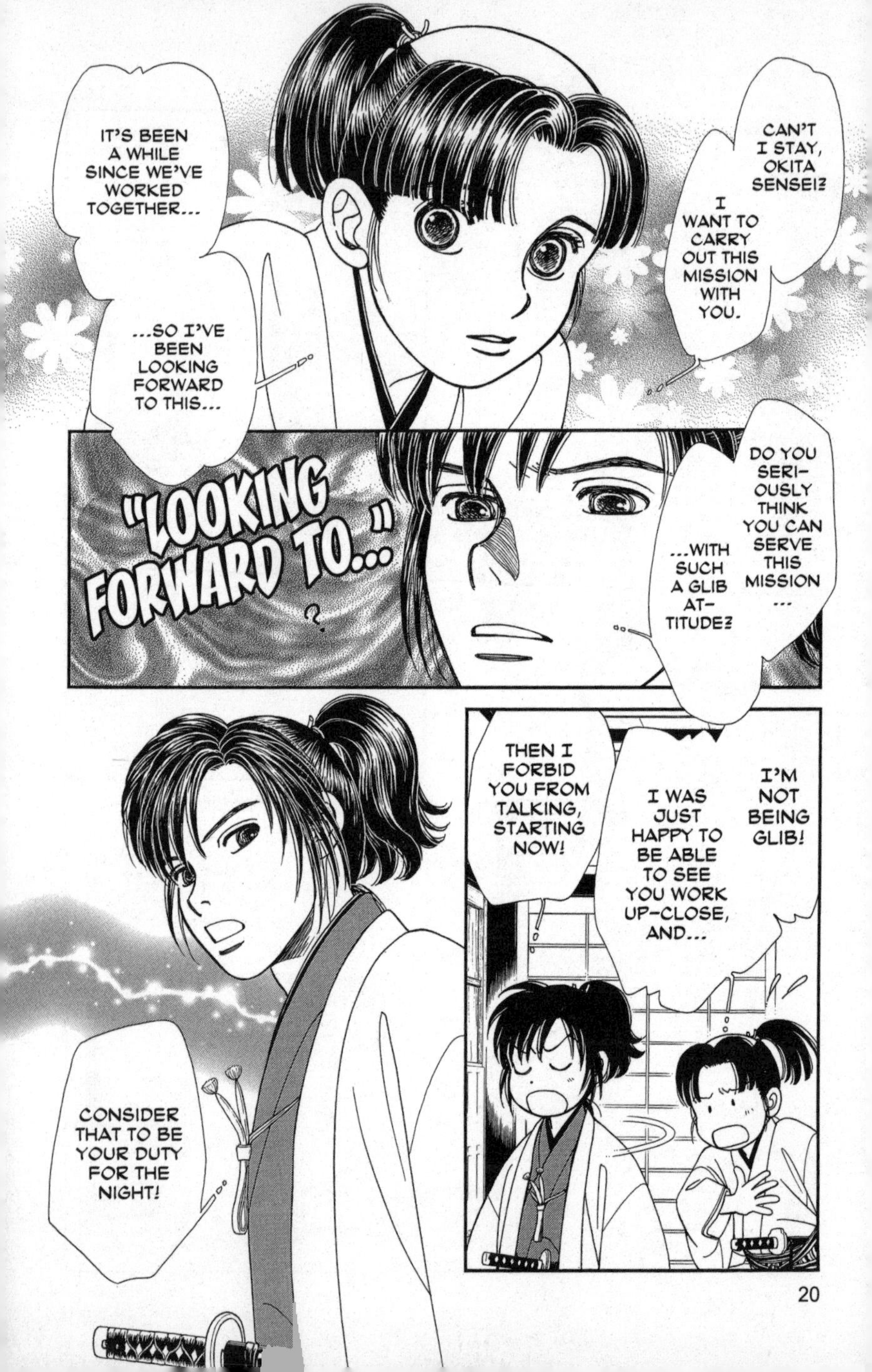
CAN'T I STAY, OKITA SENSEI?
I WANT TO CARRY OUT THIS MISSION WITH YOU.
IT'S BEEN A WHILE SINCE WE'VE WORKED TOGETHER...
...SO I'VE BEEN LOOKING FORWARD TO THIS...
DO YOU SERI-OUSLY THINK YOU CAN SERVE THIS MISSION...
...WITH SUCH A GLIB AT-TITUDE?
"LOOKING FORWARD TO..."
I'M NOT BEING GLIB!
I WAS JUST HAPPY TO BE ABLE TO SEE YOU WORK UP-CLOSE, AND...
THEN I FORBID YOU FROM TALKING, STARTING NOW!
CONSIDER THAT TO BE YOUR DUTY FOR THE NIGHT!

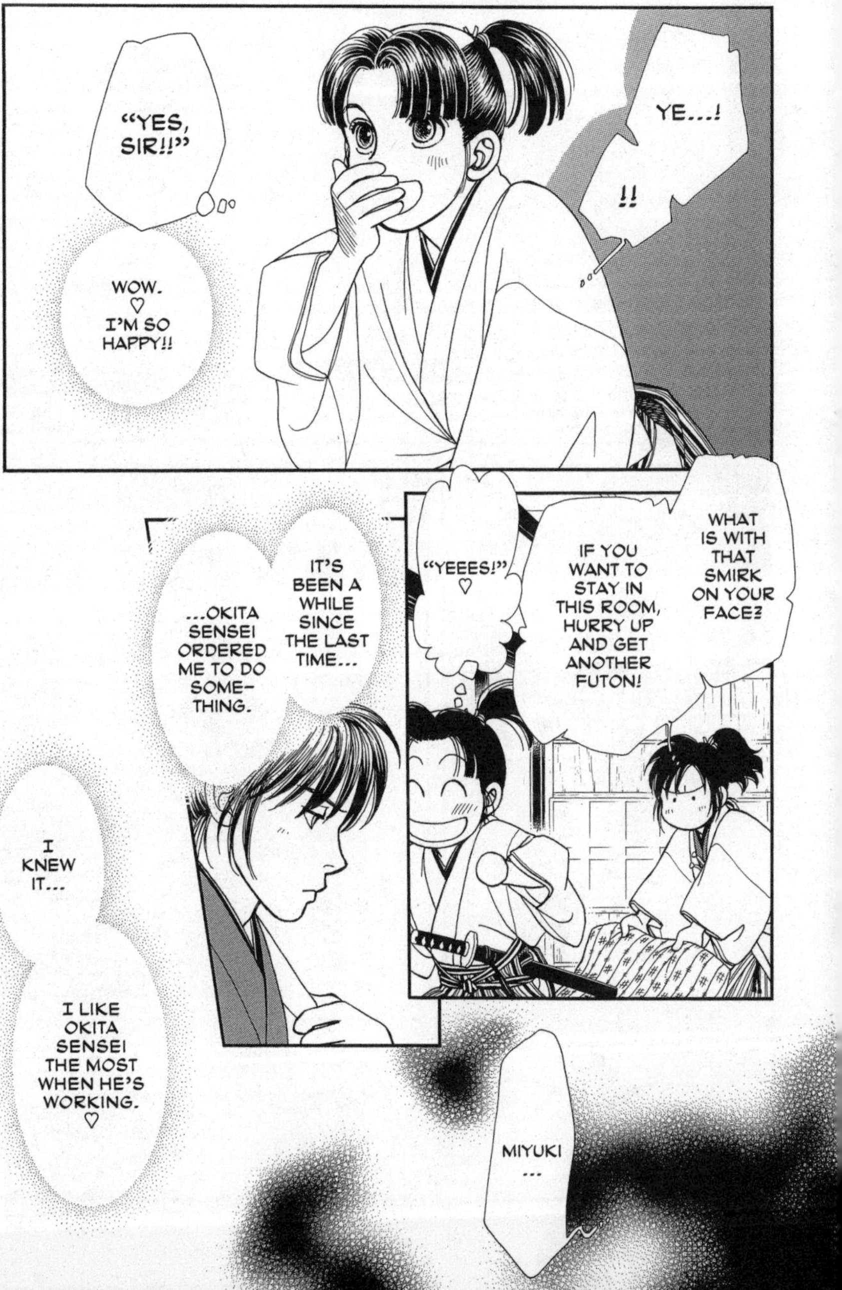
YE...!
!!
“YES, SIR!!”
WOW. ♡ I'M SO HAPPY!!
WHAT IS WITH THAT SMIRK ON YOUR FACE?
IF YOU WANT TO STAY IN THIS ROOM, HURRY UP AND GET ANOTHER FUTON!
“YEEES!” ♡
IT'S BEEN A WHILE SINCE THE LAST TIME...
...OKITA SENSEI ORDERED ME TO DO SOME-THING.
I KNEW IT...
I LIKE OKITA SENSEI THE MOST WHEN HE'S WORKING. ♡
MIYUKI ...

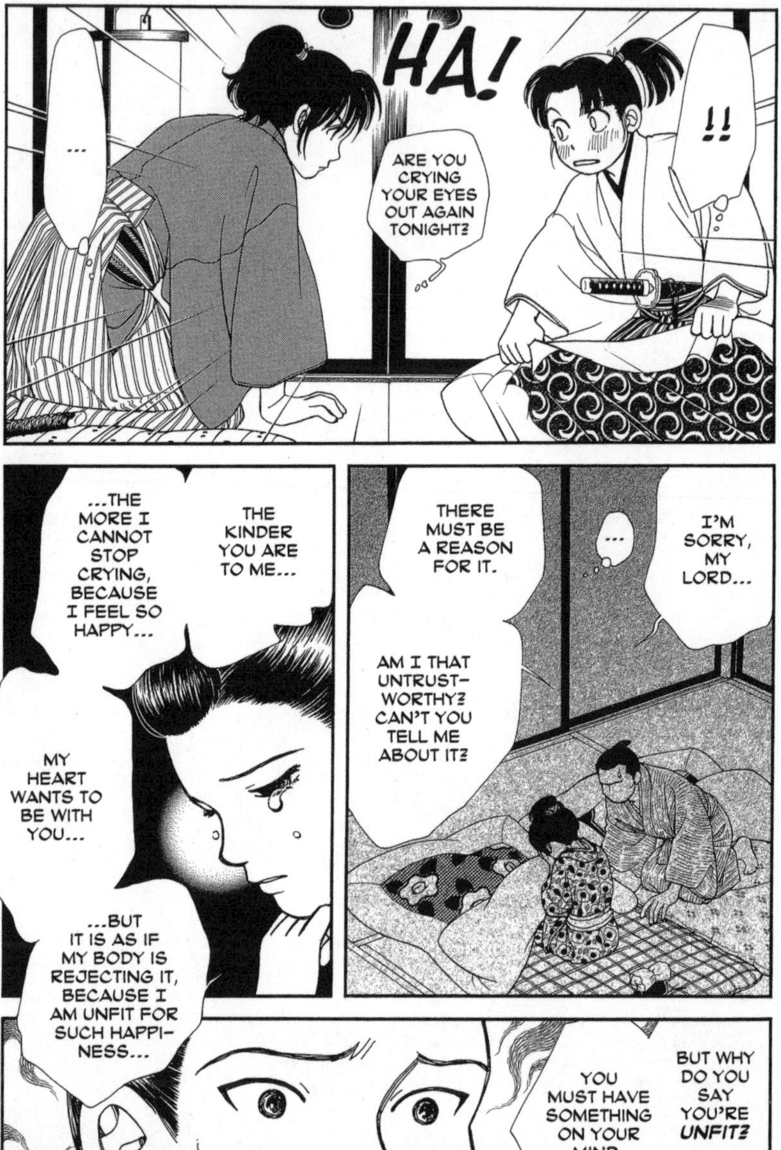
!!
HA!
ARE YOU CRYING YOUR EYES OUT AGAIN TONIGHT?
...
I'M SORRY, MY LORD...
...
THERE MUST BE A REASON FOR IT.
AM I THAT UNTRUST-WORTHY? CAN'T YOU TELL ME ABOUT IT?
THE KINDER YOU ARE TO ME...
...THE MORE I CANNOT STOP CRYING, BECAUSE I FEEL SO HAPPY...
MY HEART WANTS TO BE WITH YOU...
...BUT IT IS AS IF MY BODY IS REJECTING IT, BECAUSE I AM UNFIT FOR SUCH HAPPI-NESS...
BUT WHY DO YOU SAY YOU'RE *UNFIT?*
YOU MUST HAVE SOMETHING ON YOUR MIND.

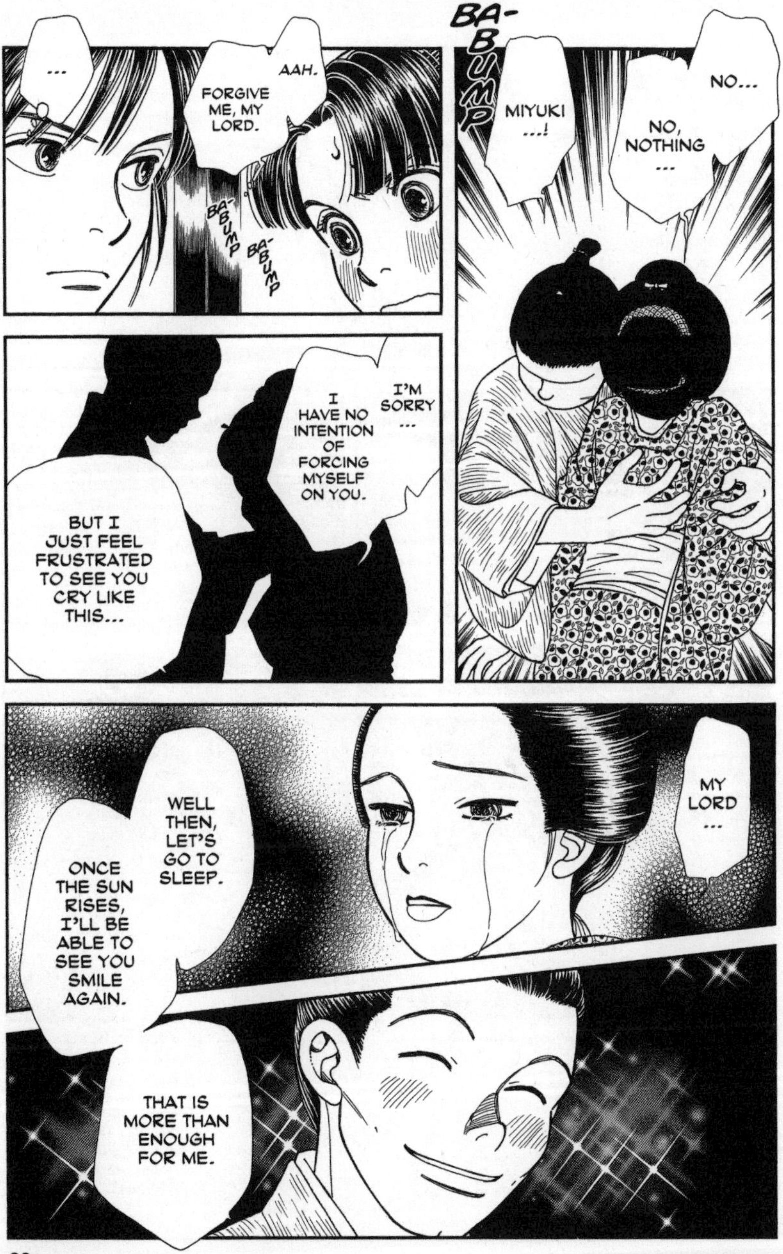
BA-BUMP
MIYUKI ...!
NO...
NO, NOTHING ...
AAH.
FORGIVE ME, MY LORD.
...
BA-BUMP
BA-BUMP
I'M SORRY ...
I HAVE NO INTENTION OF FORCING MYSELF ON YOU.
BUT I JUST FEEL FRUSTRATED TO SEE YOU CRY LIKE THIS...
MY LORD ...
WELL THEN, LET'S GO TO SLEEP.
ONCE THE SUN RISES, I'LL BE ABLE TO SEE YOU SMILE AGAIN.
THAT IS MORE THAN ENOUGH FOR ME.

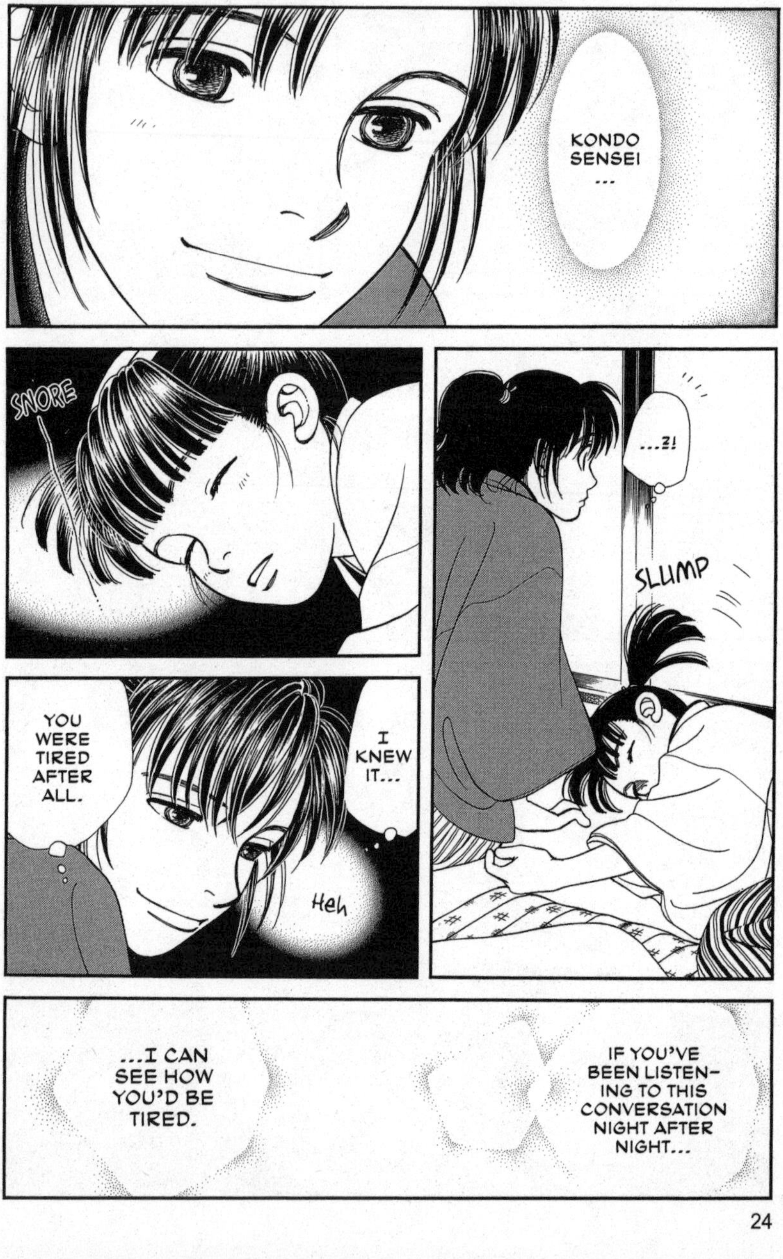
KONDO SENSEI ...
...?!
SLUMP
SNORE
I KNEW IT...
YOU WERE TIRED AFTER ALL.
Heh
IF YOU'VE BEEN LISTENING TO THIS CONVERSATION NIGHT AFTER NIGHT...
...I CAN SEE HOW YOU'D BE TIRED.

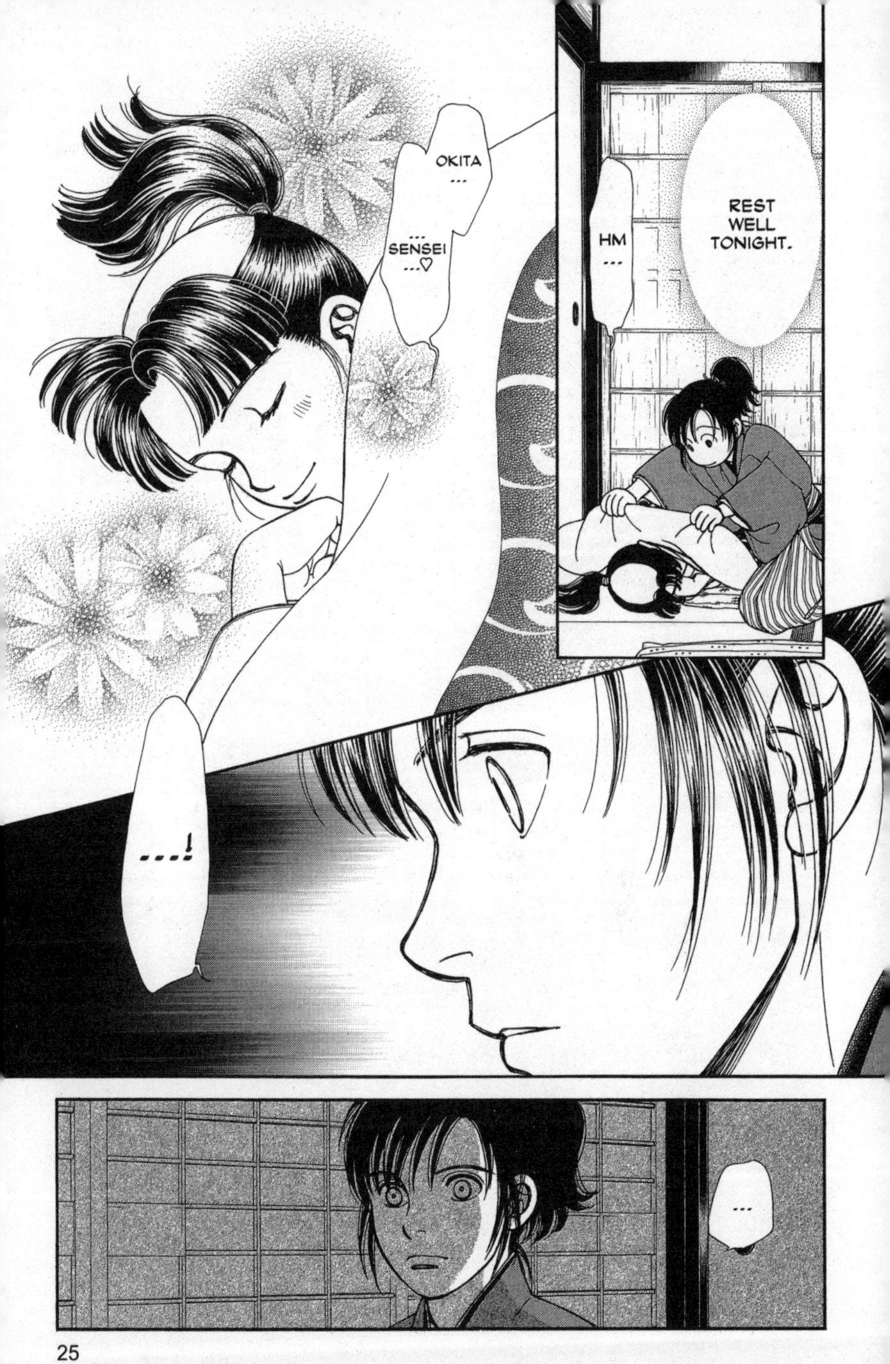
REST WELL TONIGHT.
HM ...
OKITA ...
... SENSEI ...♡
...!
...

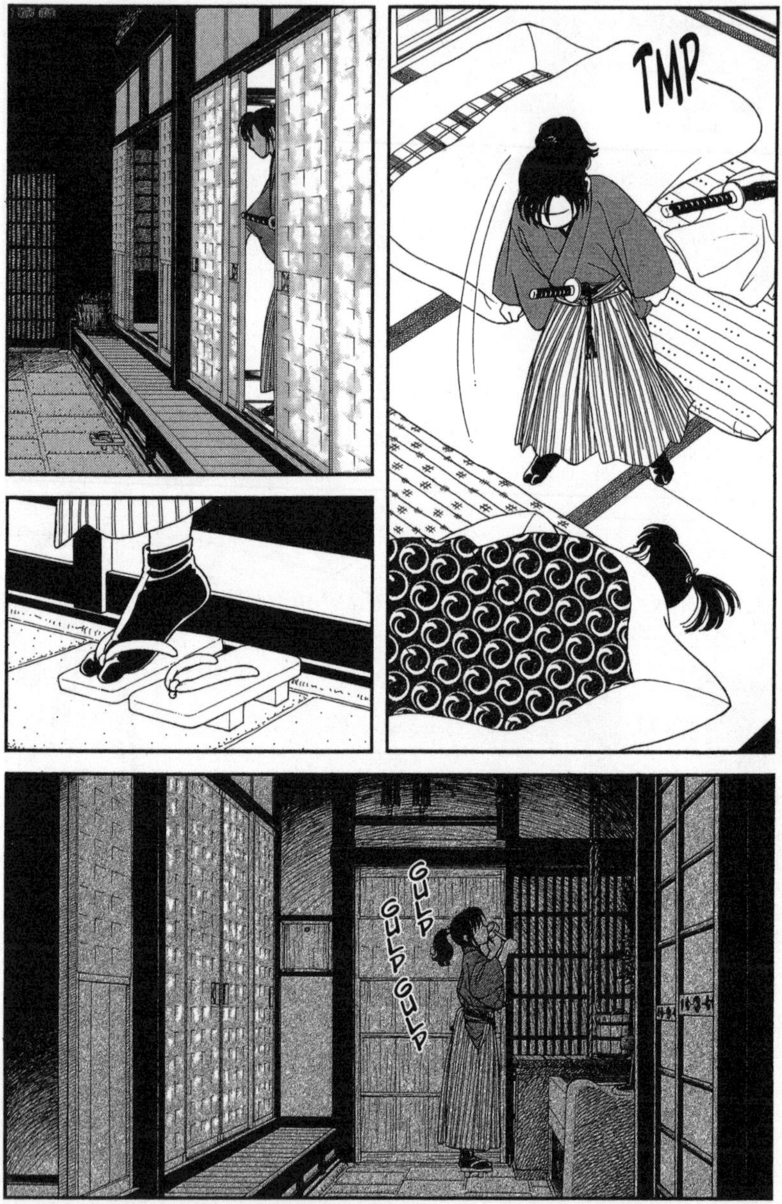
TMP
GULP
GULP GULP
GULP

Blush

COULD SHE CUT IT OUT ...?!

The limit of his self-control

Hahh

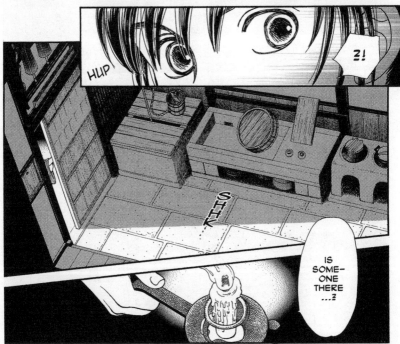

HUP

?!

SHK...

IS SOME-ONE THERE ...?

27

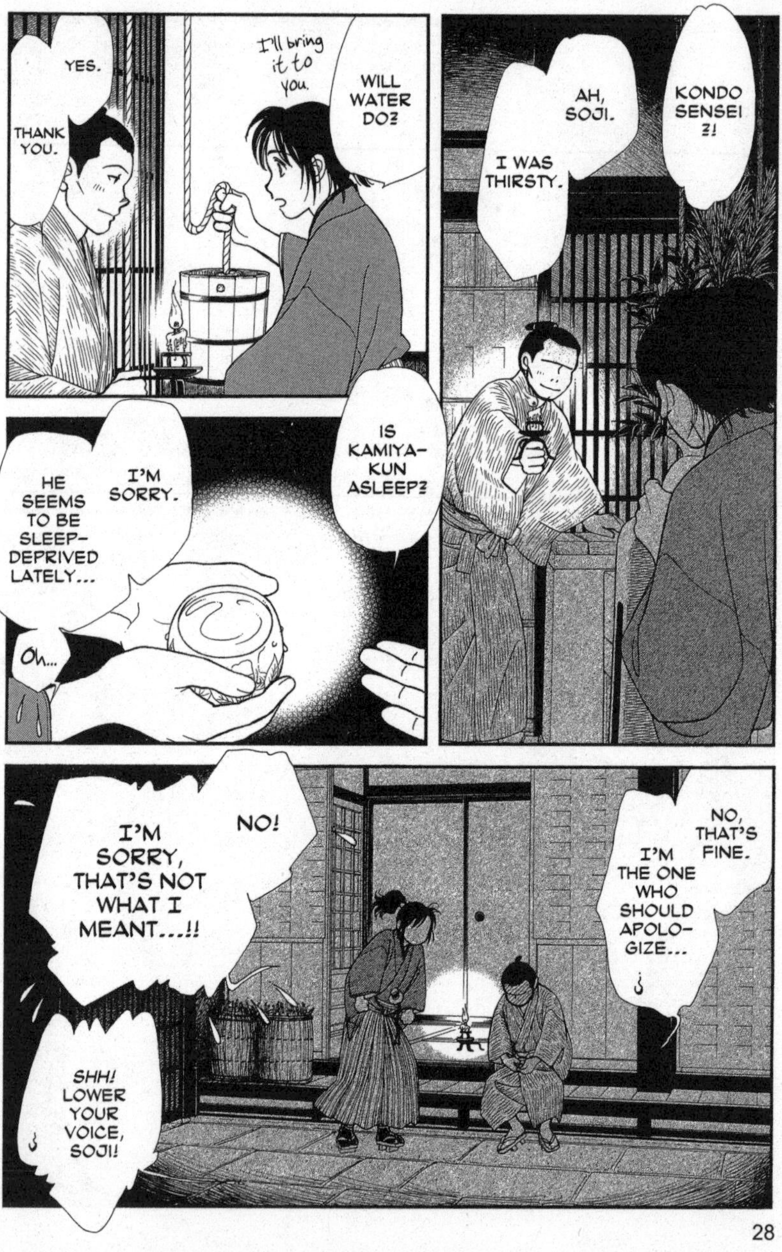
KONDO SENSEI?!
AH, SOJI.
I WAS THIRSTY.
WILL WATER DO?
I'll bring it to you.
YES.
THANK YOU.
IS KAMIYA-KUN ASLEEP?
I'M SORRY.
HE SEEMS TO BE SLEEP-DEPRIVED LATELY...
Oh...
NO, THAT'S FINE.
I'M THE ONE WHO SHOULD APOLOGIZE...
NO!
I'M SORRY, THAT'S NOT WHAT I MEANT...!!
SHH! LOWER YOUR VOICE, SOJI!

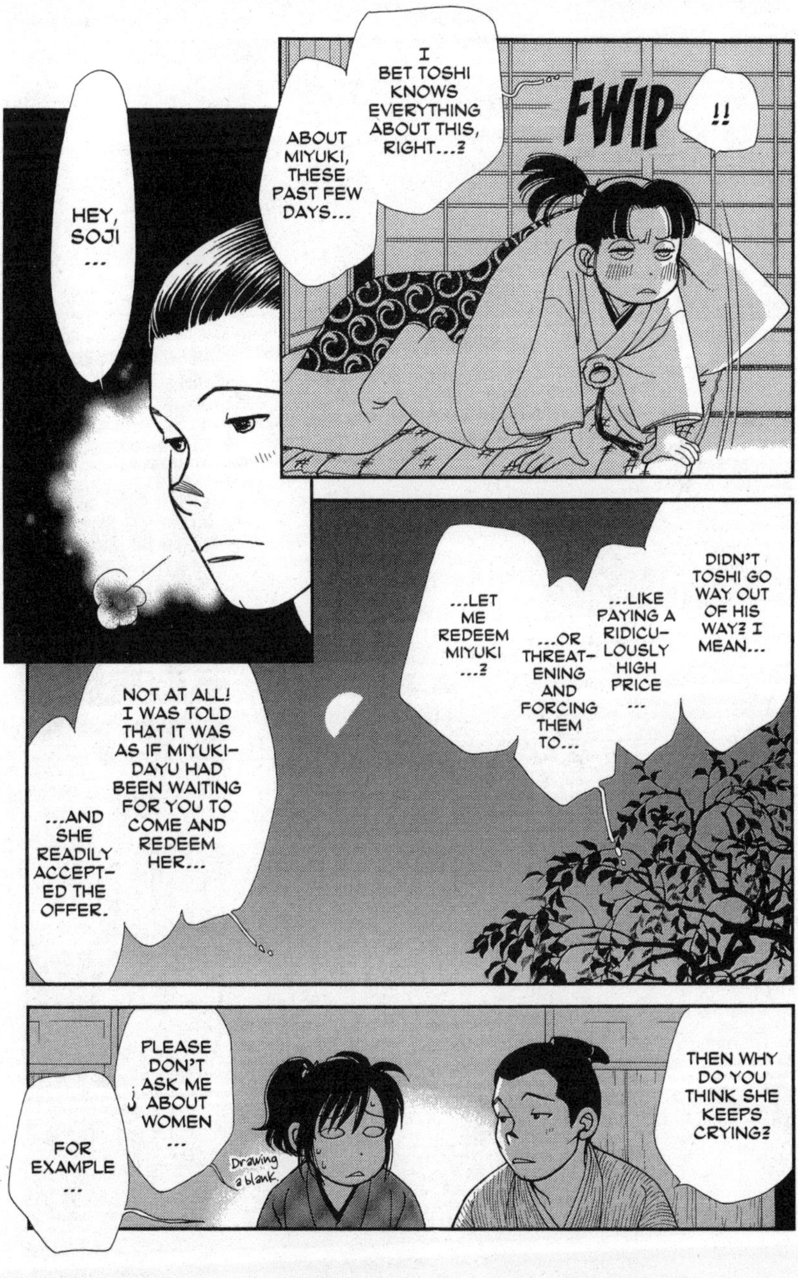
!!
FWIP
I BET TOSHI KNOWS EVERYTHING ABOUT THIS, RIGHT...?
ABOUT MIYUKI, THESE PAST FEW DAYS...
HEY, SOJI ...
DIDN'T TOSHI GO WAY OUT OF HIS WAY? I MEAN...
...LIKE PAYING A RIDICU-LOUSLY HIGH PRICE ...
...OR THREAT-ENING AND FORCING THEM TO...
...LET ME REDEEM MIYUKI ...?
NOT AT ALL! I WAS TOLD THAT IT WAS AS IF MIYUKI-DAYU HAD BEEN WAITING FOR YOU TO COME AND REDEEM HER...
...AND SHE READILY ACCEPT-ED THE OFFER.
THEN WHY DO YOU THINK SHE KEEPS CRYING?
PLEASE DON'T ASK ME ABOUT WOMEN ...
Drawing a blank.
FOR EXAMPLE ...

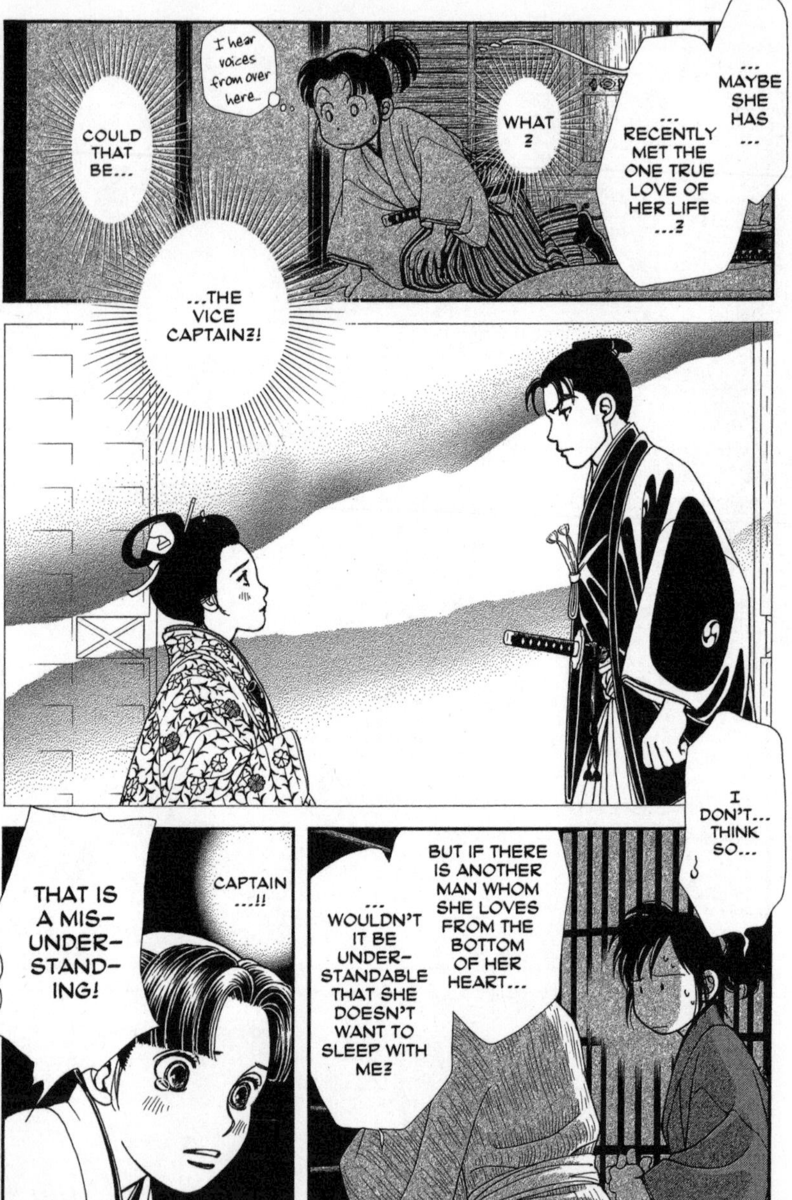
...MAYBE SHE HAS...
...RECENTLY MET THE ONE TRUE LOVE OF HER LIFE...?
WHAT?
I hear voices from over here...
COULD THAT BE...
...THE VICE CAPTAIN?!
I DON'T... THINK SO...
BUT IF THERE IS ANOTHER MAN WHOM SHE LOVES FROM THE BOTTOM OF HER HEART...
...WOULDN'T IT BE UNDER-STANDABLE THAT SHE DOESN'T WANT TO SLEEP WITH ME?
CAPTAIN...!!
THAT IS A MIS-UNDER-STAND-ING!

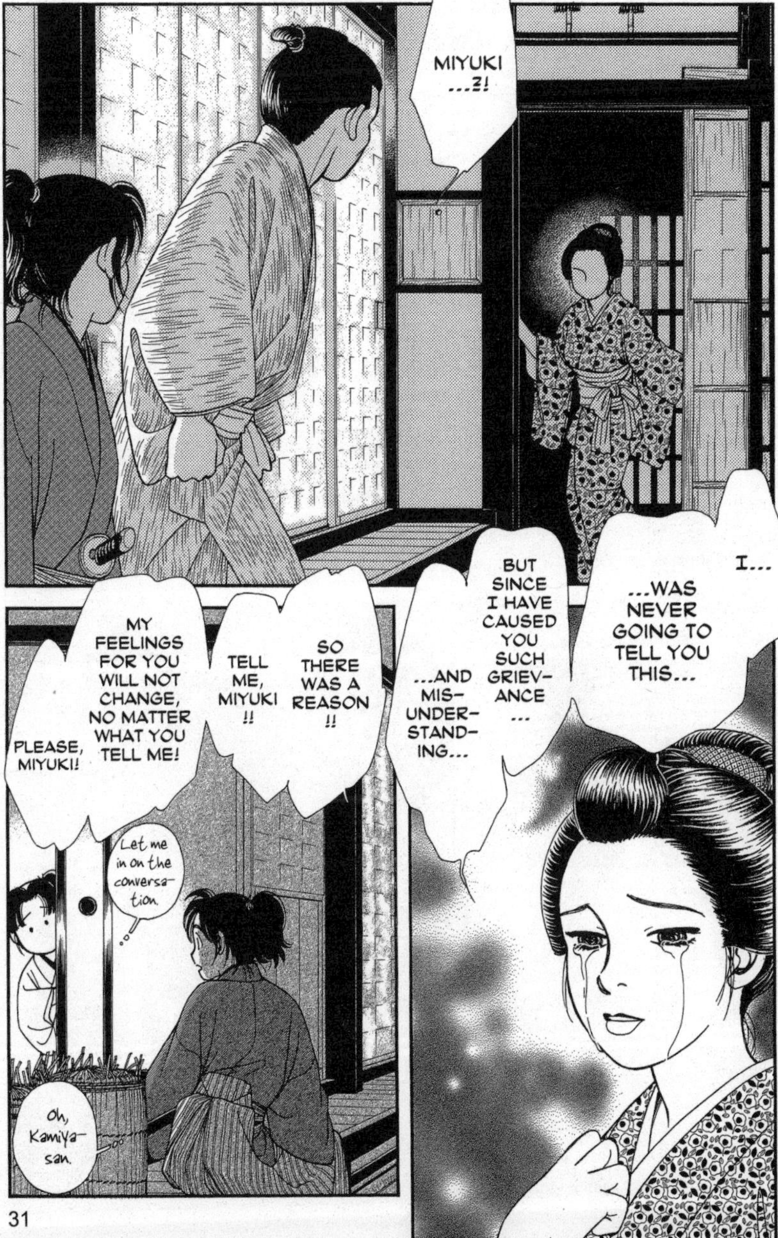
MIYUKI ...?!
I...
...WAS NEVER GOING TO TELL YOU THIS...
BUT SINCE I HAVE CAUSED YOU SUCH GRIEV-ANCE ...
...AND MIS-UNDER-STAND-ING...
SO THERE WAS A REASON !!
TELL ME, MIYUKI !!
MY FEELINGS FOR YOU WILL NOT CHANGE, NO MATTER WHAT YOU TELL ME!
PLEASE, MIYUKI!
Let me in on the conversa-tion.
Oh, Kamiya-san.

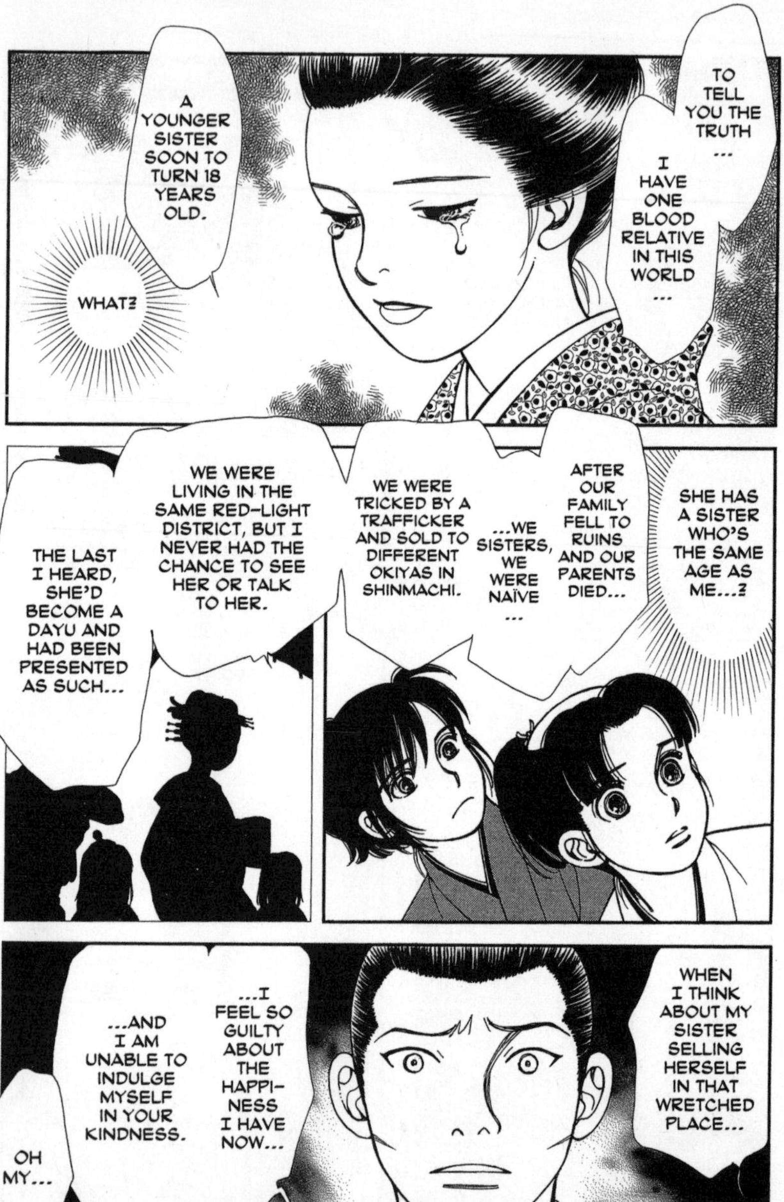
TO TELL YOU THE TRUTH...
I HAVE ONE BLOOD RELATIVE IN THIS WORLD...
A YOUNGER SISTER SOON TO TURN 18 YEARS OLD.
WHAT?
SHE HAS A SISTER WHO'S THE SAME AGE AS ME...?
AFTER OUR FAMILY FELL TO RUINS AND OUR PARENTS DIED...
...WE SISTERS, WE WERE NAÏVE...
WE WERE TRICKED BY A TRAFFICKER AND SOLD TO DIFFERENT OKIYAS IN SHINMACHI.
WE WERE LIVING IN THE SAME RED-LIGHT DISTRICT, BUT I NEVER HAD THE CHANCE TO SEE HER OR TALK TO HER.
THE LAST I HEARD, SHE'D BECOME A DAYU AND HAD BEEN PRESENTED AS SUCH...
WHEN I THINK ABOUT MY SISTER SELLING HERSELF IN THAT WRETCHED PLACE...
...I FEEL SO GUILTY ABOUT THE HAPPINESS I HAVE NOW...
...AND I AM UNABLE TO INDULGE MYSELF IN YOUR KINDNESS.
OH MY...

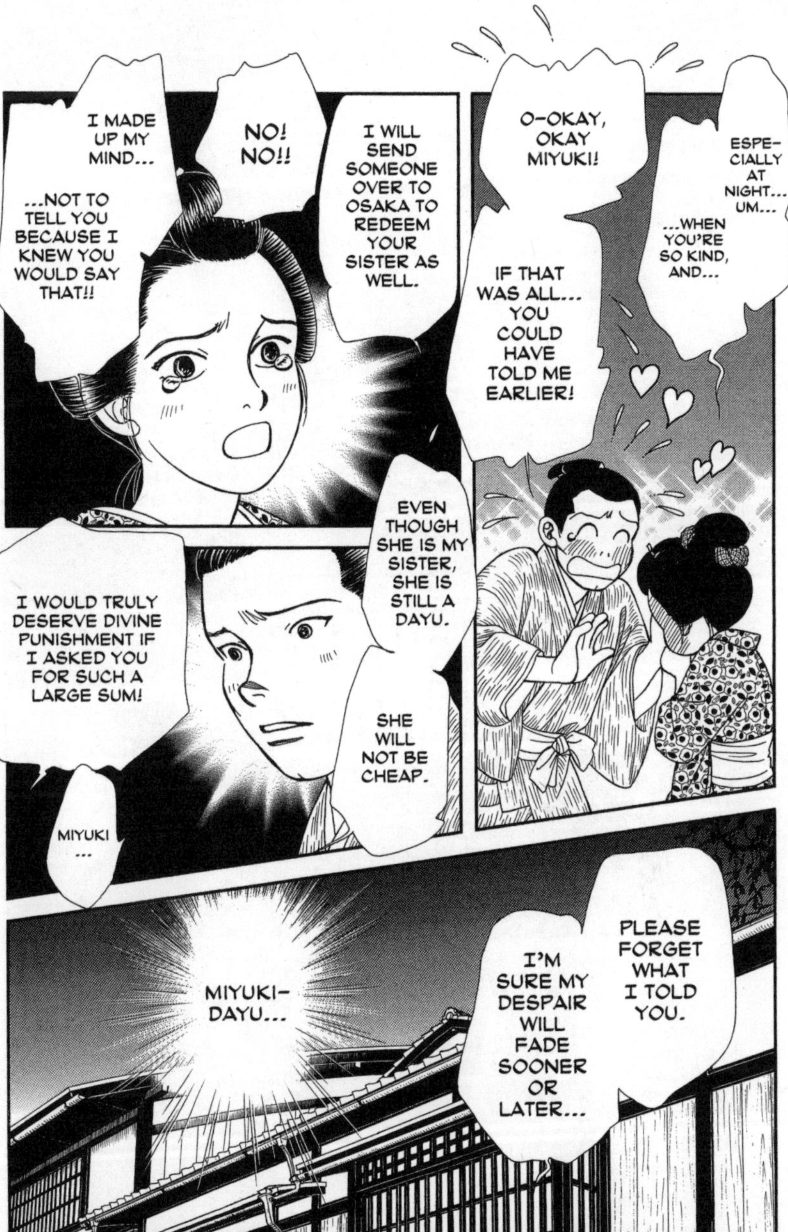
ESPE-CIALLY AT NIGHT... UM...
...WHEN YOU'RE SO KIND, AND...
O-OKAY, OKAY MIYUKI!
IF THAT WAS ALL... YOU COULD HAVE TOLD ME EARLIER!
I WILL SEND SOMEONE OVER TO OSAKA TO REDEEM YOUR SISTER AS WELL.
NO! NO!!
I MADE UP MY MIND...
...NOT TO TELL YOU BECAUSE I KNEW YOU WOULD SAY THAT!!
EVEN THOUGH SHE IS MY SISTER, SHE IS STILL A DAYU.
SHE WILL NOT BE CHEAP.
I WOULD TRULY DESERVE DIVINE PUNISHMENT IF I ASKED YOU FOR SUCH A LARGE SUM!
MIYUKI...
PLEASE FORGET WHAT I TOLD YOU.
I'M SURE MY DESPAIR WILL FADE SOONER OR LATER...
MIYUKI-DAYU...

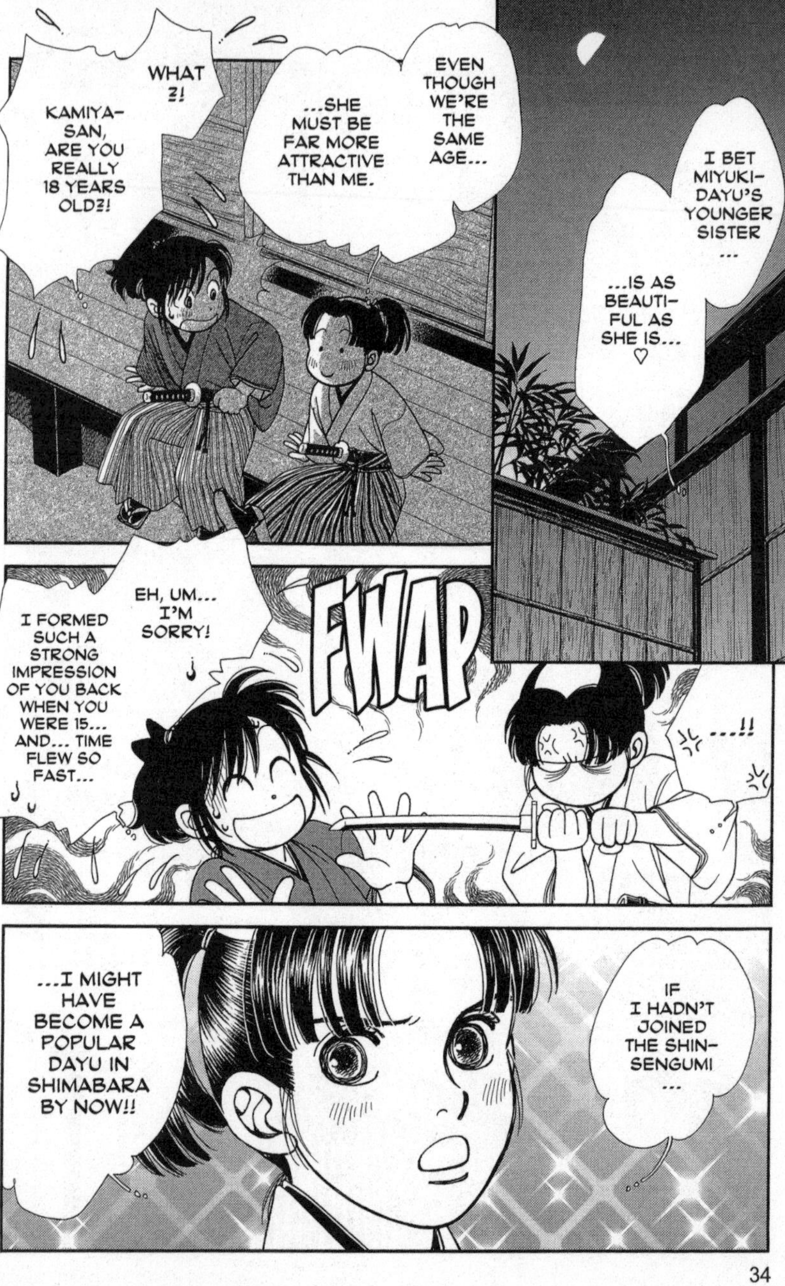
I BET MIYUKI-DAYU'S YOUNGER SISTER...
...IS AS BEAUTIFUL AS SHE IS... ♡
EVEN THOUGH WE'RE THE SAME AGE...
...SHE MUST BE FAR MORE ATTRACTIVE THAN ME.
WHAT?!
KAMIYA-SAN, ARE YOU REALLY 18 YEARS OLD?!
FWAP
...!!
EH, UM... I'M SORRY!
I FORMED SUCH A STRONG IMPRESSION OF YOU BACK WHEN YOU WERE 15... AND... TIME FLEW SO FAST...
IF I HADN'T JOINED THE SHIN-SENGUMI...
...I MIGHT HAVE BECOME A POPULAR DAYU IN SHIMABARA BY NOW!!

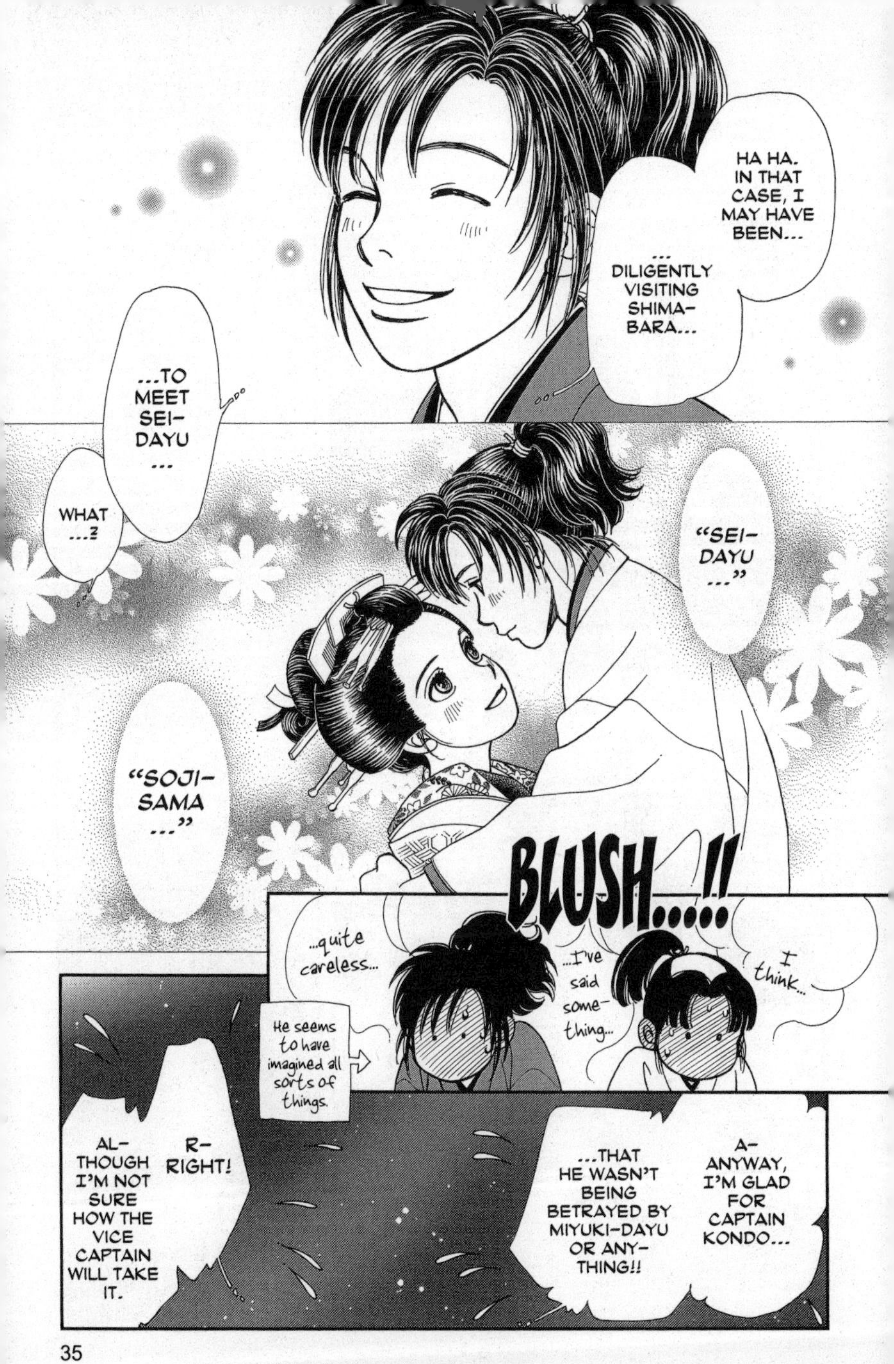
HA HA. IN THAT CASE, I MAY HAVE BEEN...
...DILIGENTLY VISITING SHIMA-BARA...
...TO MEET SEI-DAYU...
WHAT ...?
"SEI-DAYU..."
"SOJI-SAMA..."
BLUSH...!!
I think...
...I've said something...
...quite careless...
He seems to have imagined all sorts of things.
A-ANYWAY, I'M GLAD FOR CAPTAIN KONDO...
...THAT HE WASN'T BEING BETRAYED BY MIYUKI-DAYU OR ANYTHING!!
R-RIGHT!
ALTHOUGH I'M NOT SURE HOW THE VICE CAPTAIN WILL TAKE IT.

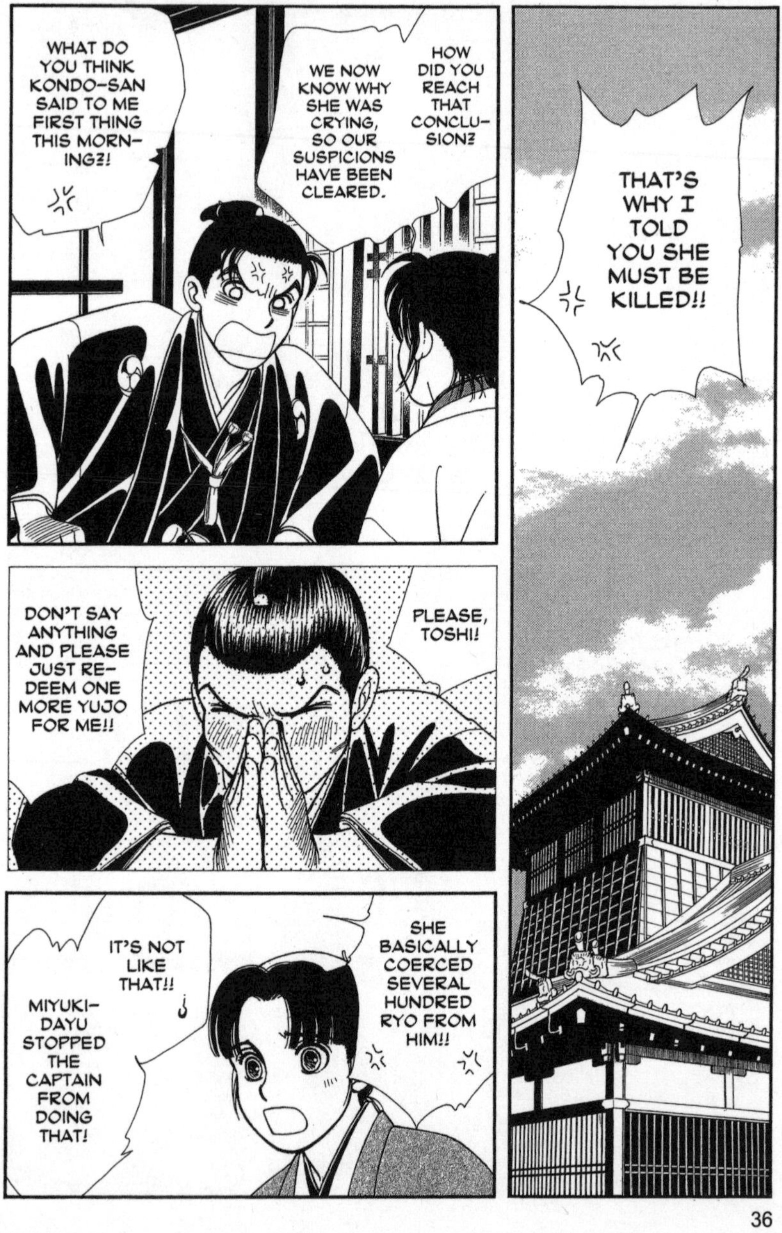
THAT'S WHY I TOLD YOU SHE MUST BE KILLED!!
HOW DID YOU REACH THAT CONCLUSION?
WE NOW KNOW WHY SHE WAS CRYING, SO OUR SUSPICIONS HAVE BEEN CLEARED.
WHAT DO YOU THINK KONDO-SAN SAID TO ME FIRST THING THIS MORNING?!
PLEASE, TOSHI!
DON'T SAY ANYTHING AND PLEASE JUST REDEEM ONE MORE YUJO FOR ME!!
SHE BASICALLY COERCED SEVERAL HUNDRED RYO FROM HIM!!
IT'S NOT LIKE THAT!!
MIYUKI-DAYU STOPPED THE CAPTAIN FROM DOING THAT!

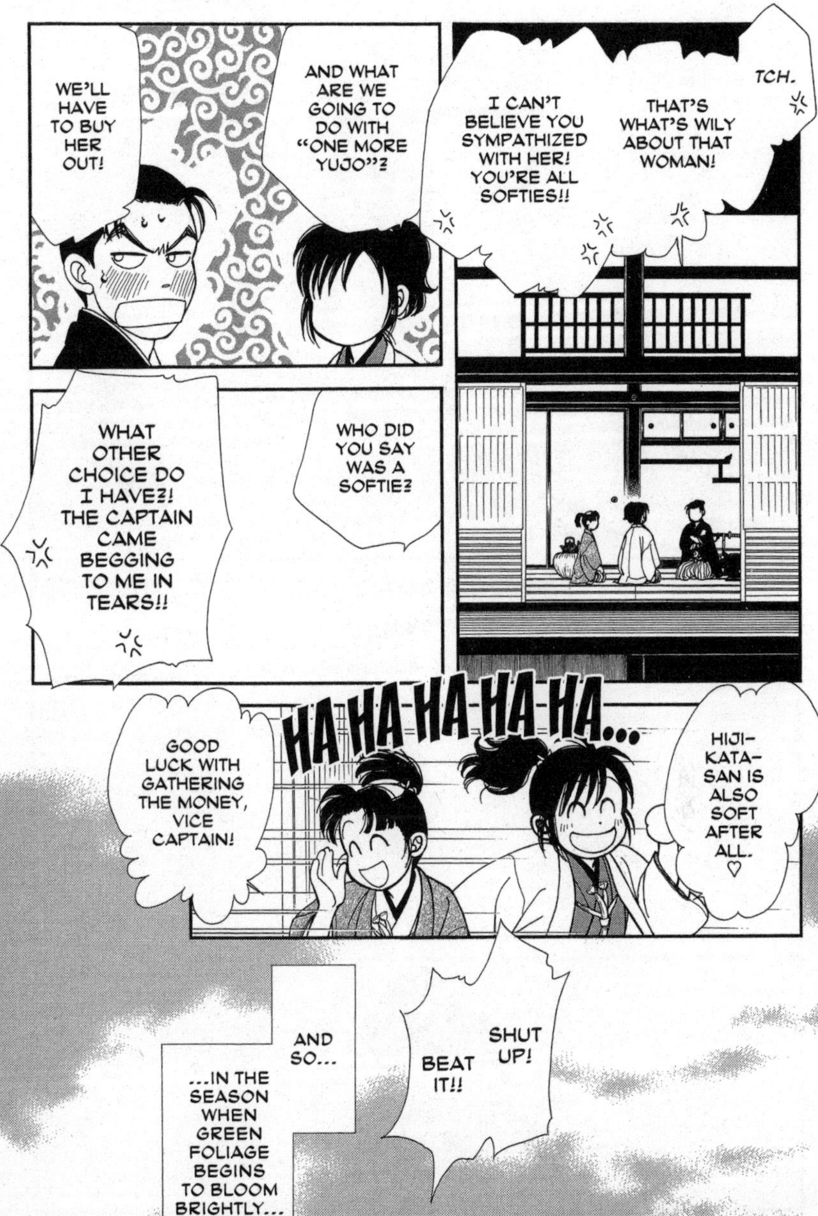
TCH.
THAT'S WHAT'S WILY ABOUT THAT WOMAN!
I CAN'T BELIEVE YOU SYMPATHIZED WITH HER! YOU'RE ALL SOFTIES!!
AND WHAT ARE WE GOING TO DO WITH "ONE MORE YUJO"?
WE'LL HAVE TO BUY HER OUT!
WHO DID YOU SAY WAS A SOFTIE?
WHAT OTHER CHOICE DO I HAVE?! THE CAPTAIN CAME BEGGING TO ME IN TEARS!!
HIJI-KATA-SAN IS ALSO SOFT AFTER ALL. ♡
HA HA HA HA HA...
GOOD LUCK WITH GATHERING THE MONEY, VICE CAPTAIN!
SHUT UP!
BEAT IT!!
AND SO...
...IN THE SEASON WHEN GREEN FOLIAGE BEGINS TO BLOOM BRIGHTLY...

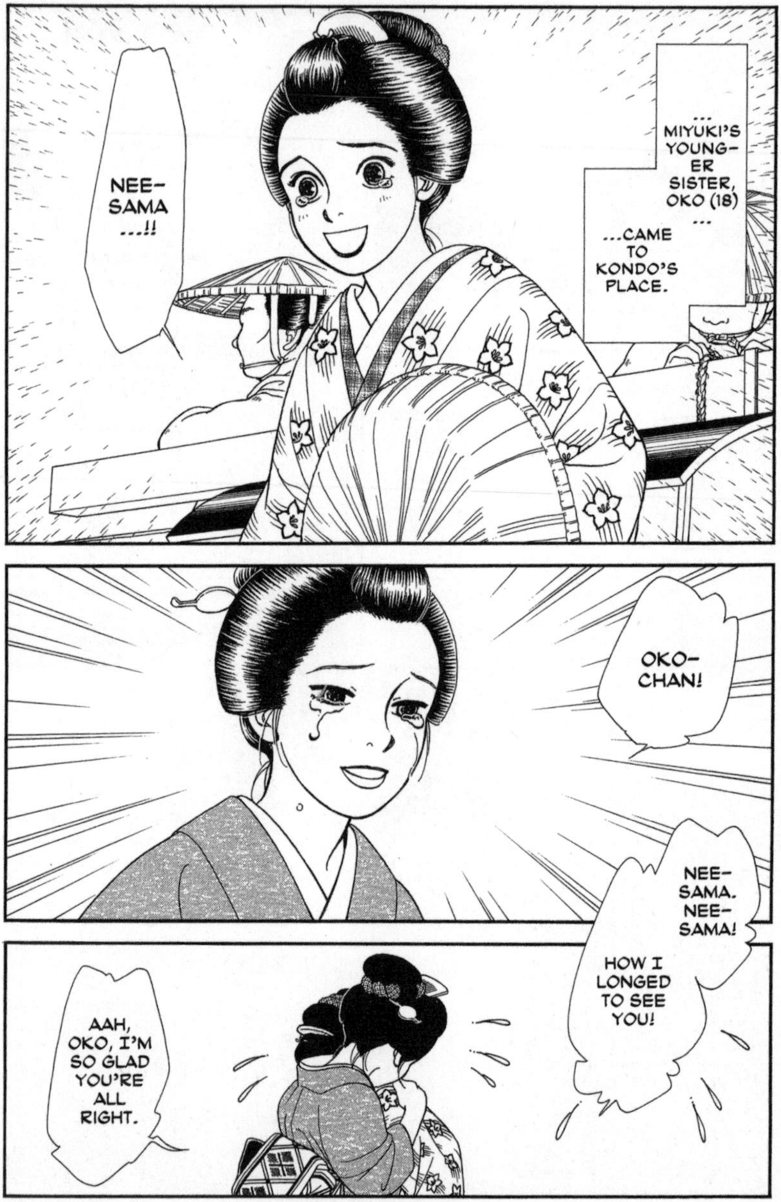

...MIYUKI'S YOUNGER SISTER, OKO (18)...
...CAME TO KONDO'S PLACE.
NEE-SAMA...!!
OKO-CHAN!
NEE-SAMA. NEE-SAMA!
HOW I LONGED TO SEE YOU!
AAH, OKO, I'M SO GLAD YOU'RE ALL RIGHT.

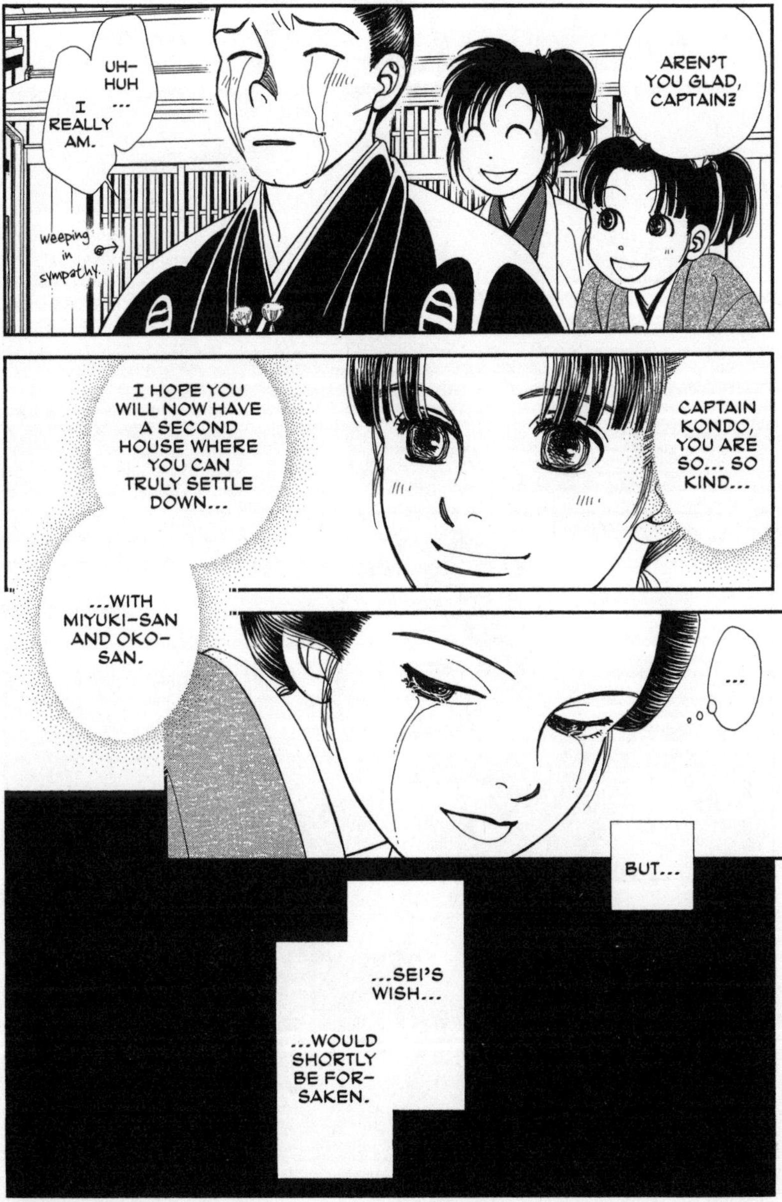
AREN'T YOU GLAD, CAPTAIN?
UH-HUH ... I REALLY AM.
weeping in sympathy.
CAPTAIN KONDO, YOU ARE SO... SO KIND...
I HOPE YOU WILL NOW HAVE A SECOND HOUSE WHERE YOU CAN TRULY SETTLE DOWN...
...WITH MIYUKI-SAN AND OKO-SAN.
...
BUT...
...SEI'S WISH...
...WOULD SHORTLY BE FOR-SAKEN.

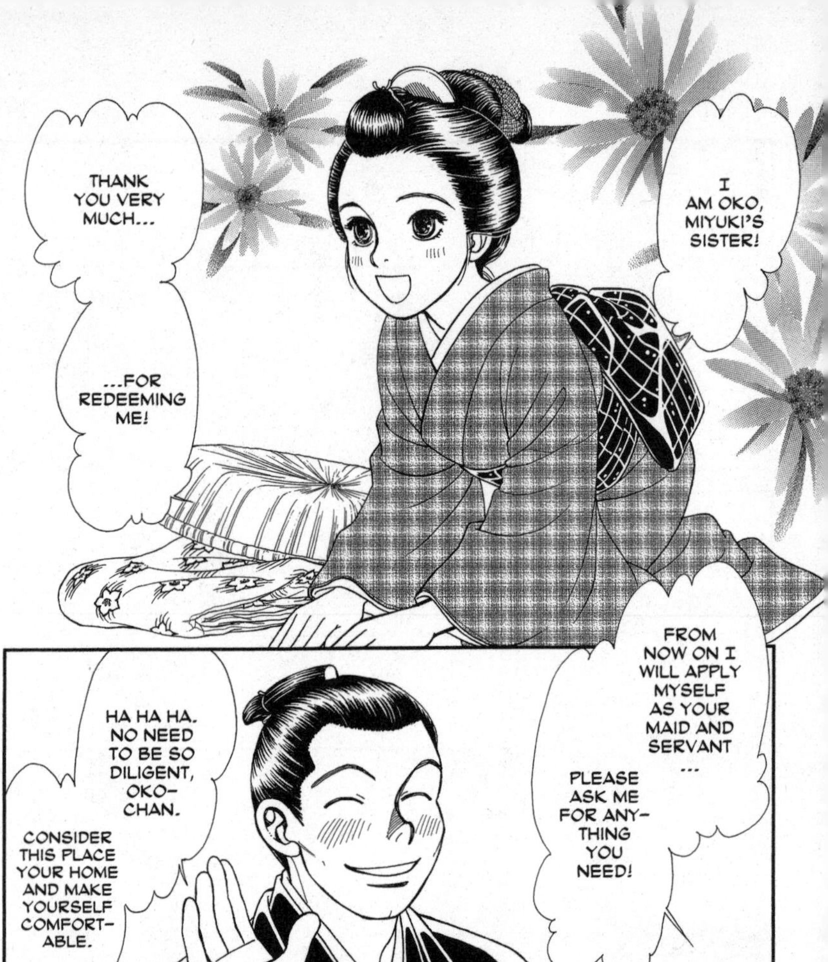
I AM OKO, MIYUKI'S SISTER!
THANK YOU VERY MUCH...
...FOR REDEEMING ME!
FROM NOW ON I WILL APPLY MYSELF AS YOUR MAID AND SERVANT...
PLEASE ASK ME FOR ANYTHING YOU NEED!
HA HA HA. NO NEED TO BE SO DILIGENT, OKO-CHAN.
CONSIDER THIS PLACE YOUR HOME AND MAKE YOURSELF COMFORTABLE.

KAZE HIKARU IROHA KARUTA

"ME" め

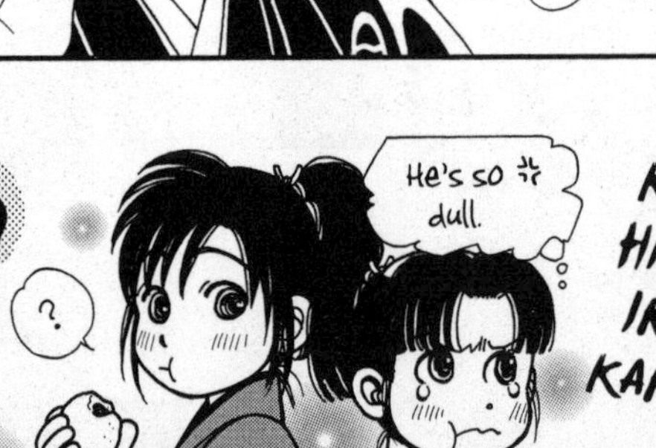
He's so dull.
?

MEKUSO HANAKUSO WO NAJIRU.
"POT COMPLAINING THAT THE KETTLE IS BLACK."

by Beni Shake-san from Tokyo

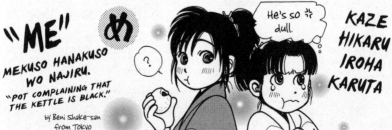

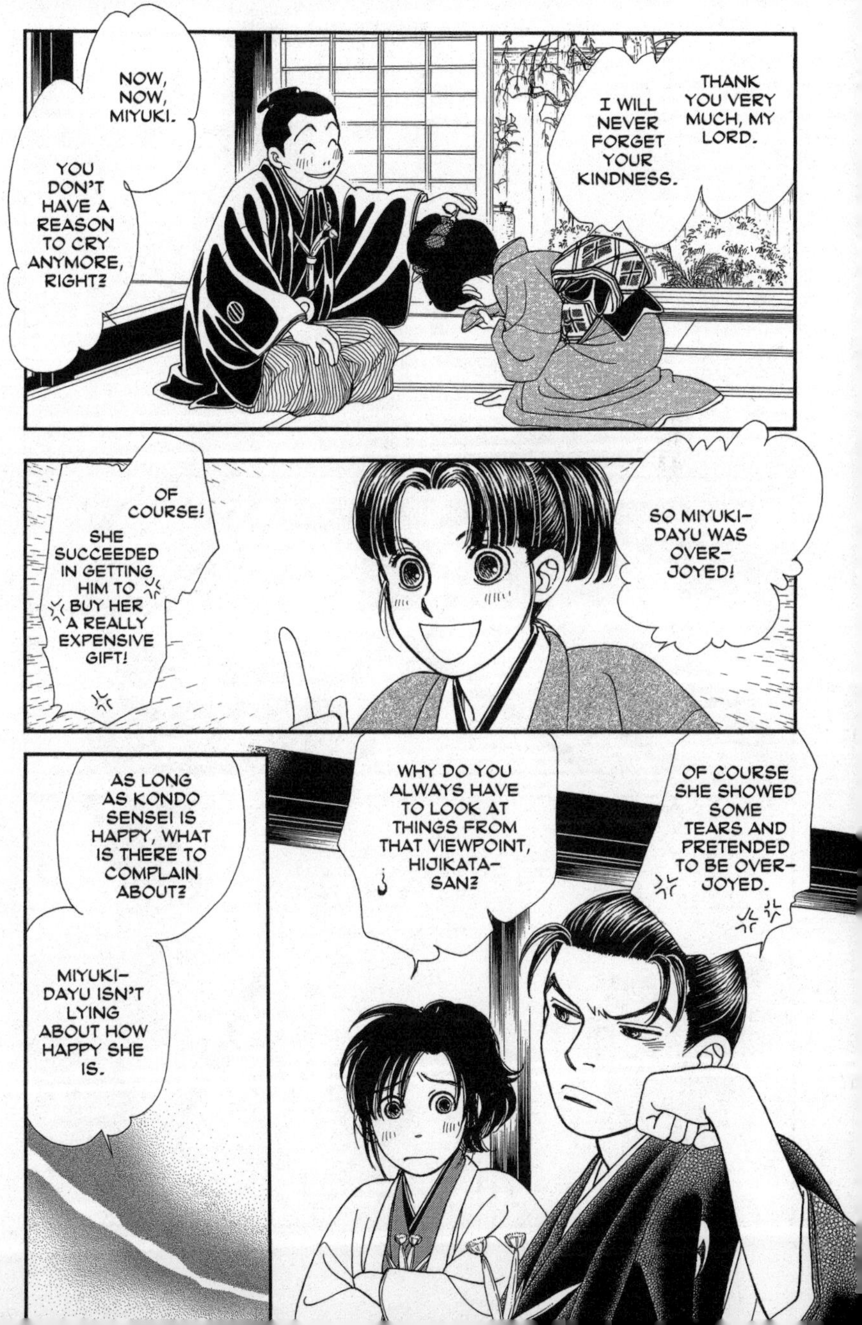
THANK YOU VERY MUCH, MY LORD.
I WILL NEVER FORGET YOUR KINDNESS.
NOW, NOW, MIYUKI.
YOU DON'T HAVE A REASON TO CRY ANYMORE, RIGHT?
SO MIYUKI-DAYU WAS OVER-JOYED!
OF COURSE!
SHE SUCCEEDED IN GETTING HIM TO BUY HER A REALLY EXPENSIVE GIFT!
OF COURSE SHE SHOWED SOME TEARS AND PRETENDED TO BE OVER-JOYED.
WHY DO YOU ALWAYS HAVE TO LOOK AT THINGS FROM THAT VIEWPOINT, HIJIKATA-SAN?
AS LONG AS KONDO SENSEI IS HAPPY, WHAT IS THERE TO COMPLAIN ABOUT?
MIYUKI-DAYU ISN'T LYING ABOUT HOW HAPPY SHE IS.

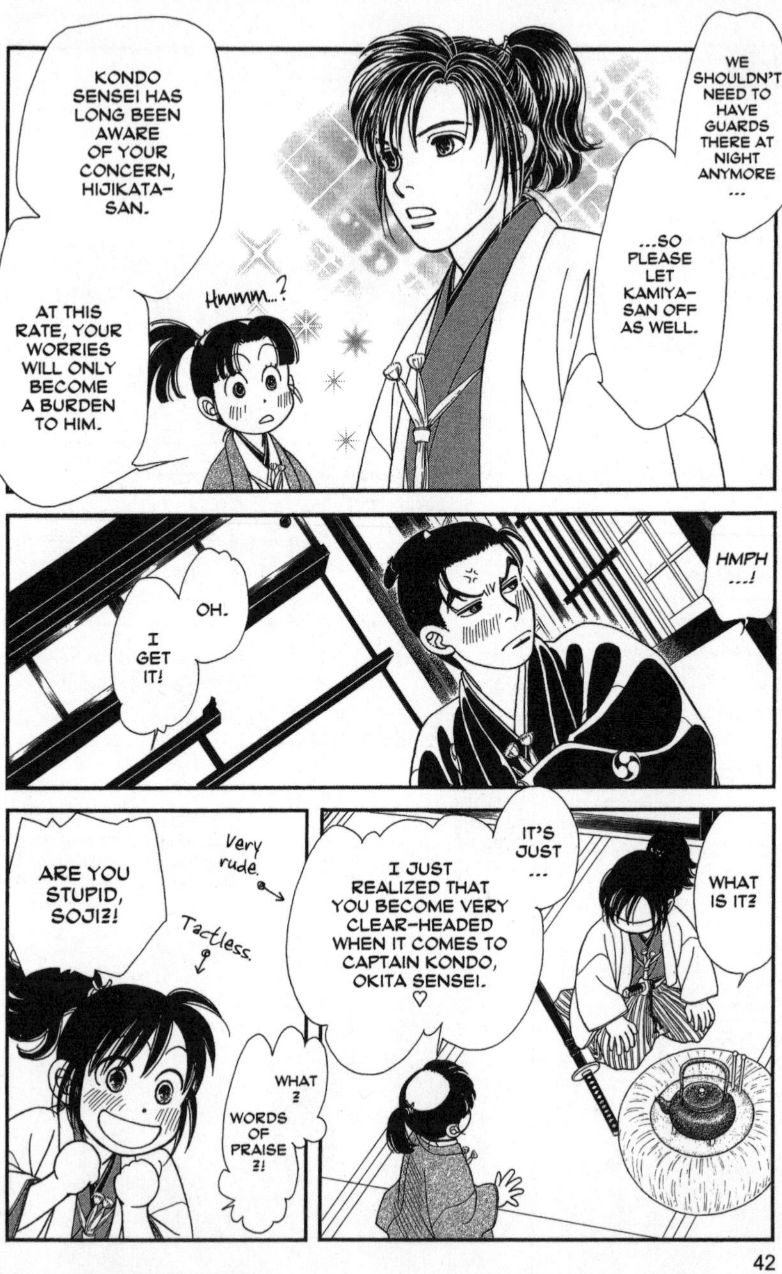
WE SHOULDN'T NEED TO HAVE GUARDS THERE AT NIGHT ANYMORE ...
...SO PLEASE LET KAMIYA-SAN OFF AS WELL.
Hmmm...?
KONDO SENSEI HAS LONG BEEN AWARE OF YOUR CONCERN, HIJIKATA-SAN.
AT THIS RATE, YOUR WORRIES WILL ONLY BECOME A BURDEN TO HIM.
HMPH ...!
OH.
I GET IT!
WHAT IS IT?
IT'S JUST ...
I JUST REALIZED THAT YOU BECOME VERY CLEAR-HEADED WHEN IT COMES TO CAPTAIN KONDO, OKITA SENSEI. ♡
WHAT ?
WORDS OF PRAISE ?!
Very rude.
Tactless.
ARE YOU STUPID, SOJI?!

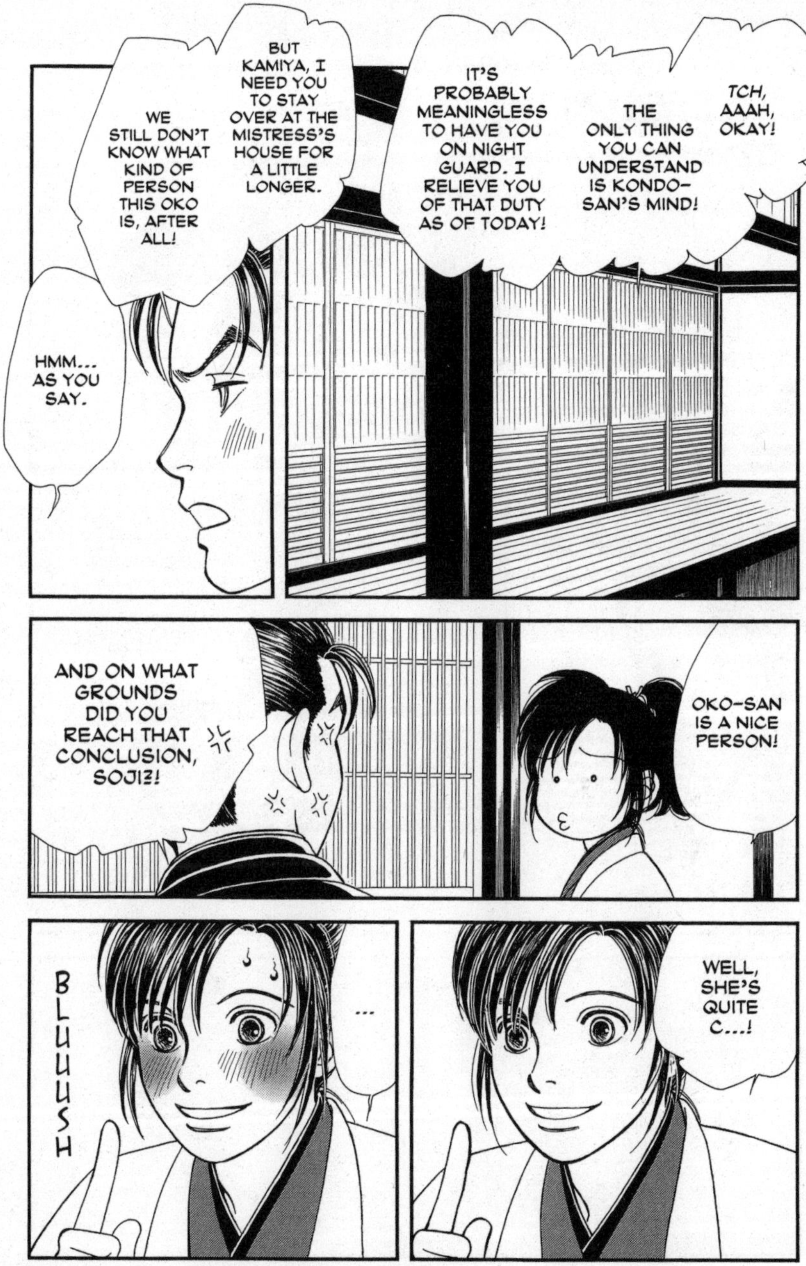
TCH, AAAH, OKAY!
THE ONLY THING YOU CAN UNDERSTAND IS KONDO-SAN'S MIND!
IT'S PROBABLY MEANINGLESS TO HAVE YOU ON NIGHT GUARD. I RELIEVE YOU OF THAT DUTY AS OF TODAY!
BUT KAMIYA, I NEED YOU TO STAY OVER AT THE MISTRESS'S HOUSE FOR A LITTLE LONGER.
WE STILL DON'T KNOW WHAT KIND OF PERSON THIS OKO IS, AFTER ALL!
HMM... AS YOU SAY.
OKO-SAN IS A NICE PERSON!
AND ON WHAT GROUNDS DID YOU REACH THAT CONCLUSION, SOJI?!
WELL, SHE'S QUITE C...!
...
BLUUUSH

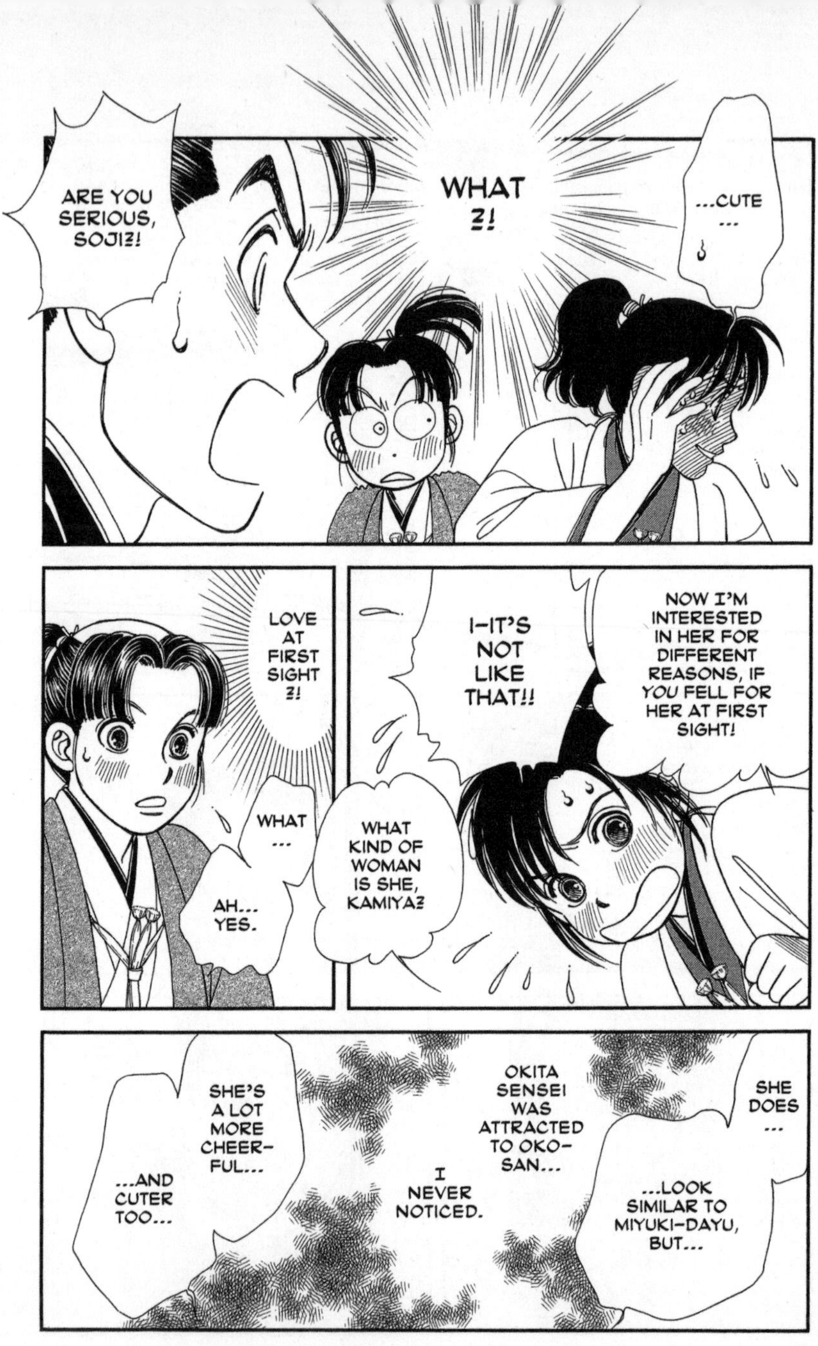
...CUTE ...
WHAT ?!
ARE YOU SERIOUS, SOJI?!
NOW I'M INTERESTED IN HER FOR DIFFERENT REASONS, IF *YOU* FELL FOR HER AT FIRST SIGHT!
I-IT'S NOT LIKE THAT!!
WHAT KIND OF WOMAN IS SHE, KAMIYA?
LOVE AT FIRST SIGHT ?!
WHAT ...
AH... YES.
SHE DOES ...
...LOOK SIMILAR TO MIYUKI-DAYU, BUT...
OKITA SENSEI WAS ATTRACTED TO OKO-SAN...
I NEVER NOTICED.
SHE'S A LOT MORE CHEER-FUL...
...AND CUTER TOO...

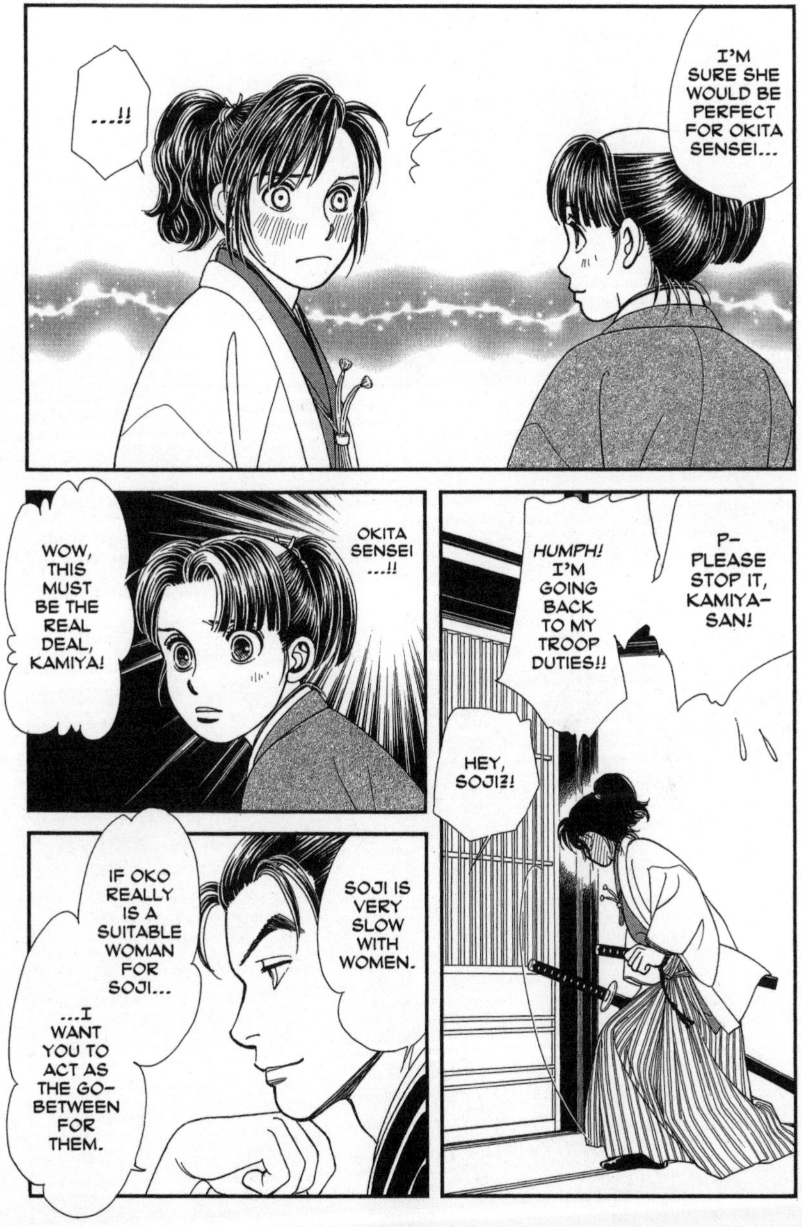
I'M SURE SHE WOULD BE PERFECT FOR OKITA SENSEI...
...!!
P-PLEASE STOP IT, KAMIYA-SAN!
HUMPH! I'M GOING BACK TO MY TROOP DUTIES!!
HEY, SOJI?!
OKITA SENSEI ...!!
WOW, THIS MUST BE THE REAL DEAL, KAMIYA!
SOJI IS VERY SLOW WITH WOMEN.
IF OKO REALLY IS A SUITABLE WOMAN FOR SOJI...
...I WANT YOU TO ACT AS THE GO-BETWEEN FOR THEM.

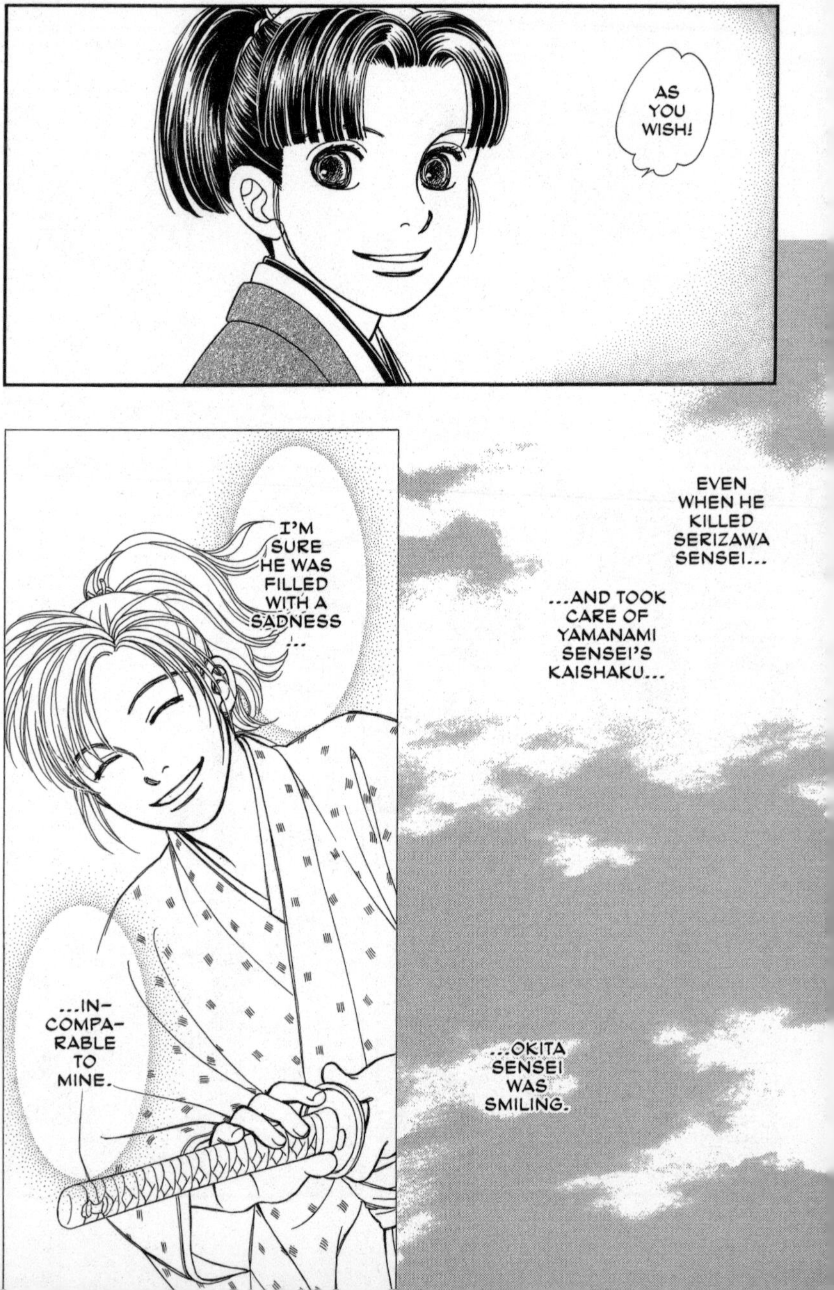
AS YOU WISH!
EVEN WHEN HE KILLED SERIZAWA SENSEI...
...AND TOOK CARE OF YAMANAMI SENSEI'S KAISHAKU...
...OKITA SENSEI WAS SMILING.
I'M SURE HE WAS FILLED WITH A SADNESS...
...IN-COMPA-RABLE TO MINE.

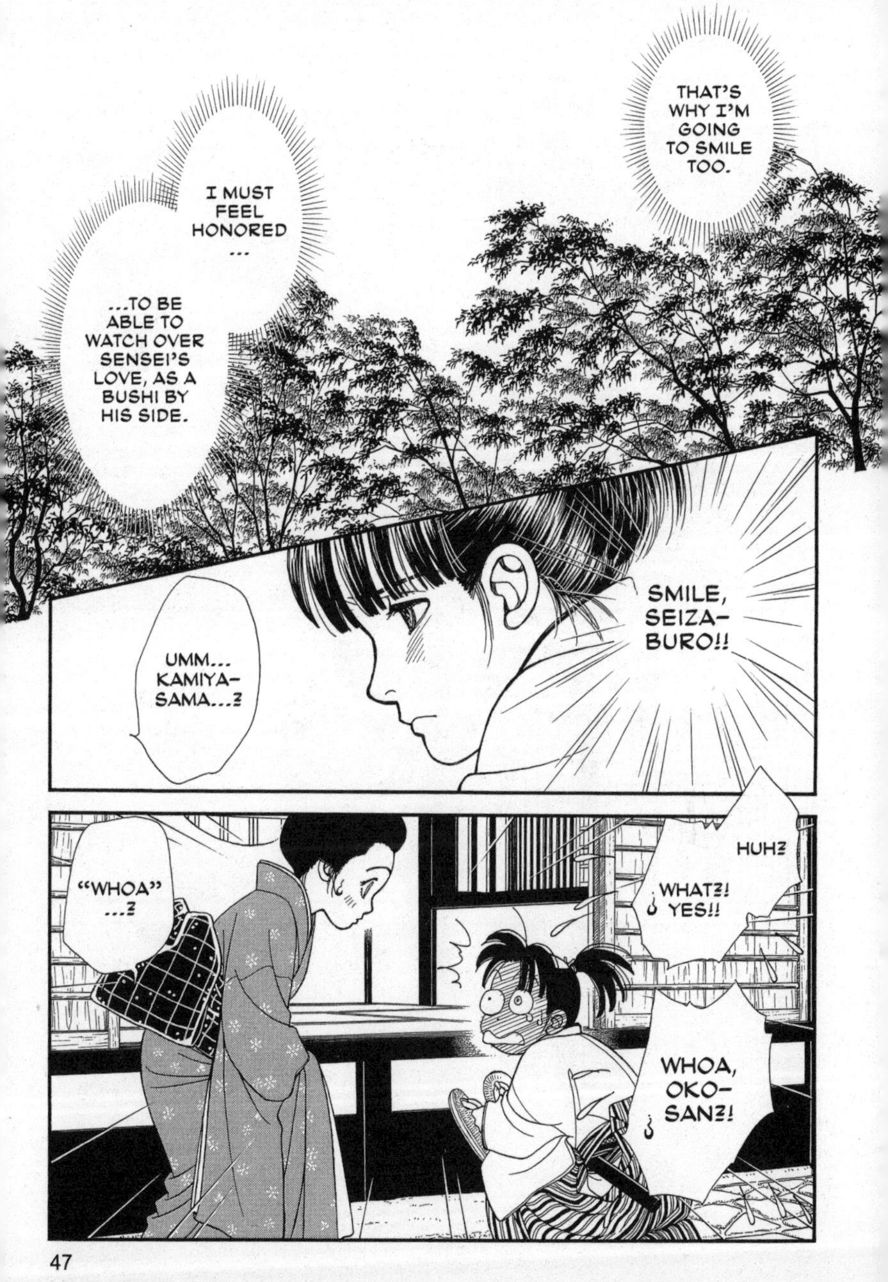
THAT'S WHY I'M GOING TO SMILE TOO.
I MUST FEEL HONORED ...
...TO BE ABLE TO WATCH OVER SENSEI'S LOVE, AS A BUSHI BY HIS SIDE.
SMILE, SEIZA-BURO!!
UMM... KAMIYA-SAMA...?
HUH?
WHAT?! YES!!
WHOA, OKO-SAN?!
"WHOA" ...?

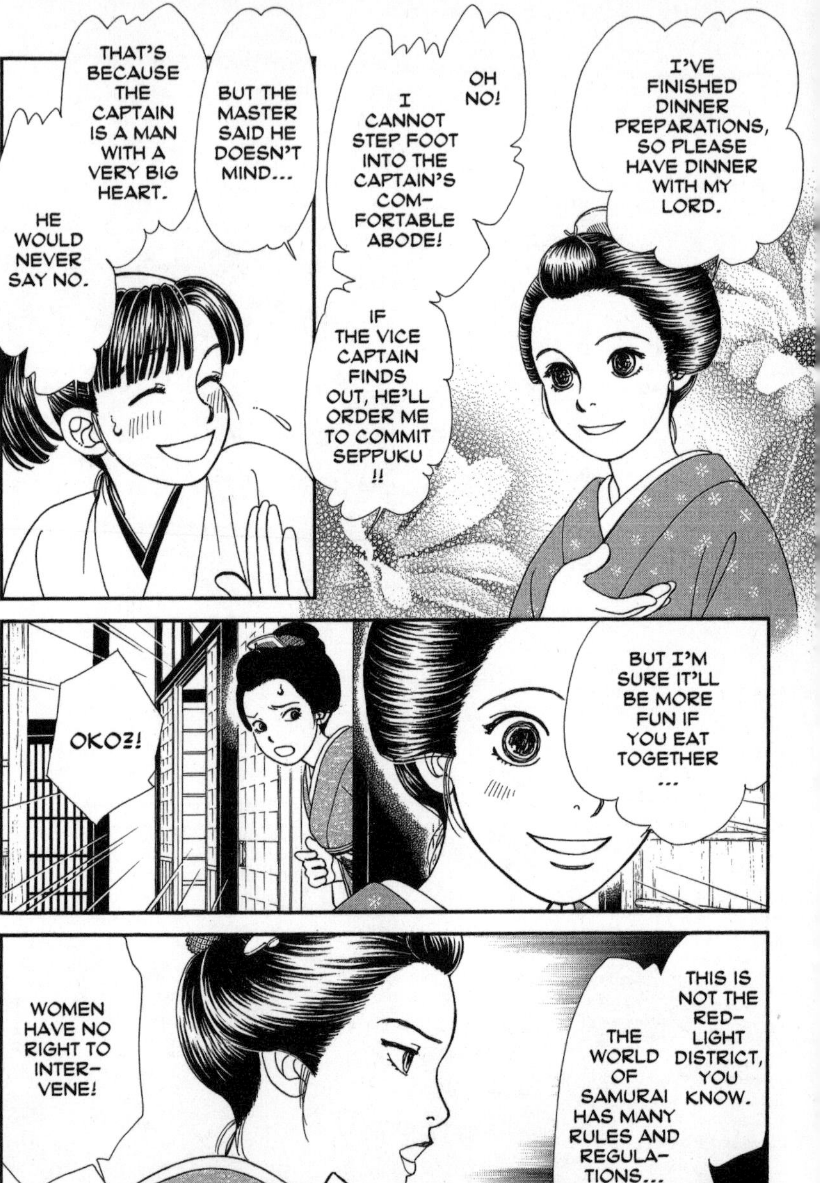
I'VE FINISHED DINNER PREPARATIONS, SO PLEASE HAVE DINNER WITH MY LORD.
OH NO!
I CANNOT STEP FOOT INTO THE CAPTAIN'S COM-FORTABLE ABODE!
IF THE VICE CAPTAIN FINDS OUT, HE'LL ORDER ME TO COMMIT SEPPUKU!!
BUT THE MASTER SAID HE DOESN'T MIND...
THAT'S BECAUSE THE CAPTAIN IS A MAN WITH A VERY BIG HEART.
HE WOULD NEVER SAY NO.
BUT I'M SURE IT'LL BE MORE FUN IF YOU EAT TOGETHER ...
OKO?!
THIS IS NOT THE RED-LIGHT DISTRICT, YOU KNOW.
THE WORLD OF SAMURAI HAS MANY RULES AND REGULA-TIONS...
WOMEN HAVE NO RIGHT TO INTER-VENE!

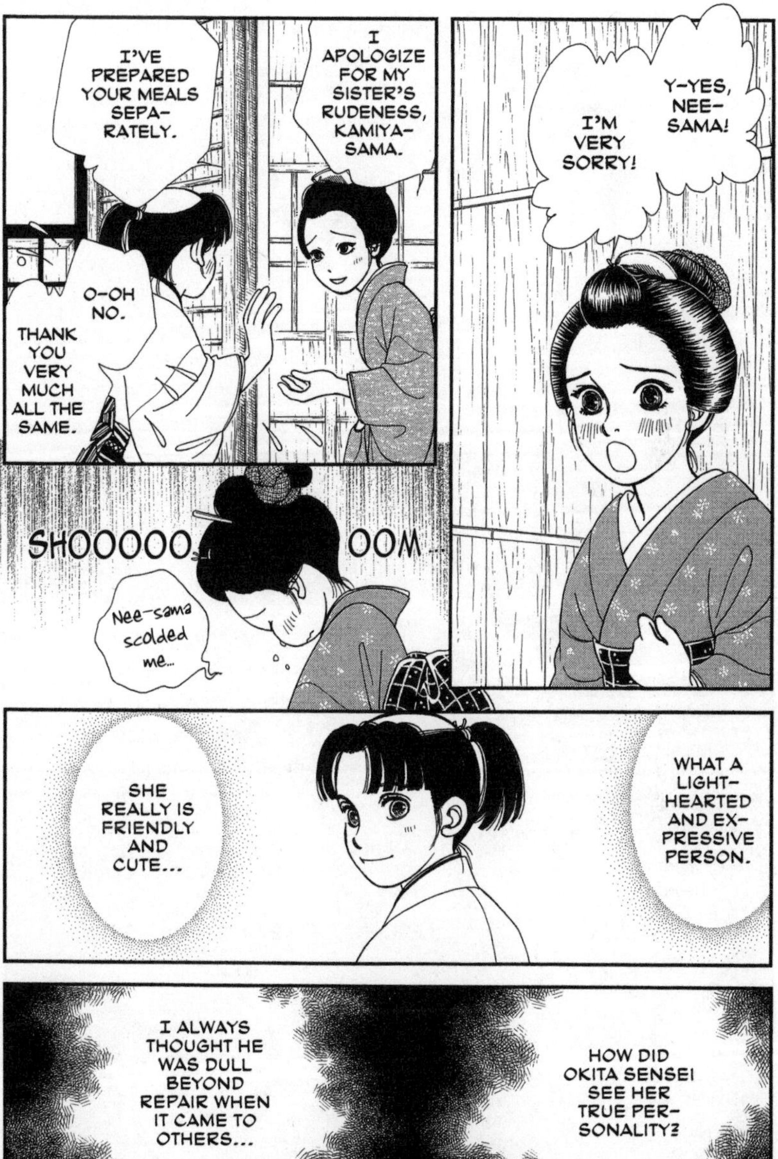
Y-YES, NEE-SAMA!
I'M VERY SORRY!
I APOLOGIZE FOR MY SISTER'S RUDENESS, KAMIYA-SAMA.
I'VE PREPARED YOUR MEALS SEPA-RATELY.
O-OH NO.
THANK YOU VERY MUCH ALL THE SAME.
SHOOOOOOOM...
Nee-sama scolded me...
WHAT A LIGHT-HEARTED AND EX-PRESSIVE PERSON.
SHE REALLY IS FRIENDLY AND CUTE...
HOW DID OKITA SENSEI SEE HER TRUE PER-SONALITY?
I ALWAYS THOUGHT HE WAS DULL BEYOND REPAIR WHEN IT CAME TO OTHERS...

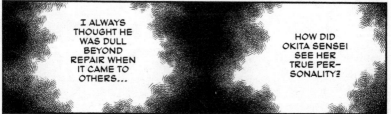

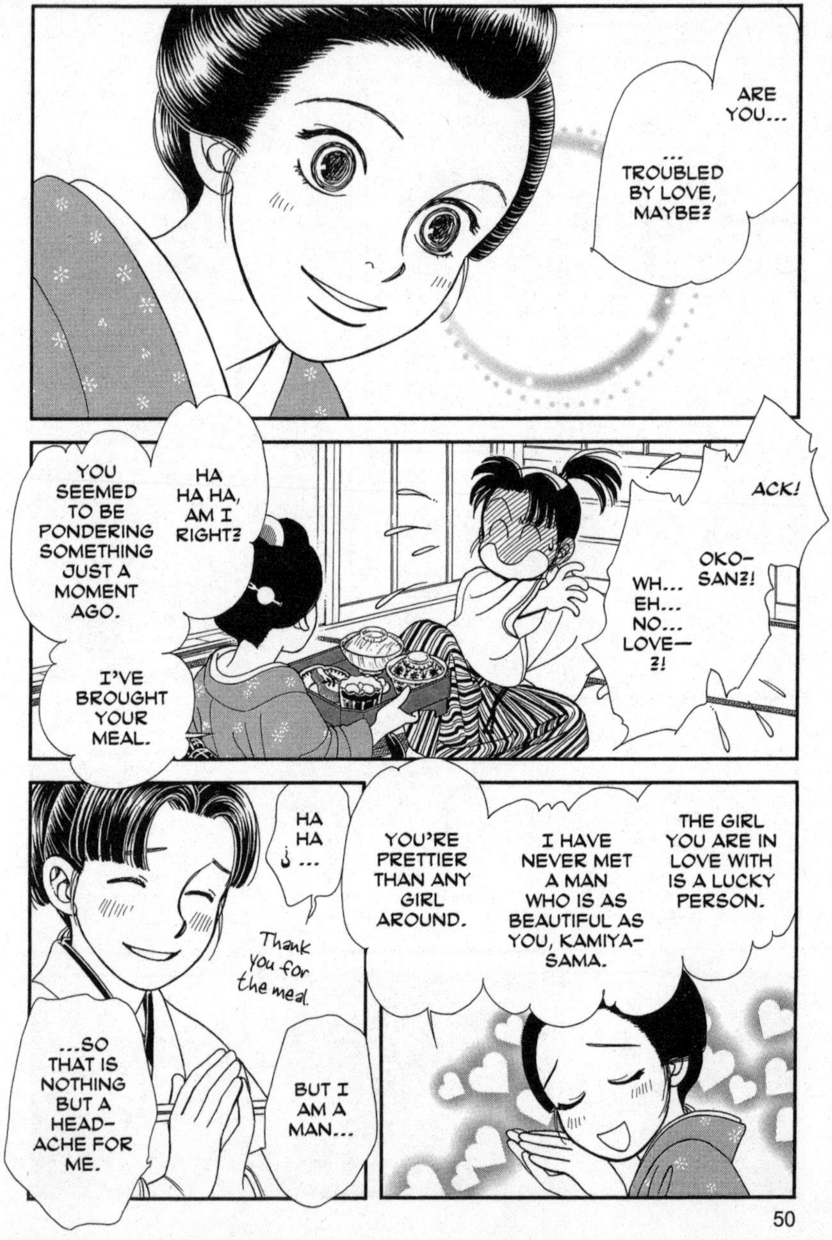
ARE YOU...
...TROUBLED BY LOVE, MAYBE?
ACK!
OKO-SAN?!
WH... EH... NO... LOVE—?!
HA HA HA, AM I RIGHT?
YOU SEEMED TO BE PONDERING SOMETHING JUST A MOMENT AGO.
I'VE BROUGHT YOUR MEAL.
THE GIRL YOU ARE IN LOVE WITH IS A LUCKY PERSON.
I HAVE NEVER MET A MAN WHO IS AS BEAUTIFUL AS YOU, KAMIYA-SAMA.
YOU'RE PRETTIER THAN ANY GIRL AROUND.
HA HA ¿...
Thank you for the meal.
BUT I AM A MAN...
...SO THAT IS NOTHING BUT A HEADACHE FOR ME.

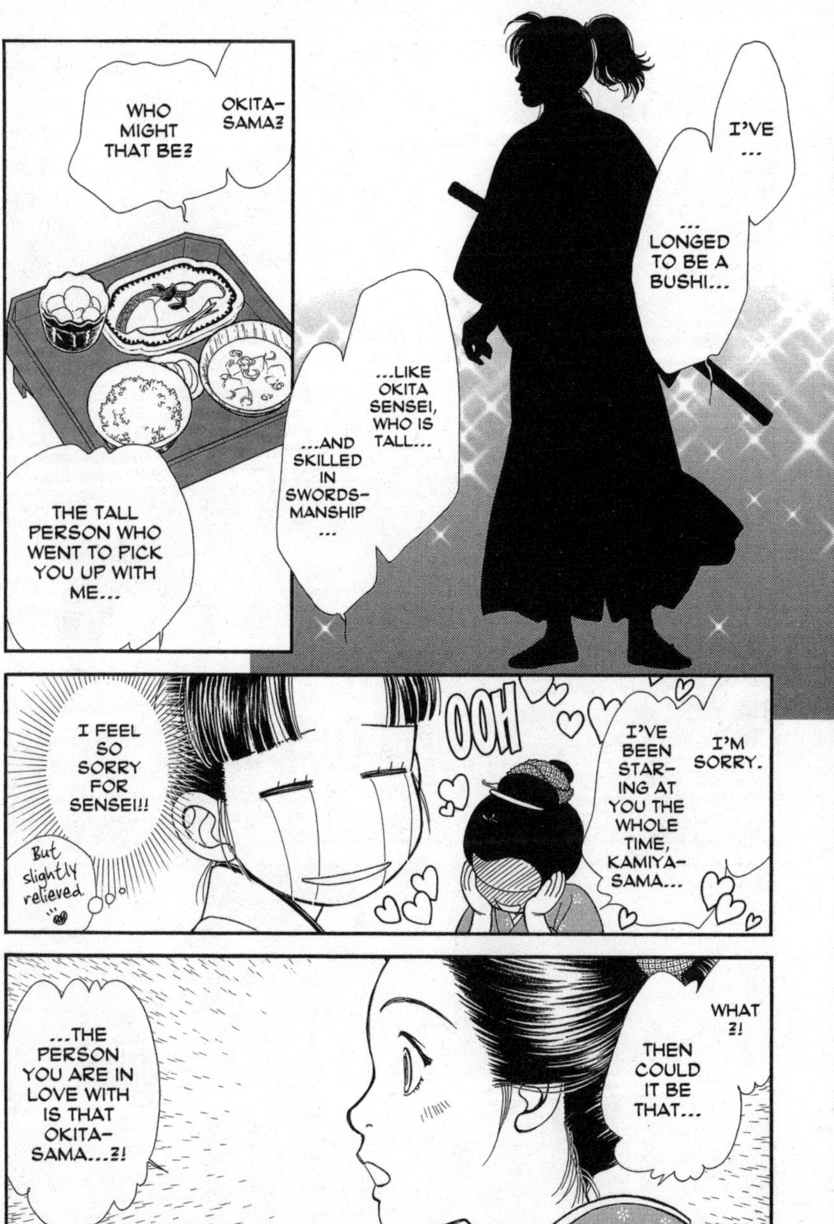
I'VE ...
... LONGED TO BE A BUSHI...
...LIKE OKITA SENSEI, WHO IS TALL...
...AND SKILLED IN SWORDSMANSHIP ...
OKITA-SAMA?
WHO MIGHT THAT BE?
THE TALL PERSON WHO WENT TO PICK YOU UP WITH ME...
I'M SORRY.
I'VE BEEN STARING AT YOU THE WHOLE TIME, KAMIYA-SAMA...
OOH
I FEEL SO SORRY FOR SENSEI!!
But slightly relieved
WHAT?!
THEN COULD IT BE THAT...
...THE PERSON YOU ARE IN LOVE WITH IS THAT OKITA-SAMA...?!

WHAT
?!

OKO!!

EH...

WHAT

I NEVER IMAGINED SUCH BUSHI TRADITIONS CARRIED ON INTO THIS DAY AND AGE!!

THIS IS THE FIRST TIME I'VE SEEN THIS! IT'S CALLED *SHUDO*, RIGHT?

HOW NICE. ♡

OOH, AM I RIGHT ?!

SUPER CURIOUS!

I'M SORRY, MIYUKI NEE-SAMA!

YES!!

HOW RUDE! WOMEN MUST LEAVE AS SOON AS THEY'VE FINISHED SERVING THE FOOD!

I'M SORRY.

YOU'RE SUCH A BAD GIRL!!

COME WITH ME, OKO-CHAN!

OH NO...

I'M SORRY SHE'S SUCH AN UNMAN-NERLY GIRL, KAMIYA-SAMA.

MIYUKI-DAYU...

...MUST BE VERY FOND OF OKO-SAN.

She seems to enjoy even scolding her.

OKO-SAN...

SHE'S LIKE THE SPRING SUNSHINE...

...EVEN THE LOFTY MIYUKI-DAYU SEEMS TO LOWER HERSELF TO THE GROUND AND RELAX...

WHEN OKO-SAN IS AROUND...

BUT MIYUKI NEE-SAMA...

HEY...

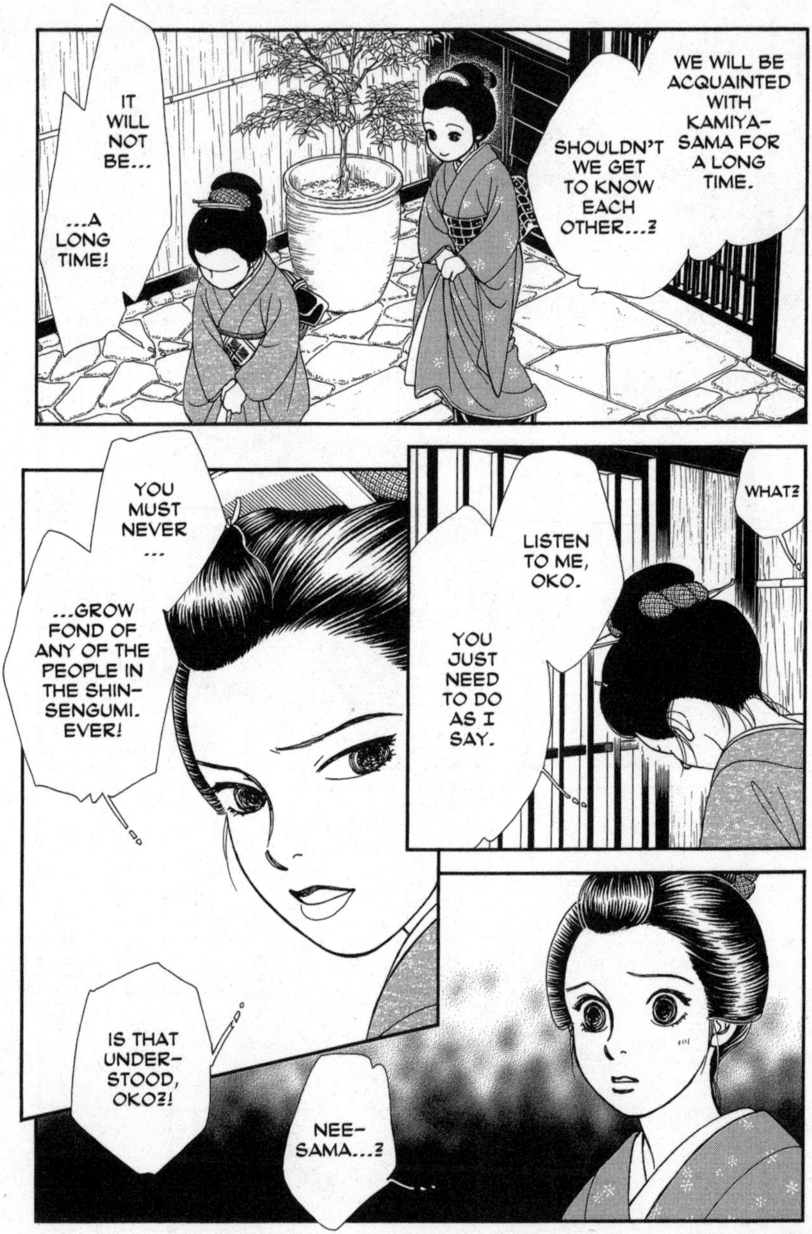
WE WILL BE ACQUAINTED WITH KAMIYA-SAMA FOR A LONG TIME.
SHOULDN'T WE GET TO KNOW EACH OTHER...?
IT WILL NOT BE...
...A LONG TIME!
WHAT?
LISTEN TO ME, OKO.
YOU JUST NEED TO DO AS I SAY.
YOU MUST NEVER...
...GROW FOND OF ANY OF THE PEOPLE IN THE SHIN-SENGUMI. EVER!
IS THAT UNDERSTOOD, OKO?!
NEE-SAMA...?

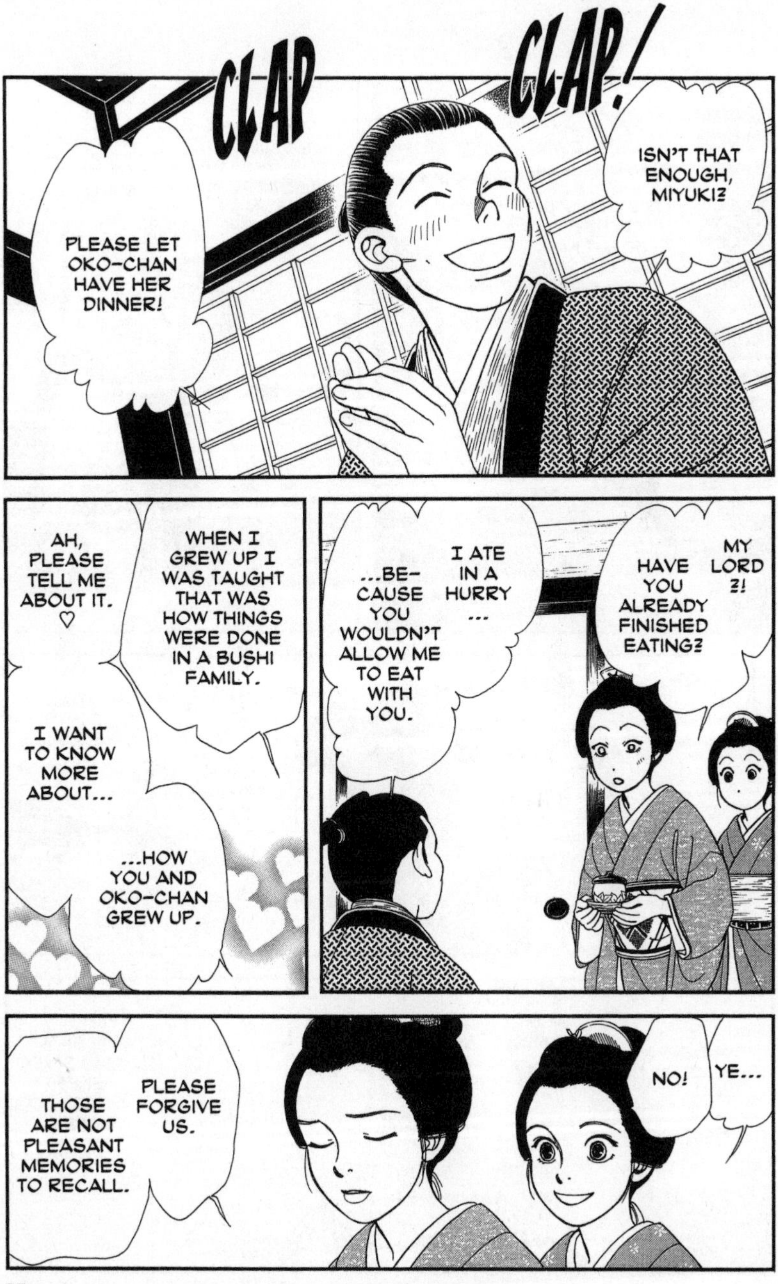
CLAP CLAP!
ISN'T THAT ENOUGH, MIYUKI?
PLEASE LET OKO-CHAN HAVE HER DINNER!
MY LORD?!
HAVE YOU ALREADY FINISHED EATING?
I ATE IN A HURRY...
...BE-CAUSE YOU WOULDN'T ALLOW ME TO EAT WITH YOU.
WHEN I GREW UP I WAS TAUGHT THAT WAS HOW THINGS WERE DONE IN A BUSHI FAMILY.
AH, PLEASE TELL ME ABOUT IT. ♡
I WANT TO KNOW MORE ABOUT...
...HOW YOU AND OKO-CHAN GREW UP.
YE...
NO!
PLEASE FORGIVE US.
THOSE ARE NOT PLEASANT MEMORIES TO RECALL.

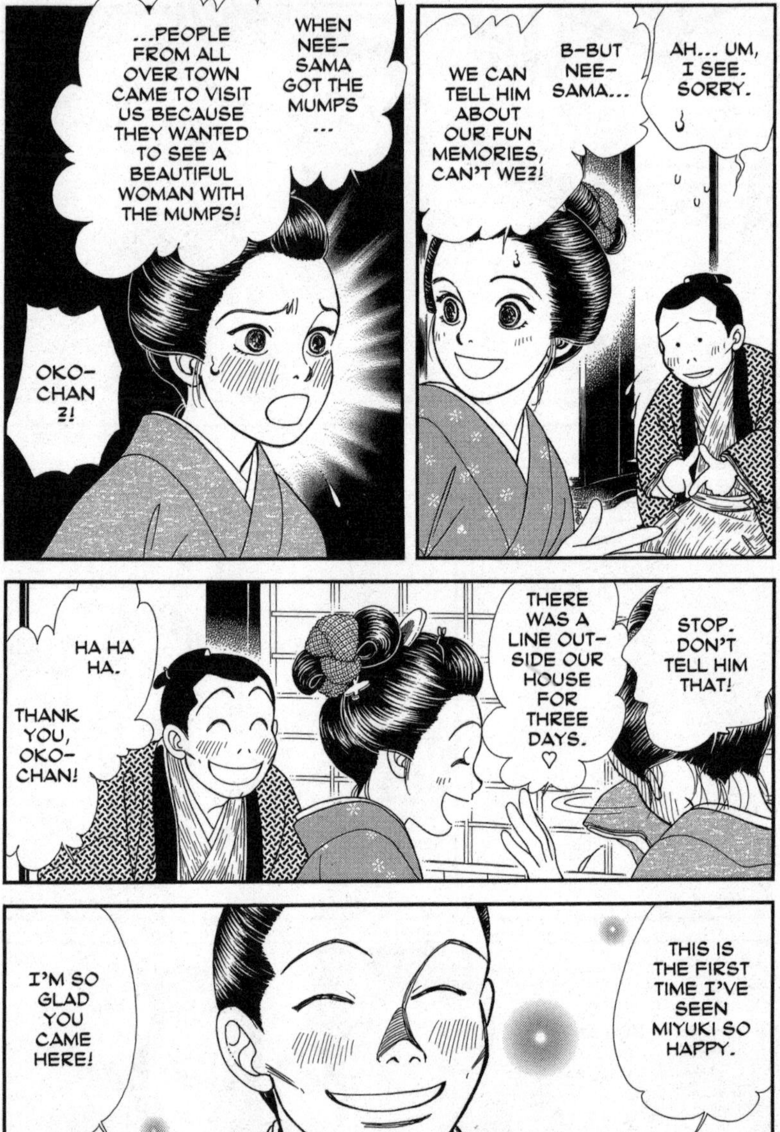
AH... UM, I SEE. SORRY.
B-BUT NEE-SAMA...
WE CAN TELL HIM ABOUT OUR FUN MEMORIES, CAN'T WE?!
WHEN NEE-SAMA GOT THE MUMPS ...
...PEOPLE FROM ALL OVER TOWN CAME TO VISIT US BECAUSE THEY WANTED TO SEE A BEAUTIFUL WOMAN WITH THE MUMPS!
OKO-CHAN?!
STOP. DON'T TELL HIM THAT!
THERE WAS A LINE OUTSIDE OUR HOUSE FOR THREE DAYS. ♡
HA HA HA.
THANK YOU, OKO-CHAN!
THIS IS THE FIRST TIME I'VE SEEN MIYUKI SO HAPPY.
I'M SO GLAD YOU CAME HERE!

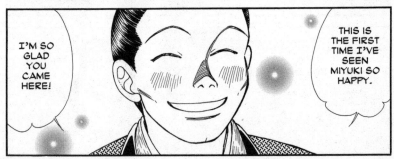

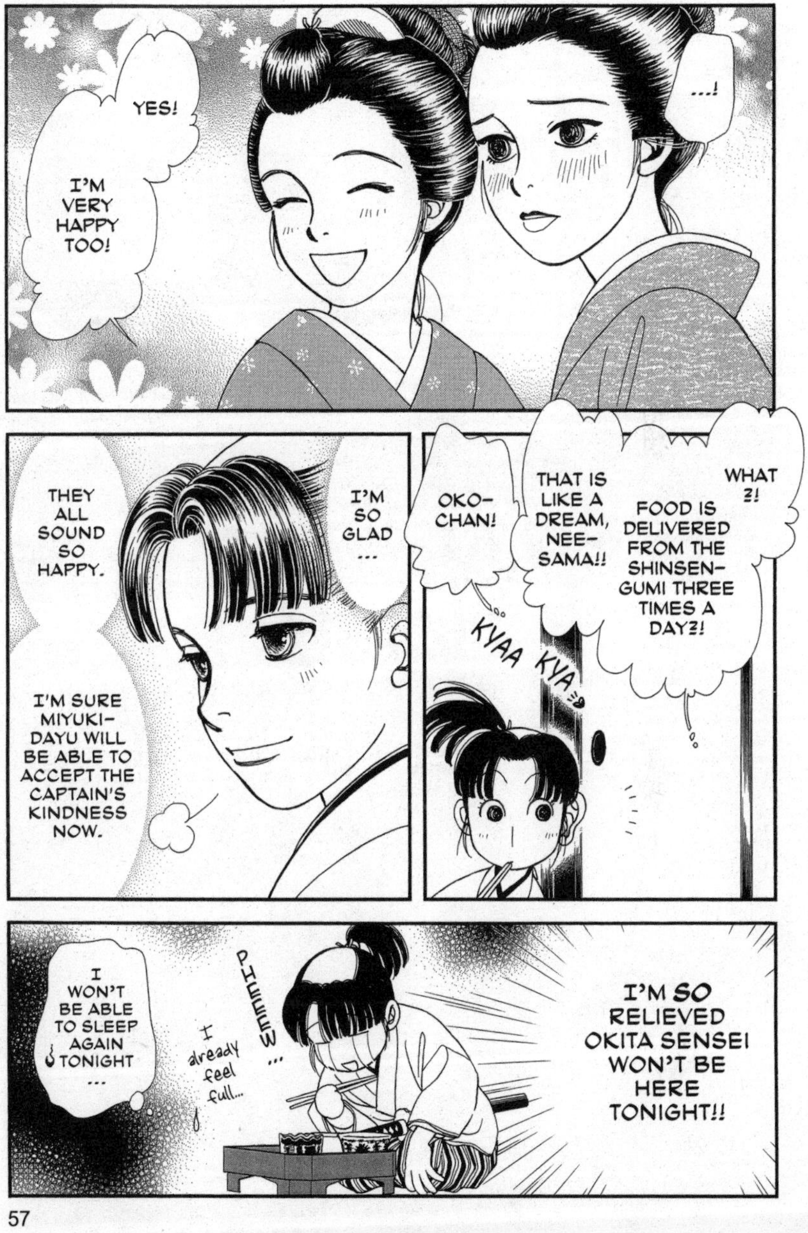
...!
YES!
I'M VERY HAPPY TOO!
WHAT?!
FOOD IS DELIVERED FROM THE SHINSEN-GUMI THREE TIMES A DAY?!
THAT IS LIKE A DREAM, NEE-SAMA!!
OKO-CHAN!
KYAA KYA
I'M SO GLAD...
THEY ALL SOUND SO HAPPY.
I'M SURE MIYUKI-DAYU WILL BE ABLE TO ACCEPT THE CAPTAIN'S KINDNESS NOW.
I'M SO RELIEVED OKITA SENSEI WON'T BE HERE TONIGHT!!
PHEEEW...
I already feel full...
I WON'T BE ABLE TO SLEEP AGAIN TONIGHT...

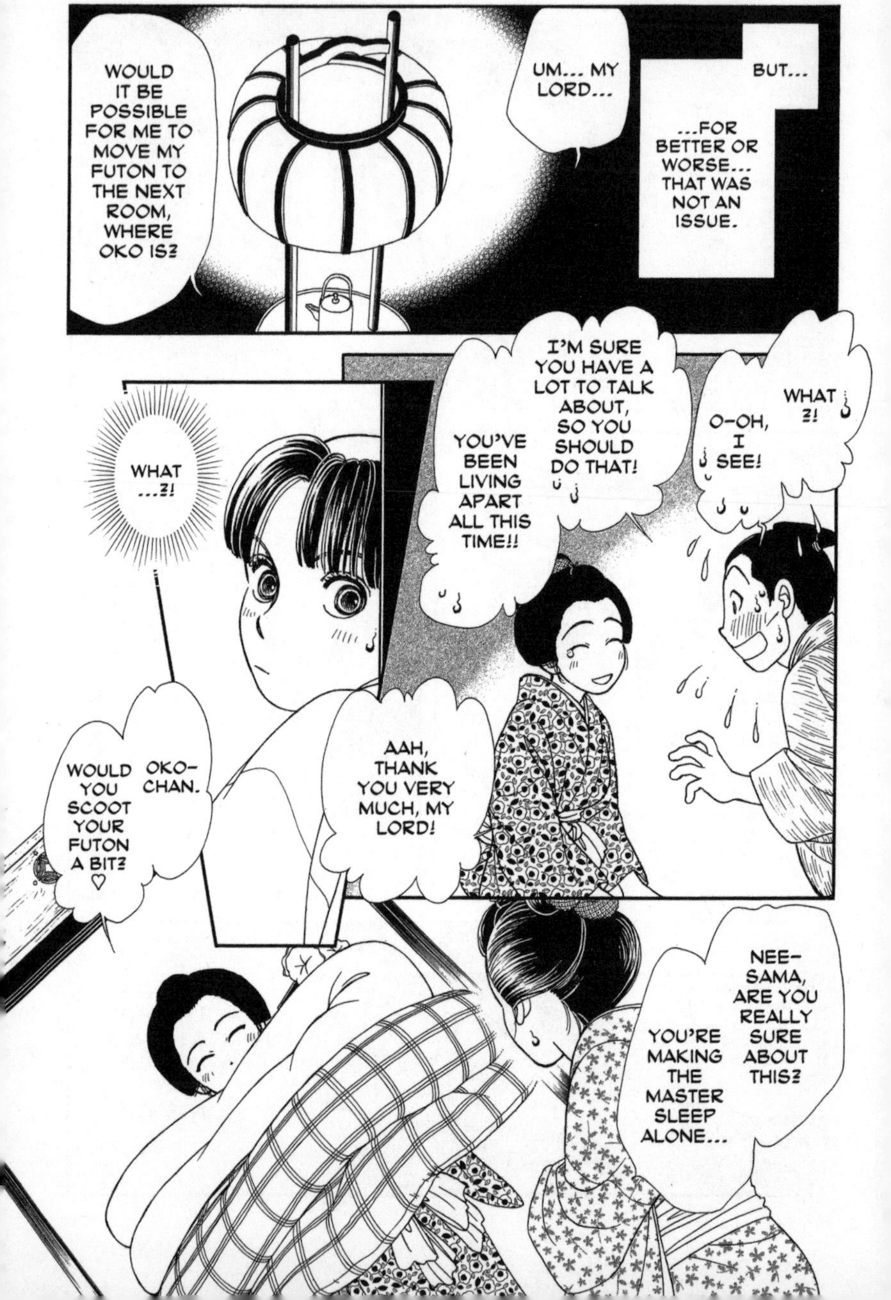
BUT...
...FOR BETTER OR WORSE... THAT WAS NOT AN ISSUE.
UM... MY LORD...
WOULD IT BE POSSIBLE FOR ME TO MOVE MY FUTON TO THE NEXT ROOM, WHERE OKO IS?
WHAT?!
O-OH, I SEE!
I'M SURE YOU HAVE A LOT TO TALK ABOUT, SO YOU SHOULD DO THAT!
YOU'VE BEEN LIVING APART ALL THIS TIME!!
AAH, THANK YOU VERY MUCH, MY LORD!
WHAT...?!
OKO-CHAN.
WOULD YOU SCOOT YOUR FUTON A BIT? ♡
NEE-SAMA, ARE YOU REALLY SURE ABOUT THIS?
YOU'RE MAKING THE MASTER SLEEP ALONE...

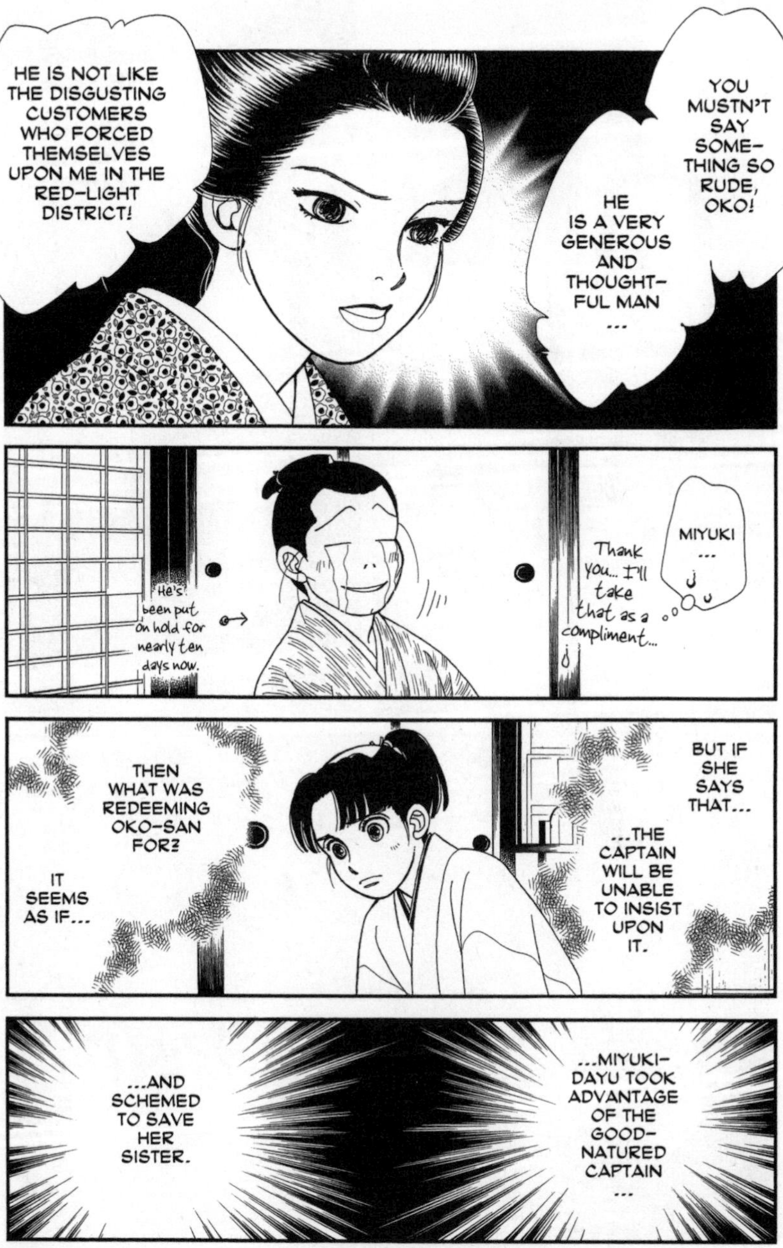
YOU MUSTN'T SAY SOME-THING SO RUDE, OKO!
HE IS A VERY GENEROUS AND THOUGHT-FUL MAN ...
HE IS NOT LIKE THE DISGUSTING CUSTOMERS WHO FORCED THEMSELVES UPON ME IN THE RED-LIGHT DISTRICT!
MIYUKI ...
Thank you... I'll take that as a compliment...
He's been put on hold for nearly ten days now.
BUT IF SHE SAYS THAT...
...THE CAPTAIN WILL BE UNABLE TO INSIST UPON IT.
THEN WHAT WAS REDEEMING OKO-SAN FOR?
IT SEEMS AS IF...
...MIYUKI-DAYU TOOK ADVANTAGE OF THE GOOD-NATURED CAPTAIN ...
...AND SCHEMED TO SAVE HER SISTER.

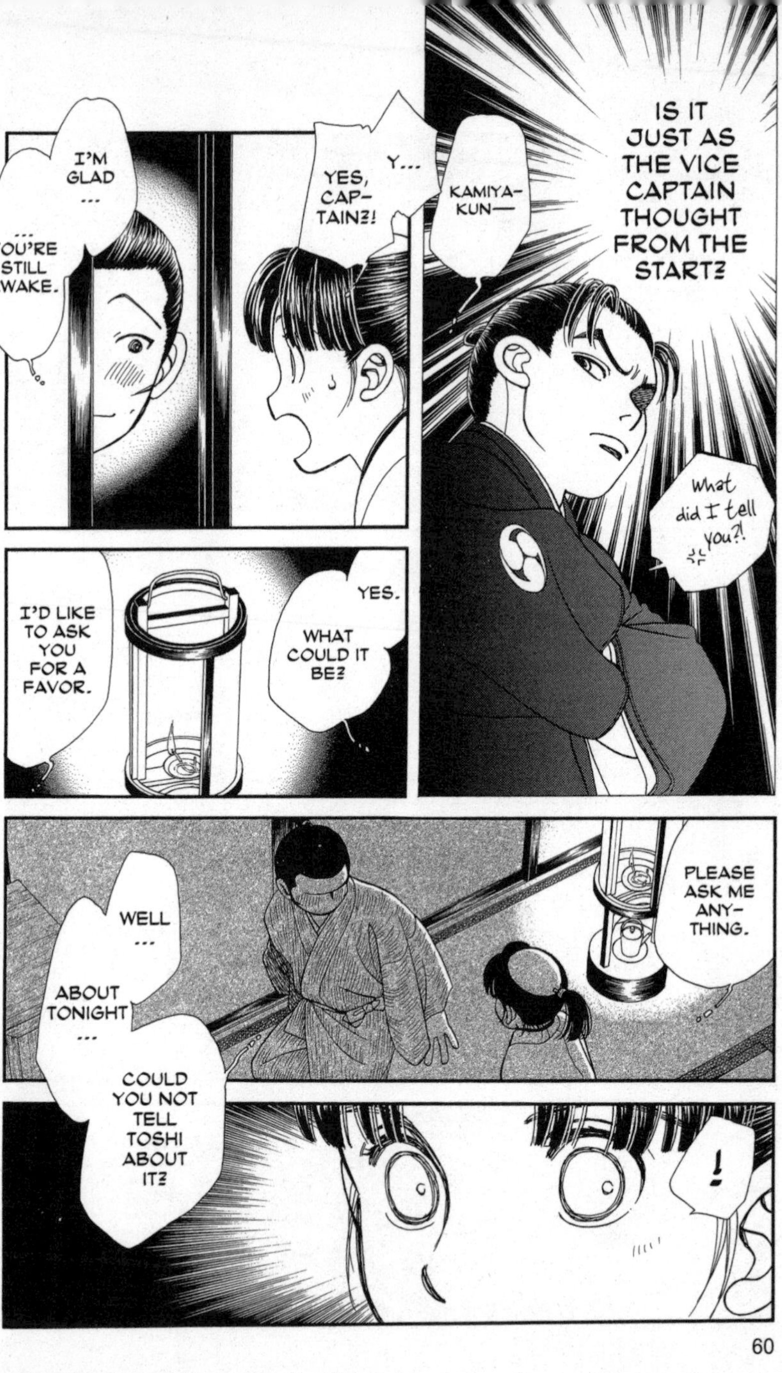
IS IT JUST AS THE VICE CAPTAIN THOUGHT FROM THE START?
KAMIYA-KUN—
What did I tell you?!
Y... YES, CAPTAIN?!
I'M GLAD... ...YOU'RE STILL AWAKE.
YES. WHAT COULD IT BE?
I'D LIKE TO ASK YOU FOR A FAVOR.
PLEASE ASK ME ANYTHING.
WELL... ABOUT TONIGHT... COULD YOU NOT TELL TOSHI ABOUT IT?
!

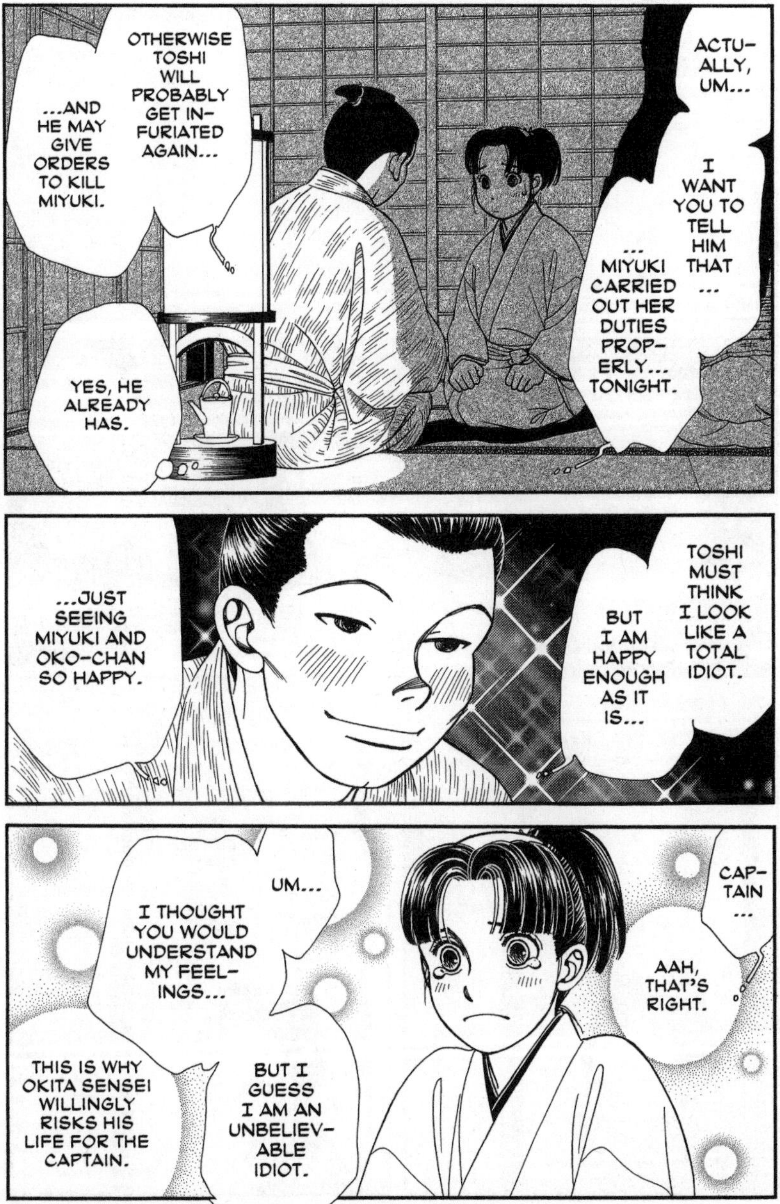
ACTUALLY, UM...
I WANT YOU TO TELL HIM THAT...
...MIYUKI CARRIED OUT HER DUTIES PROPERLY... TONIGHT.
OTHERWISE TOSHI WILL PROBABLY GET INFURIATED AGAIN...
...AND HE MAY GIVE ORDERS TO KILL MIYUKI.
YES, HE ALREADY HAS.
TOSHI MUST THINK I LOOK LIKE A TOTAL IDIOT.
BUT I AM HAPPY ENOUGH AS IT IS...
...JUST SEEING MIYUKI AND OKO-CHAN SO HAPPY.
CAPTAIN...
AAH, THAT'S RIGHT.
UM...
I THOUGHT YOU WOULD UNDERSTAND MY FEELINGS...
BUT I GUESS I AM AN UNBELIEVABLE IDIOT.
THIS IS WHY OKITA SENSEI WILLINGLY RISKS HIS LIFE FOR THE CAPTAIN.

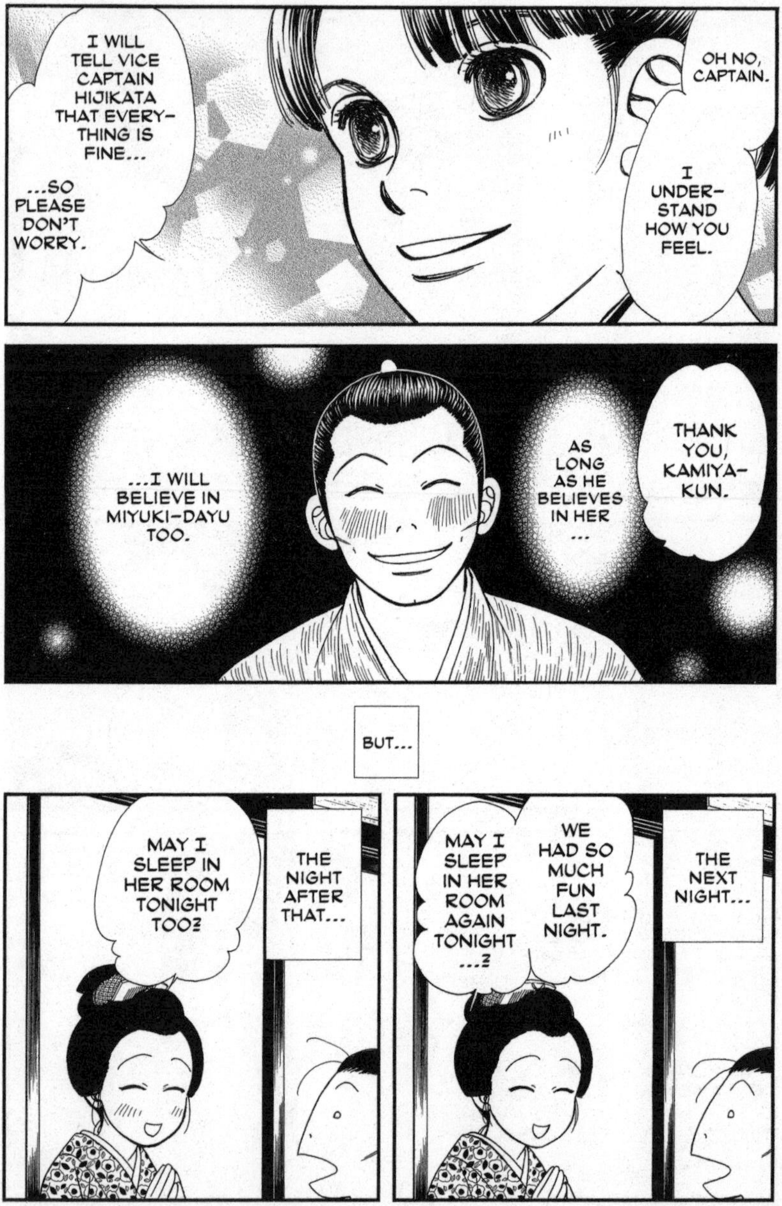
OH NO, CAPTAIN.
I UNDERSTAND HOW YOU FEEL.
I WILL TELL VICE CAPTAIN HIJIKATA THAT EVERYTHING IS FINE...
...SO PLEASE DON'T WORRY.
THANK YOU, KAMIYA-KUN.
AS LONG AS HE BELIEVES IN HER ...
...I WILL BELIEVE IN MIYUKI-DAYU TOO.
BUT...
THE NEXT NIGHT...
WE HAD SO MUCH FUN LAST NIGHT.
MAY I SLEEP IN HER ROOM AGAIN TONIGHT ...?
THE NIGHT AFTER THAT...
MAY I SLEEP IN HER ROOM TONIGHT TOO?

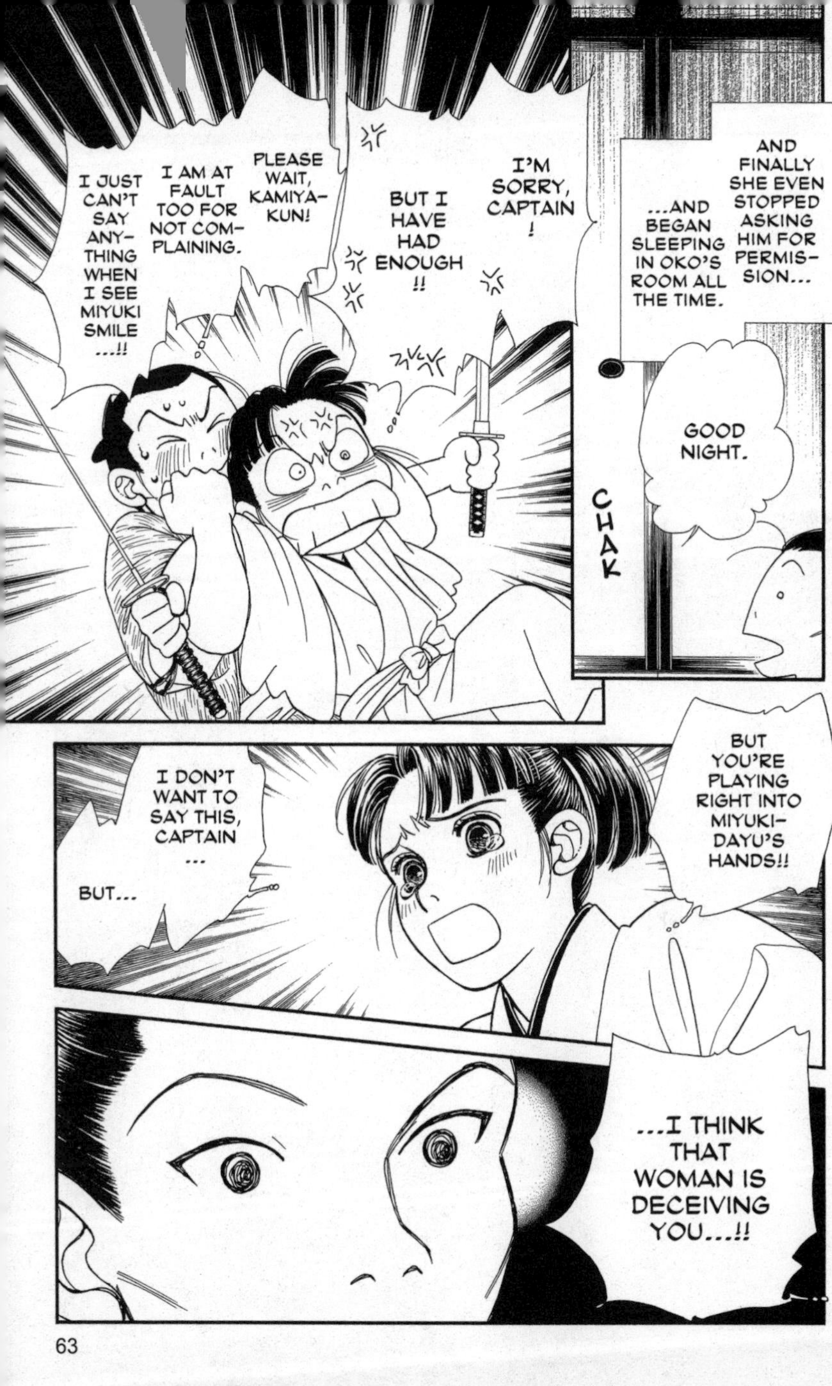
AND FINALLY SHE EVEN STOPPED ASKING HIM FOR PERMISSION...
...AND BEGAN SLEEPING IN OKO'S ROOM ALL THE TIME.
GOOD NIGHT.
CHAK
I'M SORRY, CAPTAIN!
BUT I HAVE HAD ENOUGH!!
PLEASE WAIT, KAMIYA-KUN!
I AM AT FAULT TOO FOR NOT COMPLAINING.
I JUST CAN'T SAY ANYTHING WHEN I SEE MIYUKI SMILE...!!
BUT YOU'RE PLAYING RIGHT INTO MIYUKI-DAYU'S HANDS!!
I DON'T WANT TO SAY THIS, CAPTAIN...
BUT...
...I THINK THAT WOMAN IS DECEIVING YOU...!!

*Komano is a geiko Kondo was once involved with. Read all about it in Volume 9.♡

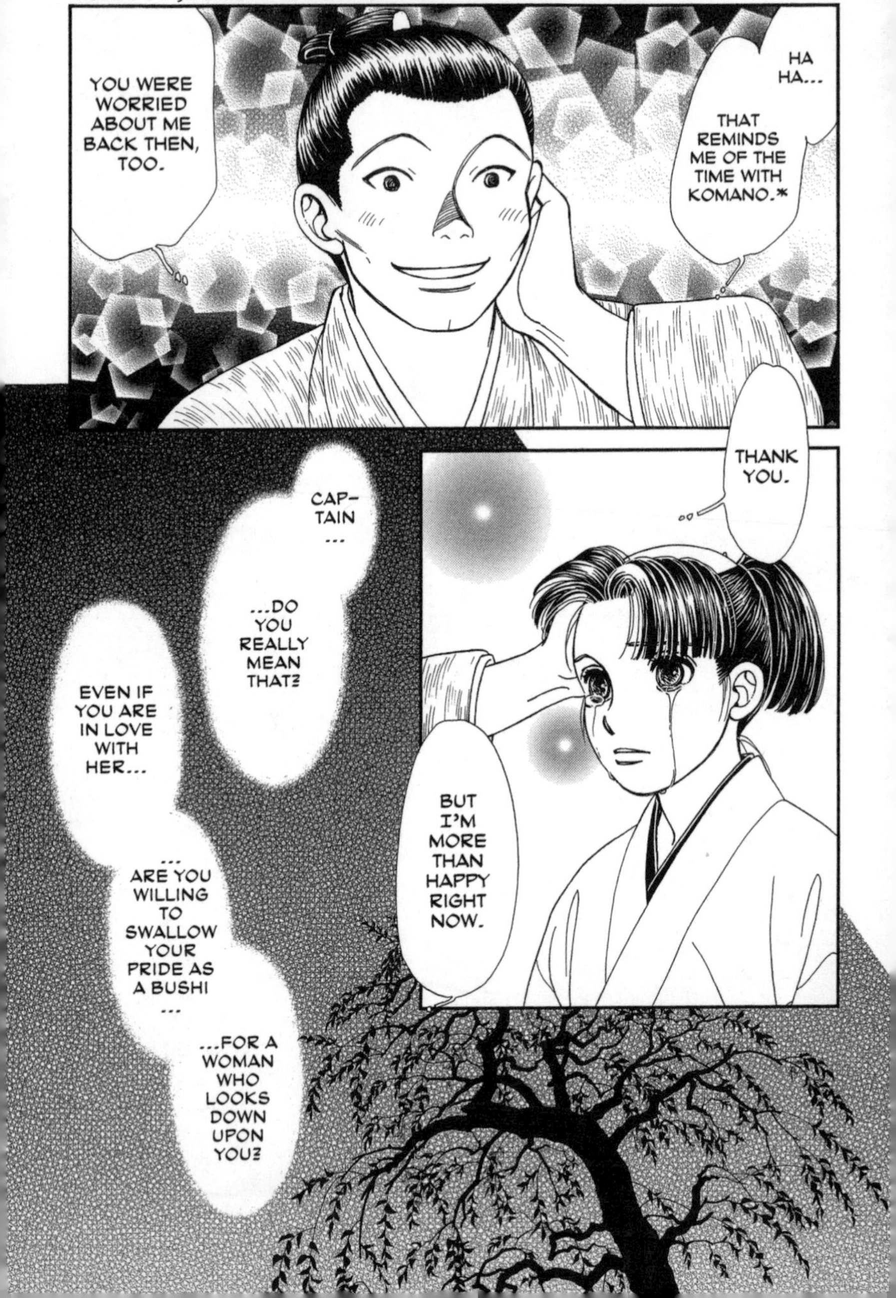
HA HA...
THAT REMINDS ME OF THE TIME WITH KOMANO.*
YOU WERE WORRIED ABOUT ME BACK THEN, TOO.
THANK YOU.
BUT I'M MORE THAN HAPPY RIGHT NOW.
CAPTAIN...
...DO YOU REALLY MEAN THAT?
EVEN IF YOU ARE IN LOVE WITH HER...
...ARE YOU WILLING TO SWALLOW YOUR PRIDE AS A BUSHI...
...FOR A WOMAN WHO LOOKS DOWN UPON YOU?

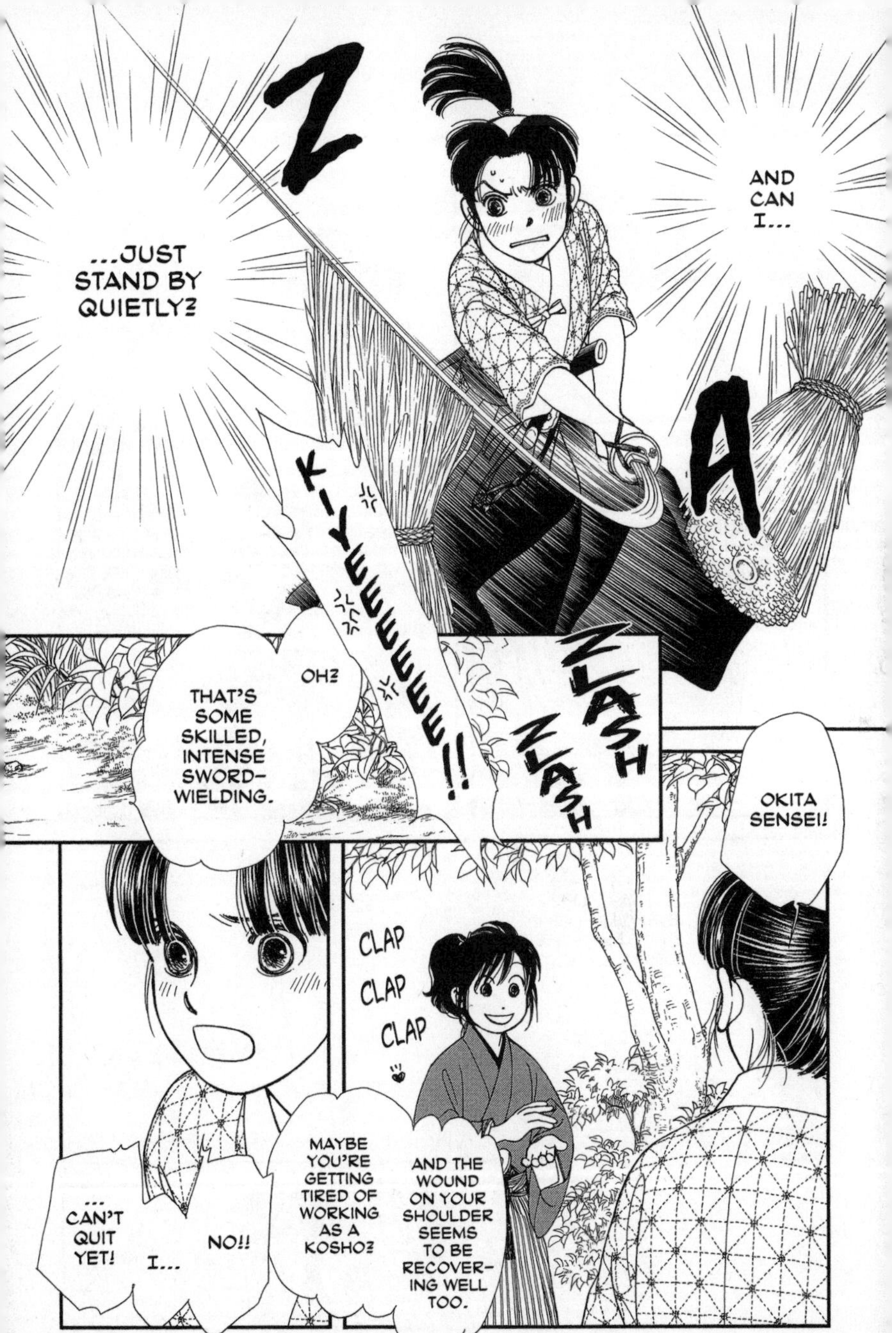
AND CAN I...
...JUST STAND BY QUIETLY?
Z
A
KIYEEEEEEE!!
ZLASH
ZLASH
OH?
THAT'S SOME SKILLED, INTENSE SWORD-WIELDING.
OKITA SENSEI!
CLAP
CLAP
CLAP
AND THE WOUND ON YOUR SHOULDER SEEMS TO BE RECOVERING WELL TOO.
MAYBE YOU'RE GETTING TIRED OF WORKING AS A KOSHO?
NO!!
I...
...CAN'T QUIT YET!

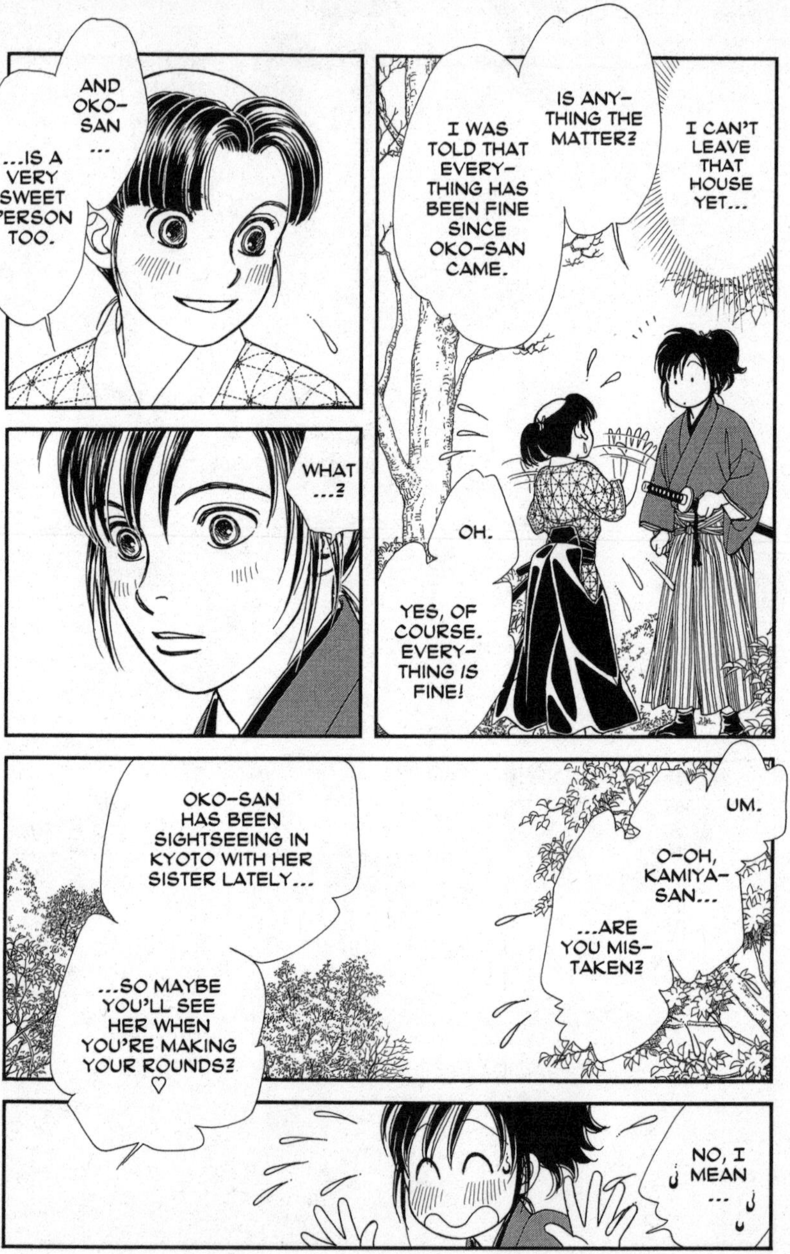
I CAN'T LEAVE THAT HOUSE YET...
IS ANYTHING THE MATTER?
I WAS TOLD THAT EVERYTHING HAS BEEN FINE SINCE OKO-SAN CAME.
OH.
YES, OF COURSE. EVERYTHING *IS* FINE!
AND OKO-SAN ...
...IS A VERY SWEET PERSON TOO.
WHAT ...?
UM.
O-OH, KAMIYA-SAN...
...ARE YOU MISTAKEN?
OKO-SAN HAS BEEN SIGHTSEEING IN KYOTO WITH HER SISTER LATELY...
...SO MAYBE YOU'LL SEE HER WHEN YOU'RE MAKING YOUR ROUNDS? ♡
NO, I MEAN ...

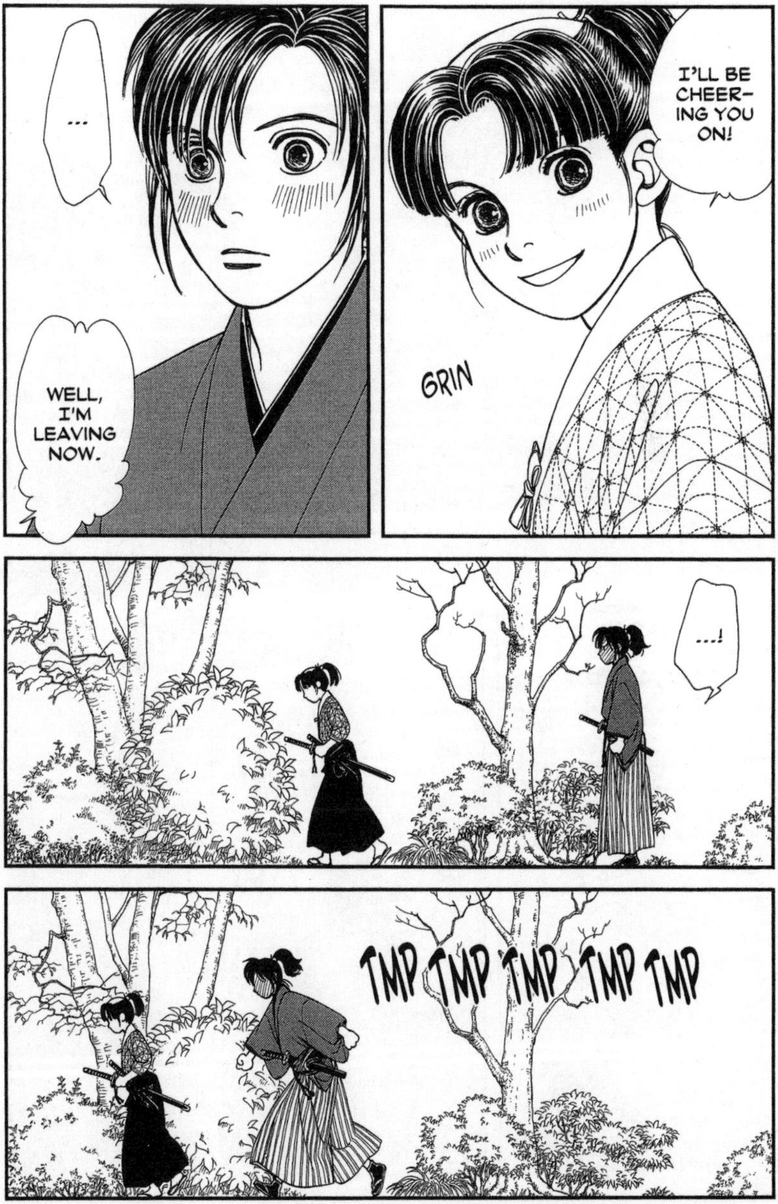
I'LL BE CHEER-ING YOU ON!
GRIN
...
WELL, I'M LEAVING NOW.
...!
TMP TMP TMP TMP TMP

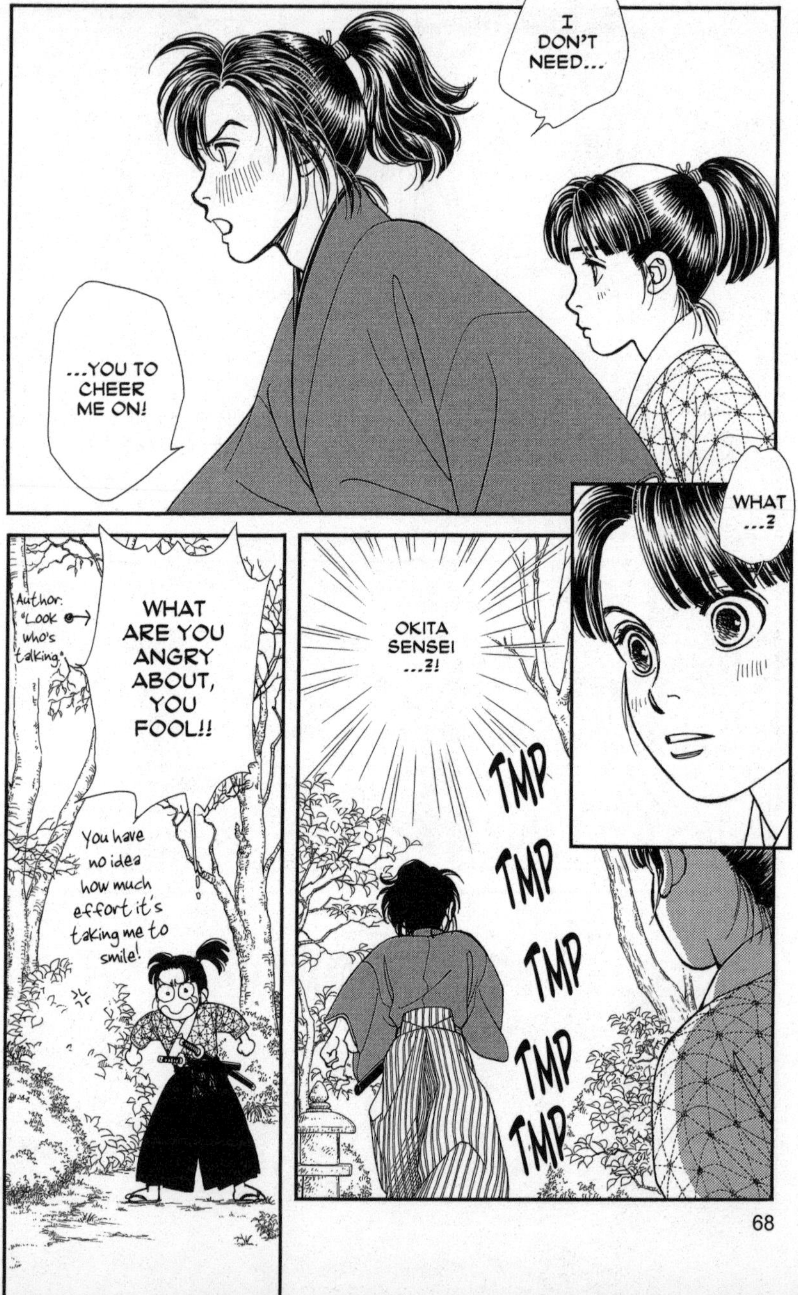
I DON'T NEED...
...YOU TO CHEER ME ON!
WHAT ...?
OKITA SENSEI ...?!
TMP
TMP
TMP
TMP
TMP
WHAT ARE YOU ANGRY ABOUT, YOU FOOL!!
You have no idea how much effort it's taking me to smile!
Author: "Look who's talking."

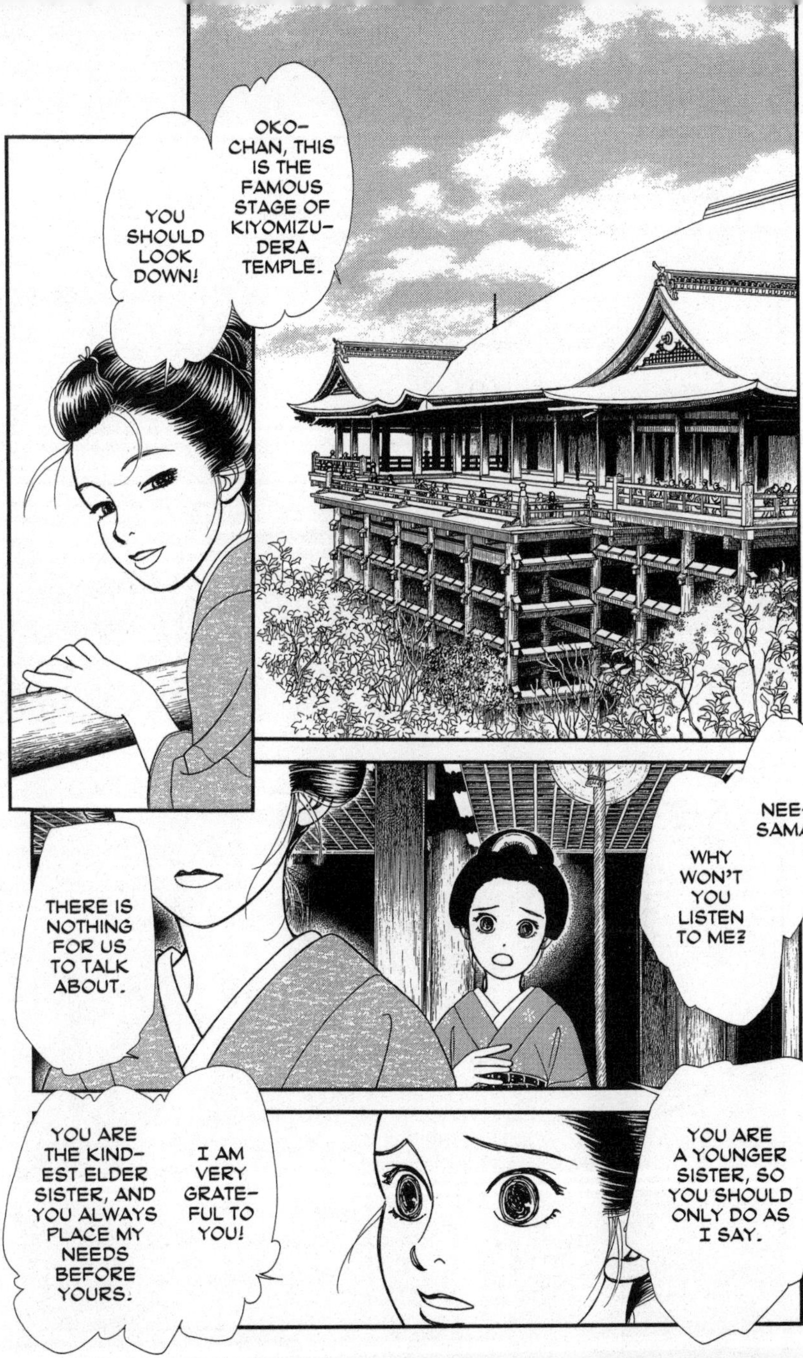
OKO-CHAN, THIS IS THE FAMOUS STAGE OF KIYOMIZU-DERA TEMPLE.
YOU SHOULD LOOK DOWN!
NEE-SAMA!
WHY WON'T YOU LISTEN TO ME?
THERE IS NOTHING FOR US TO TALK ABOUT.
YOU ARE A YOUNGER SISTER, SO YOU SHOULD ONLY DO AS I SAY.
I AM VERY GRATEFUL TO YOU!
YOU ARE THE KINDEST ELDER SISTER, AND YOU ALWAYS PLACE MY NEEDS BEFORE YOURS.

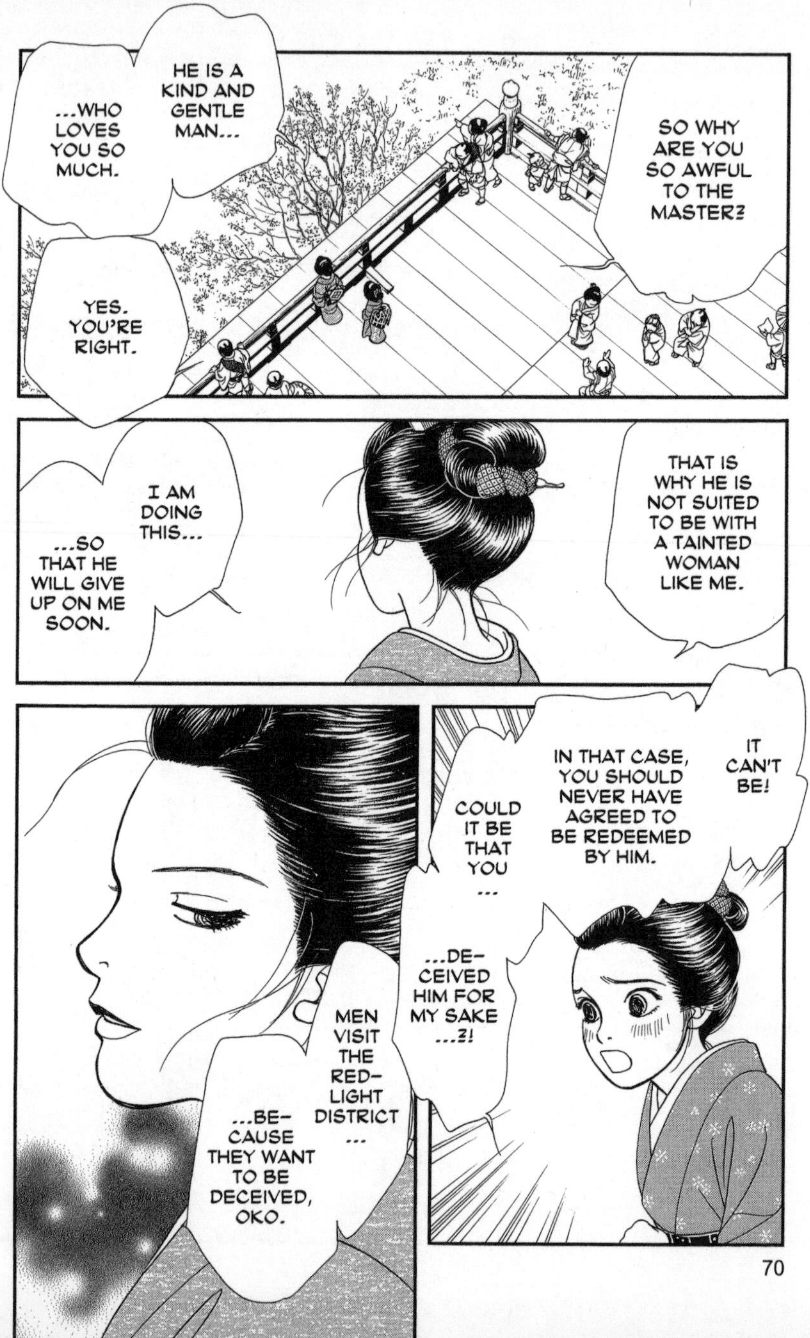
SO WHY ARE YOU SO AWFUL TO THE MASTER?
HE IS A KIND AND GENTLE MAN...
...WHO LOVES YOU SO MUCH.
YES. YOU'RE RIGHT.
THAT IS WHY HE IS NOT SUITED TO BE WITH A TAINTED WOMAN LIKE ME.
I AM DOING THIS...
...SO THAT HE WILL GIVE UP ON ME SOON.
IT CAN'T BE!
IN THAT CASE, YOU SHOULD NEVER HAVE AGREED TO BE REDEEMED BY HIM.
COULD IT BE THAT YOU ...
...DE-CEIVED HIM FOR MY SAKE ...?!
MEN VISIT THE RED-LIGHT DISTRICT ...
...BE-CAUSE THEY WANT TO BE DECEIVED, OKO.

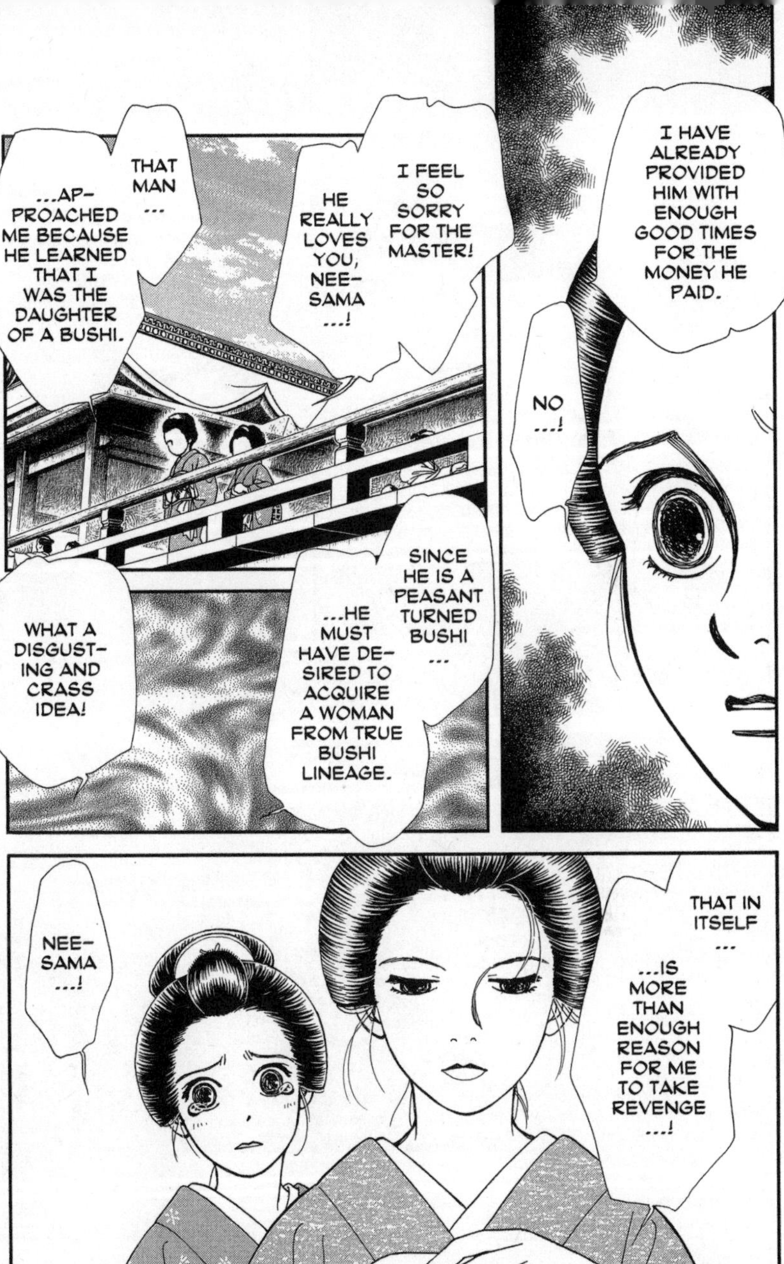
I HAVE ALREADY PROVIDED HIM WITH ENOUGH GOOD TIMES FOR THE MONEY HE PAID.
NO ...!
I FEEL SO SORRY FOR THE MASTER!
HE REALLY LOVES YOU, NEE-SAMA ...!
THAT MAN ...
...AP-PROACHED ME BECAUSE HE LEARNED THAT I WAS THE DAUGHTER OF A BUSHI.
SINCE HE IS A PEASANT TURNED BUSHI ...
...HE MUST HAVE DE-SIRED TO ACQUIRE A WOMAN FROM TRUE BUSHI LINEAGE.
WHAT A DISGUST-ING AND CRASS IDEA!
THAT IN ITSELF ...
...IS MORE THAN ENOUGH REASON FOR ME TO TAKE REVENGE ...!
NEE-SAMA ...!

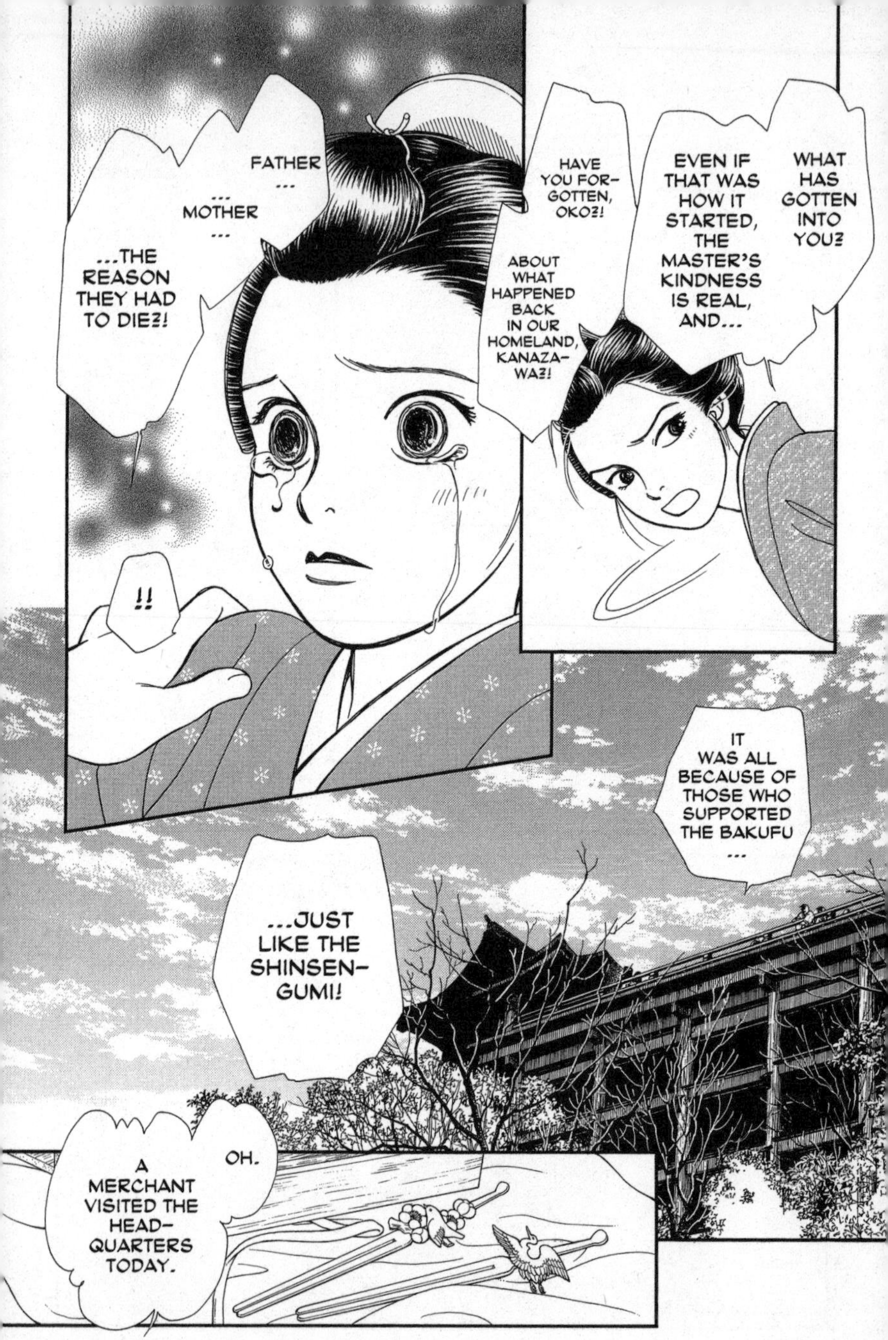
WHAT HAS GOTTEN INTO YOU?
EVEN IF THAT WAS HOW IT STARTED, THE MASTER'S KINDNESS IS REAL, AND...
HAVE YOU FORGOTTEN, OKO?!
ABOUT WHAT HAPPENED BACK IN OUR HOMELAND, KANAZAWA?!
FATHER ...
... MOTHER ...
...THE REASON THEY HAD TO DIE?!
!!
IT WAS ALL BECAUSE OF THOSE WHO SUPPORTED THE BAKUFU ...
...JUST LIKE THE SHINSEN-GUMI!
OH.
A MERCHANT VISITED THE HEAD-QUARTERS TODAY.

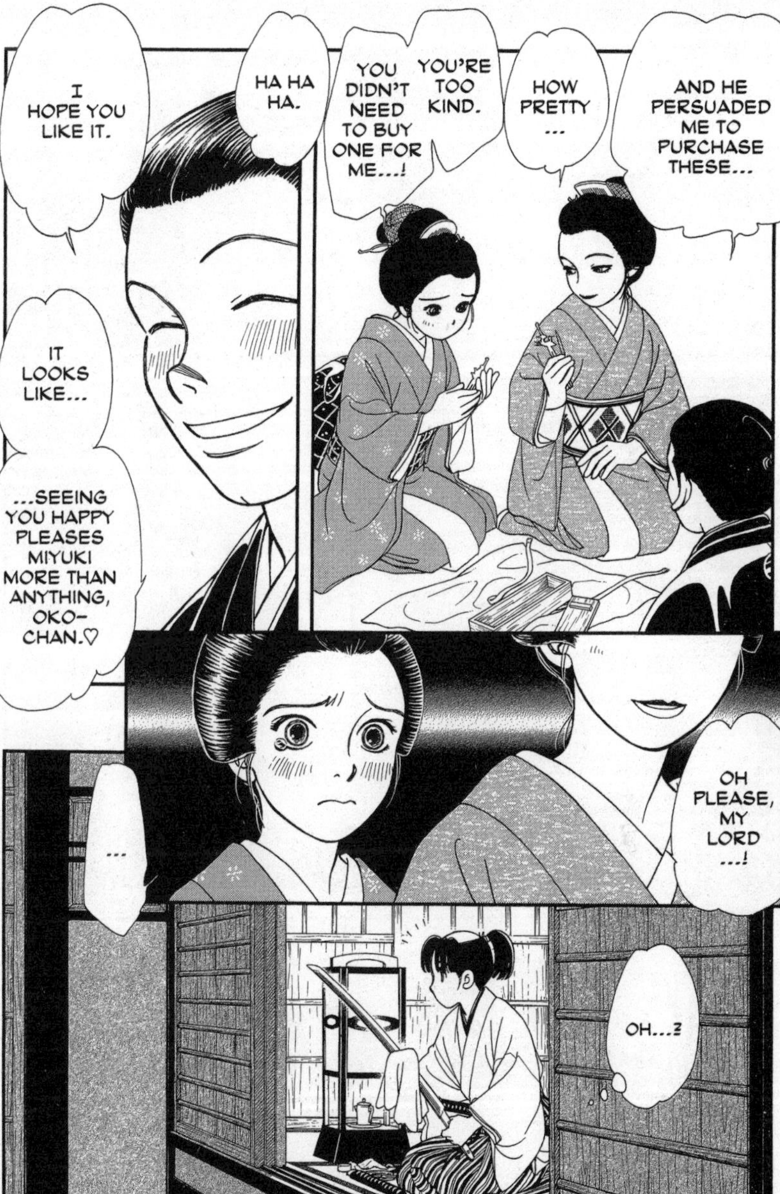
AND HE PERSUADED ME TO PURCHASE THESE...
HOW PRETTY ...
YOU'RE TOO KIND.
YOU DIDN'T NEED TO BUY ONE FOR ME...!
HA HA HA.
I HOPE YOU LIKE IT.
IT LOOKS LIKE...
...SEEING YOU HAPPY PLEASES MIYUKI MORE THAN ANYTHING, OKO-CHAN.♡
OH PLEASE, MY LORD ...!
...
OH...?

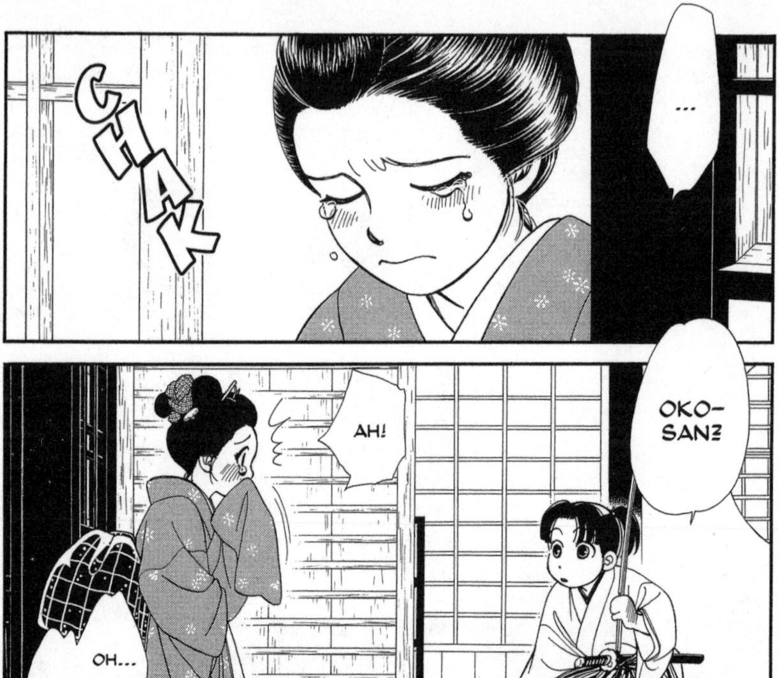
...
CHAK
OKO-SAN?
AH!
OH... KAMIYA-SAMA.

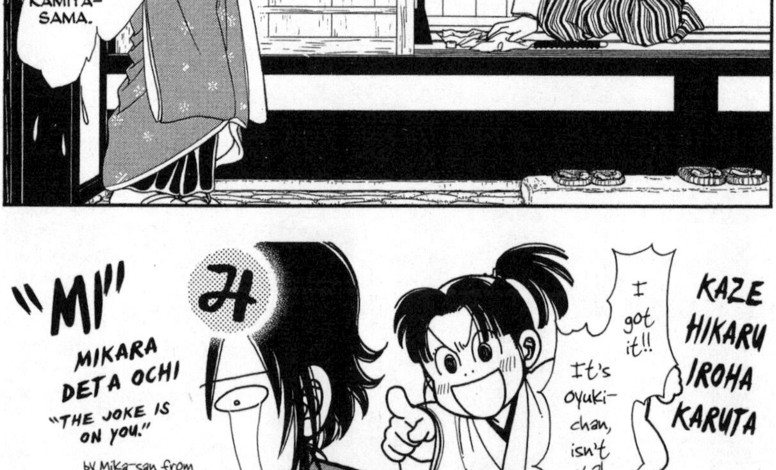
KAZE HIKARU IROHA KARUTA
I got it!!
It's oyuki-chan, isn't it?!
み
"MI"
MIKARA DETA OCHI
"THE JOKE IS ON YOU."
by Mika-san from HOKKAIDO

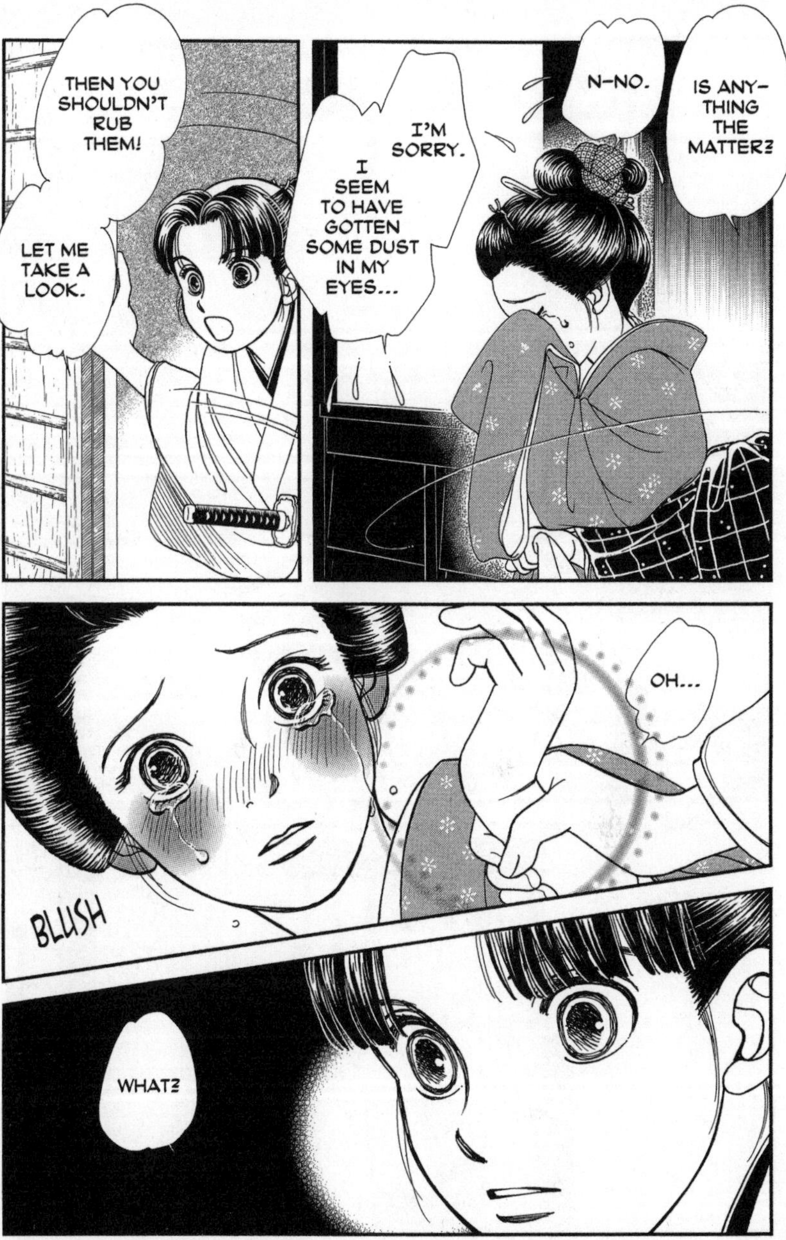
IS ANY-THING THE MATTER?
N-NO.
I'M SORRY.
I SEEM TO HAVE GOTTEN SOME DUST IN MY EYES...
THEN YOU SHOULDN'T RUB THEM!
LET ME TAKE A LOOK.
OH...
BLUSH
WHAT?

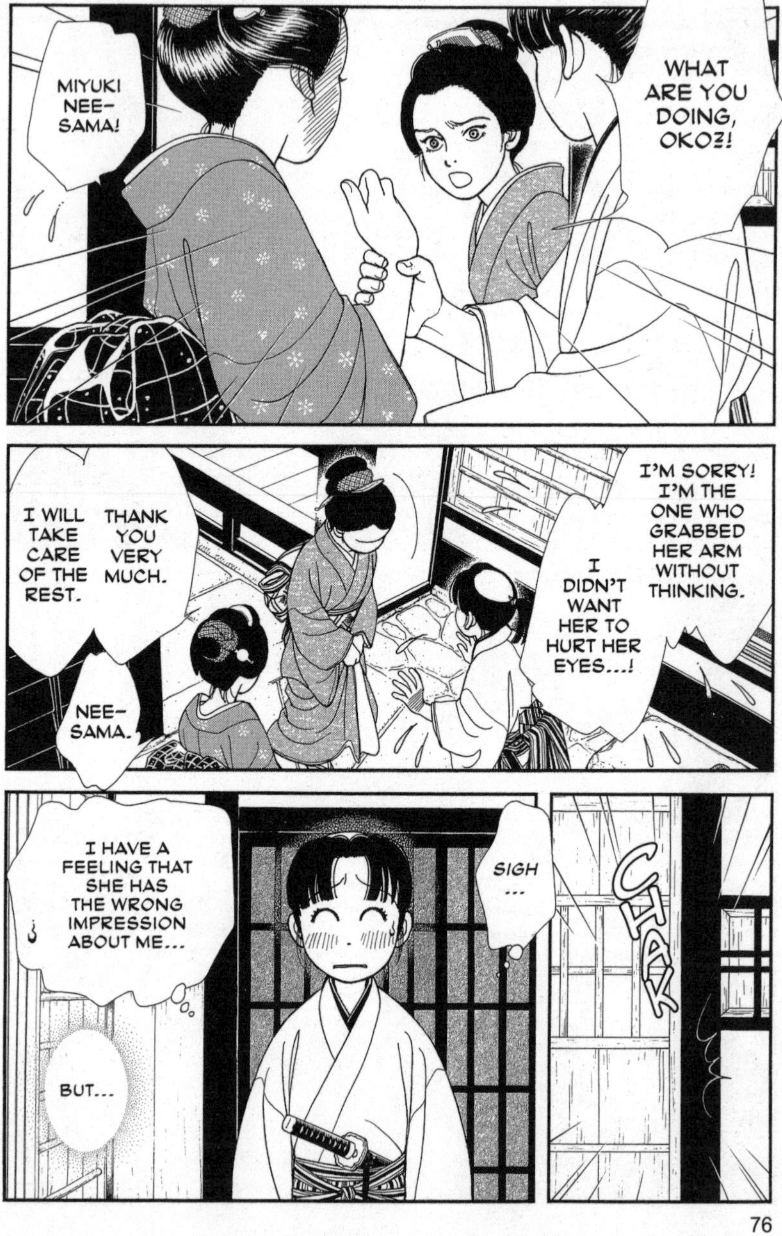
WHAT ARE YOU DOING, OKO?!
MIYUKI NEE-SAMA!
I'M SORRY! I'M THE ONE WHO GRABBED HER ARM WITHOUT THINKING.
I DIDN'T WANT HER TO HURT HER EYES...!
THANK YOU VERY MUCH.
I WILL TAKE CARE OF THE REST.
NEE-SAMA.
CHAK
SIGH...
I HAVE A FEELING THAT SHE HAS THE WRONG IMPRESSION ABOUT ME...
BUT...

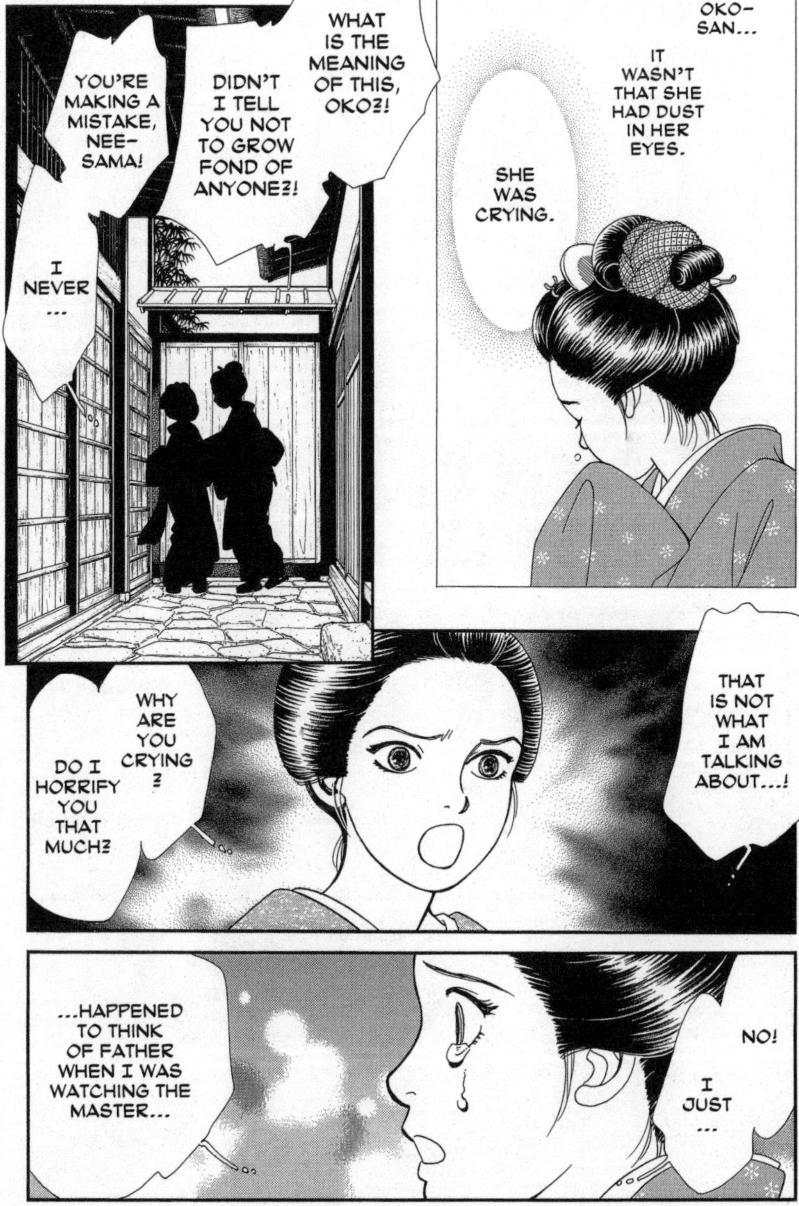
OKO-SAN...
IT WASN'T THAT SHE HAD DUST IN HER EYES.
SHE WAS CRYING.
WHAT IS THE MEANING OF THIS, OKO?!
DIDN'T I TELL YOU NOT TO GROW FOND OF ANYONE?!
YOU'RE MAKING A MISTAKE, NEE-SAMA!
I NEVER...
THAT IS NOT WHAT I AM TALKING ABOUT...!
WHY ARE YOU CRYING?
DO I HORRIFY YOU THAT MUCH?
NO!
I JUST...
...HAPPENED TO THINK OF FATHER WHEN I WAS WATCHING THE MASTER...

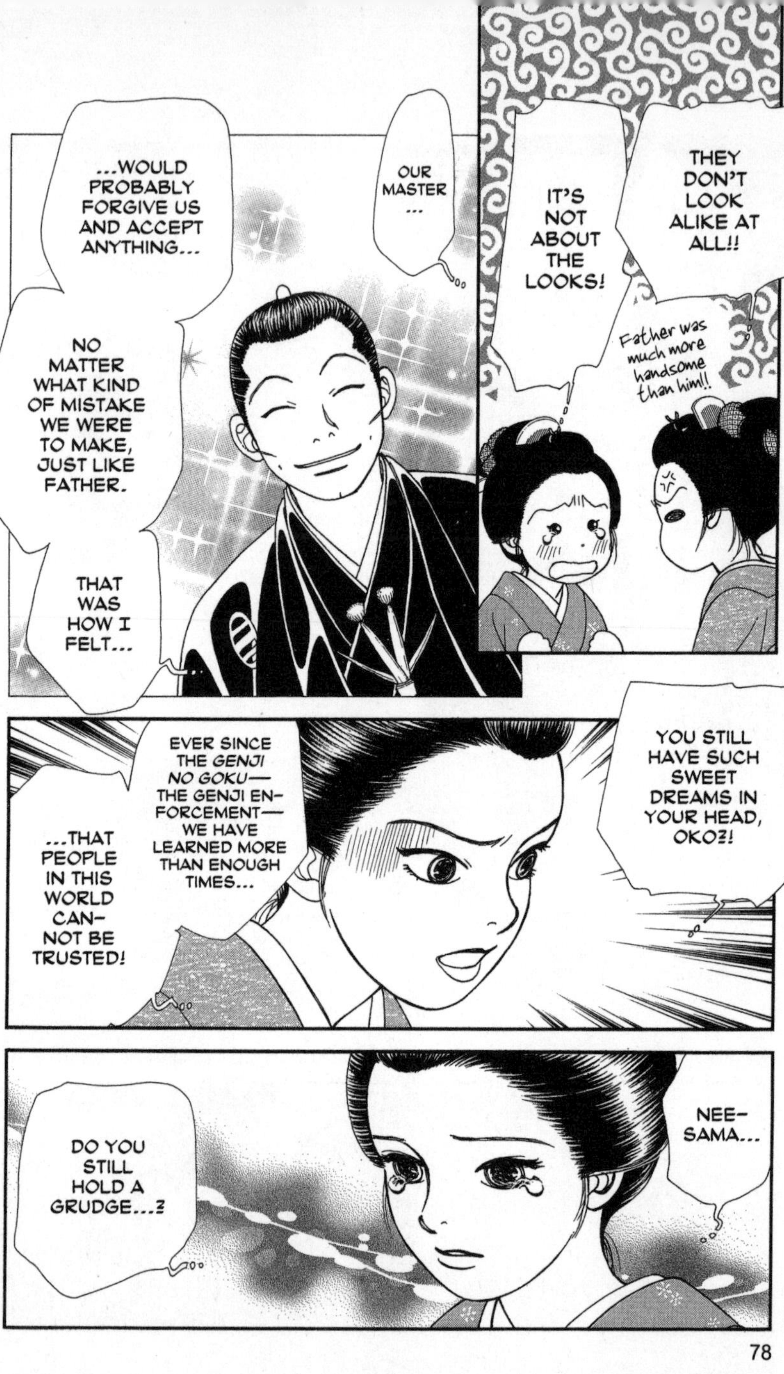
THEY DON'T LOOK ALIKE AT ALL!!
IT'S NOT ABOUT THE LOOKS!
Father was much more handsome than him!!
OUR MASTER ...
...WOULD PROBABLY FORGIVE US AND ACCEPT ANYTHING...
NO MATTER WHAT KIND OF MISTAKE WE WERE TO MAKE, JUST LIKE FATHER.
THAT WAS HOW I FELT...
YOU STILL HAVE SUCH SWEET DREAMS IN YOUR HEAD, OKO?!
EVER SINCE THE *GENJI NO GOKU*—THE GENJI ENFORCEMENT—WE HAVE LEARNED MORE THAN ENOUGH TIMES...
...THAT PEOPLE IN THIS WORLD CANNOT BE TRUSTED!
NEE-SAMA...
DO YOU STILL HOLD A GRUDGE...?

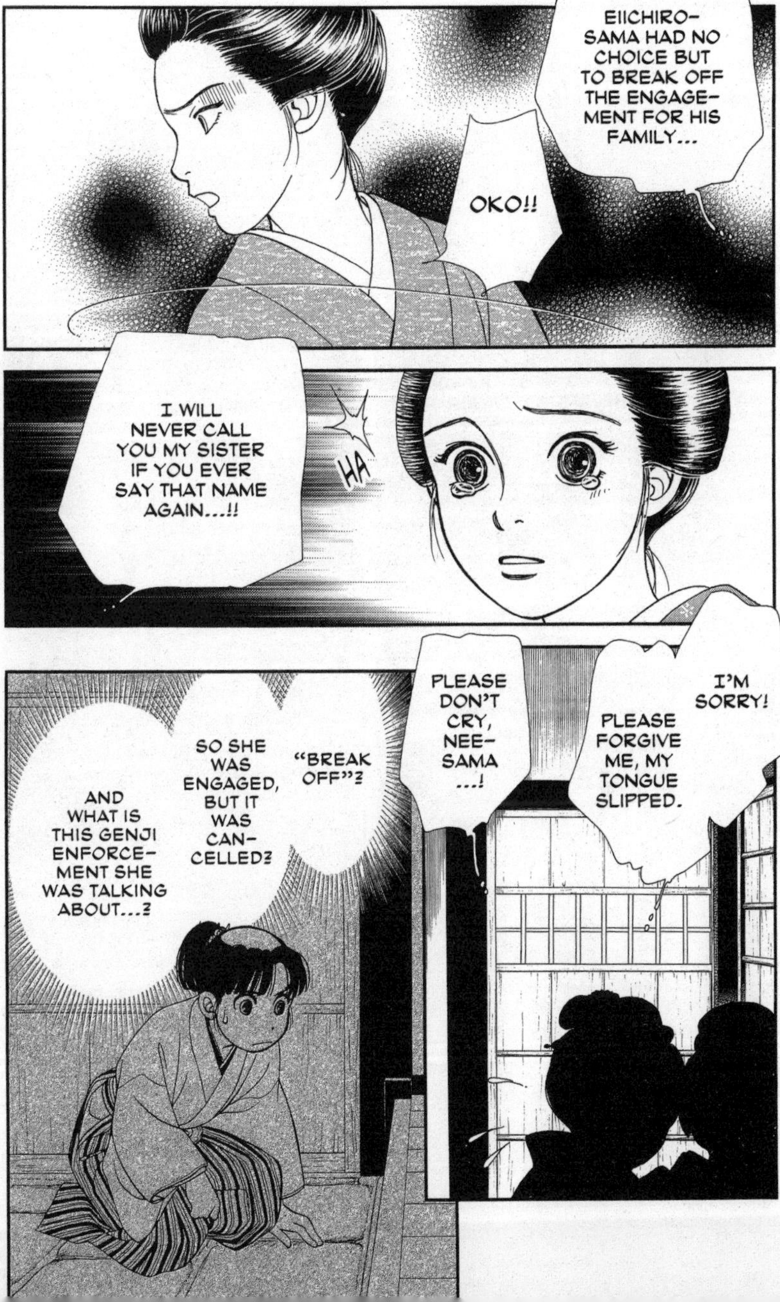
EIICHIRO-SAMA HAD NO CHOICE BUT TO BREAK OFF THE ENGAGEMENT FOR HIS FAMILY...
OKO!!
I WILL NEVER CALL YOU MY SISTER IF YOU EVER SAY THAT NAME AGAIN...!!
HA
I'M SORRY!
PLEASE FORGIVE ME, MY TONGUE SLIPPED.
PLEASE DON'T CRY, NEE-SAMA ...!
"BREAK OFF"?
SO SHE WAS ENGAGED, BUT IT WAS CANCELLED?
AND WHAT IS THIS GENJI ENFORCEMENT SHE WAS TALKING ABOUT...?

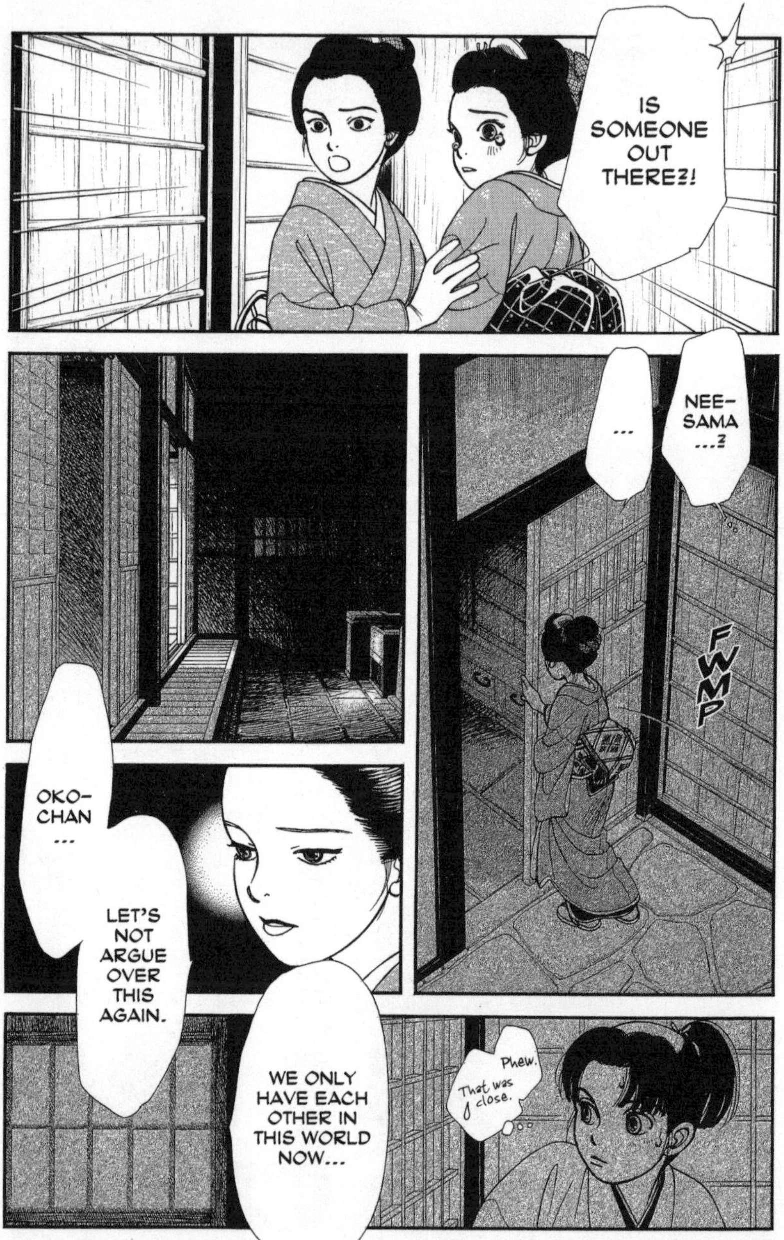
IS SOMEONE OUT THERE?!
NEE-SAMA...?
...
FWMP
OKO-CHAN...
LET'S NOT ARGUE OVER THIS AGAIN.
WE ONLY HAVE EACH OTHER IN THIS WORLD NOW...
Phew.
That was close.

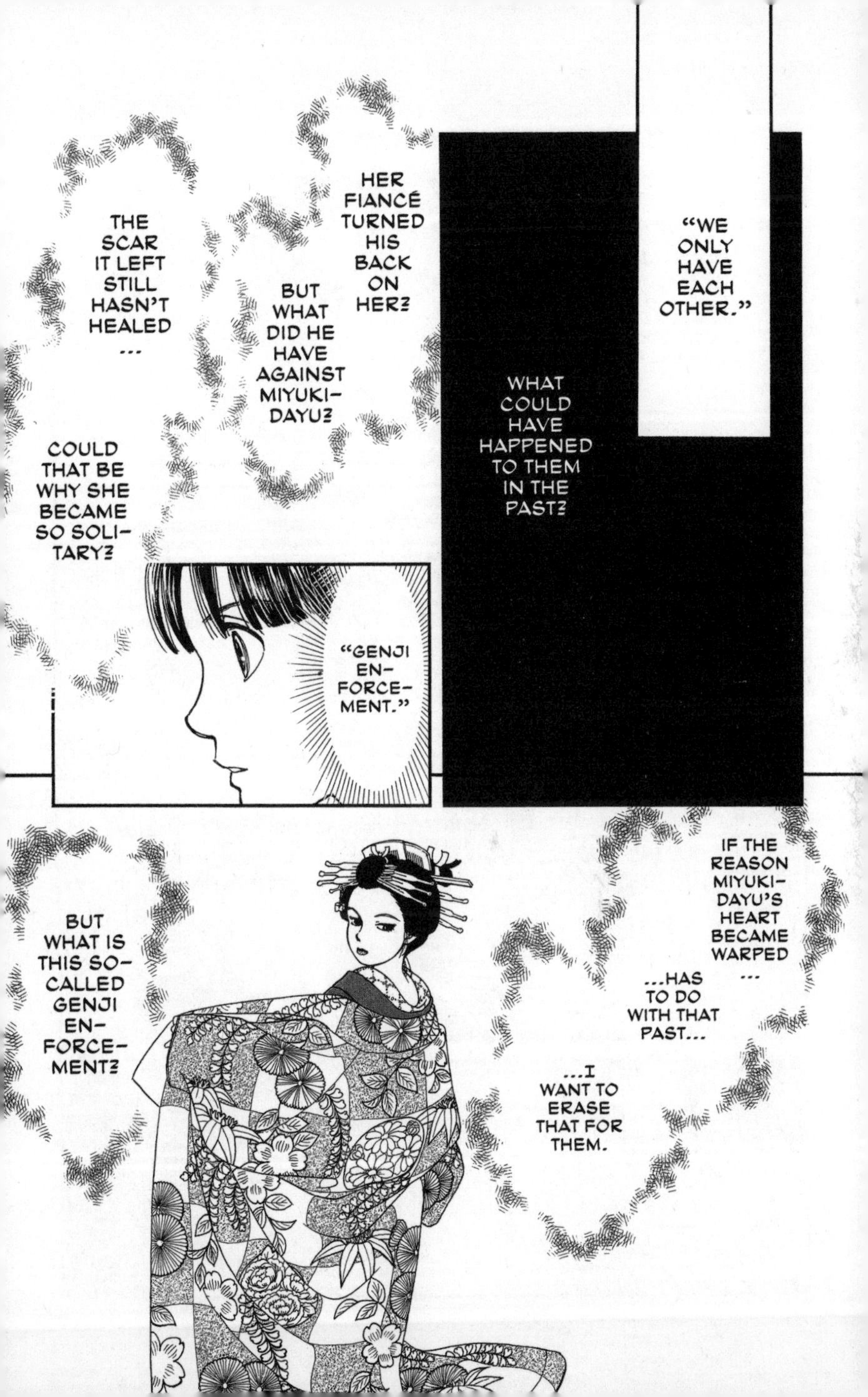
"WE ONLY HAVE EACH OTHER."
WHAT COULD HAVE HAPPENED TO THEM IN THE PAST?
HER FIANCÉ TURNED HIS BACK ON HER?
BUT WHAT DID HE HAVE AGAINST MIYUKI-DAYU?
THE SCAR IT LEFT STILL HASN'T HEALED...
COULD THAT BE WHY SHE BECAME SO SOLITARY?
"GENJI ENFORCEMENT."
IF THE REASON MIYUKI-DAYU'S HEART BECAME WARPED...
...HAS TO DO WITH THAT PAST...
...I WANT TO ERASE THAT FOR THEM.
BUT WHAT IS THIS SO-CALLED GENJI ENFORCEMENT?

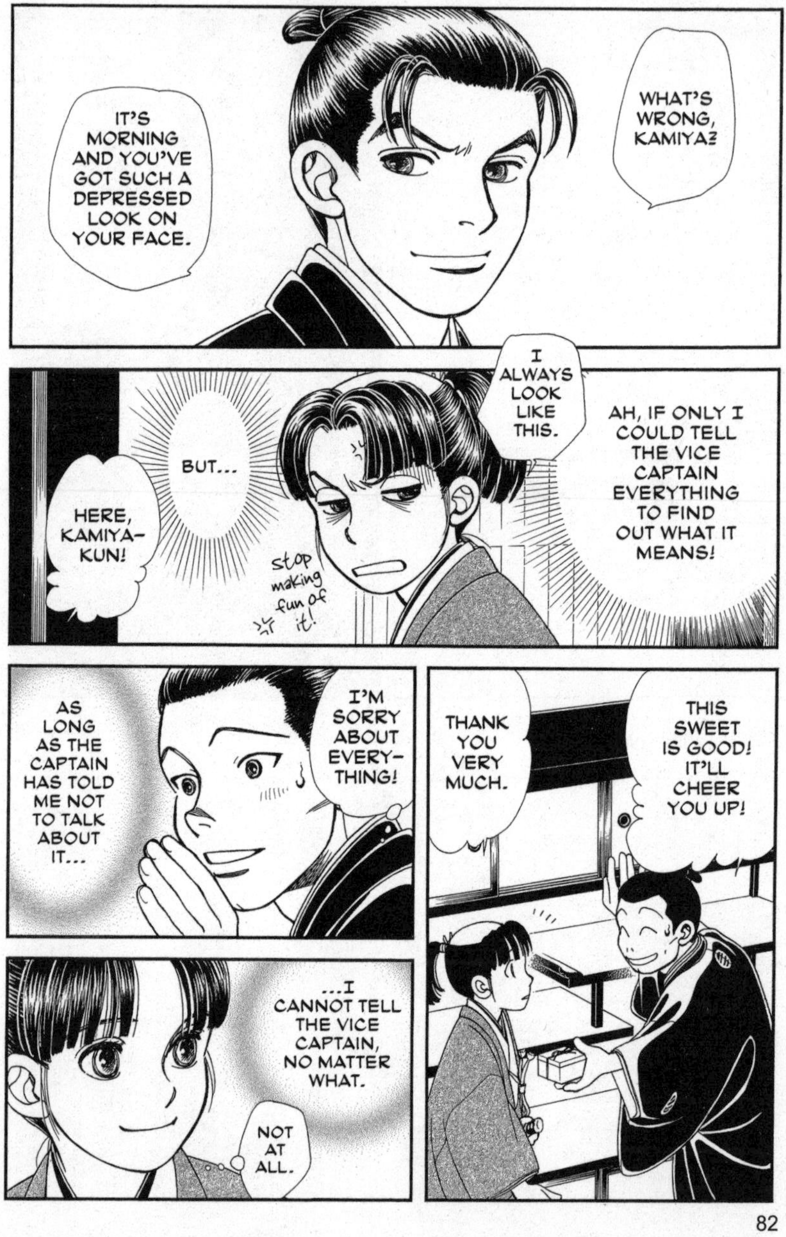
WHAT'S WRONG, KAMIYA?
IT'S MORNING AND YOU'VE GOT SUCH A DEPRESSED LOOK ON YOUR FACE.
I ALWAYS LOOK LIKE THIS.
AH, IF ONLY I COULD TELL THE VICE CAPTAIN EVERYTHING TO FIND OUT WHAT IT MEANS!
stop making fun of it!
BUT...
HERE, KAMIYA-KUN!
THIS SWEET IS GOOD! IT'LL CHEER YOU UP!
THANK YOU VERY MUCH.
I'M SORRY ABOUT EVERYTHING!
AS LONG AS THE CAPTAIN HAS TOLD ME NOT TO TALK ABOUT IT...
...I CANNOT TELL THE VICE CAPTAIN, NO MATTER WHAT.
NOT AT ALL.

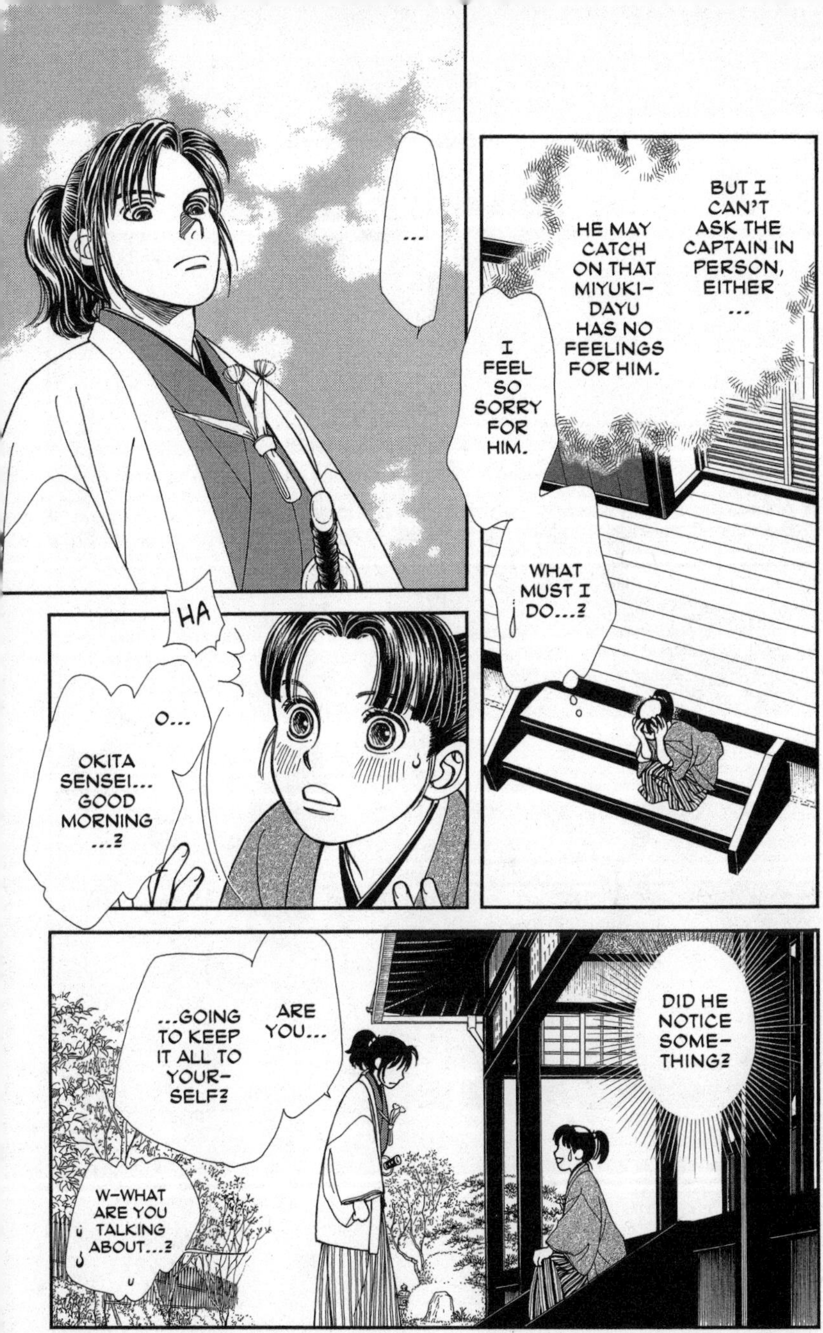
BUT I CAN'T ASK THE CAPTAIN IN PERSON, EITHER...
HE MAY CATCH ON THAT MIYUKI-DAYU HAS NO FEELINGS FOR HIM.
I FEEL SO SORRY FOR HIM.
WHAT MUST I DO...?
...
HA
O...
OKITA SENSEI... GOOD MORNING...?
DID HE NOTICE SOME-THING?
ARE YOU...
...GOING TO KEEP IT ALL TO YOUR-SELF?
W-WHAT ARE YOU TALKING ABOUT...?

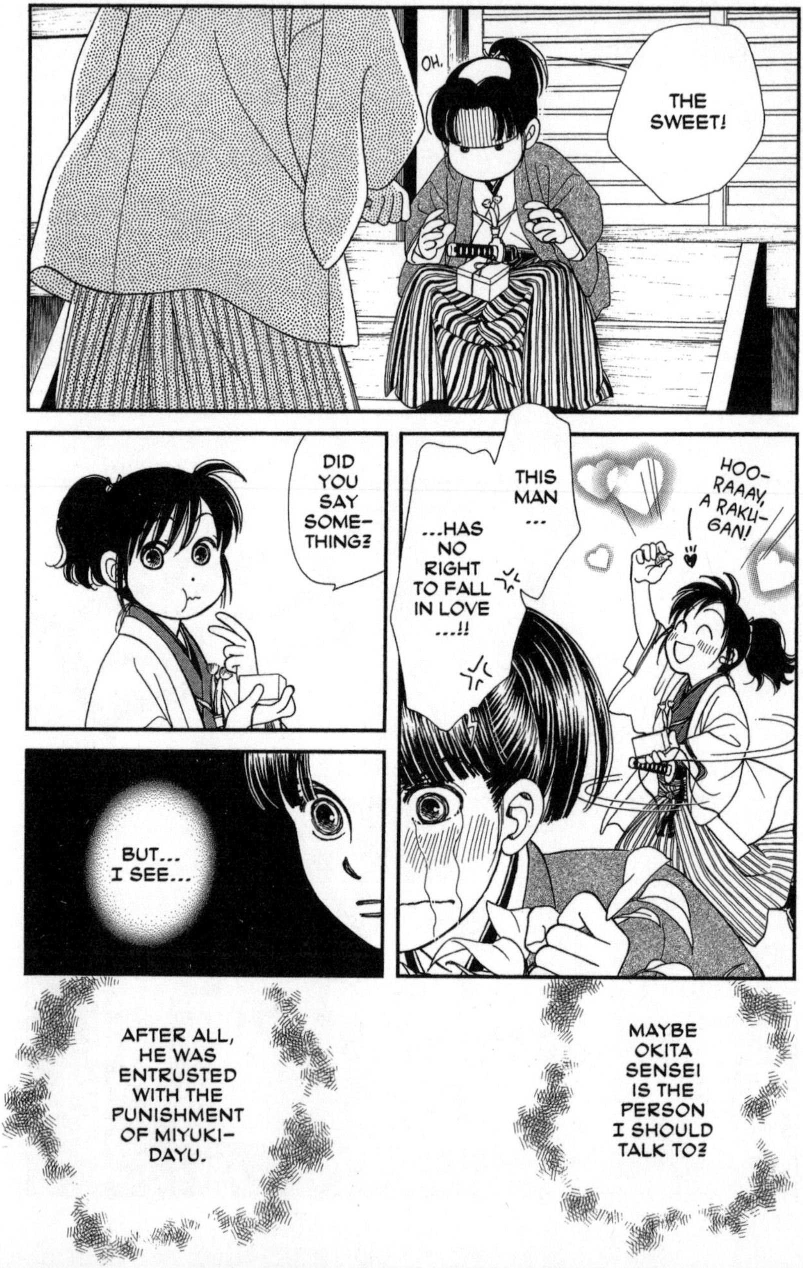
OH.
THE SWEET!
HOO-RAAAY, A RAKU-GAN!
THIS MAN...
...HAS NO RIGHT TO FALL IN LOVE...!!
DID YOU SAY SOME-THING?
BUT... I SEE...
MAYBE OKITA SENSEI IS THE PERSON I SHOULD TALK TO?
AFTER ALL, HE WAS ENTRUSTED WITH THE PUNISHMENT OF MIYUKI-DAYU.

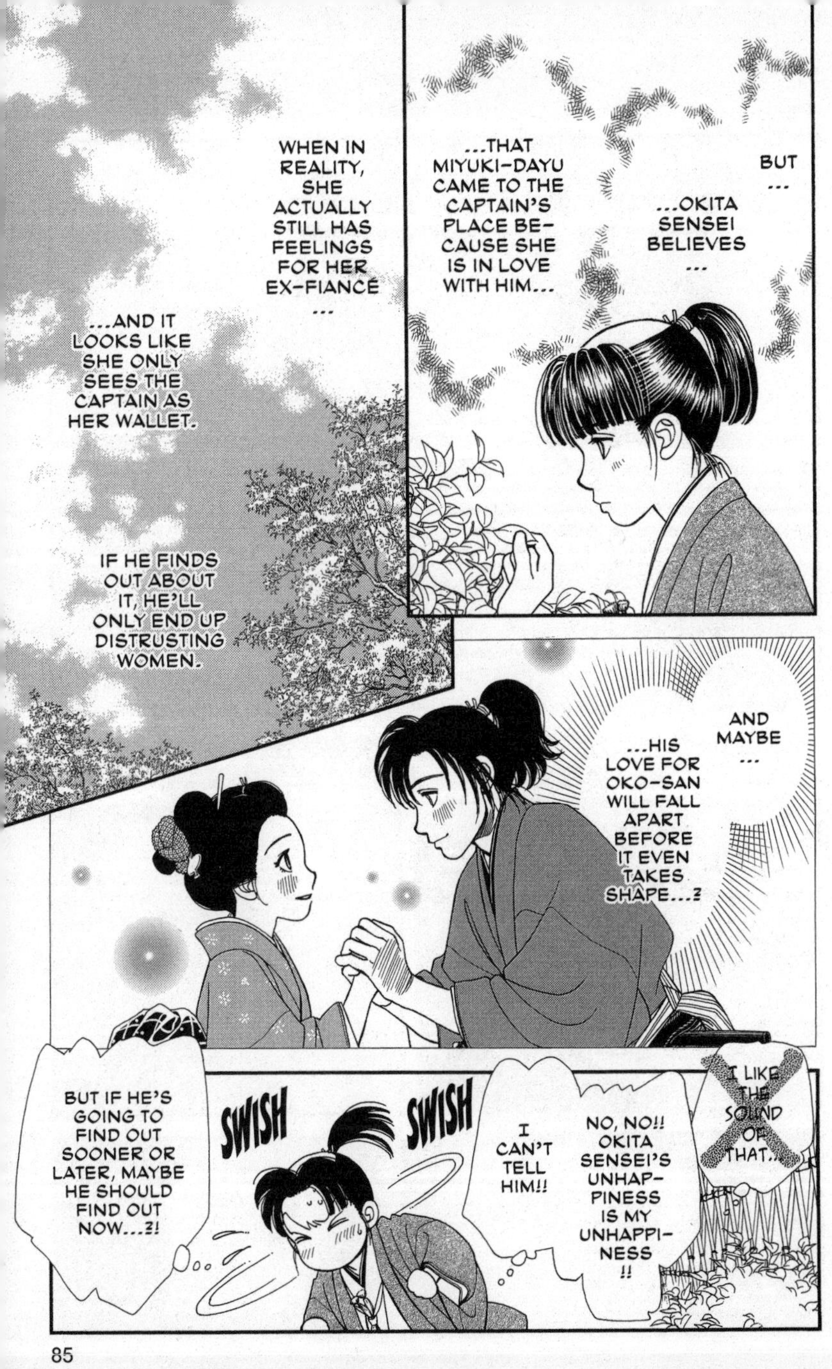

BUT ...
...OKITA SENSEI BELIEVES ...
...THAT MIYUKI-DAYU CAME TO THE CAPTAIN'S PLACE BE-CAUSE SHE IS IN LOVE WITH HIM...
WHEN IN REALITY, SHE ACTUALLY STILL HAS FEELINGS FOR HER EX-FIANCÉ ...
...AND IT LOOKS LIKE SHE ONLY SEES THE CAPTAIN AS HER WALLET.
IF HE FINDS OUT ABOUT IT, HE'LL ONLY END UP DISTRUSTING WOMEN.
AND MAYBE ...
...HIS LOVE FOR OKO-SAN WILL FALL APART BEFORE IT EVEN TAKES SHAPE...?
I LIKE THE SOUND OF THAT...
NO, NO!! OKITA SENSEI'S UNHAP-PINESS IS MY UNHAPPI-NESS !!
I CAN'T TELL HIM!!
SWISH
SWISH
BUT IF HE'S GOING TO FIND OUT SOONER OR LATER, MAYBE HE SHOULD FIND OUT NOW...?!

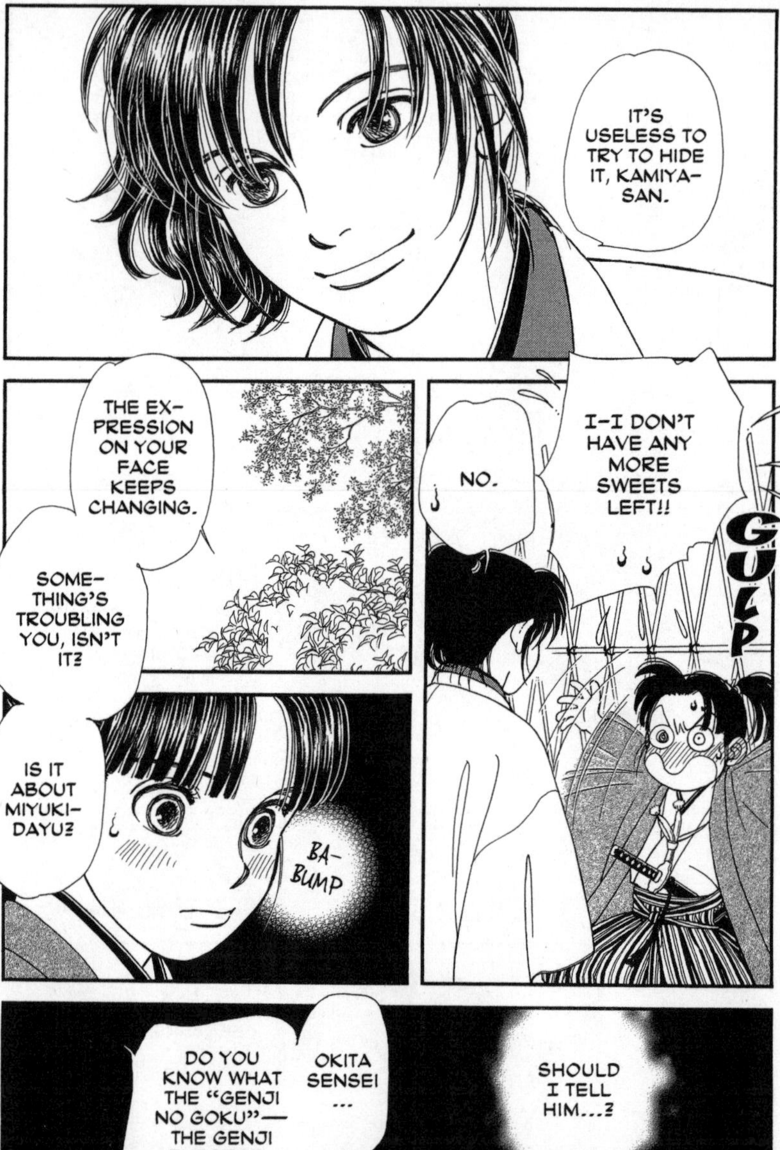
IT'S USELESS TO TRY TO HIDE IT, KAMIYA-SAN.
I-I DON'T HAVE ANY MORE SWEETS LEFT!!
NO.
GULP
THE EXPRESSION ON YOUR FACE KEEPS CHANGING.
SOMETHING'S TROUBLING YOU, ISN'T IT?
IS IT ABOUT MIYUKI-DAYU?
BA-BUMP
SHOULD I TELL HIM...?
OKITA SENSEI...
DO YOU KNOW WHAT THE "GENJI NO GOKU"—THE GENJI ENFORCEMENT—IS?

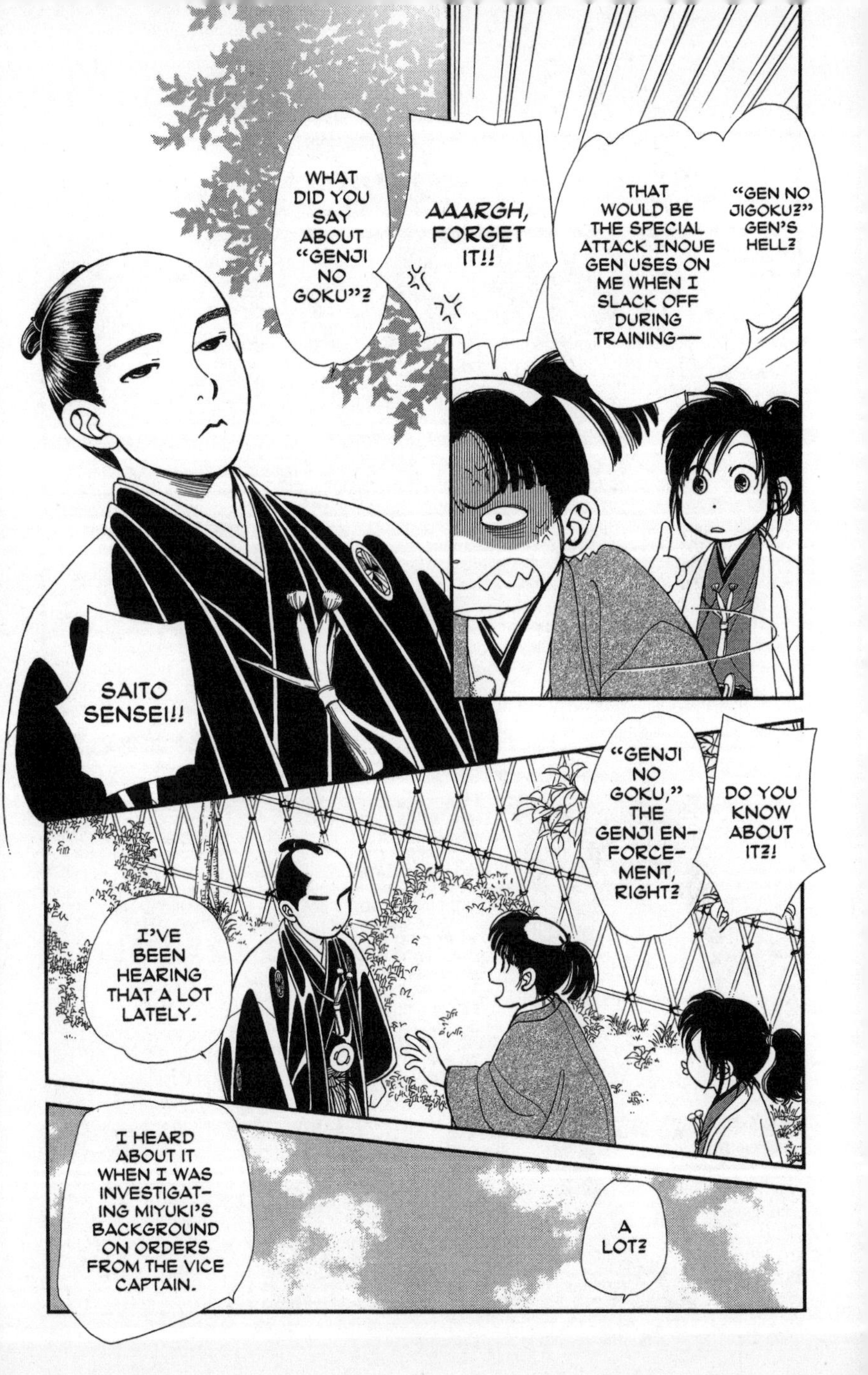
"GEN NO JIGOKU?" GEN'S HELL?
THAT WOULD BE THE SPECIAL ATTACK INOUE GEN USES ON ME WHEN I SLACK OFF DURING TRAINING—
AAARGH, FORGET IT!!
WHAT DID YOU SAY ABOUT "GENJI NO GOKU"?
SAITO SENSEI!!
DO YOU KNOW ABOUT IT?!
"GENJI NO GOKU," THE GENJI EN-FORCE-MENT, RIGHT?
I'VE BEEN HEARING THAT A LOT LATELY.
A LOT?
I HEARD ABOUT IT WHEN I WAS INVESTIGAT-ING MIYUKI'S BACKGROUND ON ORDERS FROM THE VICE CAPTAIN.

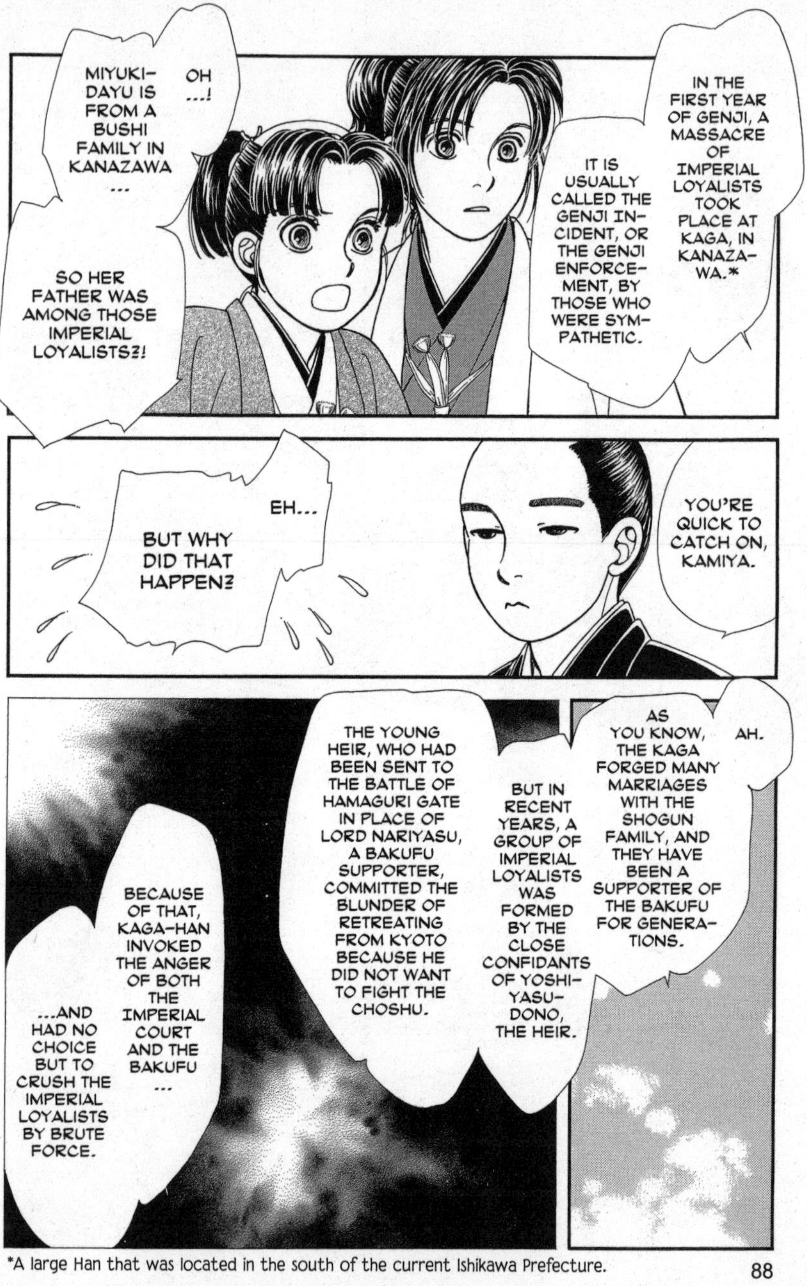
IN THE FIRST YEAR OF GENJI, A MASSACRE OF IMPERIAL LOYALISTS TOOK PLACE AT KAGA, IN KANAZAWA.*
IT IS USUALLY CALLED THE GENJI INCIDENT, OR THE GENJI ENFORCEMENT, BY THOSE WHO WERE SYMPATHETIC.
OH ...!
MIYUKI-DAYU IS FROM A BUSHI FAMILY IN KANAZAWA ...
SO HER FATHER WAS AMONG THOSE IMPERIAL LOYALISTS?!
YOU'RE QUICK TO CATCH ON, KAMIYA.
EH...
BUT WHY DID THAT HAPPEN?
AH.
AS YOU KNOW, THE KAGA FORGED MANY MARRIAGES WITH THE SHOGUN FAMILY, AND THEY HAVE BEEN A SUPPORTER OF THE BAKUFU FOR GENERATIONS.
BUT IN RECENT YEARS, A GROUP OF IMPERIAL LOYALISTS WAS FORMED BY THE CLOSE CONFIDANTS OF YOSHIYASU-DONO, THE HEIR.
THE YOUNG HEIR, WHO HAD BEEN SENT TO THE BATTLE OF HAMAGURI GATE IN PLACE OF LORD NARIYASU, A BAKUFU SUPPORTER, COMMITTED THE BLUNDER OF RETREATING FROM KYOTO BECAUSE HE DID NOT WANT TO FIGHT THE CHOSHU.
BECAUSE OF THAT, KAGA-HAN INVOKED THE ANGER OF BOTH THE IMPERIAL COURT AND THE BAKUFU ...
...AND HAD NO CHOICE BUT TO CRUSH THE IMPERIAL LOYALISTS BY BRUTE FORCE.

*A large Han that was located in the south of the current Ishikawa Prefecture.

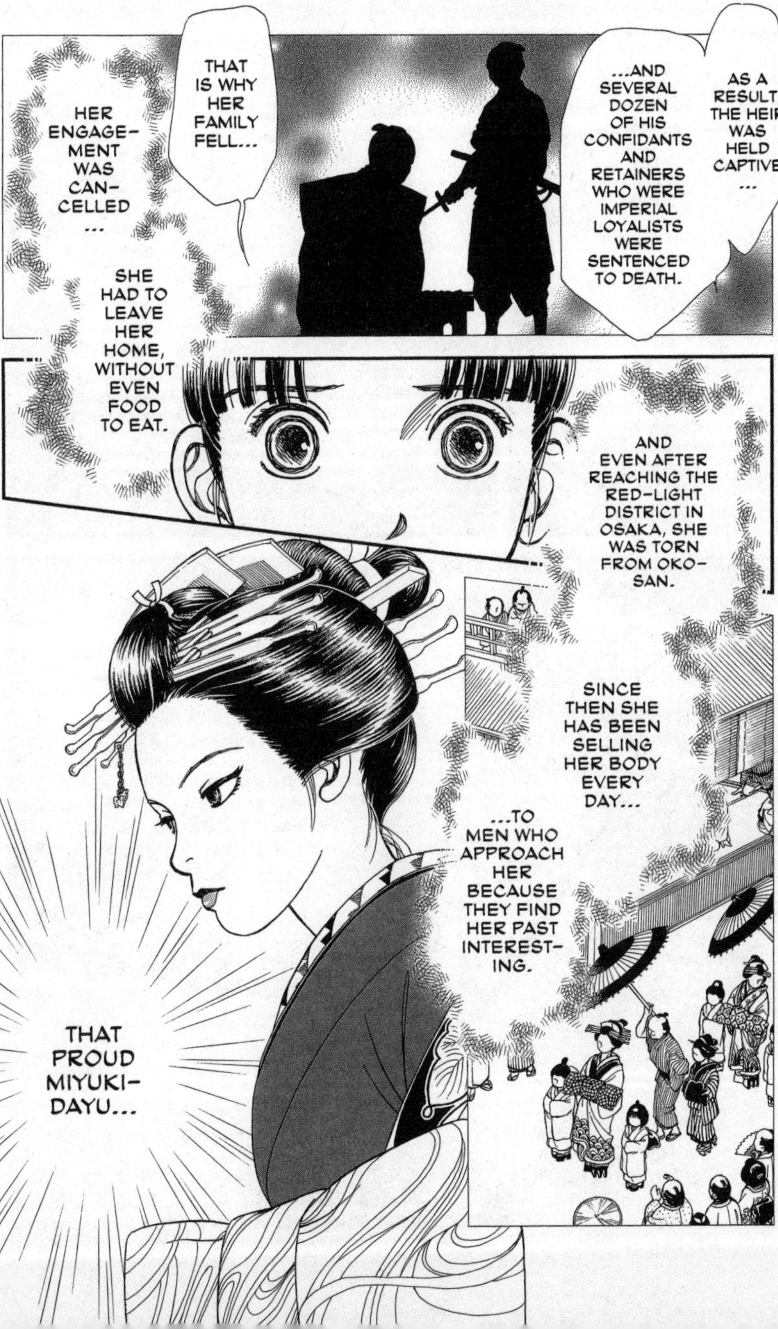
AS A RESULT, THE HEIR WAS HELD CAPTIVE ...
...AND SEVERAL DOZEN OF HIS CONFIDANTS AND RETAINERS WHO WERE IMPERIAL LOYALISTS WERE SENTENCED TO DEATH.
THAT IS WHY HER FAMILY FELL...
HER ENGAGE-MENT WAS CAN-CELLED ...
SHE HAD TO LEAVE HER HOME, WITHOUT EVEN FOOD TO EAT.
AND EVEN AFTER REACHING THE RED-LIGHT DISTRICT IN OSAKA, SHE WAS TORN FROM OKO-SAN.
SINCE THEN SHE HAS BEEN SELLING HER BODY EVERY DAY...
...TO MEN WHO APPROACH HER BECAUSE THEY FIND HER PAST INTEREST-ING.
THAT PROUD MIYUKI-DAYU...

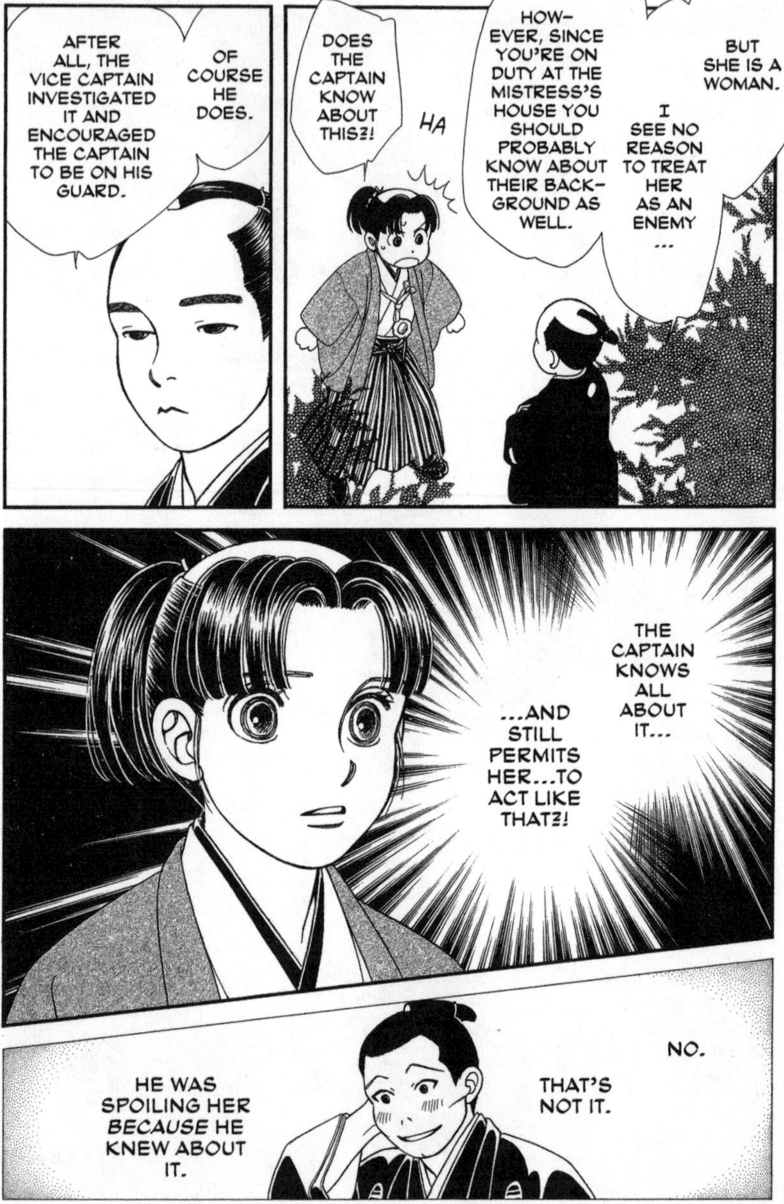
BUT SHE IS A WOMAN.
I SEE NO REASON TO TREAT HER AS AN ENEMY...
HOW-EVER, SINCE YOU'RE ON DUTY AT THE MISTRESS'S HOUSE YOU SHOULD PROBABLY KNOW ABOUT THEIR BACK-GROUND AS WELL.
HA
DOES THE CAPTAIN KNOW ABOUT THIS?!
OF COURSE HE DOES.
AFTER ALL, THE VICE CAPTAIN INVESTIGATED IT AND ENCOURAGED THE CAPTAIN TO BE ON HIS GUARD.
THE CAPTAIN KNOWS ALL ABOUT IT...
...AND STILL PERMITS HER...TO ACT LIKE THAT?!
NO.
THAT'S NOT IT.
HE WAS SPOILING HER *BECAUSE* HE KNEW ABOUT IT.

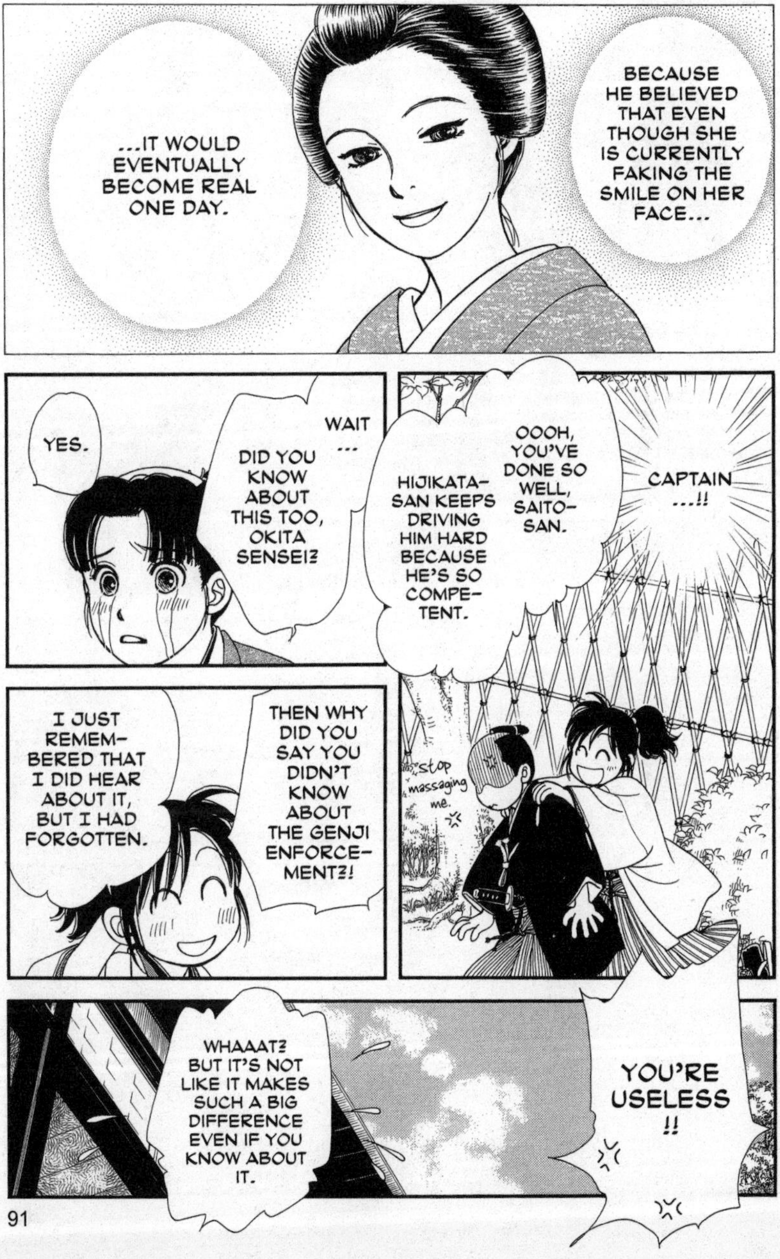
BECAUSE HE BELIEVED THAT EVEN THOUGH SHE IS CURRENTLY FAKING THE SMILE ON HER FACE...
...IT WOULD EVENTUALLY BECOME REAL ONE DAY.
CAPTAIN ...!!
OOOH, YOU'VE DONE SO WELL, SAITO-SAN.
HIJIKATA-SAN KEEPS DRIVING HIM HARD BECAUSE HE'S SO COMPETENT.
stop massaging me.
WAIT ... DID YOU KNOW ABOUT THIS TOO, OKITA SENSEI?
YES.
THEN WHY DID YOU SAY YOU DIDN'T KNOW ABOUT THE GENJI ENFORCEMENT?!
I JUST REMEMBERED THAT I DID HEAR ABOUT IT, BUT I HAD FORGOTTEN.
YOU'RE USELESS !!
WHAAAT? BUT IT'S NOT LIKE IT MAKES SUCH A BIG DIFFERENCE EVEN IF YOU KNOW ABOUT IT.

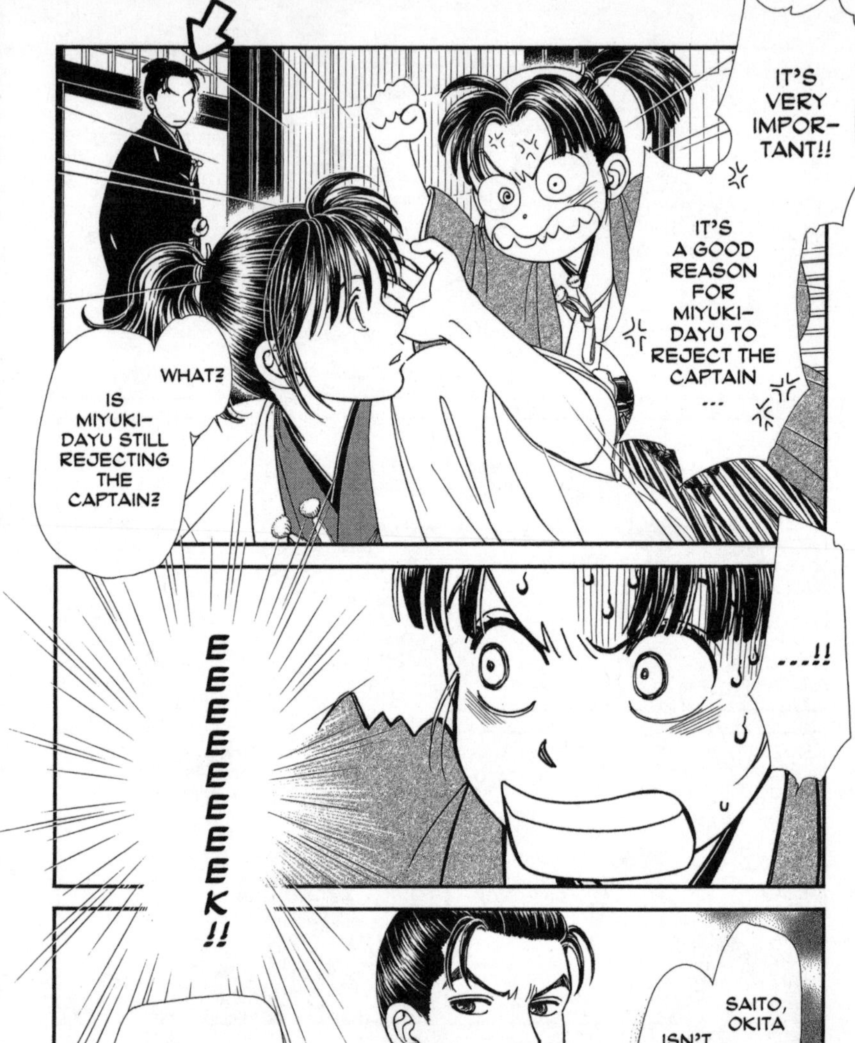
IT'S VERY IMPOR-TANT!!
IT'S A GOOD REASON FOR MIYUKI-DAYU TO REJECT THE CAPTAIN ...
WHAT?
IS MIYUKI-DAYU STILL REJECTING THE CAPTAIN?
...!!
EEEEEEEEEK!!
SAITO, OKITA ...
ISN'T IT TIME FOR YOU TO MAKE YOUR ROUNDS?
KAMIYA, I WANT YOU IN MY ROOM RIGHT NOW.

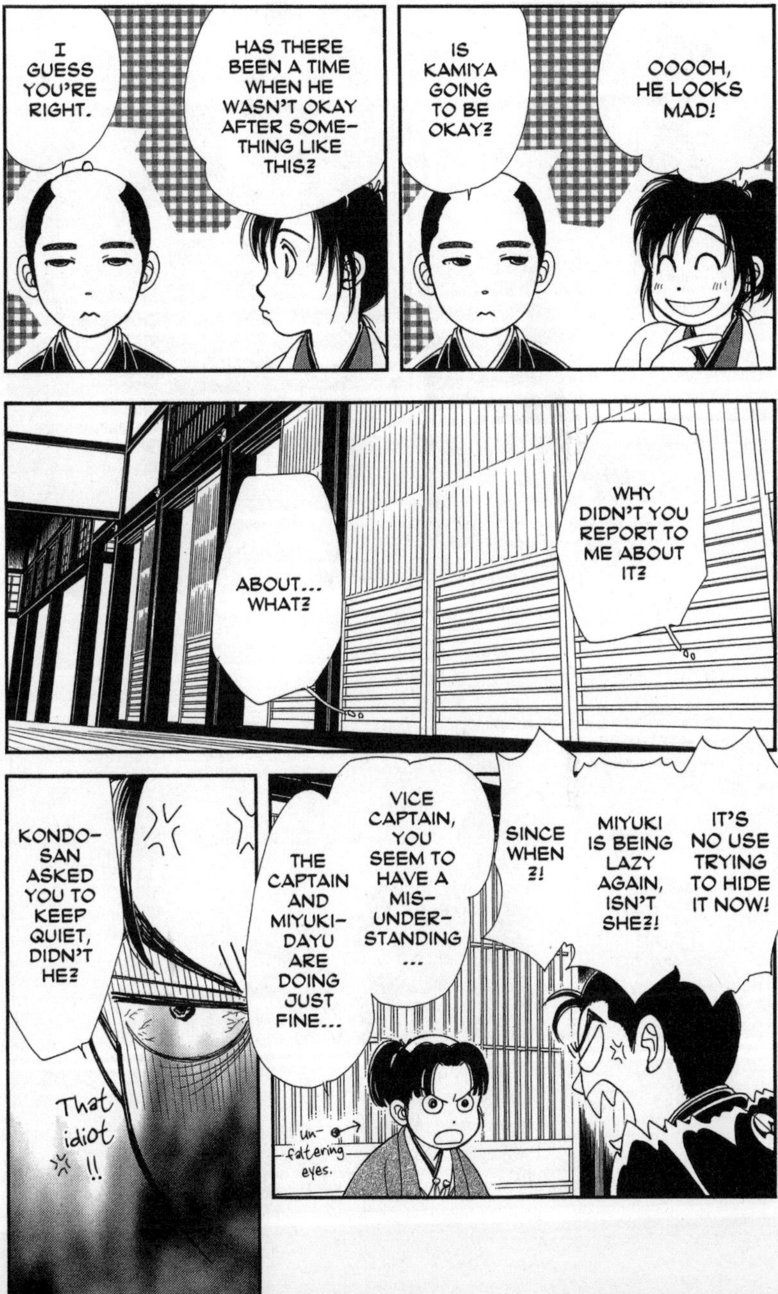
OOOOH, HE LOOKS MAD!
IS KAMIYA GOING TO BE OKAY?
HAS THERE BEEN A TIME WHEN HE WASN'T OKAY AFTER SOME-THING LIKE THIS?
I GUESS YOU'RE RIGHT.
WHY DIDN'T YOU REPORT TO ME ABOUT IT?
ABOUT... WHAT?
IT'S NO USE TRYING TO HIDE IT NOW!
MIYUKI IS BEING LAZY AGAIN, ISN'T SHE?!
SINCE WHEN ?!
VICE CAPTAIN, YOU SEEM TO HAVE A MIS-UNDER-STANDING...
THE CAPTAIN AND MIYUKI-DAYU ARE DOING JUST FINE...
un-faltering eyes.
KONDO-SAN ASKED YOU TO KEEP QUIET, DIDN'T HE?
That idiot !!

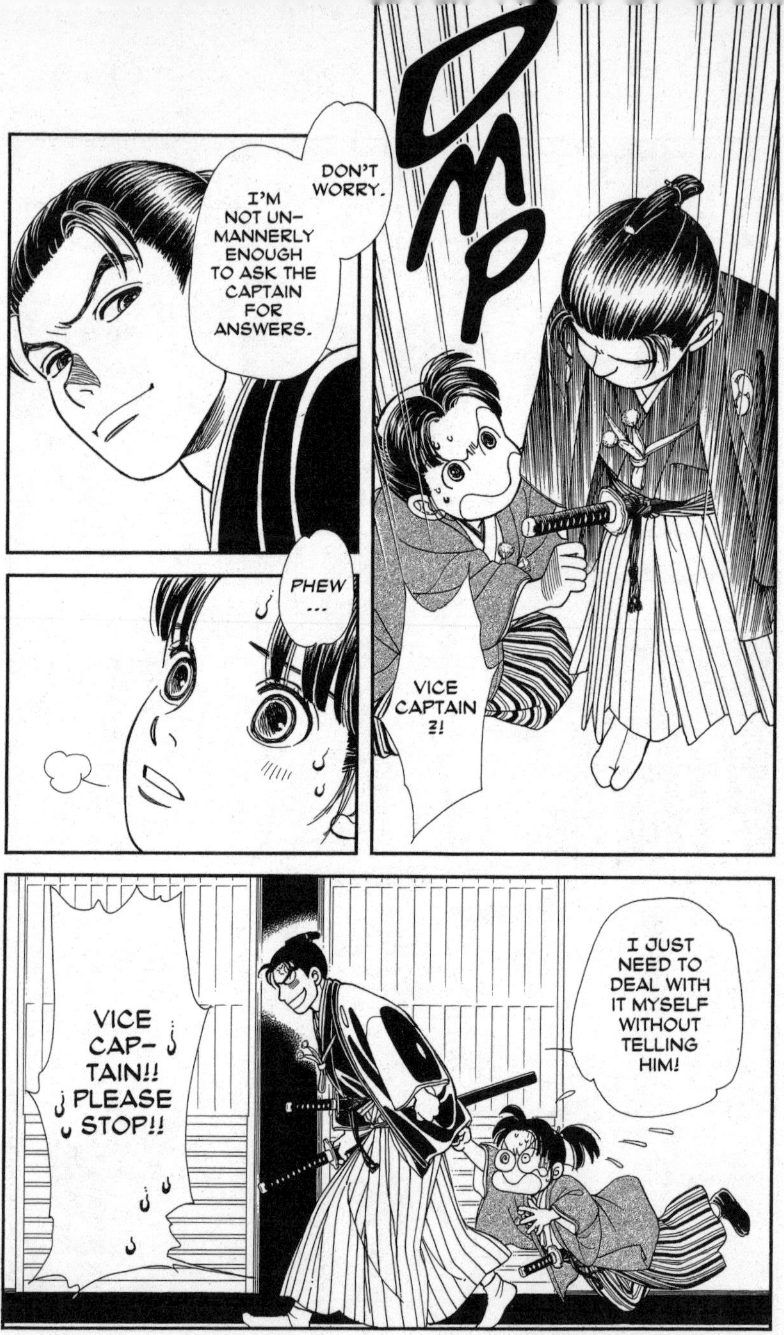
OMP
VICE CAPTAIN?!
DON'T WORRY. I'M NOT UN-MANNERLY ENOUGH TO ASK THE CAPTAIN FOR ANSWERS.
PHEW...
I JUST NEED TO DEAL WITH IT MYSELF WITHOUT TELLING HIM!
VICE CAP-TAIN!! PLEASE STOP!!

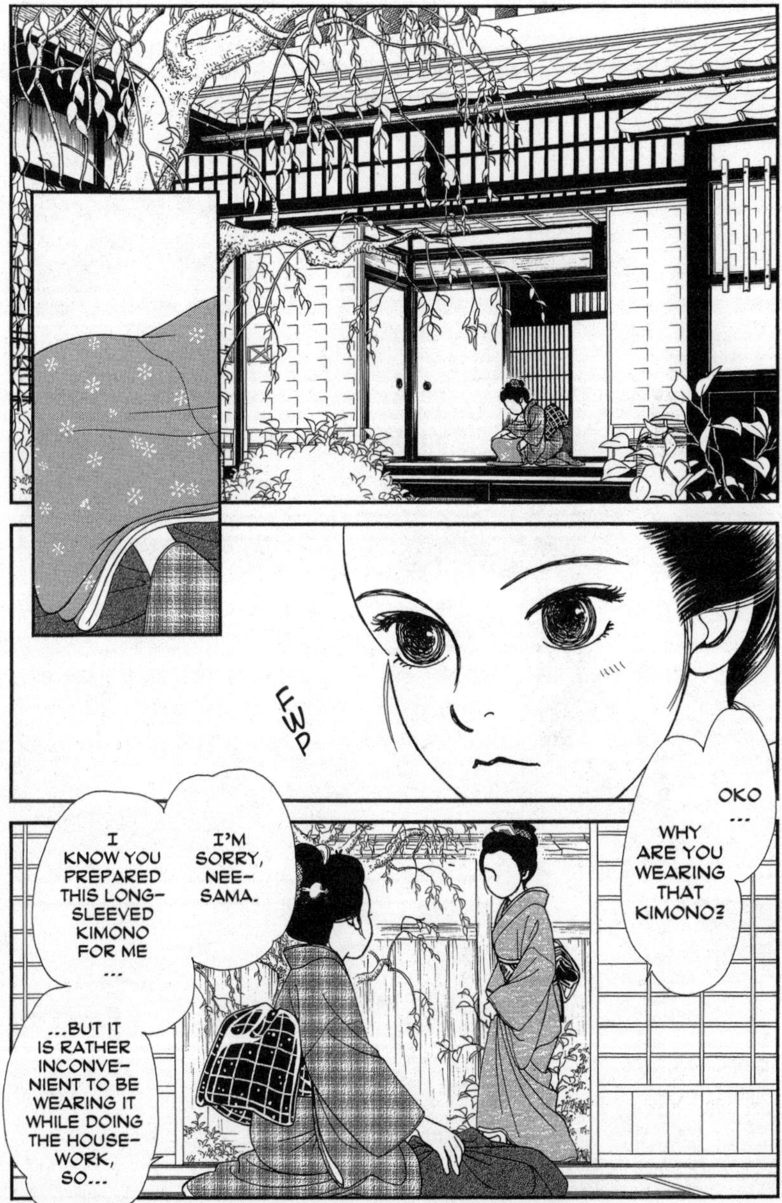
FWP
OKO... WHY ARE YOU WEARING THAT KIMONO?
I'M SORRY, NEE-SAMA.
I KNOW YOU PREPARED THIS LONG-SLEEVED KIMONO FOR ME...
...BUT IT IS RATHER INCONVENIENT TO BE WEARING IT WHILE DOING THE HOUSEWORK, SO...

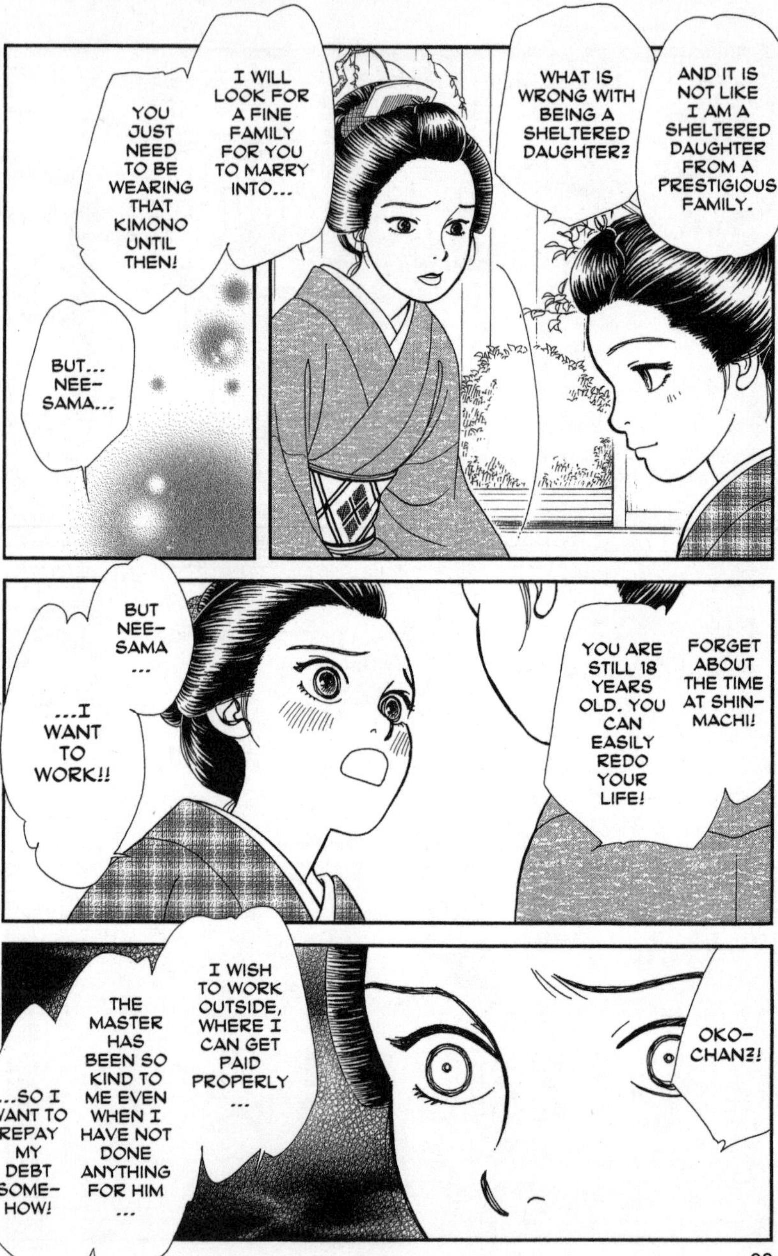
AND IT IS NOT LIKE I AM A SHELTERED DAUGHTER FROM A PRESTIGIOUS FAMILY.
WHAT IS WRONG WITH BEING A SHELTERED DAUGHTER?
I WILL LOOK FOR A FINE FAMILY FOR YOU TO MARRY INTO...
YOU JUST NEED TO BE WEARING THAT KIMONO UNTIL THEN!
BUT... NEE-SAMA...
FORGET ABOUT THE TIME AT SHIN-MACHI!
YOU ARE STILL 18 YEARS OLD. YOU CAN EASILY REDO YOUR LIFE!
BUT NEE-SAMA ... ...I WANT TO WORK!!
OKO-CHAN?!
I WISH TO WORK OUTSIDE, WHERE I CAN GET PAID PROPERLY ...
THE MASTER HAS BEEN SO KIND TO ME EVEN WHEN I HAVE NOT DONE ANYTHING FOR HIM ...
...SO I WANT TO REPAY MY DEBT SOME-HOW!

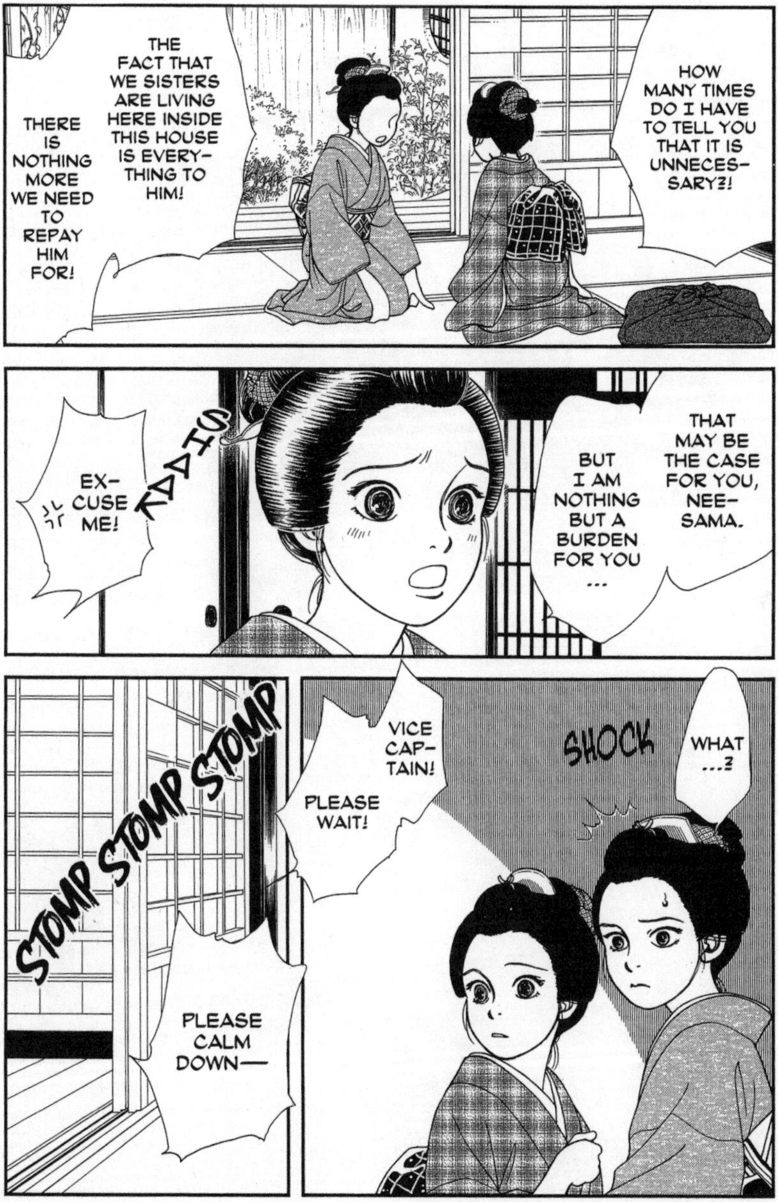
HOW MANY TIMES DO I HAVE TO TELL YOU THAT IT IS UNNECES-SARY?!
THE FACT THAT WE SISTERS ARE LIVING HERE INSIDE THIS HOUSE IS EVERY-THING TO HIM!
THERE IS NOTHING MORE WE NEED TO REPAY HIM FOR!
THAT MAY BE THE CASE FOR YOU, NEE-SAMA.
BUT I AM NOTHING BUT A BURDEN FOR YOU ...
SHAAK
EX-CUSE ME!
WHAT ...?
SHOCK
VICE CAP-TAIN!
PLEASE WAIT!
STOMP STOMP STOMP
PLEASE CALM DOWN—

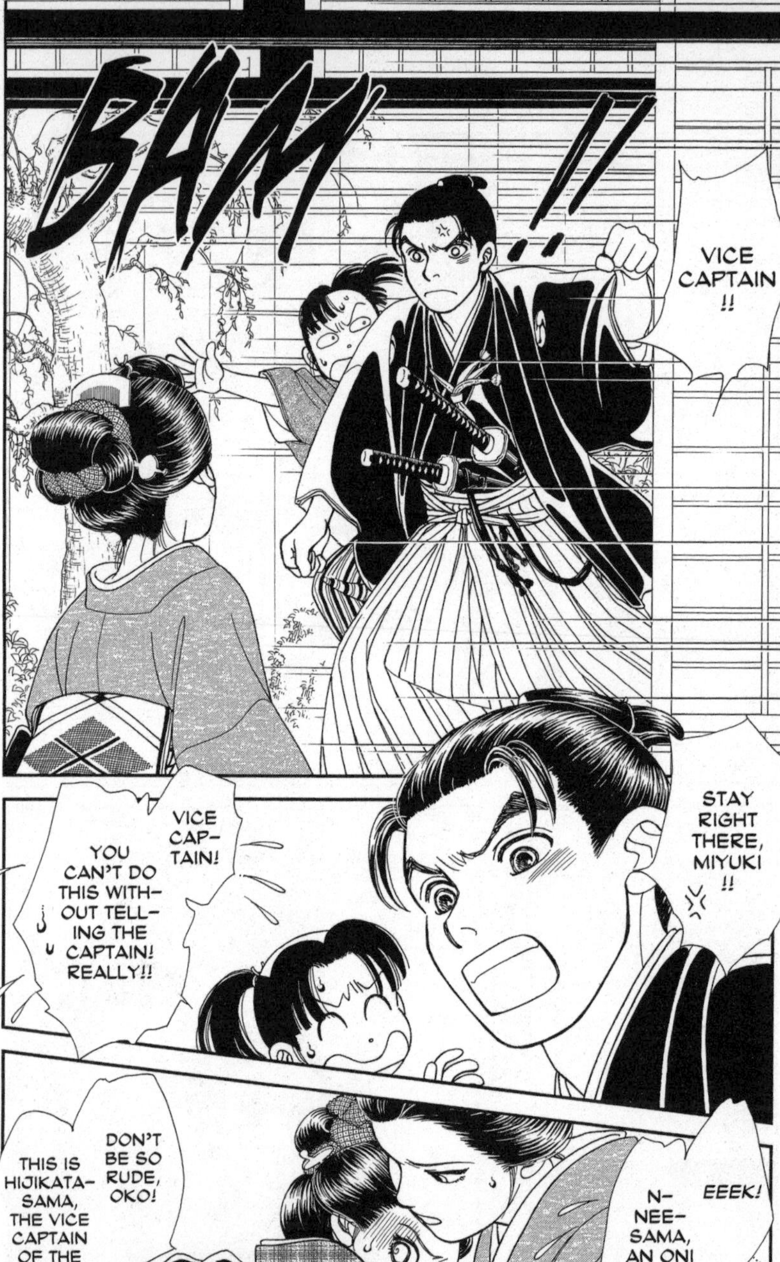
BAM !!
VICE CAPTAIN !!
STAY RIGHT THERE, MIYUKI !!
VICE CAPTAIN!
YOU CAN'T DO THIS WITHOUT TELLING THE CAPTAIN! REALLY!!
EEEK!
N-NEE-SAMA, AN ONI ...
DON'T BE SO RUDE, OKO!
THIS IS HIJIKATA-SAMA, THE VICE CAPTAIN OF THE SHINSENGUMI.

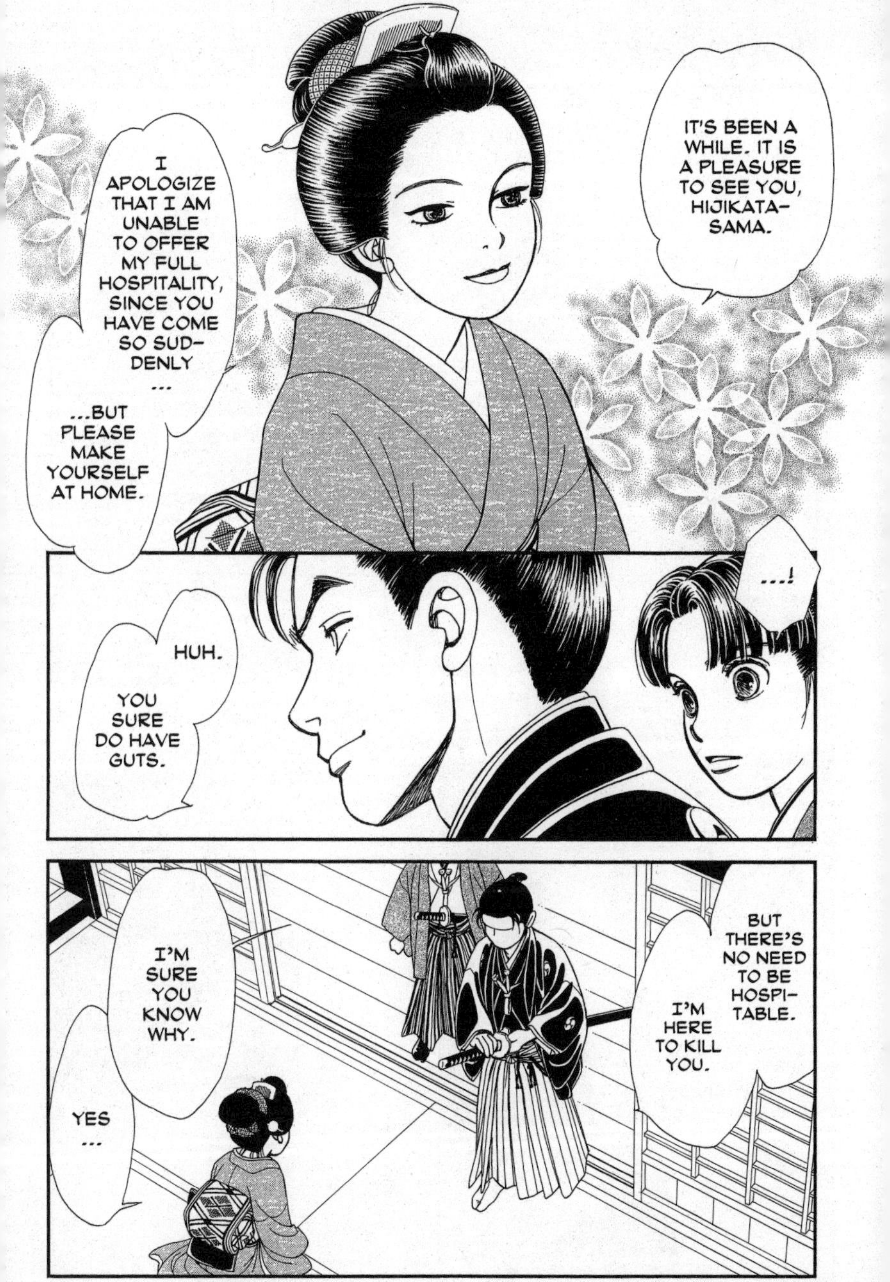
IT'S BEEN A WHILE. IT IS A PLEASURE TO SEE YOU, HIJIKATA-SAMA.
I APOLOGIZE THAT I AM UNABLE TO OFFER MY FULL HOSPITALITY, SINCE YOU HAVE COME SO SUD-DENLY ...
...BUT PLEASE MAKE YOURSELF AT HOME.
...!
HUH.
YOU SURE DO HAVE GUTS.
BUT THERE'S NO NEED TO BE HOSPI-TABLE.
I'M HERE TO KILL YOU.
I'M SURE YOU KNOW WHY.
YES ...

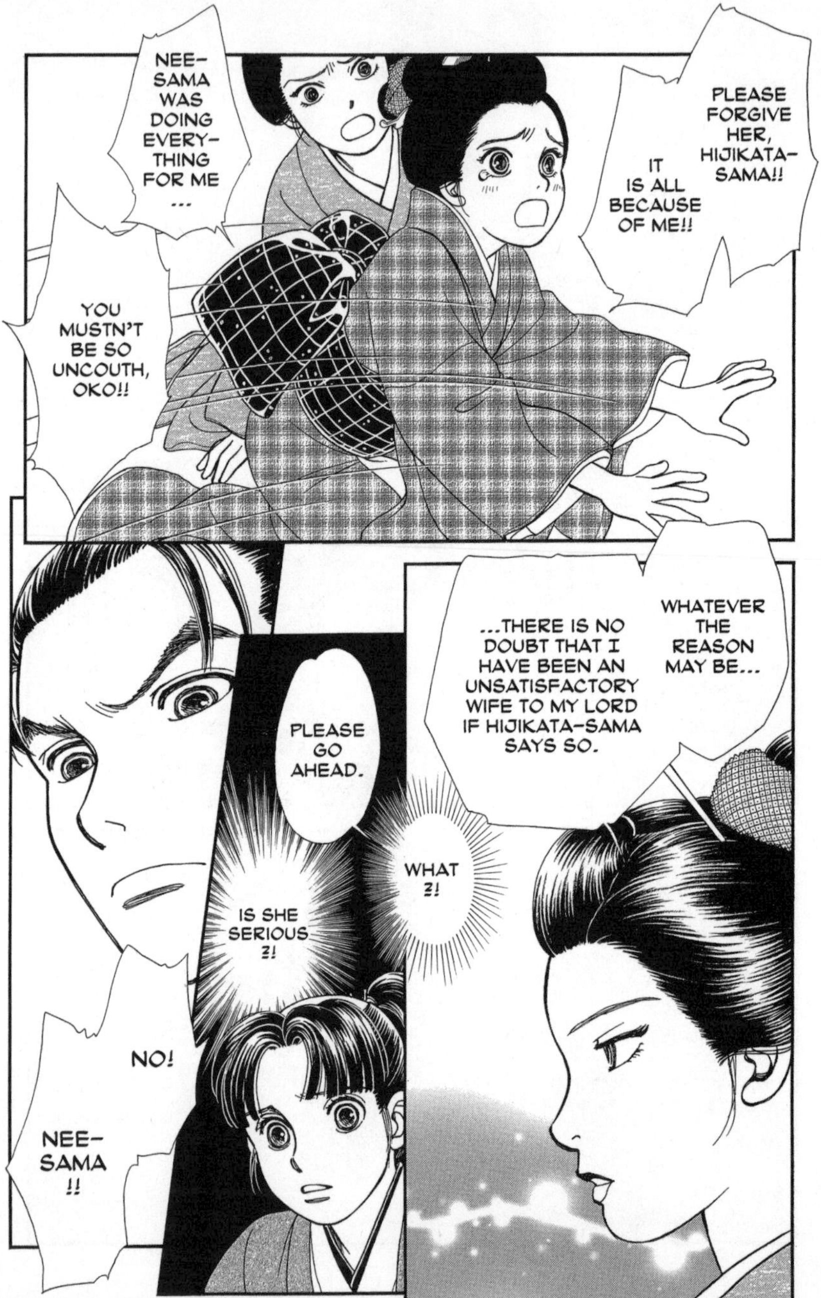
PLEASE FORGIVE HER, HIJIKATA-SAMA!!
IT IS ALL BECAUSE OF ME!!
NEE-SAMA WAS DOING EVERY-THING FOR ME ...
YOU MUSTN'T BE SO UNCOUTH, OKO!!
WHATEVER THE REASON MAY BE...
...THERE IS NO DOUBT THAT I HAVE BEEN AN UNSATISFACTORY WIFE TO MY LORD IF HIJIKATA-SAMA SAYS SO.
PLEASE GO AHEAD.
WHAT?!
IS SHE SERIOUS?!
NO!
NEE-SAMA!!

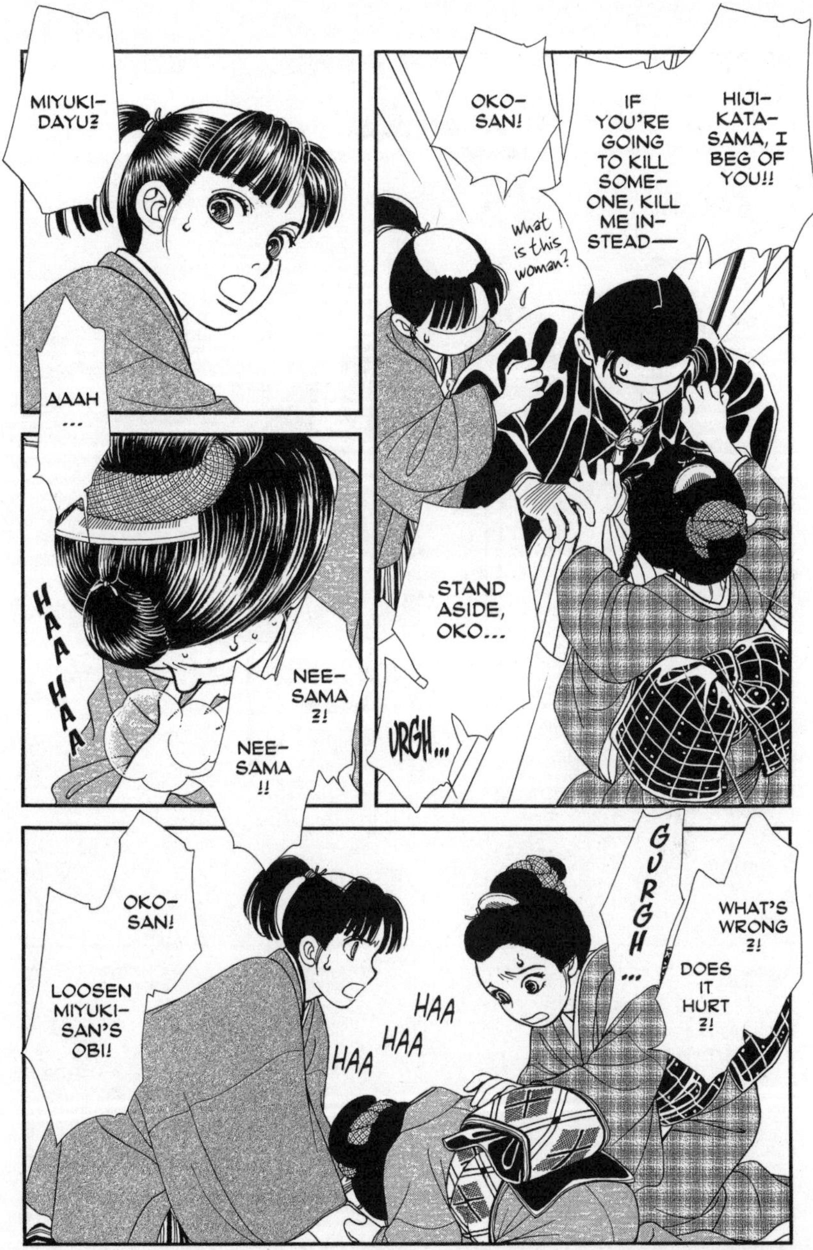
HIJI-KATA-SAMA, I BEG OF YOU!!
IF YOU'RE GOING TO KILL SOME-ONE, KILL ME IN-STEAD—
OKO-SAN!
what is this woman?
STAND ASIDE, OKO...
URGH...
MIYUKI-DAYU?
AAAH ...
HAA HAA
NEE-SAMA?!
NEE-SAMA!!
WHAT'S WRONG?!
DOES IT HURT?!
GURGH...
HAA
HAA
HAA
OKO-SAN!
LOOSEN MIYUKI-SAN'S OBI!

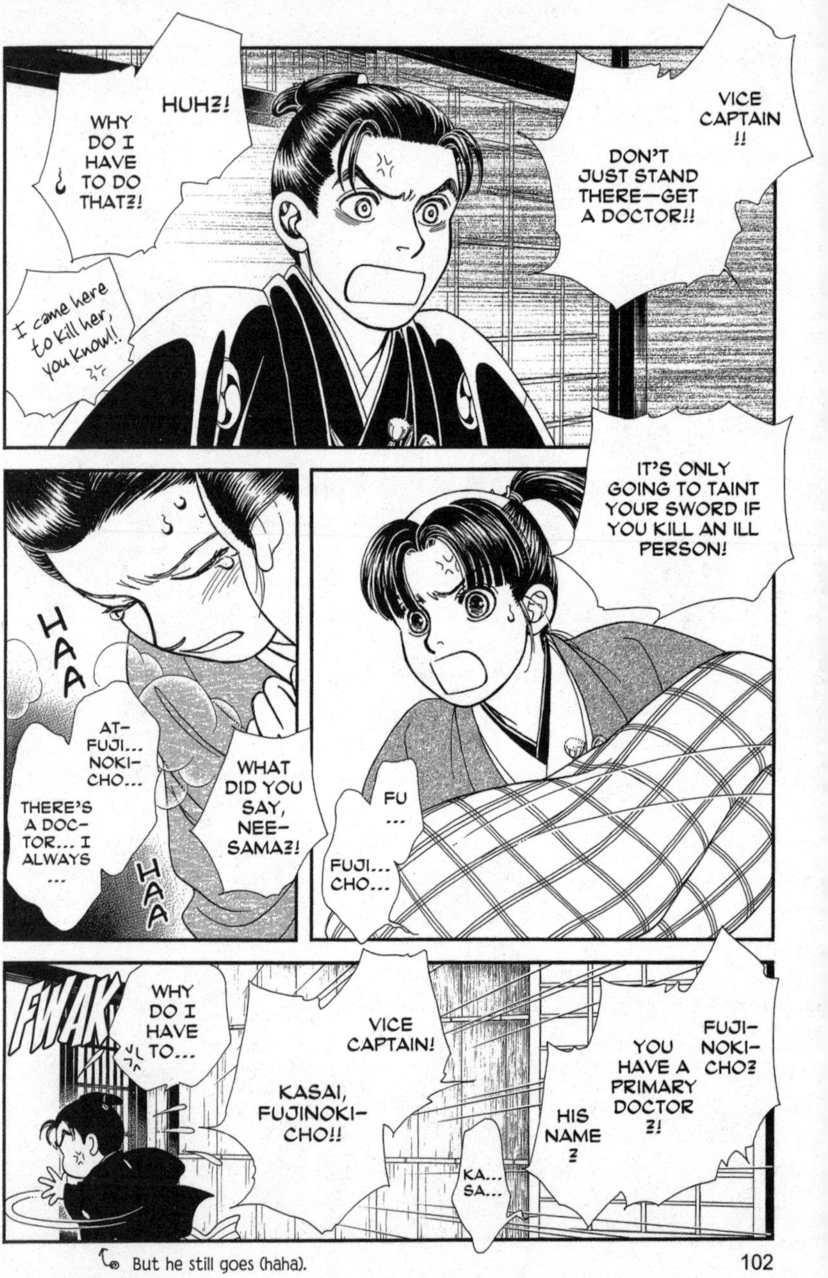
VICE CAPTAIN!!
DON'T JUST STAND THERE—GET A DOCTOR!!
HUH?!
WHY DO I HAVE TO DO THAT?!
I came here to kill her, you know!!
IT'S ONLY GOING TO TAINT YOUR SWORD IF YOU KILL AN ILL PERSON!
FU...
FUJI... CHO...
WHAT DID YOU SAY, NEE-SAMA?!
AT-FUJI... NOKI-CHO...
THERE'S A DOC-TOR... I ALWAYS...
HAA
HAA
FUJI-NOKI-CHO?
YOU HAVE A PRIMARY DOCTOR?!
HIS NAME?
KA... SA...
VICE CAPTAIN!
KASAI, FUJINOKI-CHO!!
WHY DO I HAVE TO...
FWAK

But he still goes (haha).

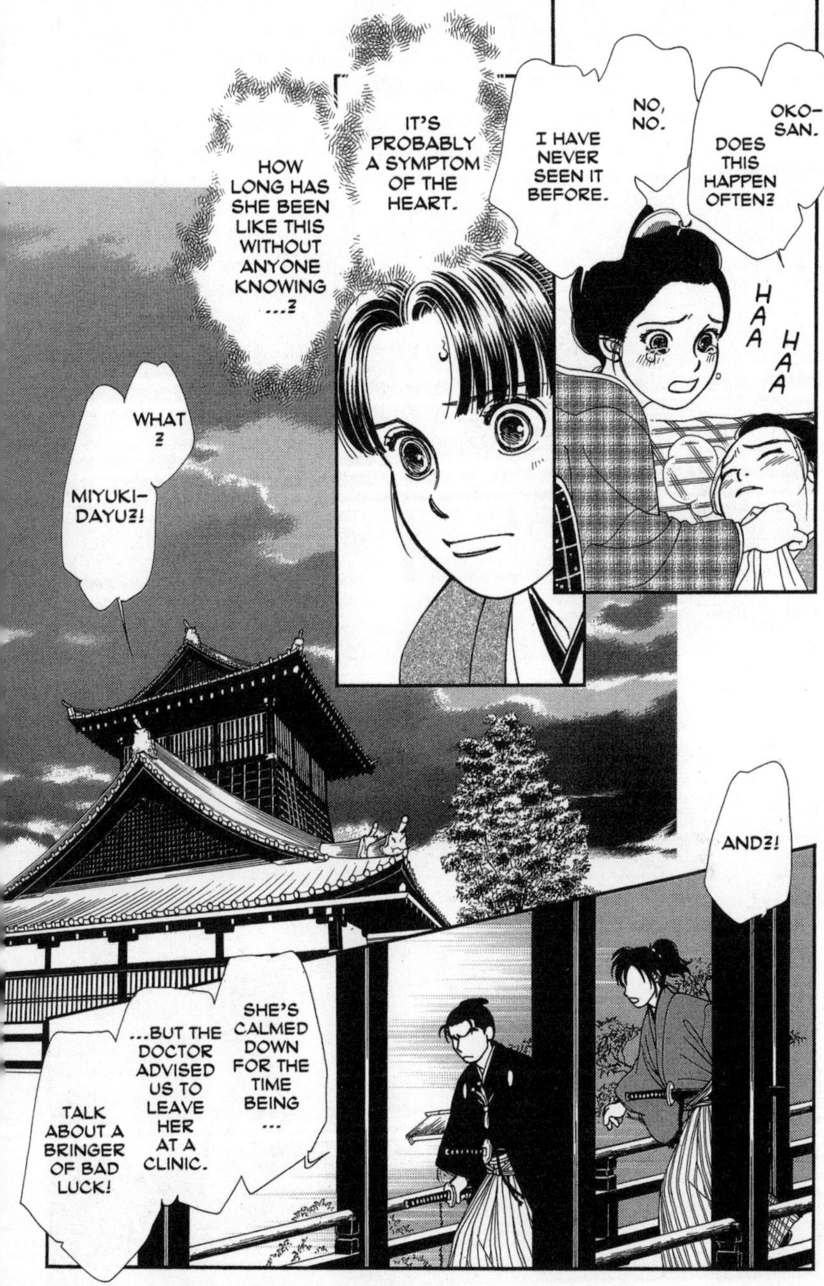
OKO-SAN.
DOES THIS HAPPEN OFTEN?
NO, NO.
I HAVE NEVER SEEN IT BEFORE.
HAA HAA
IT'S PROBABLY A SYMPTOM OF THE HEART.
HOW LONG HAS SHE BEEN LIKE THIS WITHOUT ANYONE KNOWING...?
WHAT?
MIYUKI-DAYU?!
AND?!
SHE'S CALMED DOWN FOR THE TIME BEING...
...BUT THE DOCTOR ADVISED US TO LEAVE HER AT A CLINIC.
TALK ABOUT A BRINGER OF BAD LUCK!

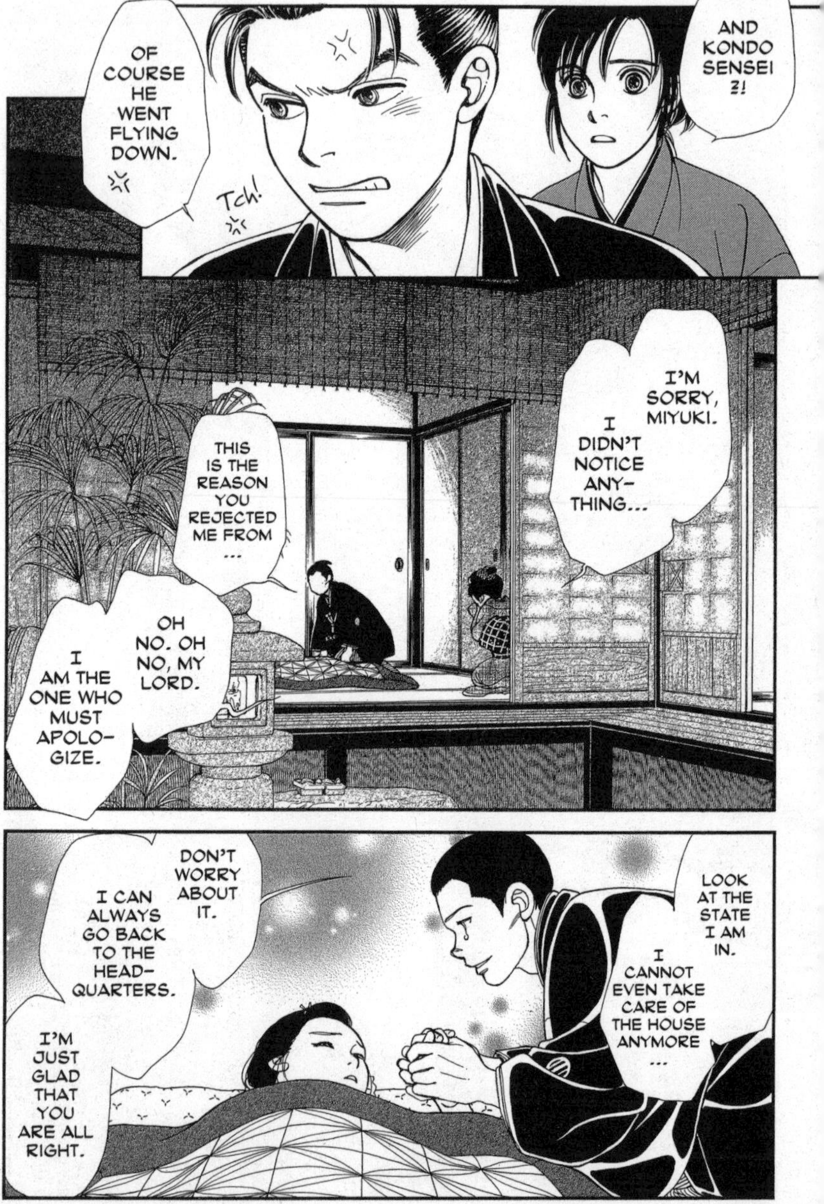
AND KONDO SENSEI?!
OF COURSE HE WENT FLYING DOWN.
Tch!
I'M SORRY, MIYUKI.
I DIDN'T NOTICE ANYTHING...
THIS IS THE REASON YOU REJECTED ME FROM...
OH NO. OH NO, MY LORD.
I AM THE ONE WHO MUST APOLOGIZE.
LOOK AT THE STATE I AM IN.
I CANNOT EVEN TAKE CARE OF THE HOUSE ANYMORE...
DON'T WORRY ABOUT IT.
I CAN ALWAYS GO BACK TO THE HEADQUARTERS.
I'M JUST GLAD THAT YOU ARE ALL RIGHT.

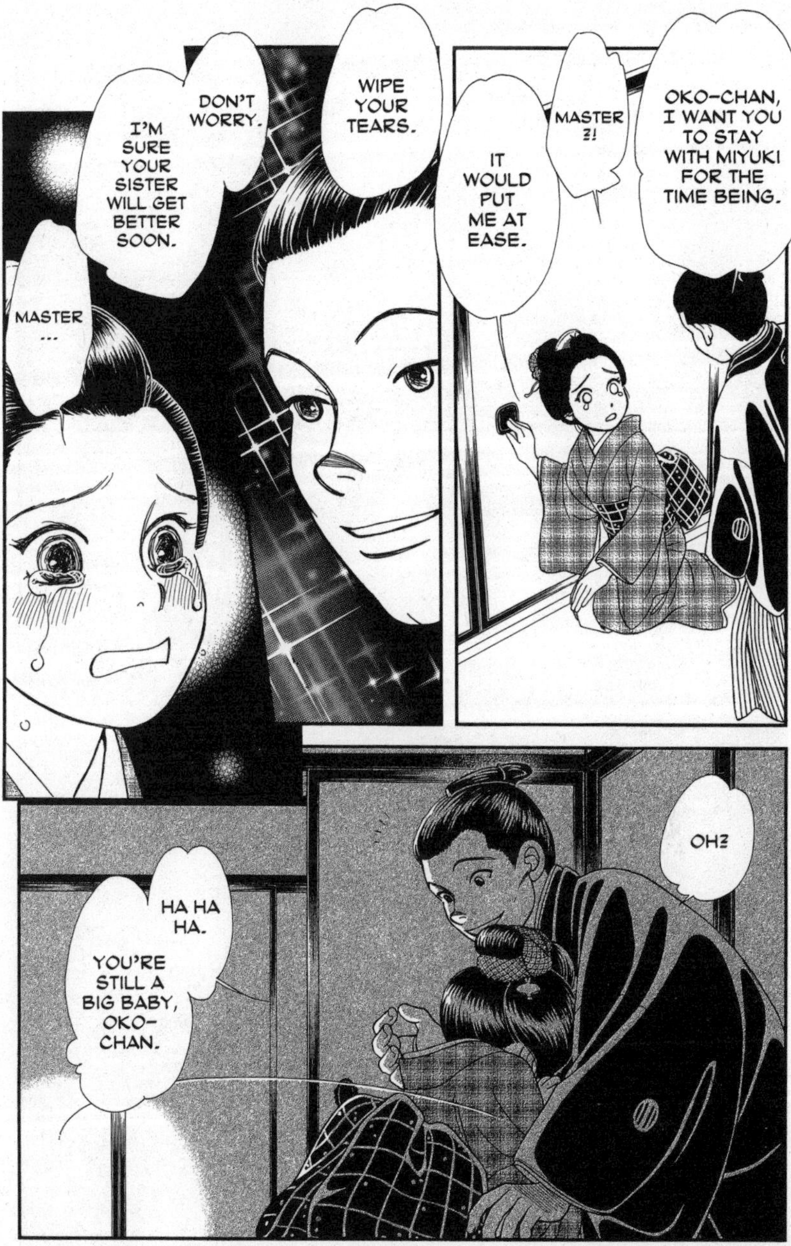
OKO-CHAN, I WANT YOU TO STAY WITH MIYUKI FOR THE TIME BEING.
MASTER?!
IT WOULD PUT ME AT EASE.
WIPE YOUR TEARS.
DON'T WORRY.
I'M SURE YOUR SISTER WILL GET BETTER SOON.
MASTER...
OH?
HA HA HA.
YOU'RE STILL A BIG BABY, OKO-CHAN.

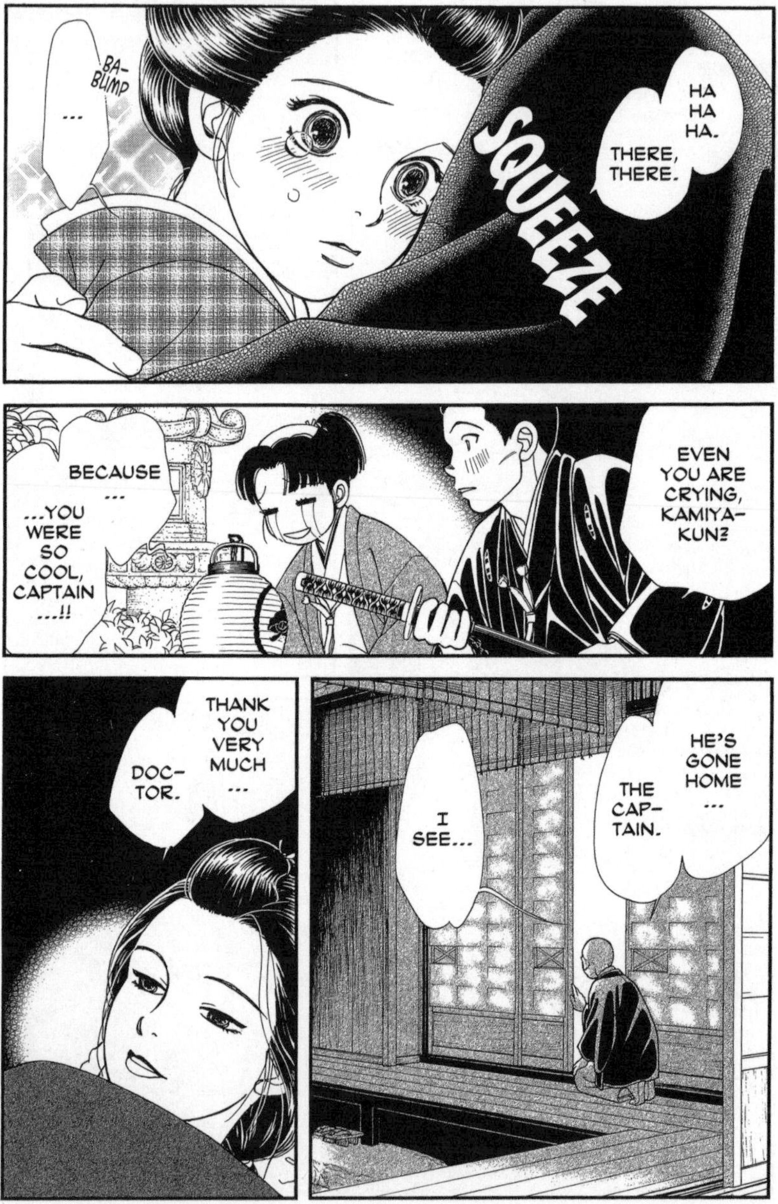
HA HA HA. THERE, THERE.
SQUEEZE
BA-BUMP
...
EVEN YOU ARE CRYING, KAMIYA-KUN?
BECAUSE ...
...YOU WERE SO COOL, CAPTAIN ...!!
HE'S GONE HOME ...
THE CAP-TAIN.
I SEE...
THANK YOU VERY MUCH ...
DOC-TOR.

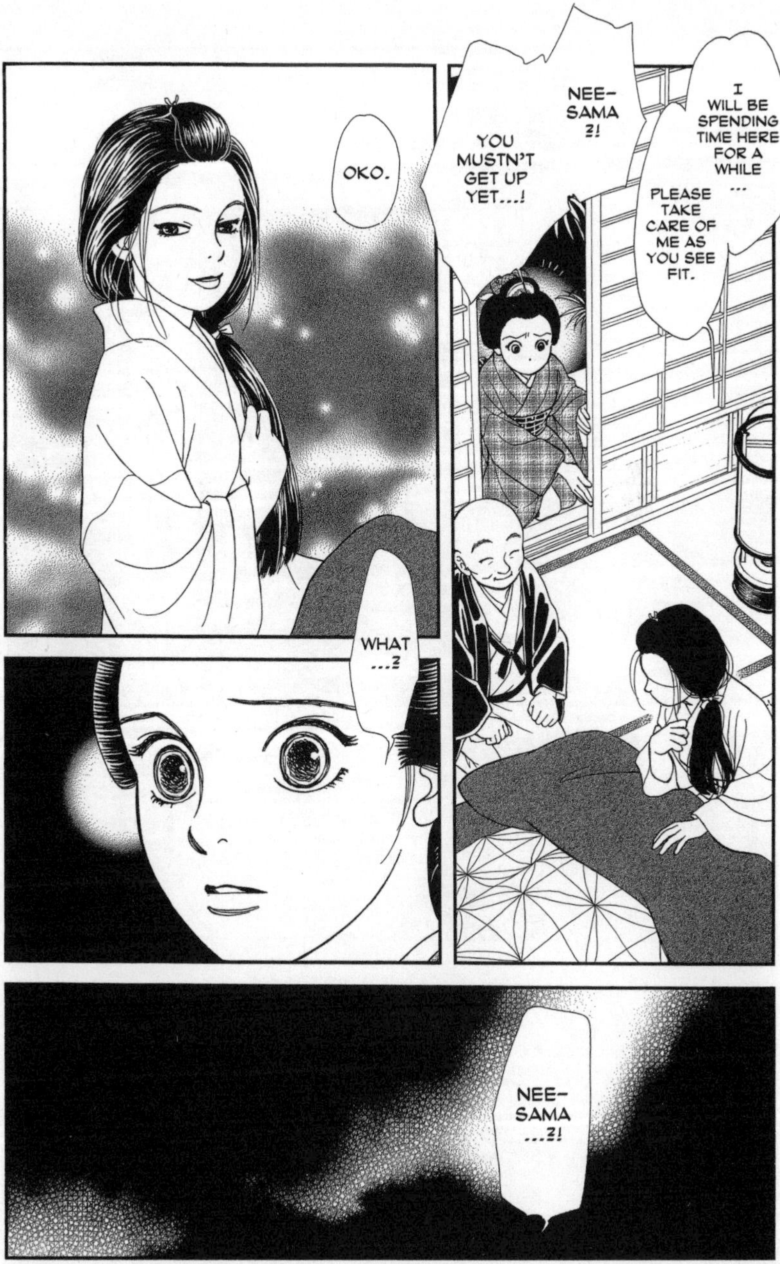
I WILL BE SPENDING TIME HERE FOR A WHILE ...
PLEASE TAKE CARE OF ME AS YOU SEE FIT.
NEE-SAMA?!
YOU MUSTN'T GET UP YET...!
OKO.
WHAT...?
NEE-SAMA...?!

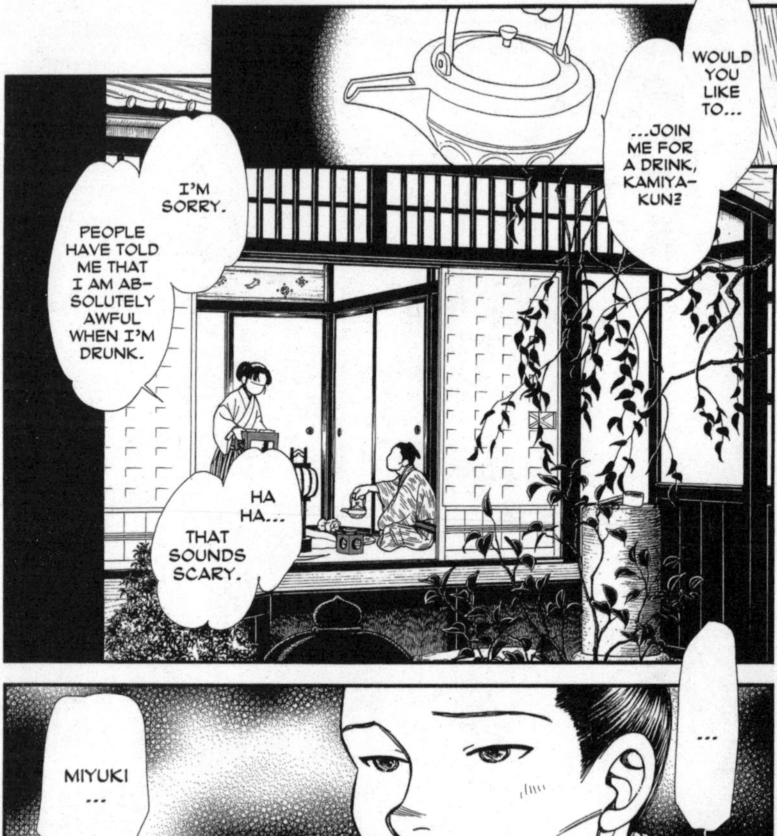
WOULD YOU LIKE TO...
...JOIN ME FOR A DRINK, KAMIYA-KUN?
I'M SORRY.
PEOPLE HAVE TOLD ME THAT I AM ABSOLUTELY AWFUL WHEN I'M DRUNK.
HA HA... THAT SOUNDS SCARY.
...
MIYUKI ...

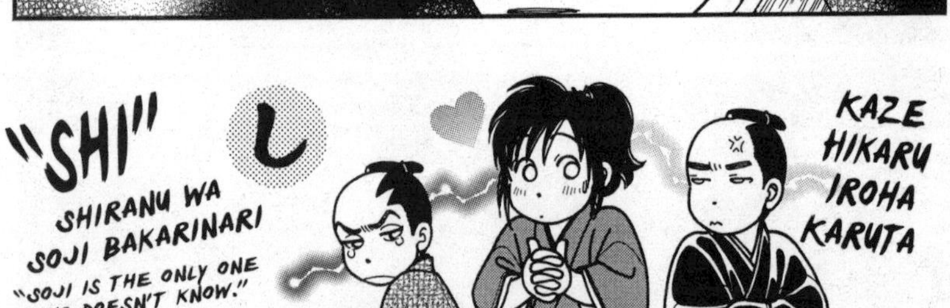
KAZE HIKARU IROHA KARUTA
"SHI"
し
SHIRANU WA SOJI BAKARINARI
"SOJI IS THE ONLY ONE WHO DOESN'T KNOW."
by Aoi-san from Tokyo

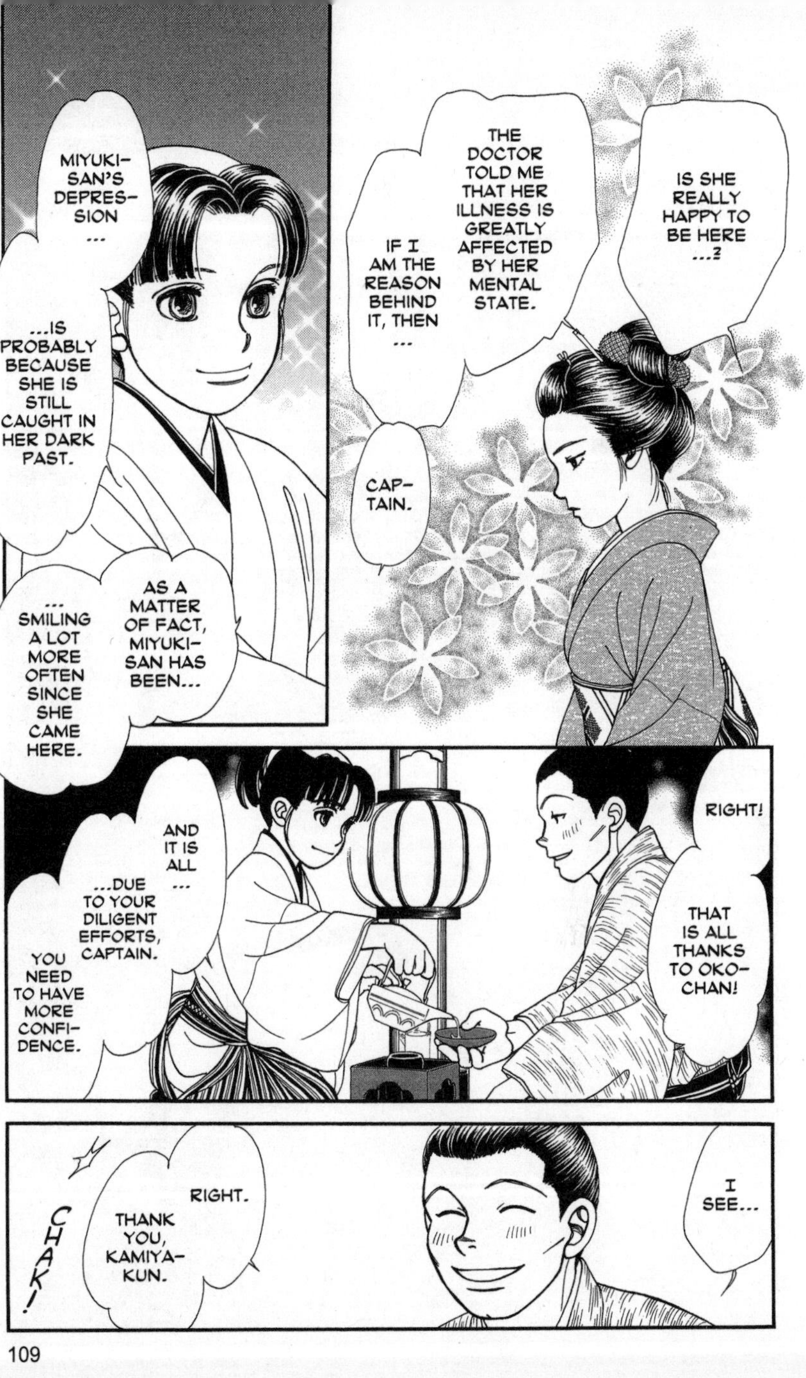
IS SHE REALLY HAPPY TO BE HERE ...?
THE DOCTOR TOLD ME THAT HER ILLNESS IS GREATLY AFFECTED BY HER MENTAL STATE.
IF I AM THE REASON BEHIND IT, THEN ...
CAPTAIN.
MIYUKI-SAN'S DEPRESSION ...
...IS PROBABLY BECAUSE SHE IS STILL CAUGHT IN HER DARK PAST.
AS A MATTER OF FACT, MIYUKI-SAN HAS BEEN...
... SMILING A LOT MORE OFTEN SINCE SHE CAME HERE.
RIGHT!
THAT IS ALL THANKS TO OKO-CHAN!
AND IT IS ALL ...
...DUE TO YOUR DILIGENT EFFORTS, CAPTAIN.
YOU NEED TO HAVE MORE CONFIDENCE.
I SEE...
RIGHT.
THANK YOU, KAMIYA-KUN.
CHAKI!

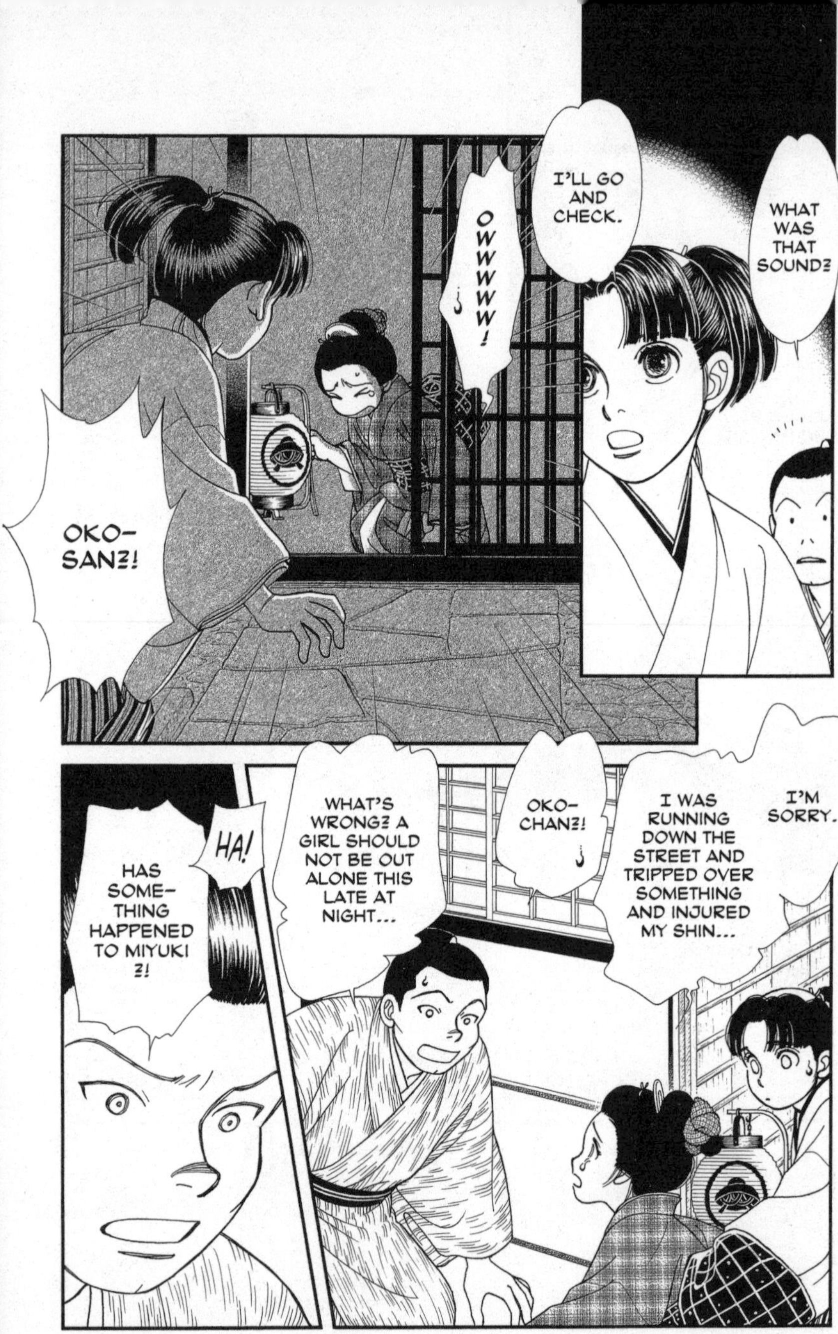
WHAT WAS THAT SOUND?
I'LL GO AND CHECK.
OWWWWW!
OKO-SAN?!
I'M SORRY.
I WAS RUNNING DOWN THE STREET AND TRIPPED OVER SOMETHING AND INJURED MY SHIN...
OKO-CHAN?!
WHAT'S WRONG? A GIRL SHOULD NOT BE OUT ALONE THIS LATE AT NIGHT...
HA!
HAS SOMETHING HAPPENED TO MIYUKI?!

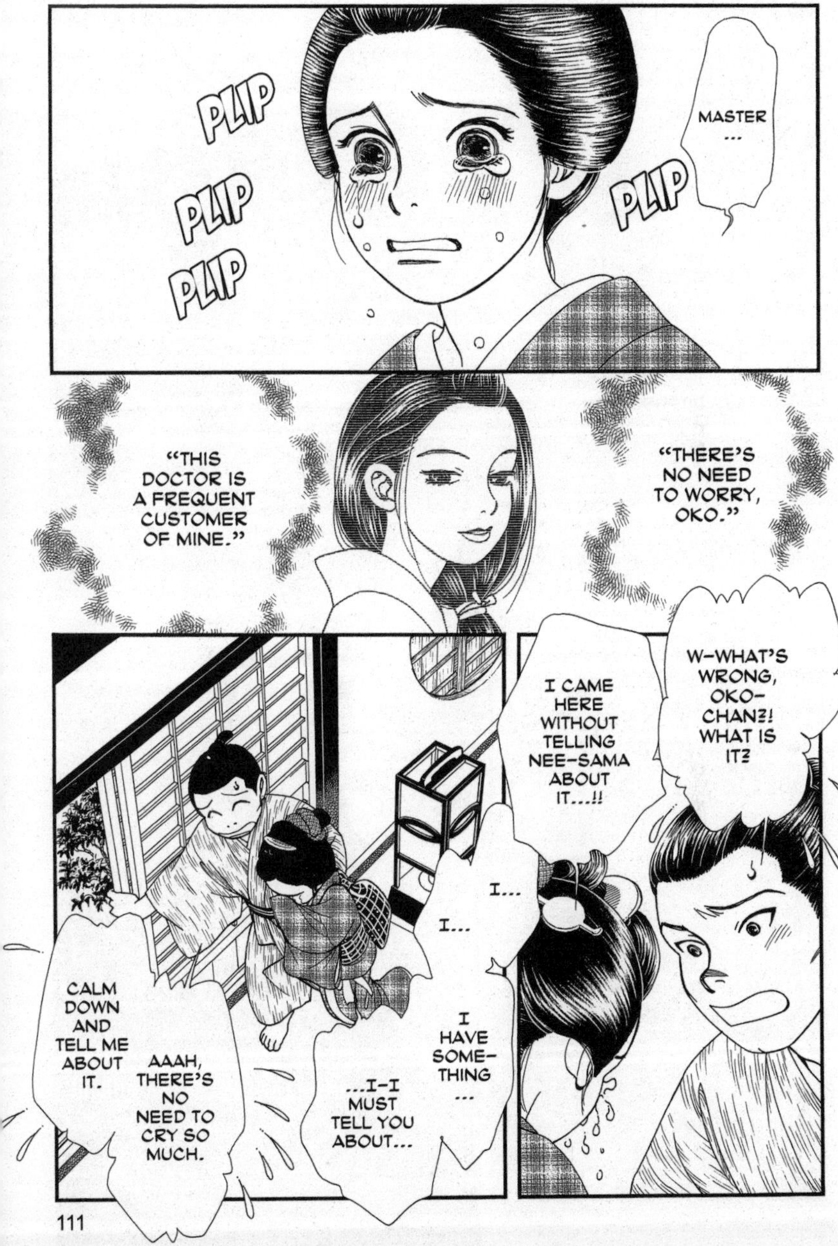
MASTER ...
PLIP
PLIP
PLIP
PLIP
"THERE'S NO NEED TO WORRY, OKO."
"THIS DOCTOR IS A FREQUENT CUSTOMER OF MINE."
W-WHAT'S WRONG, OKO-CHAN?! WHAT IS IT?
I CAME HERE WITHOUT TELLING NEE-SAMA ABOUT IT...!!
I...
I...
I HAVE SOMETHING ...
...I-I MUST TELL YOU ABOUT...
AAAH, THERE'S NO NEED TO CRY SO MUCH.
CALM DOWN AND TELL ME ABOUT IT.

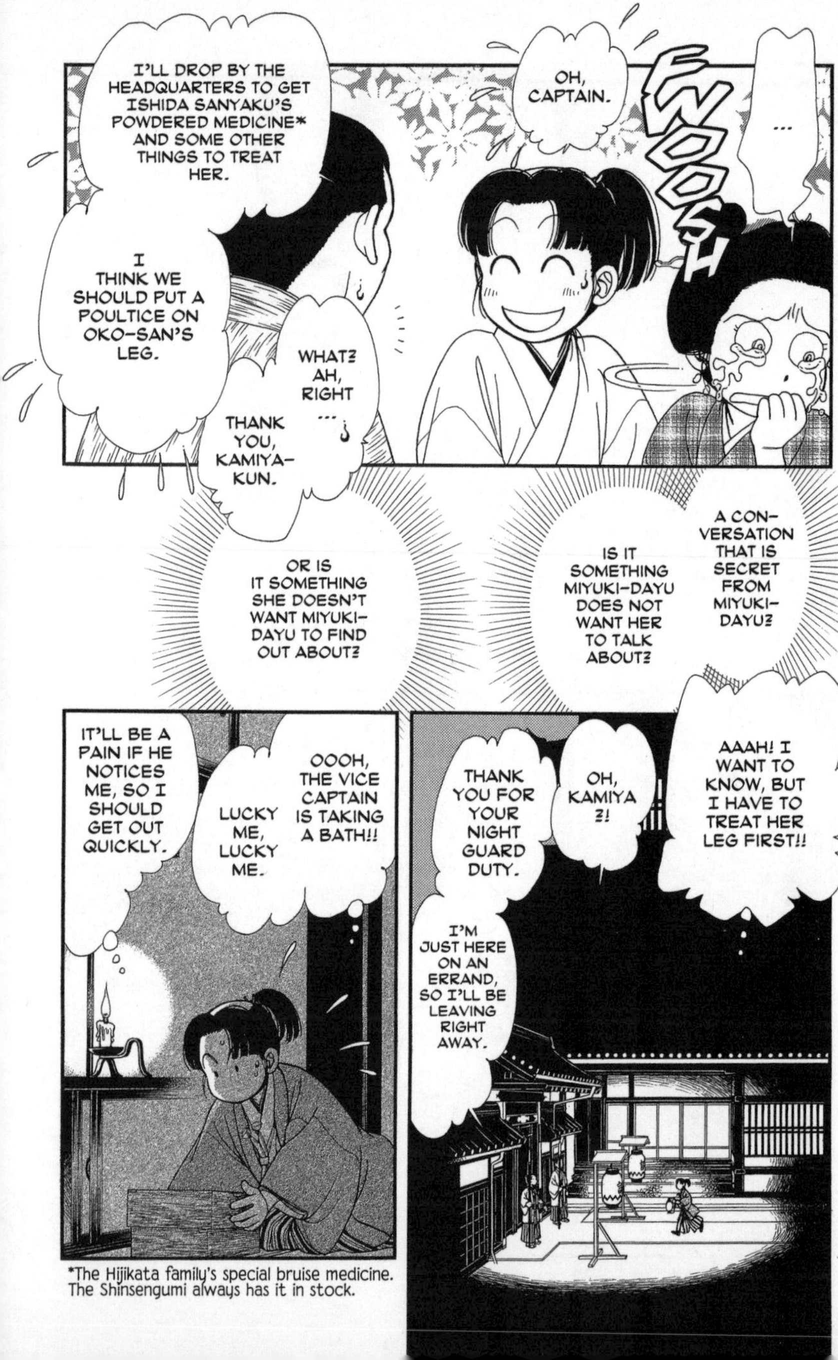
...
FWOOSH
OH, CAPTAIN.
I THINK WE SHOULD PUT A POULTICE ON OKO-SAN'S LEG.
I'LL DROP BY THE HEADQUARTERS TO GET ISHIDA SANYAKU'S POWDERED MEDICINE* AND SOME OTHER THINGS TO TREAT HER.
WHAT? AH, RIGHT...
THANK YOU, KAMIYA-KUN.
A CON-VERSATION THAT IS SECRET FROM MIYUKI-DAYU?
IS IT SOMETHING MIYUKI-DAYU DOES NOT WANT HER TO TALK ABOUT?
OR IS IT SOMETHING SHE DOESN'T WANT MIYUKI-DAYU TO FIND OUT ABOUT?
AAAH! I WANT TO KNOW, BUT I HAVE TO TREAT HER LEG FIRST!!
OH, KAMIYA?!
THANK YOU FOR YOUR NIGHT GUARD DUTY.
I'M JUST HERE ON AN ERRAND, SO I'LL BE LEAVING RIGHT AWAY.
OOOH, THE VICE CAPTAIN IS TAKING A BATH!!
LUCKY ME, LUCKY ME.
IT'LL BE A PAIN IF HE NOTICES ME, SO I SHOULD GET OUT QUICKLY.

*The Hijikata family's special bruise medicine. The Shinsengumi always has it in stock.

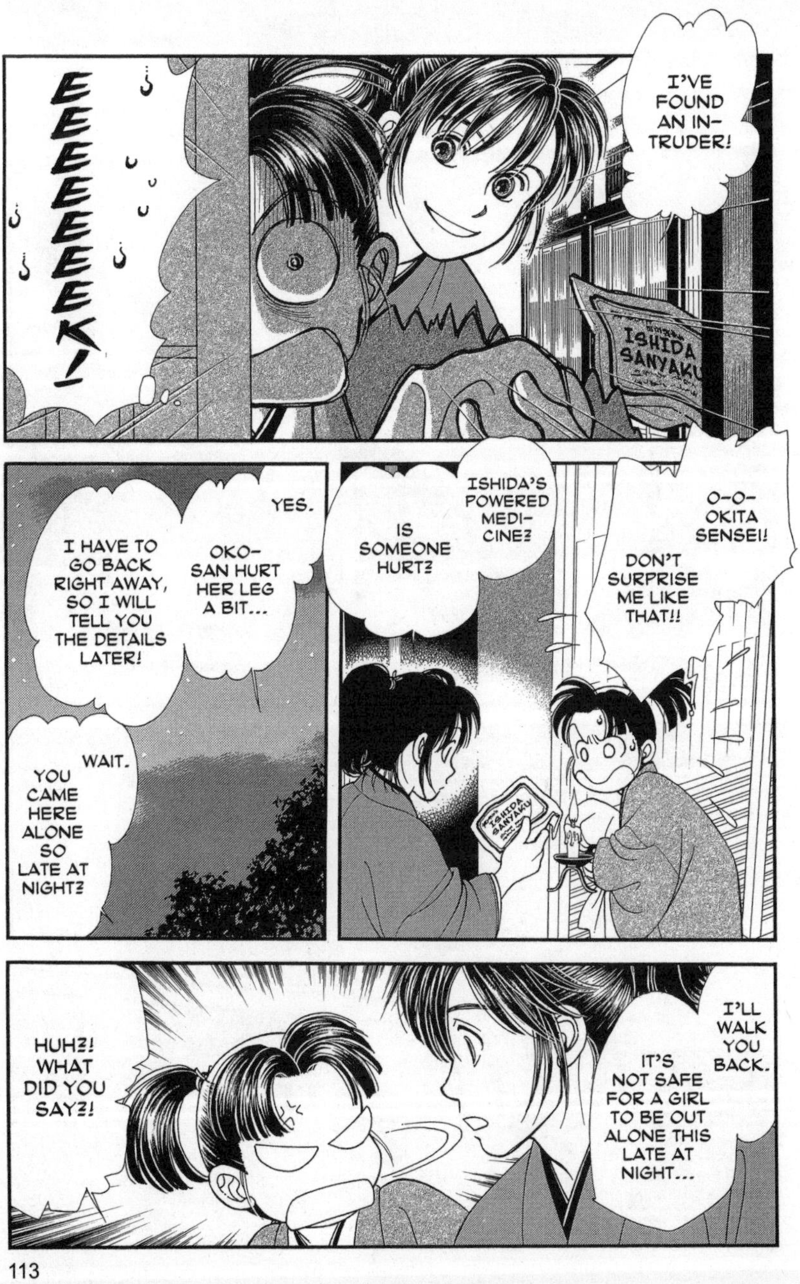
I'VE FOUND AN INTRUDER!
ISHIDA SANYAKU
EEEEEEEK!
O-O-OKITA SENSEI!
DON'T SURPRISE ME LIKE THAT!!
ISHIDA'S POWERED MEDICINE?
IS SOMEONE HURT?
ISHIDA SANYAKU
YES.
OKO-SAN HURT HER LEG A BIT...
I HAVE TO GO BACK RIGHT AWAY, SO I WILL TELL YOU THE DETAILS LATER!
WAIT.
YOU CAME HERE ALONE SO LATE AT NIGHT?
I'LL WALK YOU BACK.
IT'S NOT SAFE FOR A GIRL TO BE OUT ALONE THIS LATE AT NIGHT...
HUH?! WHAT DID YOU SAY?!

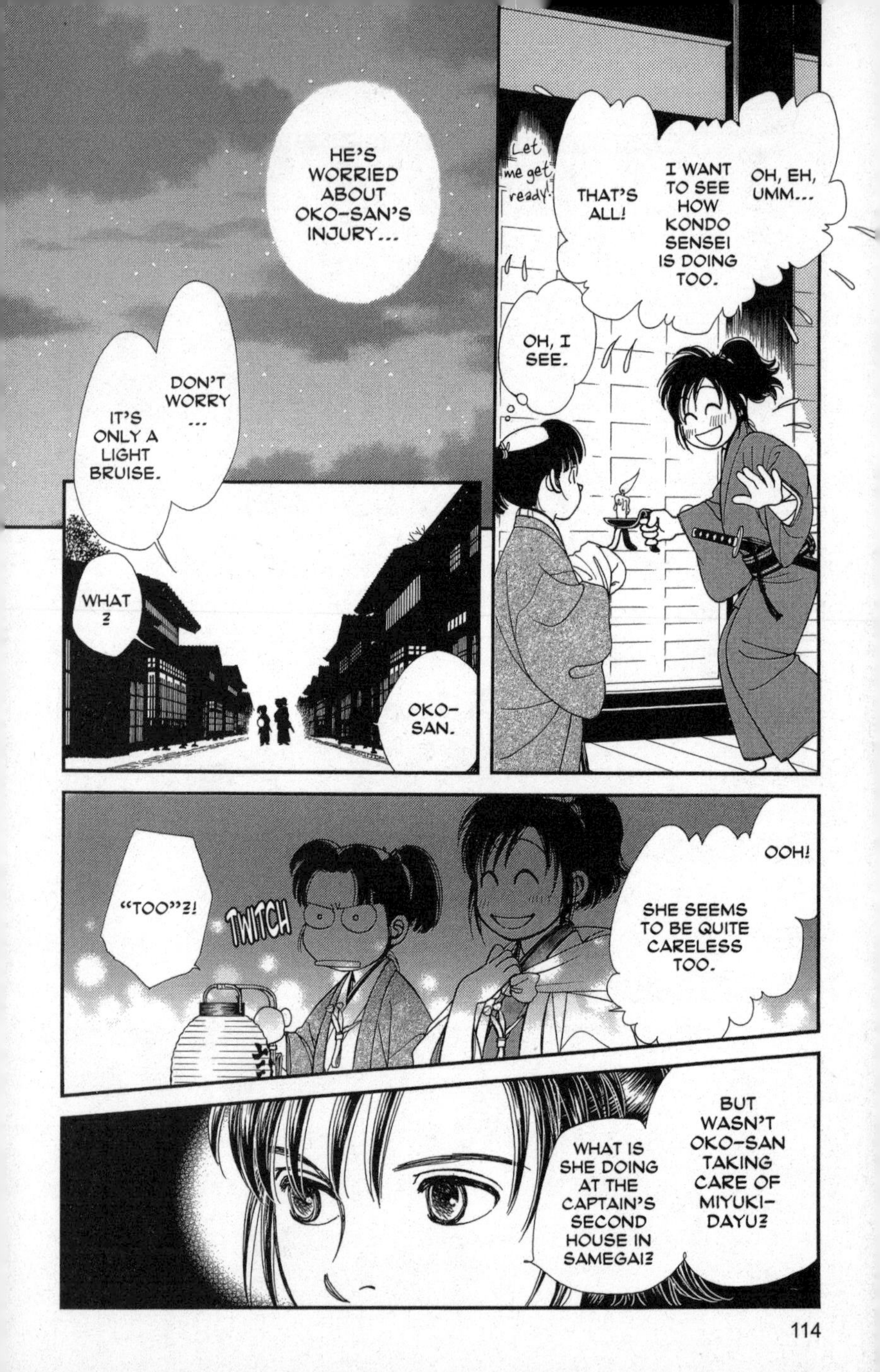
OH, EH, UMM...
I WANT TO SEE HOW KONDO SENSEI IS DOING TOO.
THAT'S ALL!
Let me get ready!
OH, I SEE.
HE'S WORRIED ABOUT OKO-SAN'S INJURY...
DON'T WORRY... IT'S ONLY A LIGHT BRUISE.
WHAT?
OKO-SAN.
OOH!
SHE SEEMS TO BE QUITE CARELESS TOO.
TWITCH
"TOO"?!
BUT WASN'T OKO-SAN TAKING CARE OF MIYUKI-DAYU?
WHAT IS SHE DOING AT THE CAPTAIN'S SECOND HOUSE IN SAMEGAI?

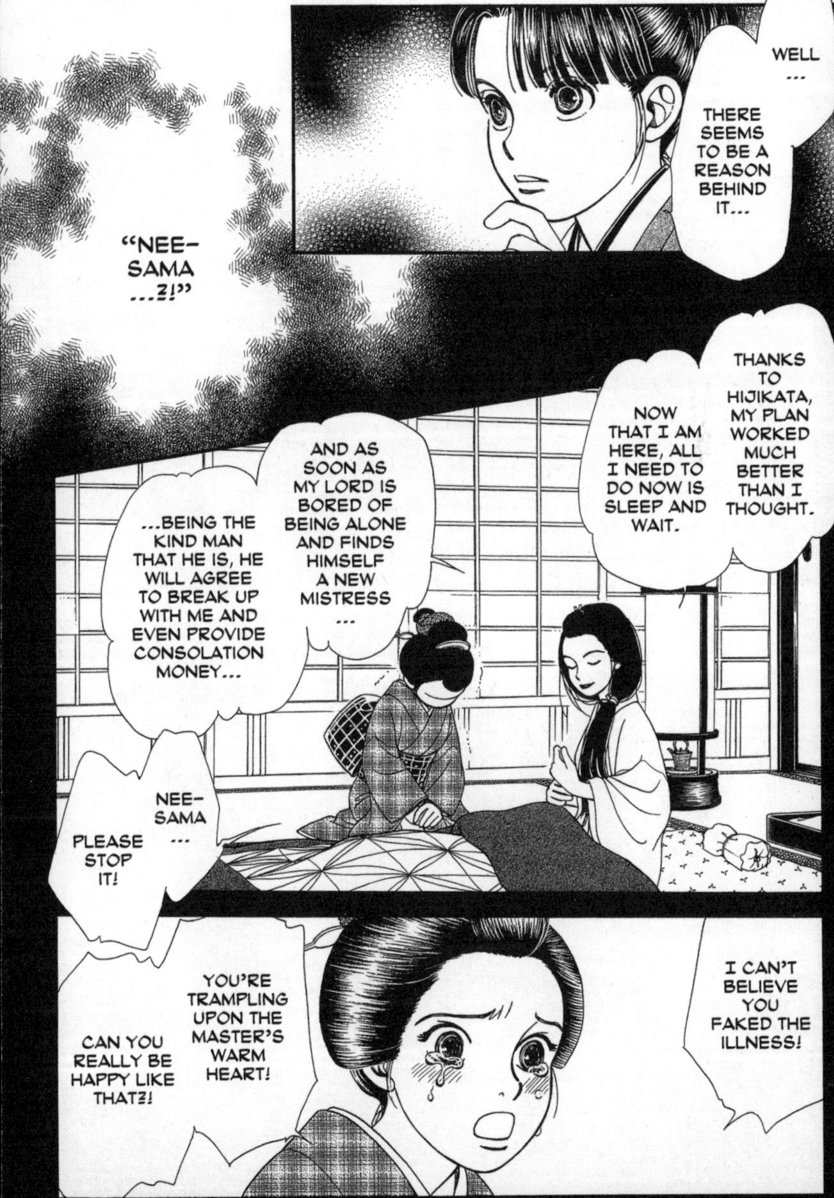
WELL...
THERE SEEMS TO BE A REASON BEHIND IT...
"NEE-SAMA...?!"
THANKS TO HIJIKATA, MY PLAN WORKED MUCH BETTER THAN I THOUGHT.
NOW THAT I AM HERE, ALL I NEED TO DO NOW IS SLEEP AND WAIT.
AND AS SOON AS MY LORD IS BORED OF BEING ALONE AND FINDS HIMSELF A NEW MISTRESS...
...BEING THE KIND MAN THAT HE IS, HE WILL AGREE TO BREAK UP WITH ME AND EVEN PROVIDE CONSOLATION MONEY...
NEE-SAMA...
PLEASE STOP IT!
I CAN'T BELIEVE YOU FAKED THE ILLNESS!
YOU'RE TRAMPLING UPON THE MASTER'S WARM HEART!
CAN YOU REALLY BE HAPPY LIKE THAT?!

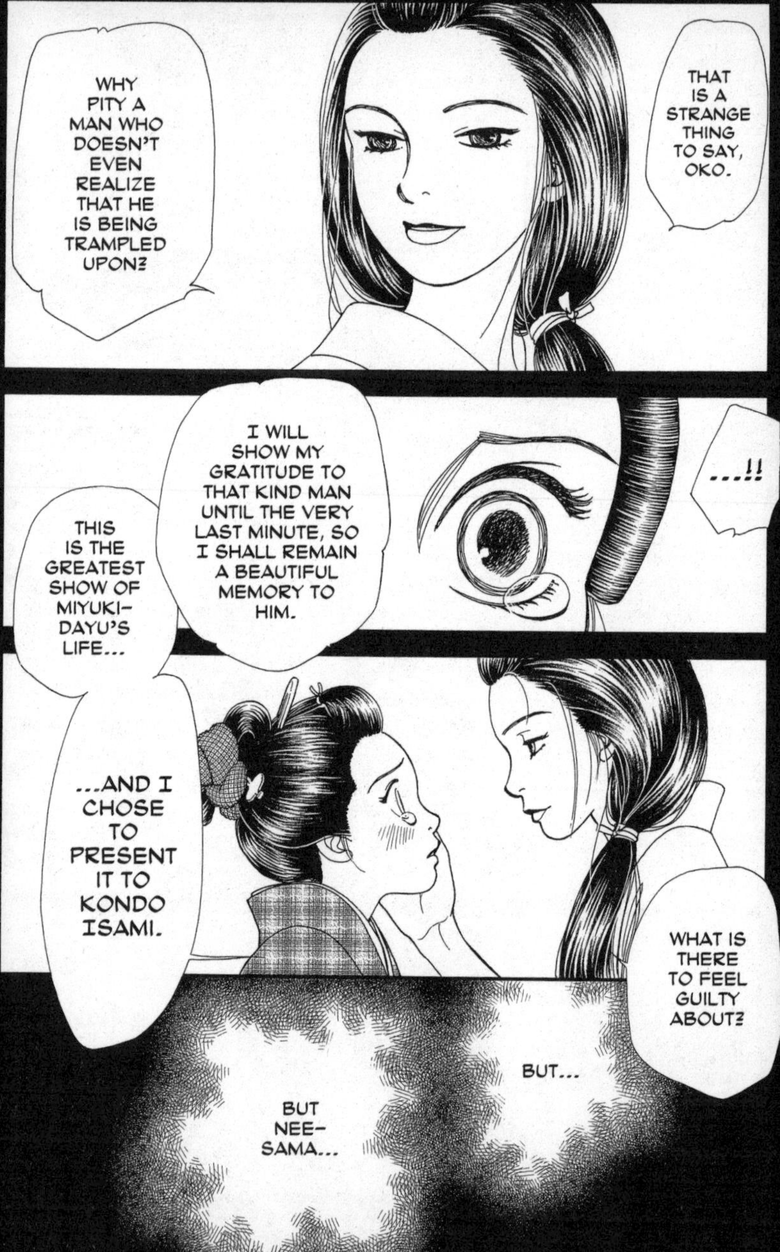
THAT IS A STRANGE THING TO SAY, OKO.
WHY PITY A MAN WHO DOESN'T EVEN REALIZE THAT HE IS BEING TRAMPLED UPON?
...!!
I WILL SHOW MY GRATITUDE TO THAT KIND MAN UNTIL THE VERY LAST MINUTE, SO I SHALL REMAIN A BEAUTIFUL MEMORY TO HIM.
THIS IS THE GREATEST SHOW OF MIYUKI-DAYU'S LIFE...
...AND I CHOSE TO PRESENT IT TO KONDO ISAMI.
WHAT IS THERE TO FEEL GUILTY ABOUT?
BUT...
BUT NEE-SAMA...

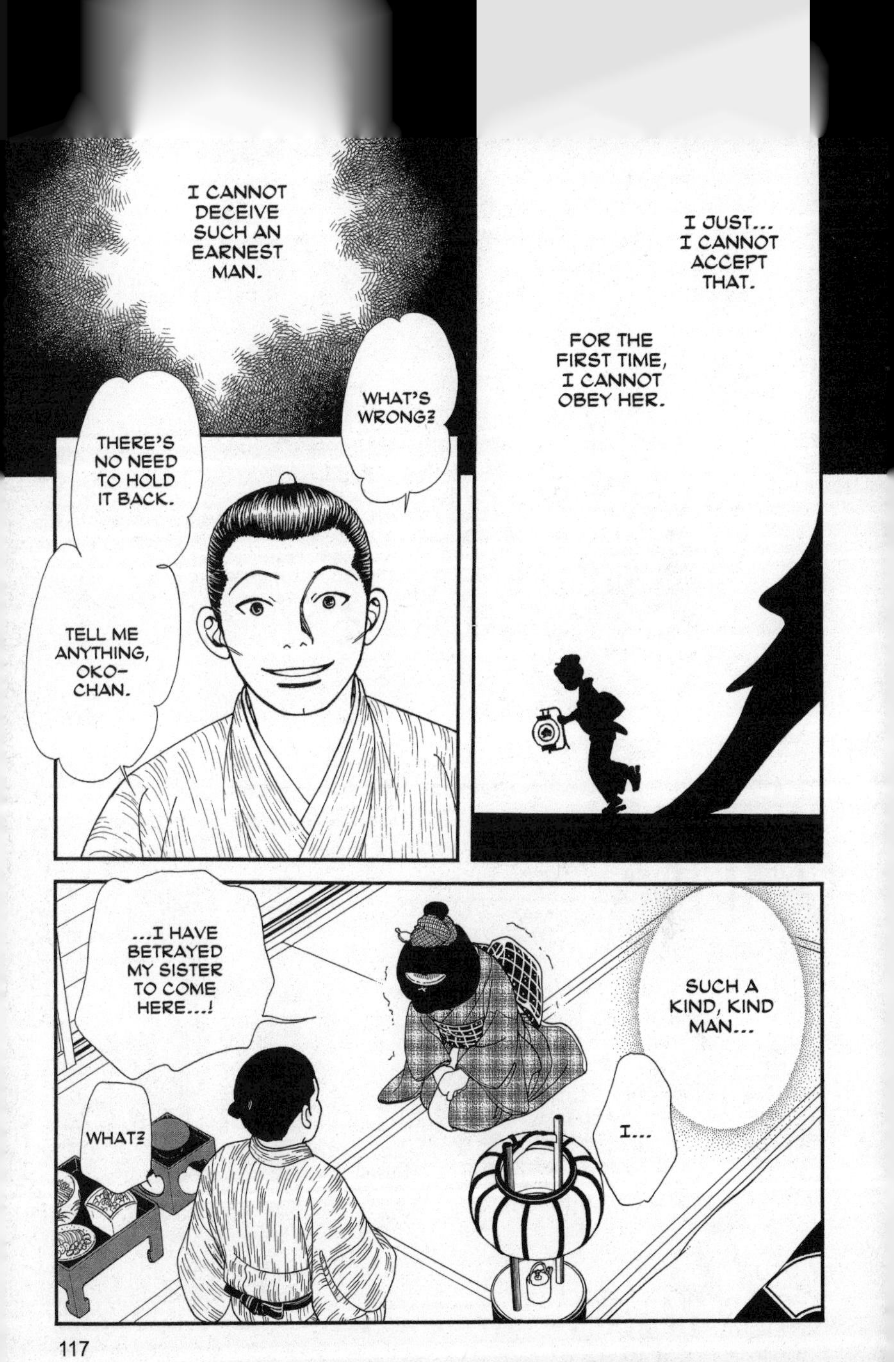
I JUST... I CANNOT ACCEPT THAT.
FOR THE FIRST TIME, I CANNOT OBEY HER.
I CANNOT DECEIVE SUCH AN EARNEST MAN.
WHAT'S WRONG?
THERE'S NO NEED TO HOLD IT BACK.
TELL ME ANYTHING, OKO-CHAN.
SUCH A KIND, KIND MAN...
I...
...I HAVE BETRAYED MY SISTER TO COME HERE...!
WHAT?

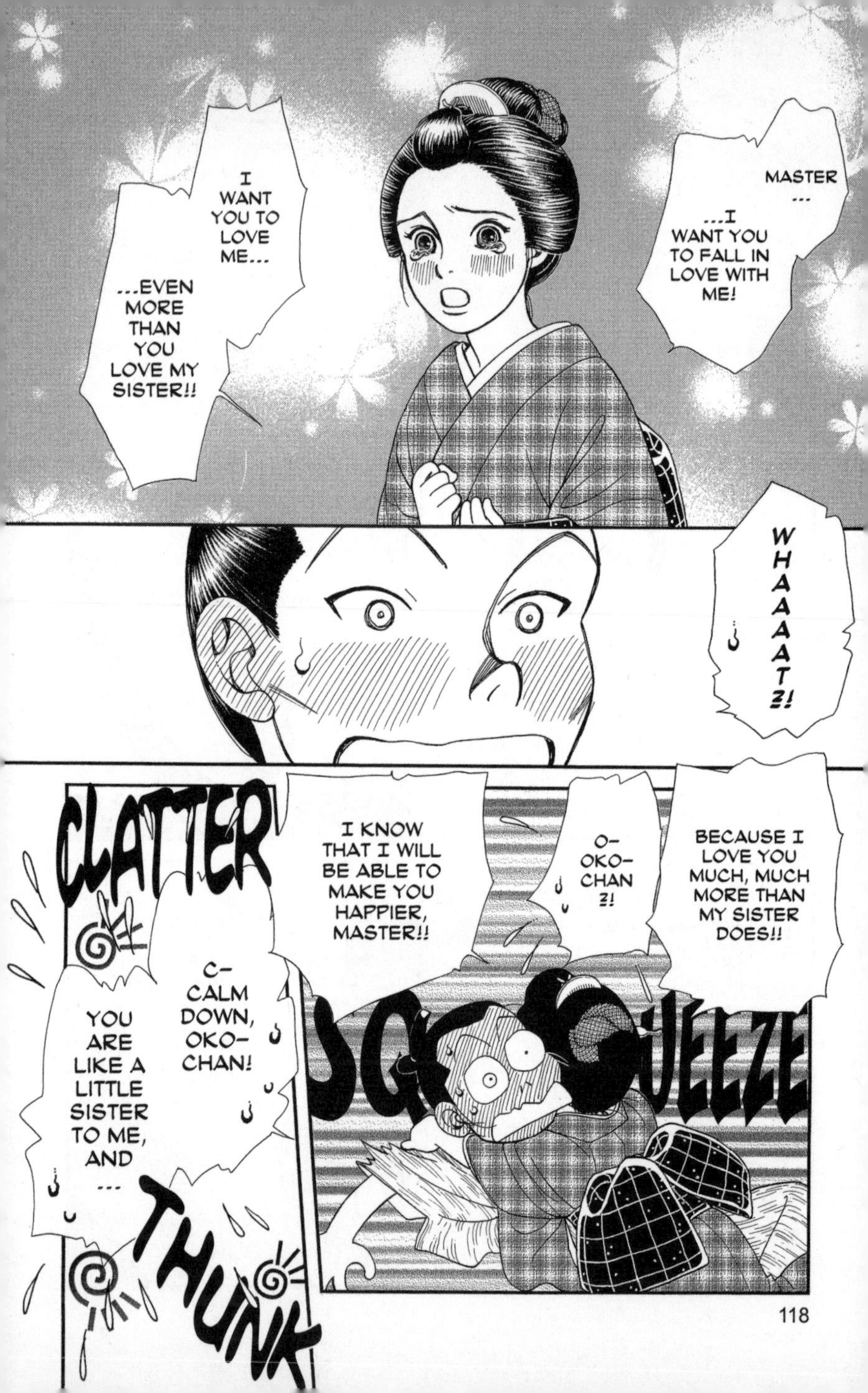
MASTER ...
...I WANT YOU TO FALL IN LOVE WITH ME!
I WANT YOU TO LOVE ME...
...EVEN MORE THAN YOU LOVE MY SISTER!!
WHAAAAAT?!
BECAUSE I LOVE YOU MUCH, MUCH MORE THAN MY SISTER DOES!!
O-OKO-CHAN?!
I KNOW THAT I WILL BE ABLE TO MAKE YOU HAPPIER, MASTER!!
CLATTER
SQUEEZE
C-CALM DOWN, OKO-CHAN!
YOU ARE LIKE A LITTLE SISTER TO ME, AND ...
THUNK

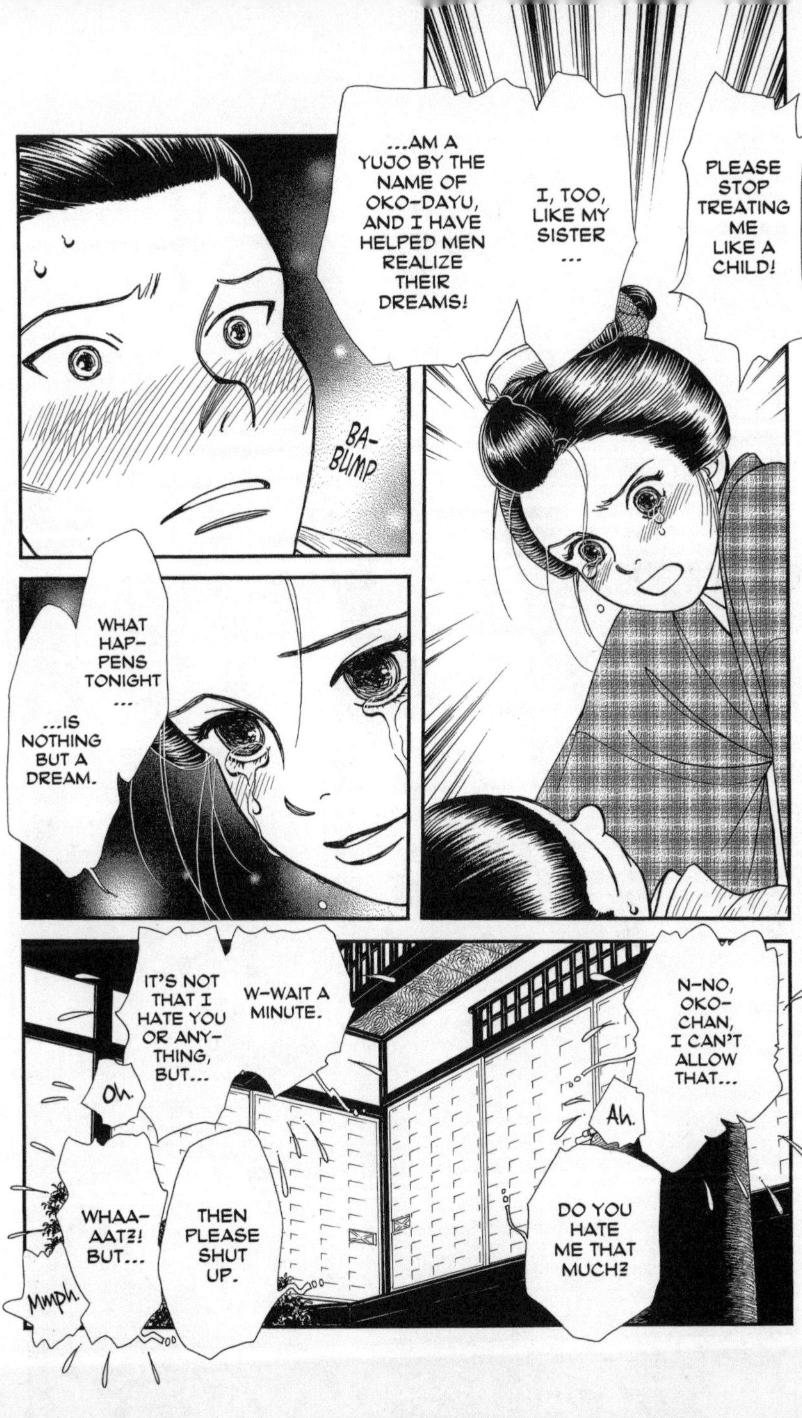
PLEASE STOP TREATING ME LIKE A CHILD!
I, TOO, LIKE MY SISTER ...
...AM A YUJO BY THE NAME OF OKO-DAYU, AND I HAVE HELPED MEN REALIZE THEIR DREAMS!
BA-BUMP
WHAT HAP-PENS TONIGHT ...
...IS NOTHING BUT A DREAM.
N-NO, OKO-CHAN, I CAN'T ALLOW THAT...
W-WAIT A MINUTE.
IT'S NOT THAT I HATE YOU OR ANY-THING, BUT...
Ah.
Oh.
DO YOU HATE ME THAT MUCH?
THEN PLEASE SHUT UP.
WHAA-AAT?! BUT...
Mmph.

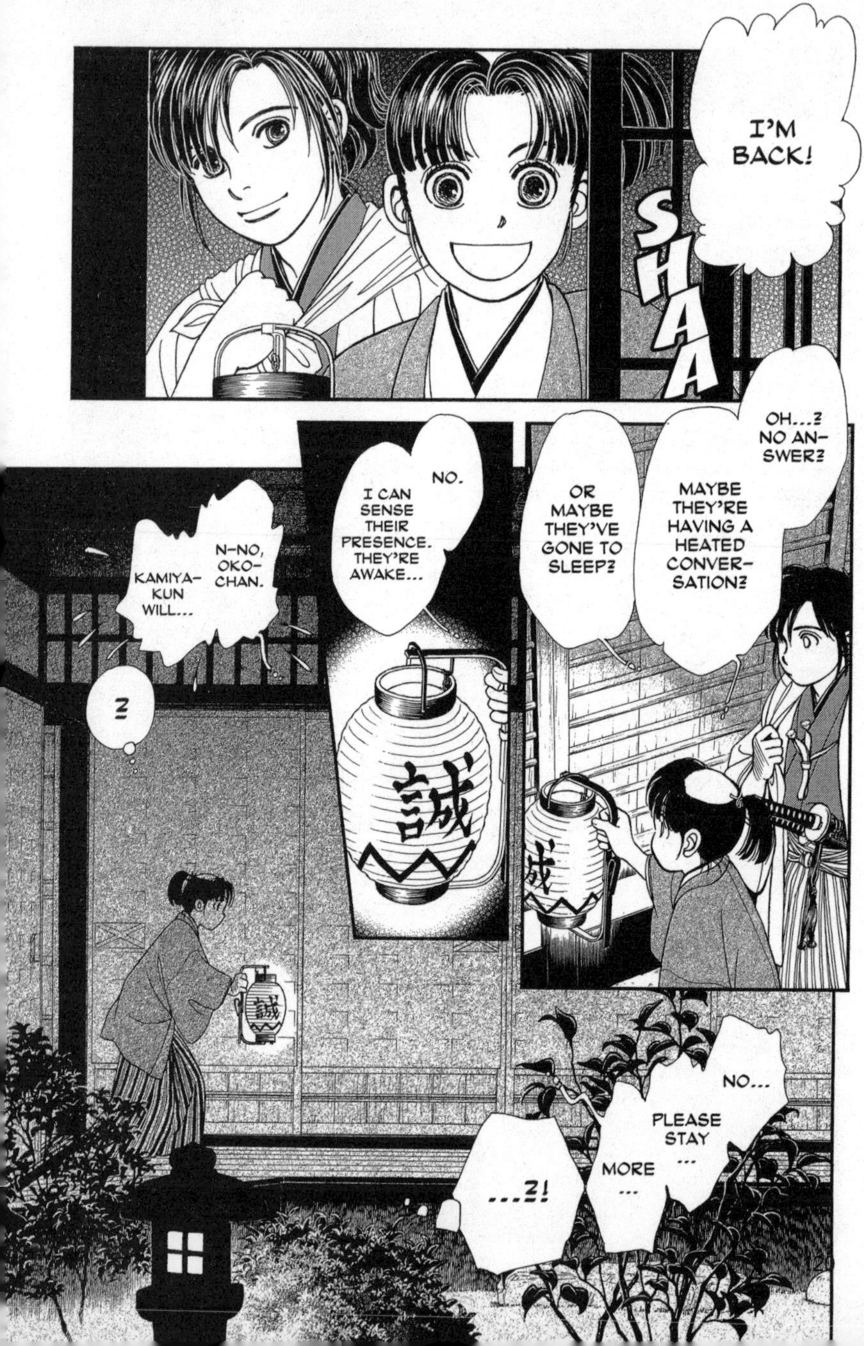
I'M BACK!
SHAA
OH...? NO ANSWER?
MAYBE THEY'RE HAVING A HEATED CONVERSATION?
OR MAYBE THEY'VE GONE TO SLEEP?
NO. I CAN SENSE THEIR PRESENCE. THEY'RE AWAKE...
N-NO, OKO-CHAN. KAMIYA-KUN WILL...
?
NO... PLEASE STAY ... MORE ...
...?!

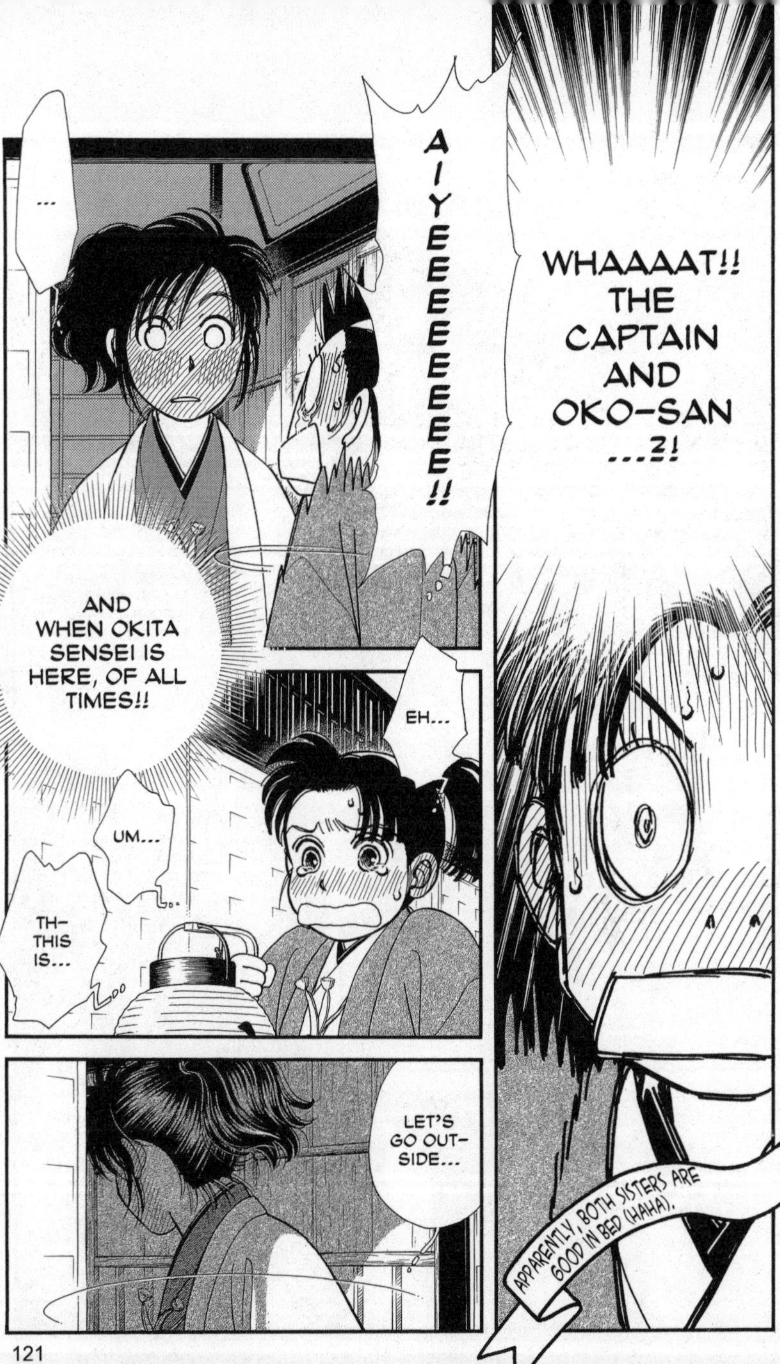
WHAAAAT!! THE CAPTAIN AND OKO-SAN ...?!
APPARENTLY, BOTH SISTERS ARE GOOD IN BED (HAHA).
...
AIYEEEEEEEEEE!!
AND WHEN OKITA SENSEI IS HERE, OF ALL TIMES!!
EH...
UM...
TH- THIS IS...
LET'S GO OUT-SIDE...

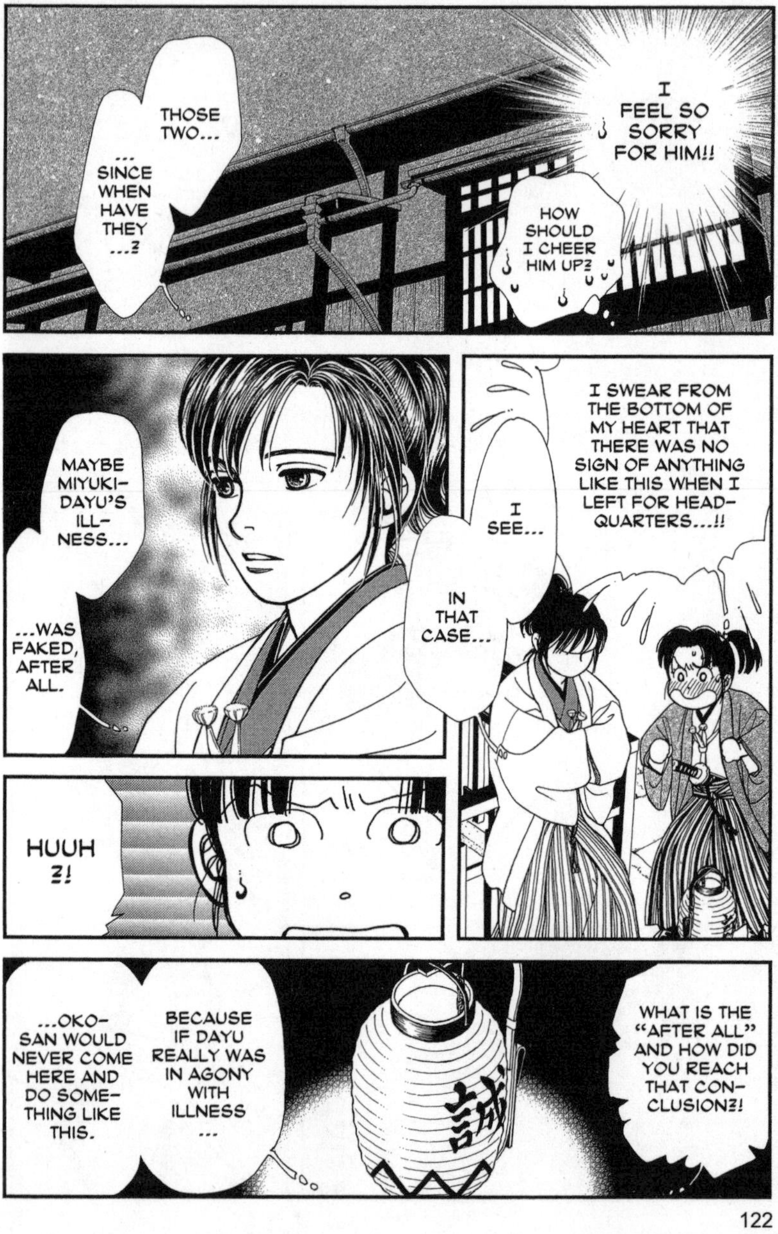
I FEEL SO SORRY FOR HIM!!
HOW SHOULD I CHEER HIM UP?
THOSE TWO...
...SINCE WHEN HAVE THEY...?
I SWEAR FROM THE BOTTOM OF MY HEART THAT THERE WAS NO SIGN OF ANYTHING LIKE THIS WHEN I LEFT FOR HEAD-QUARTERS...!!
I SEE...
IN THAT CASE...
MAYBE MIYUKI-DAYU'S ILL-NESS...
...WAS FAKED, AFTER ALL.
HUUH?!
WHAT IS THE "AFTER ALL" AND HOW DID YOU REACH THAT CON-CLUSION?!
誠
BECAUSE IF DAYU REALLY WAS IN AGONY WITH ILLNESS ...
...OKO-SAN WOULD NEVER COME HERE AND DO SOME-THING LIKE THIS.

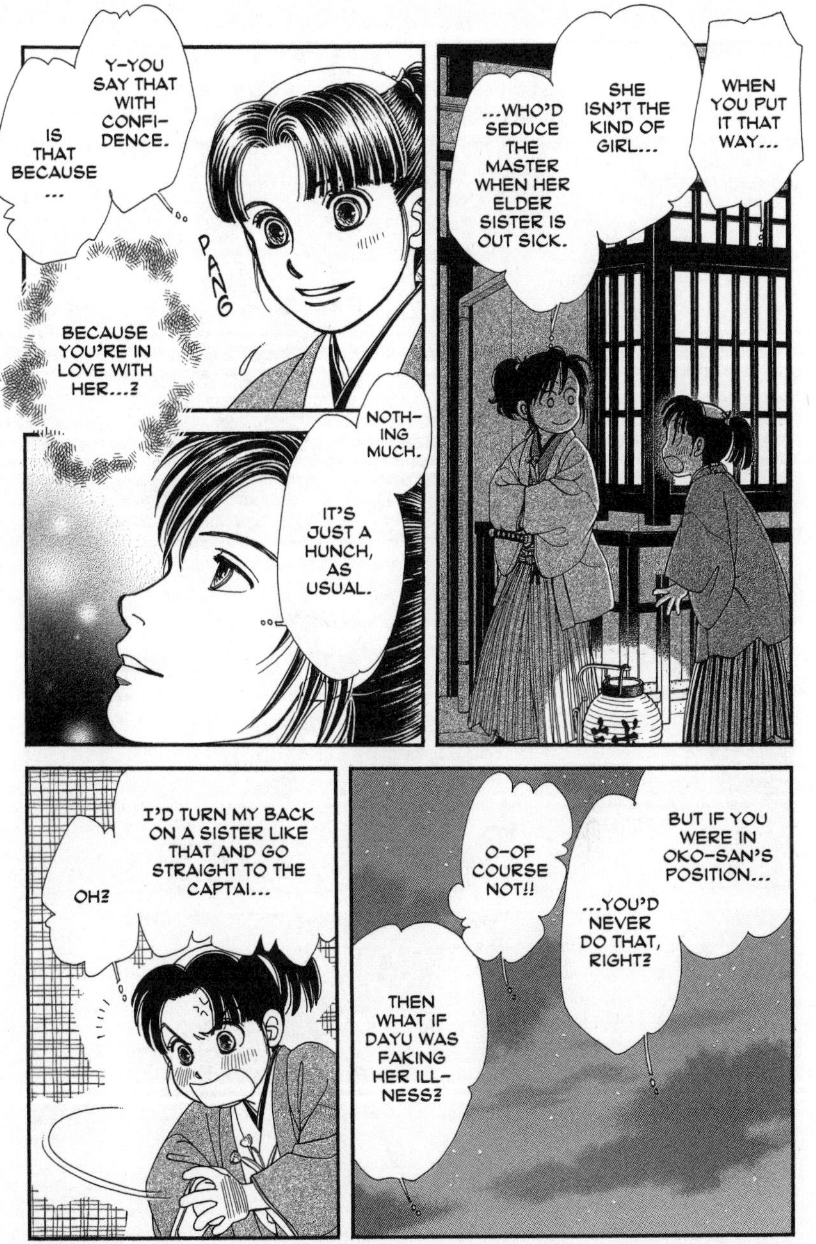
WHEN YOU PUT IT THAT WAY...
SHE ISN'T THE KIND OF GIRL...
...WHO'D SEDUCE THE MASTER WHEN HER ELDER SISTER IS OUT SICK.
Y-YOU SAY THAT WITH CONFIDENCE.
IS THAT BECAUSE ...
PANG
BECAUSE YOU'RE IN LOVE WITH HER...?
NOTHING MUCH.
IT'S JUST A HUNCH, AS USUAL.
BUT IF YOU WERE IN OKO-SAN'S POSITION...
...YOU'D NEVER DO THAT, RIGHT?
O-OF COURSE NOT!!
THEN WHAT IF DAYU WAS FAKING HER ILLNESS?
I'D TURN MY BACK ON A SISTER LIKE THAT AND GO STRAIGHT TO THE CAPTAI...
OH?

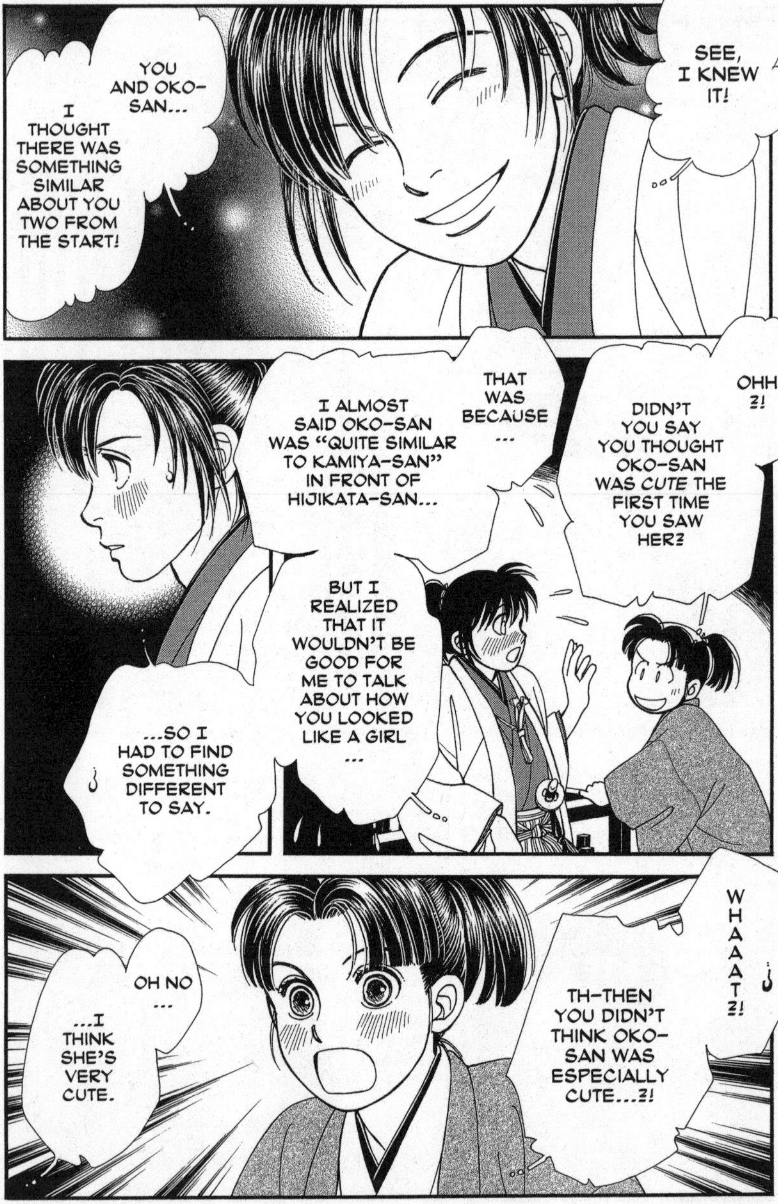
SEE, I KNEW IT!
YOU AND OKO-SAN...
I THOUGHT THERE WAS SOMETHING SIMILAR ABOUT YOU TWO FROM THE START!
OHH?!
DIDN'T YOU SAY YOU THOUGHT OKO-SAN WAS *CUTE* THE FIRST TIME YOU SAW HER?
THAT WAS BECAUSE...
I ALMOST SAID OKO-SAN WAS "QUITE SIMILAR TO KAMIYA-SAN" IN FRONT OF HIJIKATA-SAN...
BUT I REALIZED THAT IT WOULDN'T BE GOOD FOR ME TO TALK ABOUT HOW YOU LOOKED LIKE A GIRL...
...SO I HAD TO FIND SOMETHING DIFFERENT TO SAY.
WHAAAT?!
TH-THEN YOU DIDN'T THINK OKO-SAN WAS ESPECIALLY CUTE...?!
OH NO...
...I THINK SHE'S VERY CUTE.

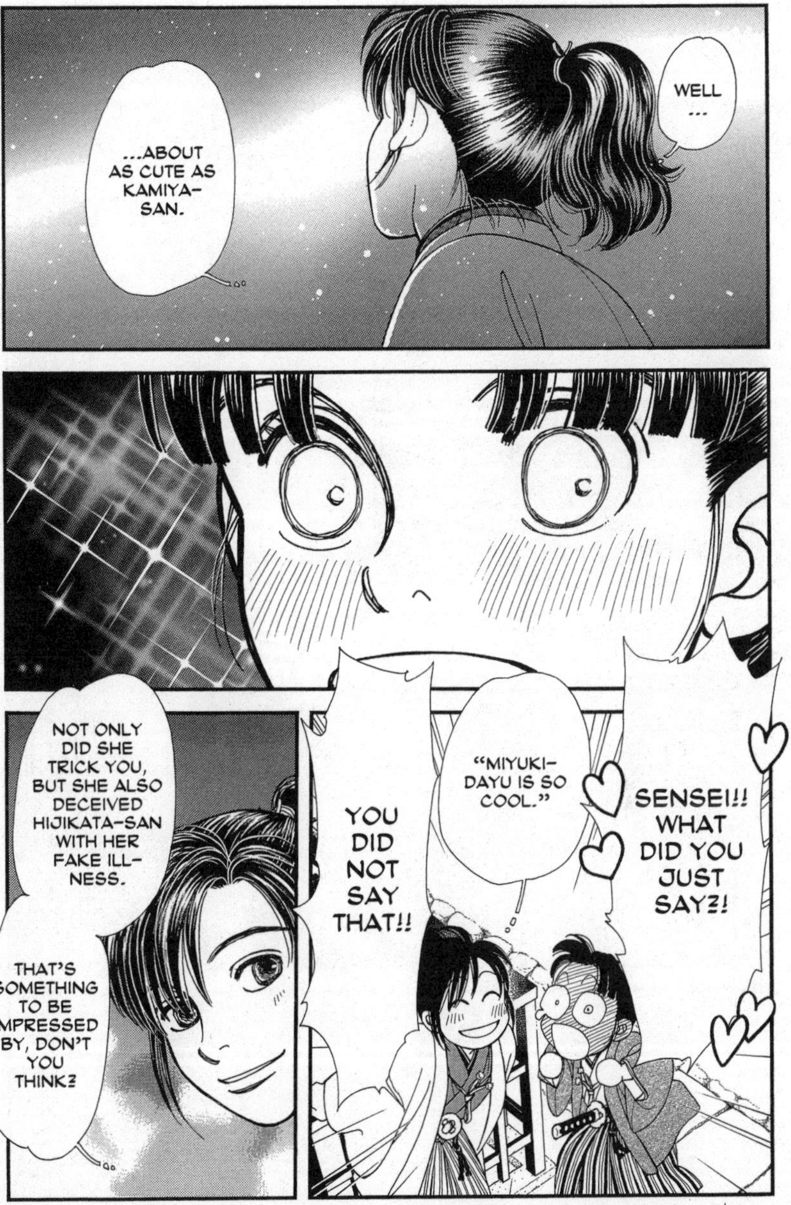
WELL...
...ABOUT AS CUTE AS KAMIYA-SAN.
SENSEI!!! WHAT DID YOU JUST SAY?!
“MIYUKI-DAYU IS SO COOL.”
YOU DID NOT SAY THAT!!
NOT ONLY DID SHE TRICK YOU, BUT SHE ALSO DECEIVED HIJIKATA-SAN WITH HER FAKE ILLNESS.
THAT'S SOMETHING TO BE IMPRESSED BY, DON'T YOU THINK?

Don't be so noisy in the middle of the night!

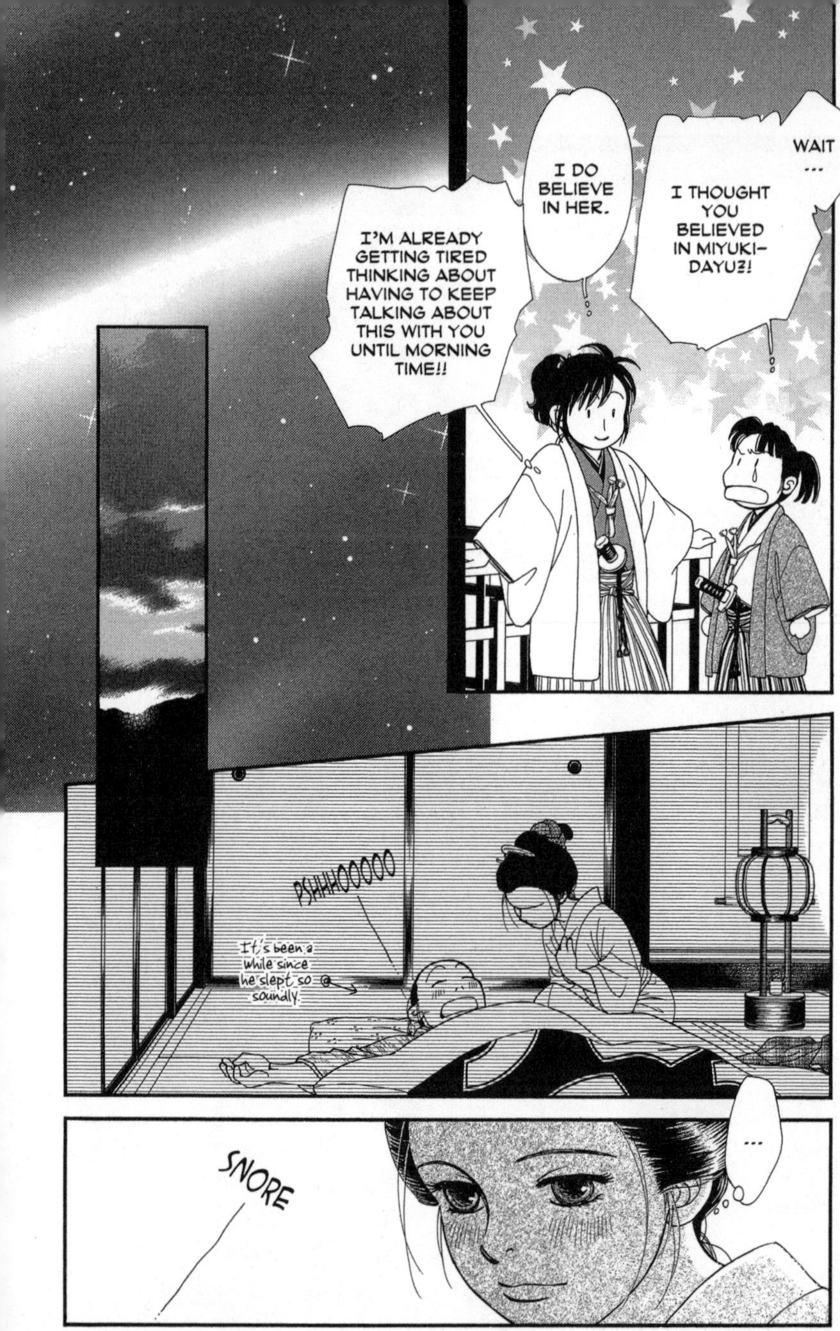
WAIT... I THOUGHT YOU BELIEVED IN MIYUKI-DAYU?!
I DO BELIEVE IN HER.
I'M ALREADY GETTING TIRED THINKING ABOUT HAVING TO KEEP TALKING ABOUT THIS WITH YOU UNTIL MORNING TIME!!
PSHHOOOOO
It's been a while since he slept so soundly.
...
SNORE

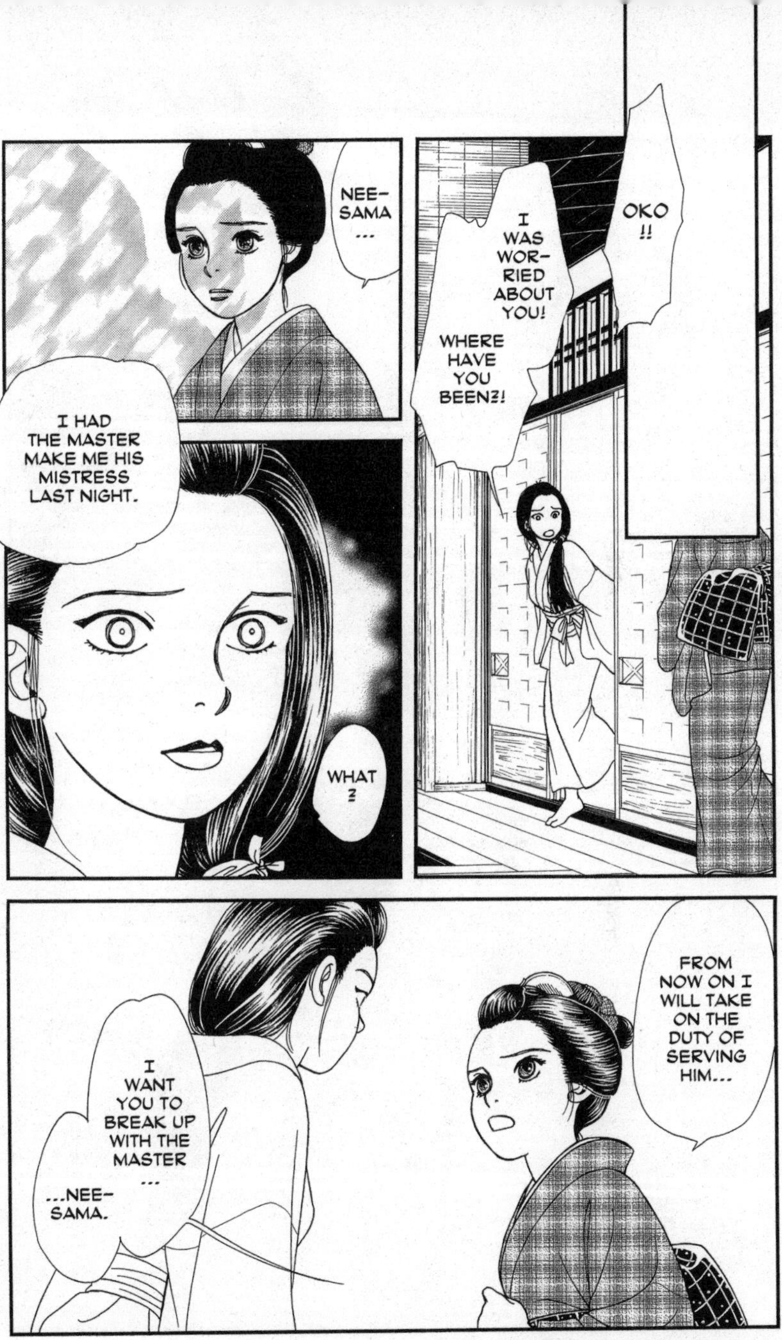
OKO !!
I WAS WORRIED ABOUT YOU! WHERE HAVE YOU BEEN?!
NEE-SAMA ...
I HAD THE MASTER MAKE ME HIS MISTRESS LAST NIGHT.
WHAT?
FROM NOW ON I WILL TAKE ON THE DUTY OF SERVING HIM...
I WANT YOU TO BREAK UP WITH THE MASTER ... ...NEE-SAMA.

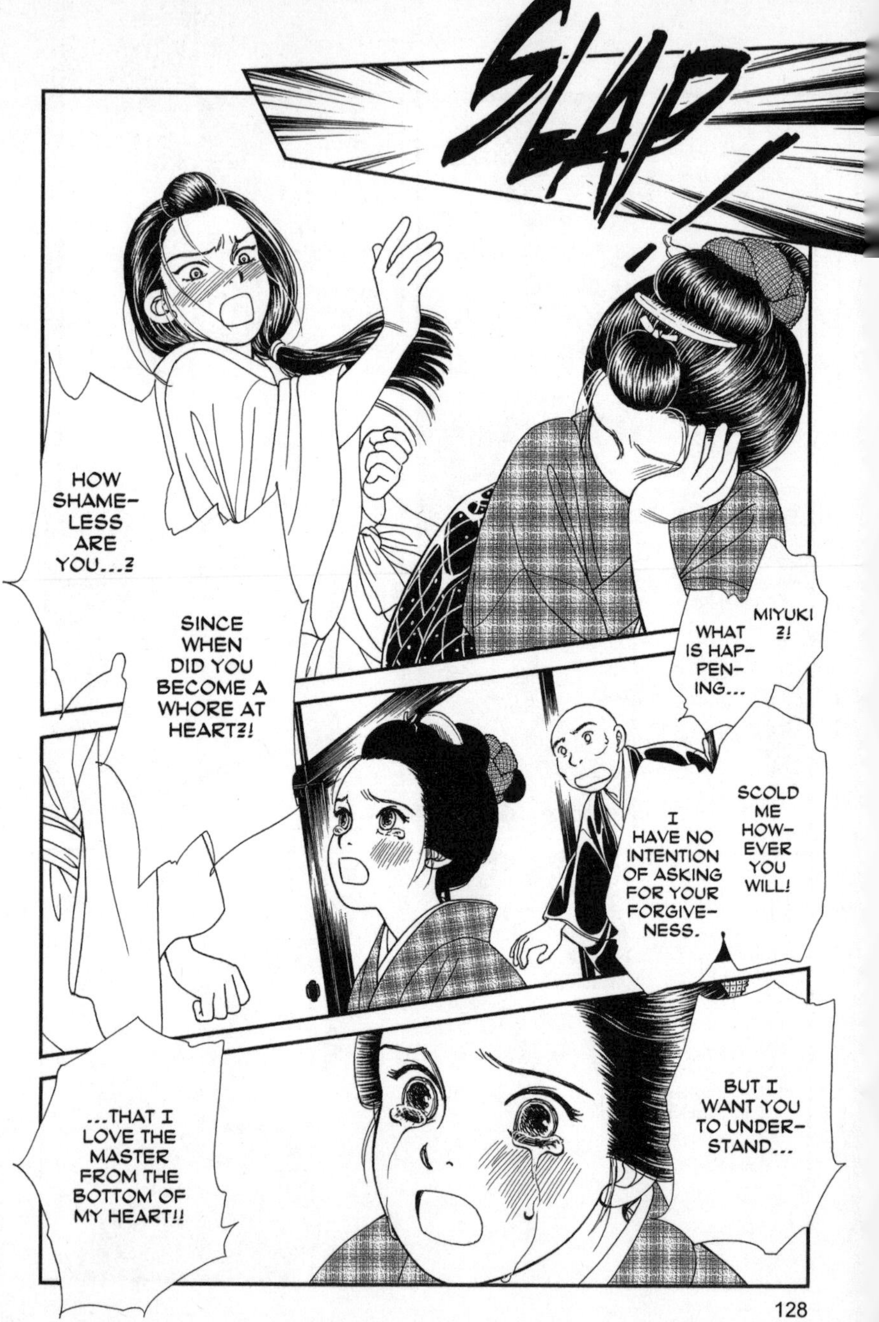
SLAP!
HOW SHAMELESS ARE YOU...?
SINCE WHEN DID YOU BECOME A WHORE AT HEART?!
MIYUKI?! WHAT IS HAPPENING...
SCOLD ME HOWEVER YOU WILL!
I HAVE NO INTENTION OF ASKING FOR YOUR FORGIVENESS.
BUT I WANT YOU TO UNDERSTAND...
...THAT I LOVE THE MASTER FROM THE BOTTOM OF MY HEART!!

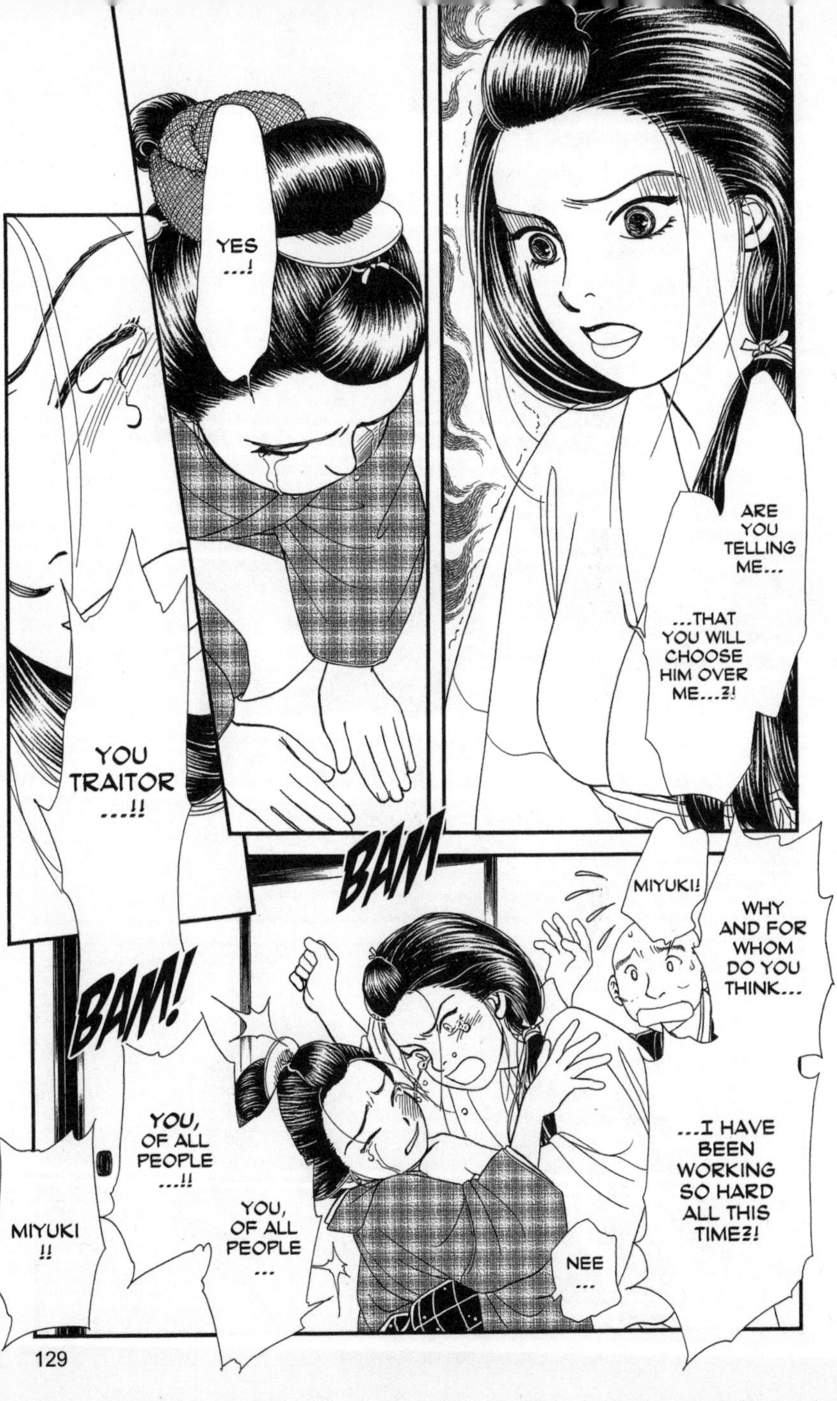
ARE YOU TELLING ME...
...THAT YOU WILL CHOOSE HIM OVER ME...?!
YES ...!
YOU TRAITOR ...!!
BAM
BAM!
MIYUKI!
WHY AND FOR WHOM DO YOU THINK...
...I HAVE BEEN WORKING SO HARD ALL THIS TIME?!
NEE ...
YOU, OF ALL PEOPLE ...
YOU, OF ALL PEOPLE ...!!
MIYUKI !!

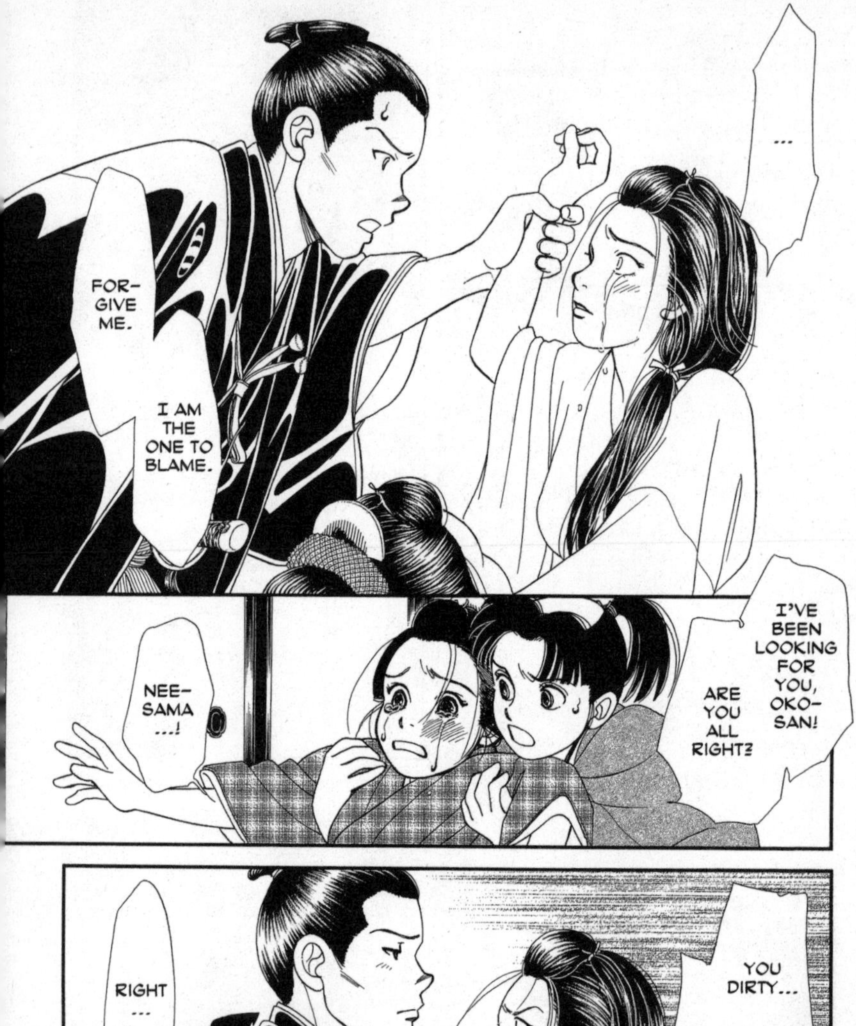
...
FOR-GIVE ME.
I AM THE ONE TO BLAME.
I'VE BEEN LOOKING FOR YOU, OKO-SAN!
ARE YOU ALL RIGHT?
NEE-SAMA ...!
YOU DIRTY...
CHEATER!
RIGHT ...
BAM!

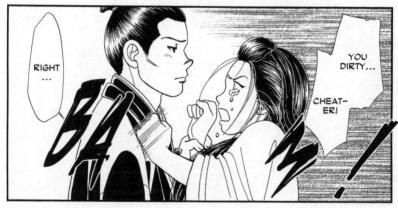

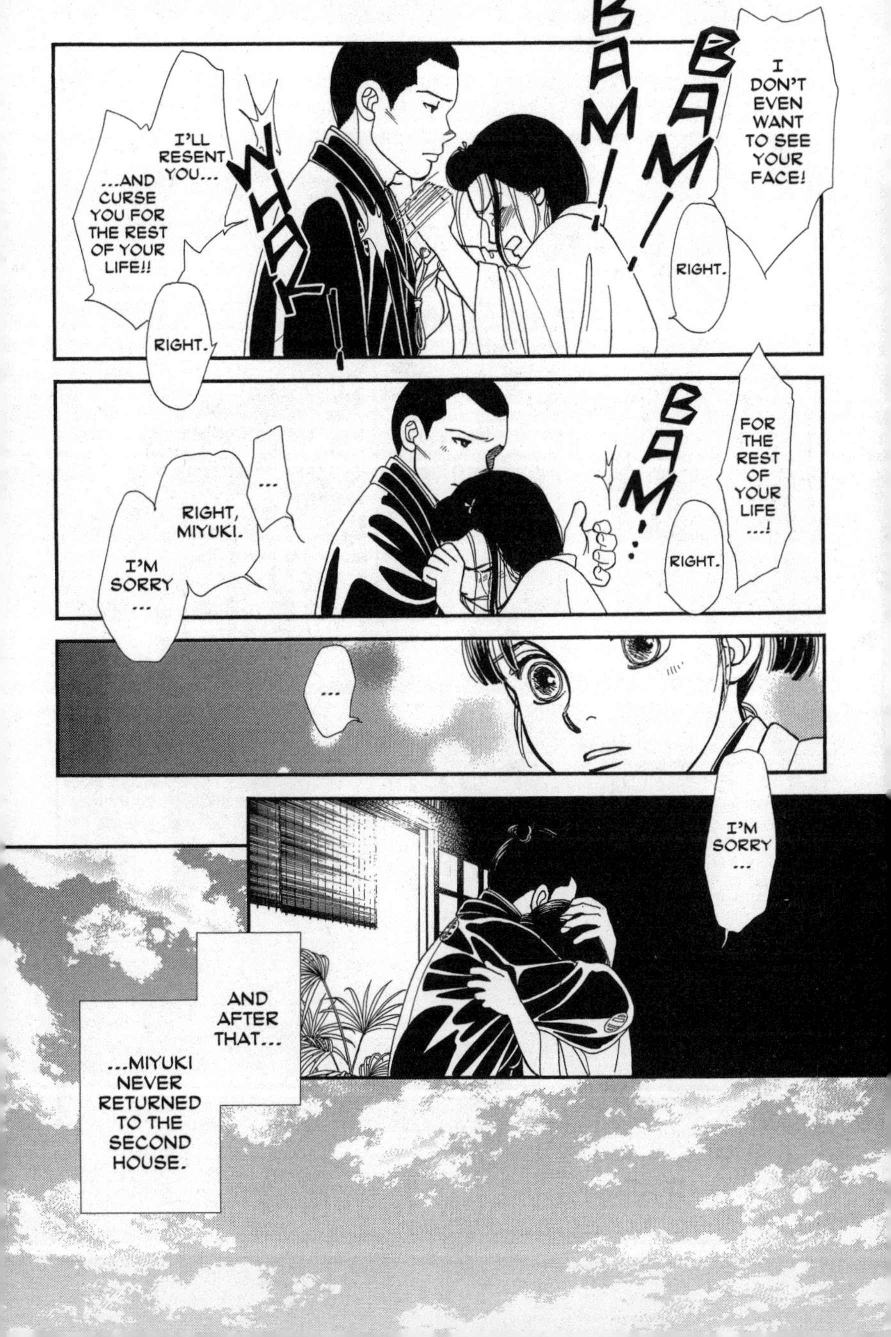
I DON'T EVEN WANT TO SEE YOUR FACE!
BAM!
BAM!
RIGHT.
I'LL RESENT YOU...
...AND CURSE YOU FOR THE REST OF YOUR LIFE!!
WHAK
RIGHT.
FOR THE REST OF YOUR LIFE...!
BAM!..
RIGHT.
...
RIGHT, MIYUKI.
I'M SORRY...
...
I'M SORRY...
AND AFTER THAT...
...MIYUKI NEVER RETURNED TO THE SECOND HOUSE.

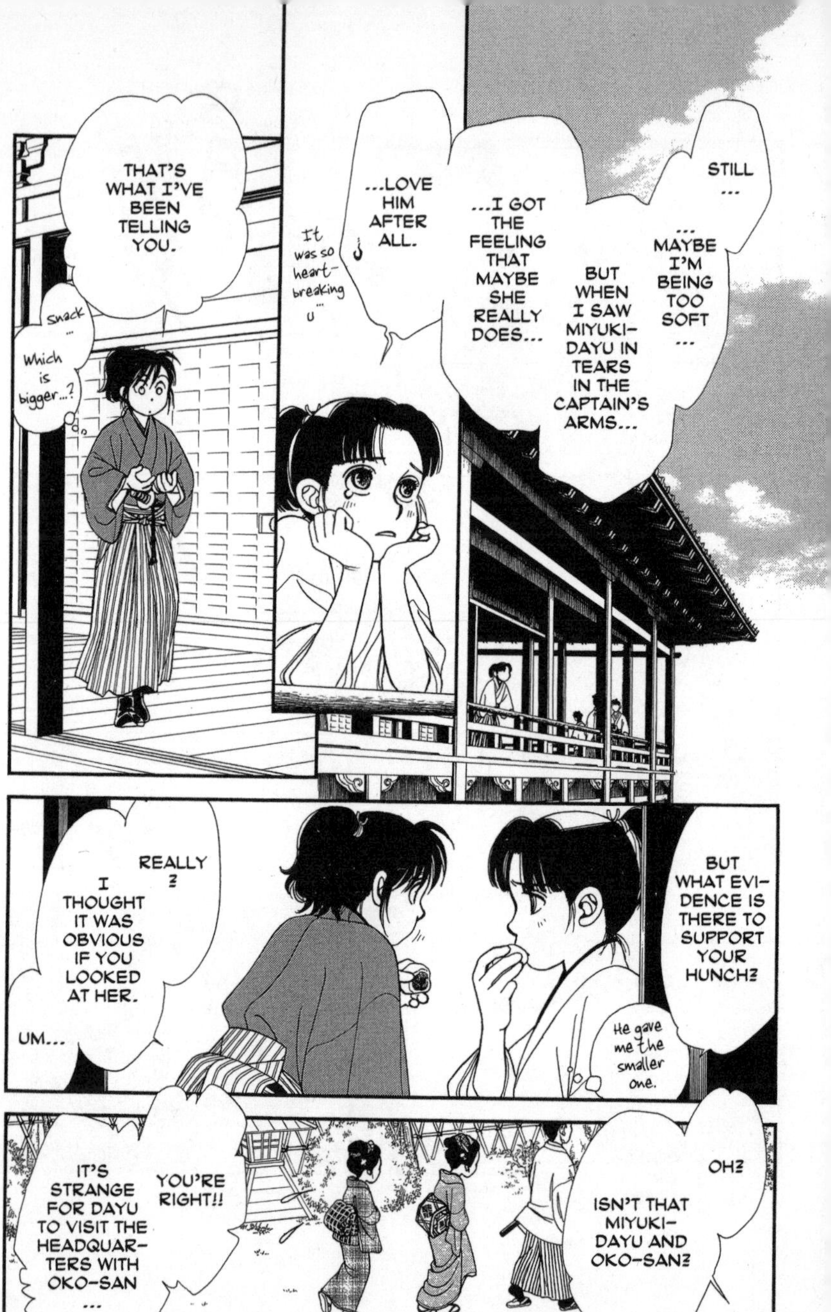
STILL...
...MAYBE I'M BEING TOO SOFT...
BUT WHEN I SAW MIYUKI-DAYU IN TEARS IN THE CAPTAIN'S ARMS...
...I GOT THE FEELING THAT MAYBE SHE REALLY DOES...
...LOVE HIM AFTER ALL.
It was so heart-breaking...
THAT'S WHAT I'VE BEEN TELLING YOU.
Snack...
Which is bigger...?
BUT WHAT EVIDENCE IS THERE TO SUPPORT YOUR HUNCH?
He gave me the smaller one.
REALLY?
I THOUGHT IT WAS OBVIOUS IF YOU LOOKED AT HER.
UM...
OH?
ISN'T THAT MIYUKI-DAYU AND OKO-SAN?
YOU'RE RIGHT!!
IT'S STRANGE FOR DAYU TO VISIT THE HEADQUARTERS WITH OKO-SAN...

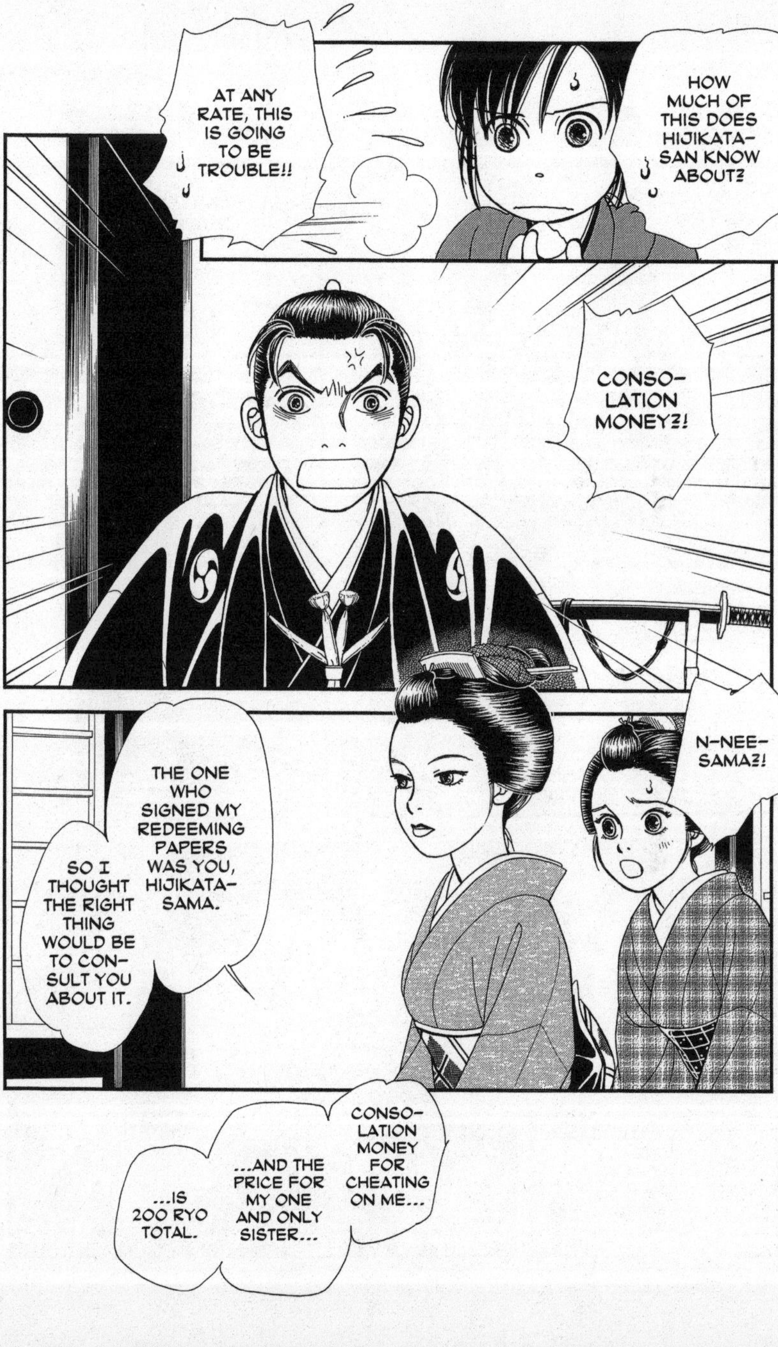
HOW MUCH OF THIS DOES HIJIKATA-SAN KNOW ABOUT?
AT ANY RATE, THIS IS GOING TO BE TROUBLE!!
CONSO-LATION MONEY?!
N-NEE-SAMA?!
THE ONE WHO SIGNED MY REDEEMING PAPERS WAS YOU, HIJIKATA-SAMA.
SO I THOUGHT THE RIGHT THING WOULD BE TO CON-SULT YOU ABOUT IT.
CONSO-LATION MONEY FOR CHEATING ON ME...
...AND THE PRICE FOR MY ONE AND ONLY SISTER...
...IS 200 RYO TOTAL.

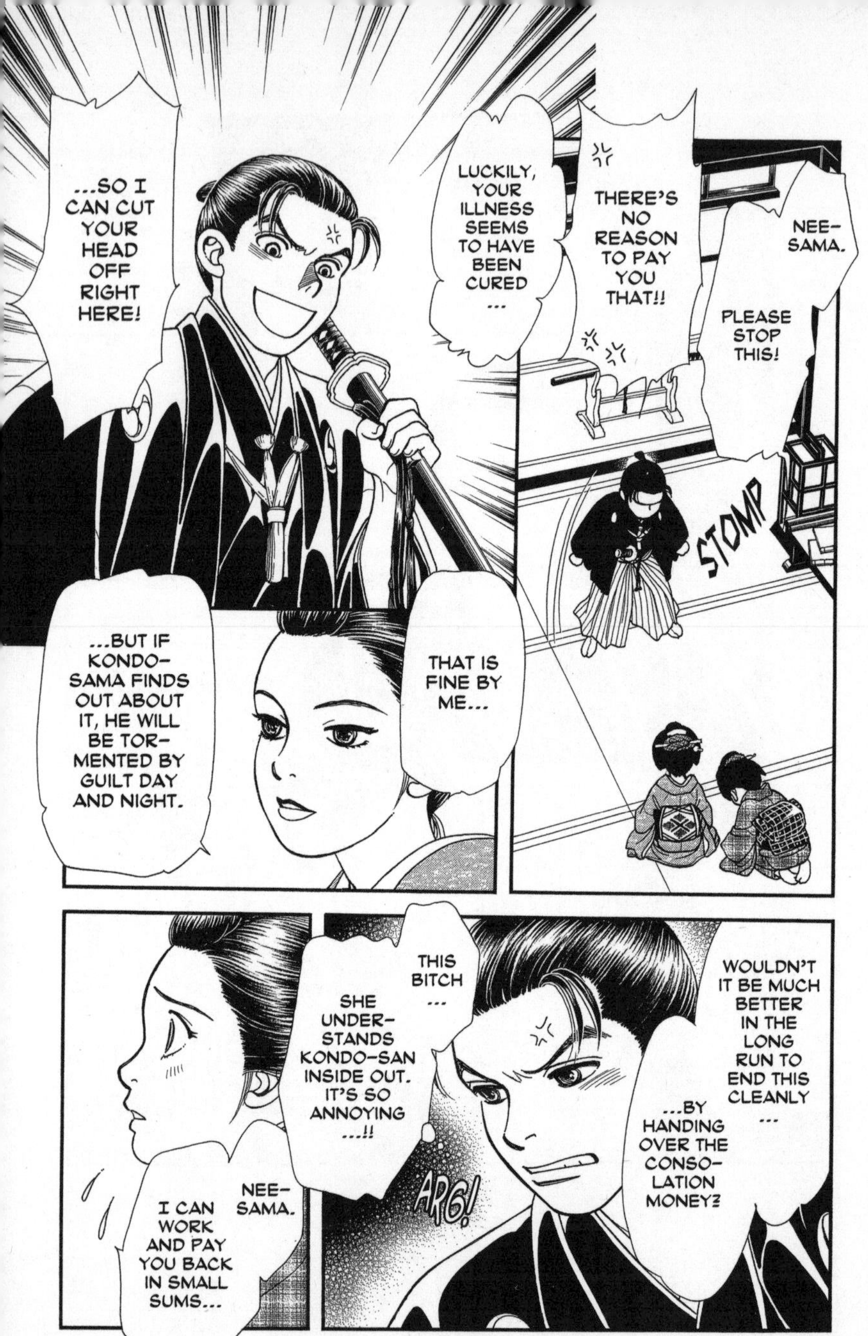
THERE'S NO REASON TO PAY YOU THAT!!
STOMP
NEE-SAMA.
PLEASE STOP THIS!
LUCKILY, YOUR ILLNESS SEEMS TO HAVE BEEN CURED...
...SO I CAN CUT YOUR HEAD OFF RIGHT HERE!
THAT IS FINE BY ME...
...BUT IF KONDO-SAMA FINDS OUT ABOUT IT, HE WILL BE TORMENTED BY GUILT DAY AND NIGHT.
WOULDN'T IT BE MUCH BETTER IN THE LONG RUN TO END THIS CLEANLY...
...BY HANDING OVER THE CONSOLATION MONEY?
THIS BITCH...
SHE UNDERSTANDS KONDO-SAN INSIDE OUT. IT'S SO ANNOYING...!!
ARG!
NEE-SAMA.
I CAN WORK AND PAY YOU BACK IN SMALL SUMS...

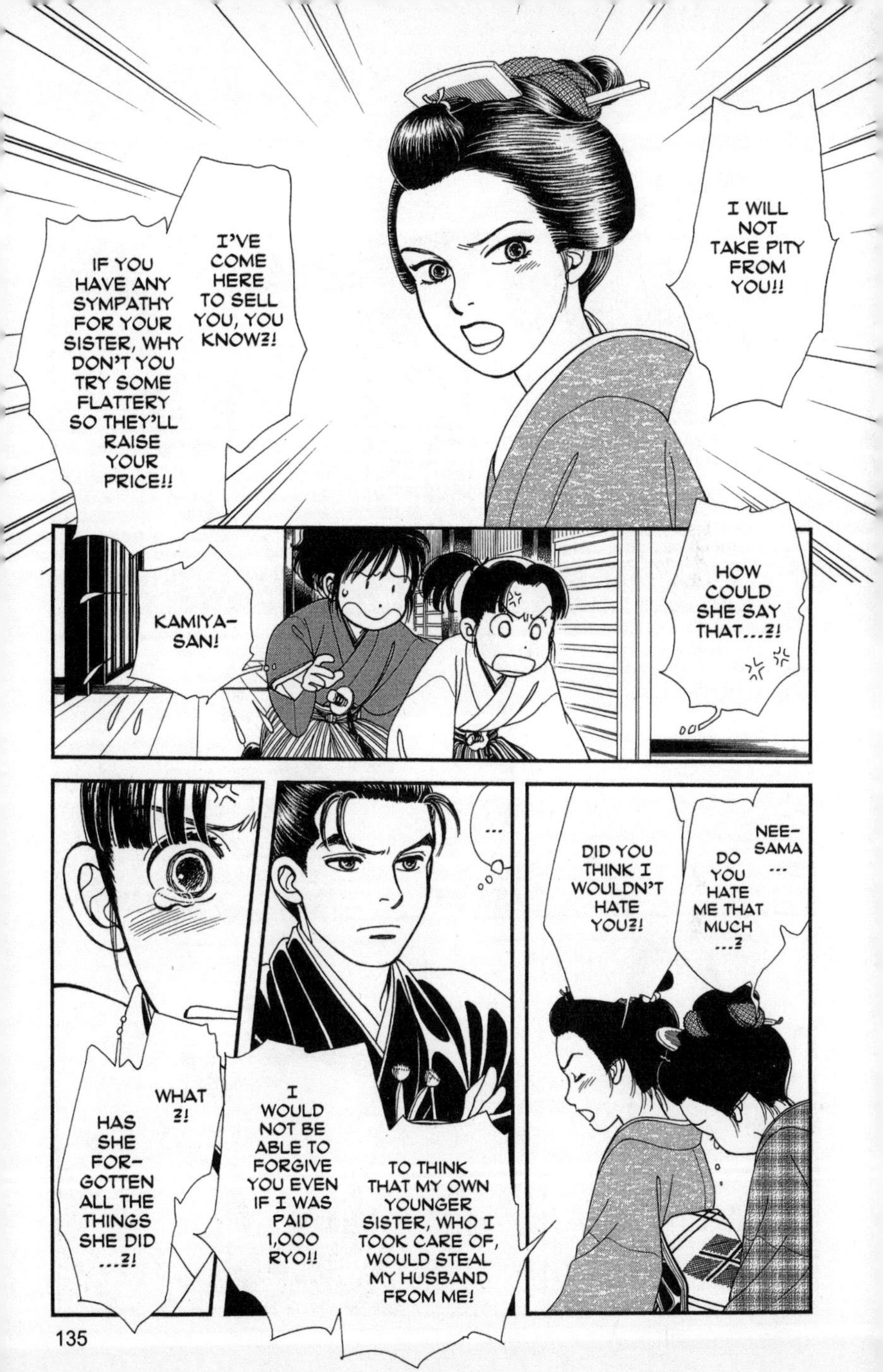

I WILL NOT TAKE PITY FROM YOU!!
I'VE COME HERE TO SELL YOU, YOU KNOW?!
IF YOU HAVE ANY SYMPATHY FOR YOUR SISTER, WHY DON'T YOU TRY SOME FLATTERY SO THEY'LL RAISE YOUR PRICE!!
HOW COULD SHE SAY THAT...?!
KAMIYA-SAN!
NEE-SAMA...
DO YOU HATE ME THAT MUCH...?
DID YOU THINK I WOULDN'T HATE YOU?!
TO THINK THAT MY OWN YOUNGER SISTER, WHO I TOOK CARE OF, WOULD STEAL MY HUSBAND FROM ME!
I WOULD NOT BE ABLE TO FORGIVE YOU EVEN IF I WAS PAID 1,000 RYO!!
...
WHAT?!
HAS SHE FORGOTTEN ALL THE THINGS SHE DID...?!

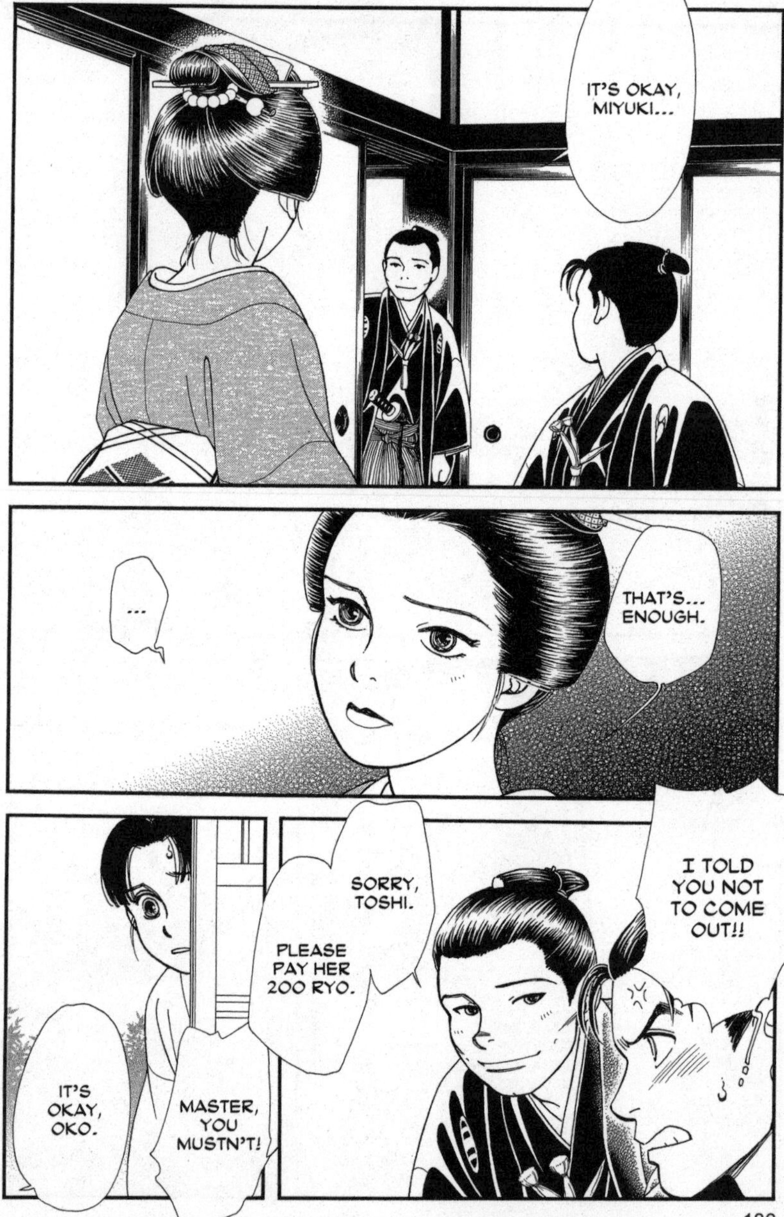
IT'S OKAY, MIYUKI...
THAT'S... ENOUGH.
...
I TOLD YOU NOT TO COME OUT!!
SORRY, TOSHI.
PLEASE PAY HER 200 RYO.
MASTER, YOU MUSTN'T!
IT'S OKAY, OKO.

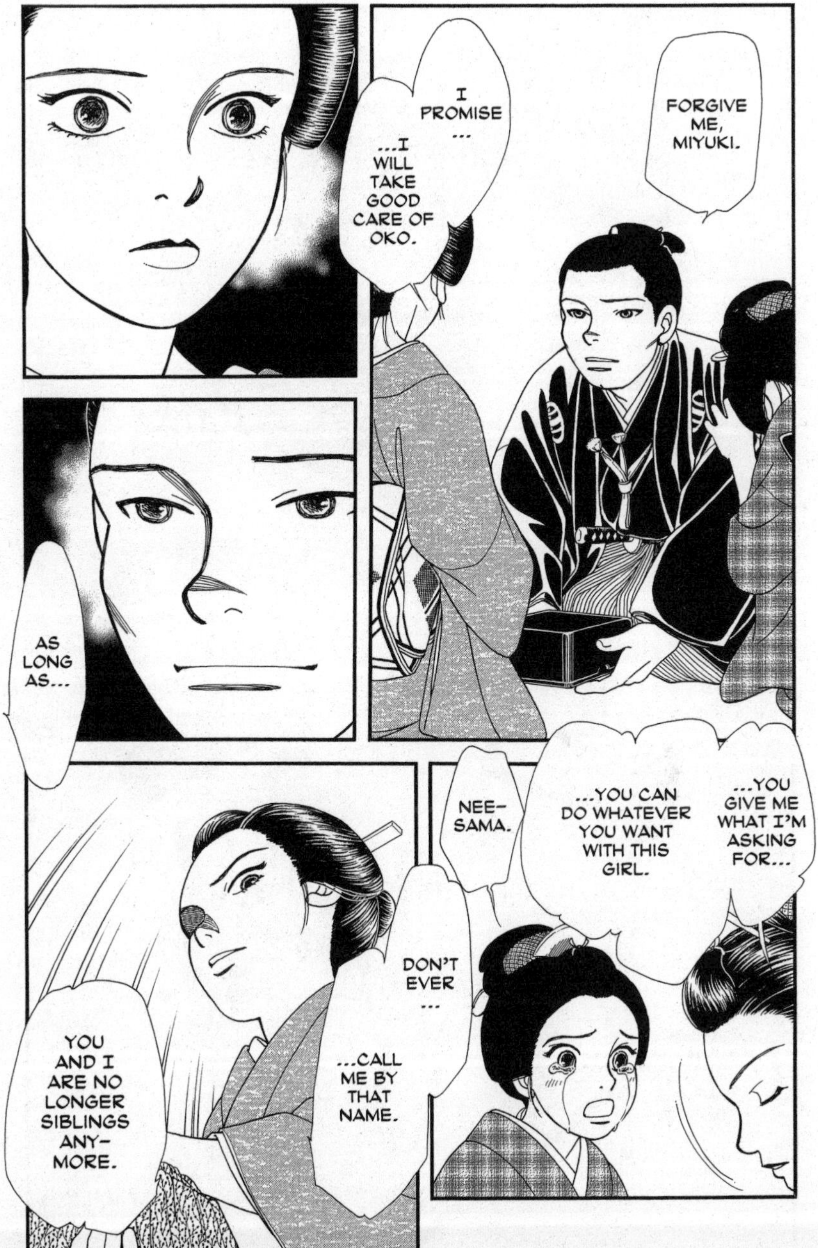
FORGIVE ME, MIYUKI.
I PROMISE ...
...I WILL TAKE GOOD CARE OF OKO.
AS LONG AS...
...YOU GIVE ME WHAT I'M ASKING FOR...
...YOU CAN DO WHATEVER YOU WANT WITH THIS GIRL.
NEE-SAMA.
DON'T EVER ...
...CALL ME BY THAT NAME.
YOU AND I ARE NO LONGER SIBLINGS ANY-MORE.

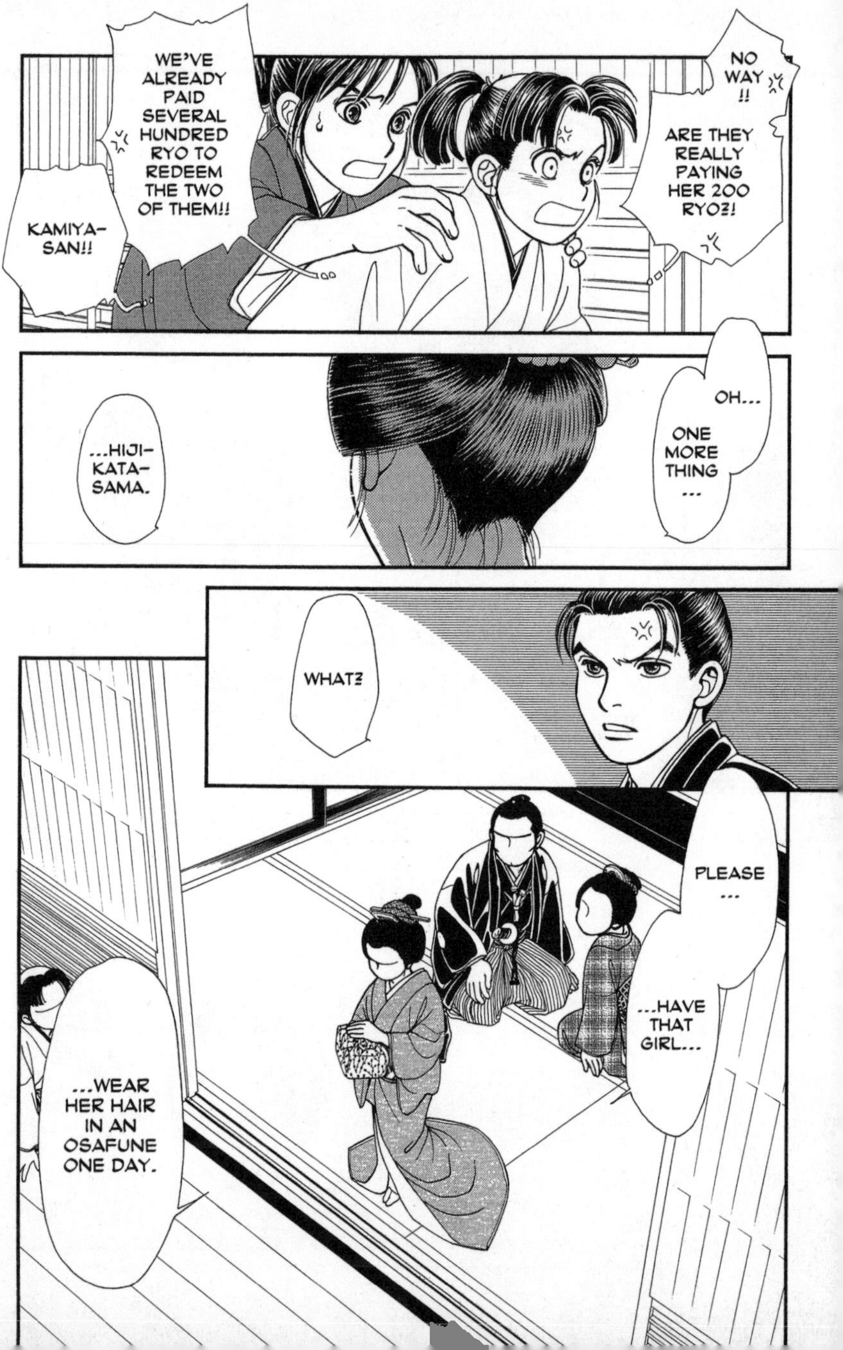
NO WAY!!
ARE THEY REALLY PAYING HER 200 RYO?!
WE'VE ALREADY PAID SEVERAL HUNDRED RYO TO REDEEM THE TWO OF THEM!!
KAMIYA-SAN!!
OH... ONE MORE THING...
...HIJI-KATA-SAMA.
WHAT?
PLEASE...
...HAVE THAT GIRL...
...WEAR HER HAIR IN AN OSAFUNE ONE DAY.

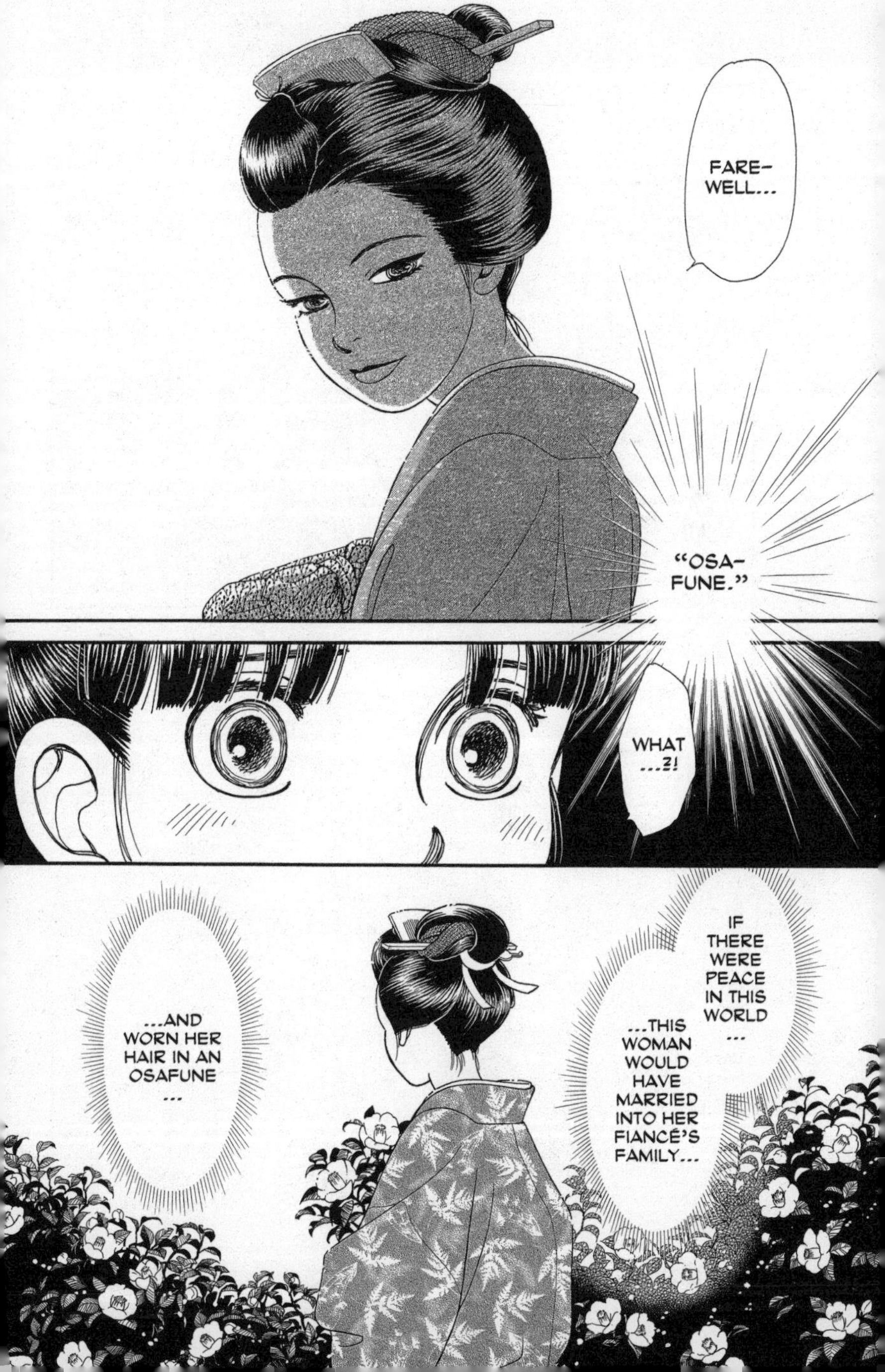
FARE-WELL...
"OSA-FUNE."
WHAT ...?!
IF THERE WERE PEACE IN THIS WORLD ...
...THIS WOMAN WOULD HAVE MARRIED INTO HER FIANCÉ'S FAMILY...
...AND WORN HER HAIR IN AN OSAFUNE ...

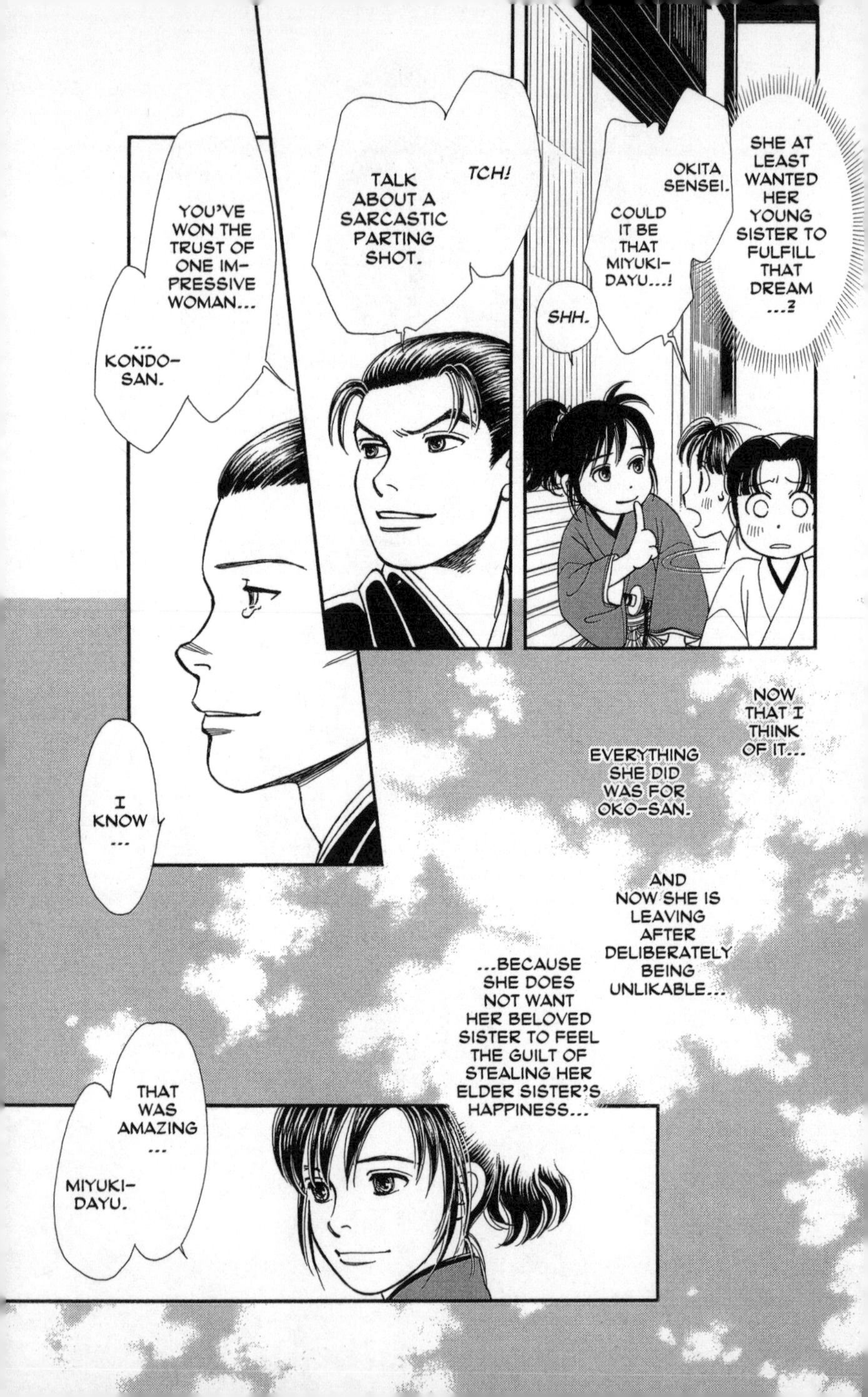
SHE AT LEAST WANTED HER YOUNG SISTER TO FULFILL THAT DREAM...?
OKITA SENSEI.
COULD IT BE THAT MIYUKI-DAYU...!
SHH.
TCH!
TALK ABOUT A SARCASTIC PARTING SHOT.
YOU'VE WON THE TRUST OF ONE IMPRESSIVE WOMAN... ...KONDO-SAN.
I KNOW...
NOW THAT I THINK OF IT...
EVERYTHING SHE DID WAS FOR OKO-SAN.
AND NOW SHE IS LEAVING AFTER DELIBERATELY BEING UNLIKABLE...
...BECAUSE SHE DOES NOT WANT HER BELOVED SISTER TO FEEL THE GUILT OF STEALING HER ELDER SISTER'S HAPPINESS...
THAT WAS AMAZING... MIYUKI-DAYU.

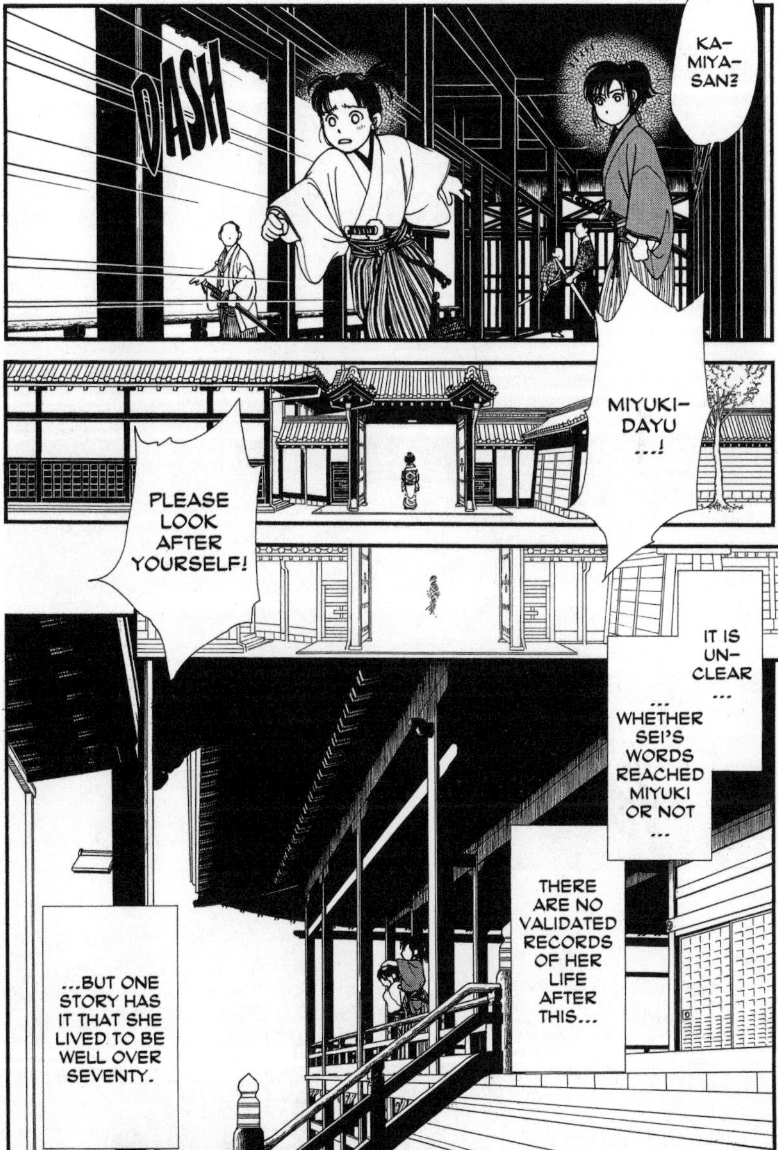
KA-MIYA-SAN?
DASH
MIYUKI-DAYU...!
PLEASE LOOK AFTER YOURSELF!
IT IS UN-CLEAR...
...WHETHER SEI'S WORDS REACHED MIYUKI OR NOT...
THERE ARE NO VALIDATED RECORDS OF HER LIFE AFTER THIS...
...BUT ONE STORY HAS IT THAT SHE LIVED TO BE WELL OVER SEVENTY.

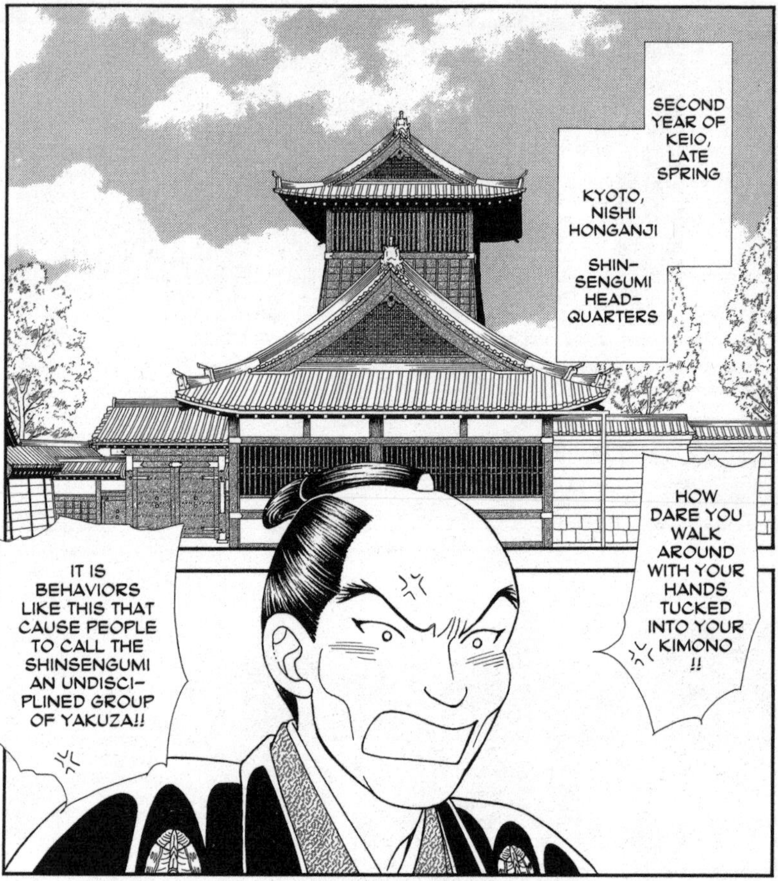
SECOND YEAR OF KEIO, LATE SPRING
KYOTO, NISHI HONGANJI
SHIN-SENGUMI HEAD-QUARTERS
HOW DARE YOU WALK AROUND WITH YOUR HANDS TUCKED INTO YOUR KIMONO !!
IT IS BEHAVIORS LIKE THIS THAT CAUSE PEOPLE TO CALL THE SHINSENGUMI AN UNDISCI-PLINED GROUP OF YAKUZA!!

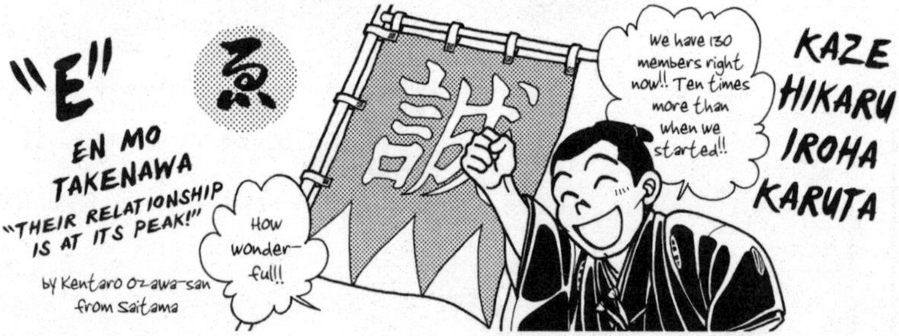
KAZE HIKARU IROHA KARUTA
We have 130 members right now!! Ten times more than when we started!!
How wonder-ful!!
"E"
ゑ
EN MO TAKENAWA
"THEIR RELATIONSHIP IS AT ITS PEAK!"
by Kentaro Ozawa-san from Saitama

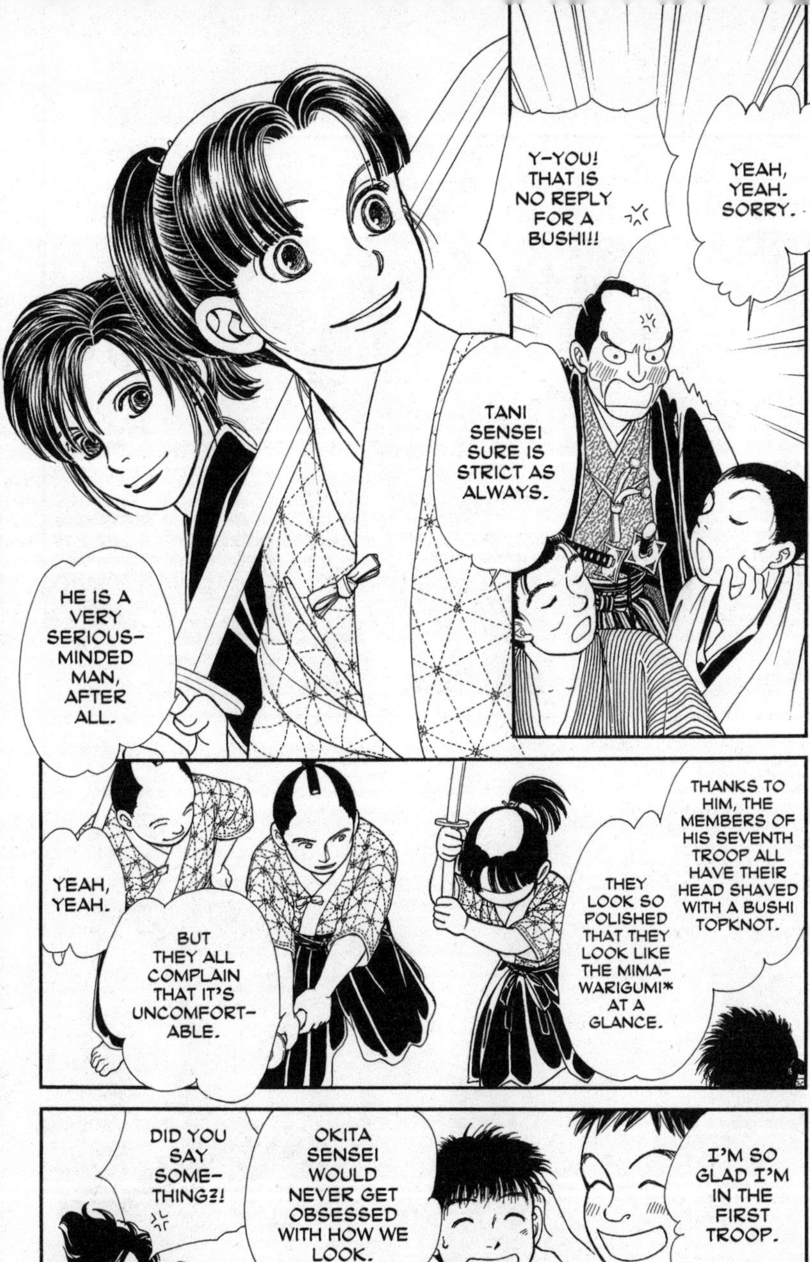
YEAH, YEAH. SORRY.
Y-YOU! THAT IS NO REPLY FOR A BUSHI!!
TANI SENSEI SURE IS STRICT AS ALWAYS.
HE IS A VERY SERIOUS-MINDED MAN, AFTER ALL.
THANKS TO HIM, THE MEMBERS OF HIS SEVENTH TROOP ALL HAVE THEIR HEAD SHAVED WITH A BUSHI TOPKNOT.
THEY LOOK SO POLISHED THAT THEY LOOK LIKE THE MIMA-WARIGUMI* AT A GLANCE.
BUT THEY ALL COMPLAIN THAT IT'S UNCOMFORT-ABLE.
YEAH, YEAH.
I'M SO GLAD I'M IN THE FIRST TROOP.
OKITA SENSEI WOULD NEVER GET OBSESSED WITH HOW WE LOOK.
DID YOU SAY SOME-THING?!

*A police force created from direct retainers of the Bakufu.

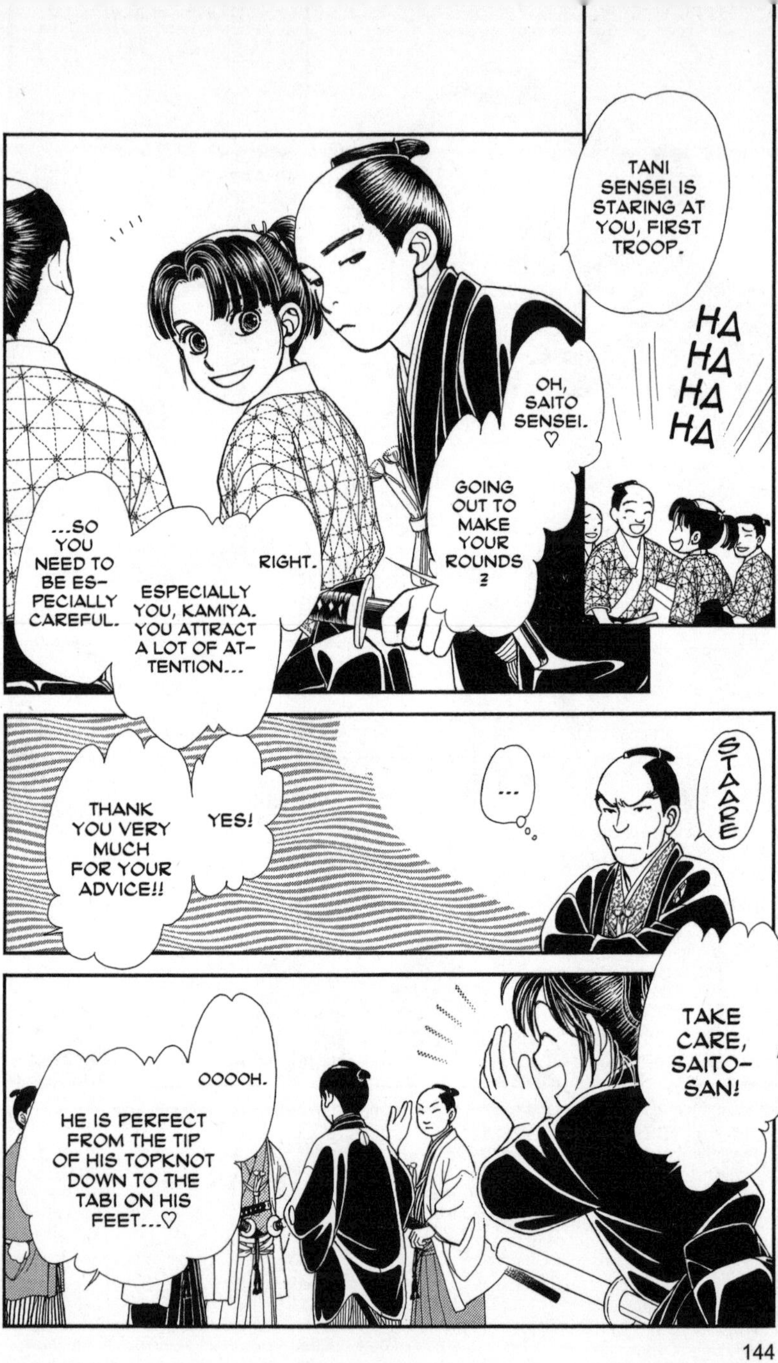
TANI SENSEI IS STARING AT YOU, FIRST TROOP.
HA HA HA HA HA
OH, SAITO SENSEI. ♡
GOING OUT TO MAKE YOUR ROUNDS?
RIGHT.
ESPECIALLY YOU, KAMIYA. YOU ATTRACT A LOT OF AT-TENTION...
...SO YOU NEED TO BE ES-PECIALLY CAREFUL.
STAARE
...
YES!
THANK YOU VERY MUCH FOR YOUR ADVICE!!
TAKE CARE, SAITO-SAN!
OOOOH.
HE IS PERFECT FROM THE TIP OF HIS TOPKNOT DOWN TO THE TABI ON HIS FEET...♡

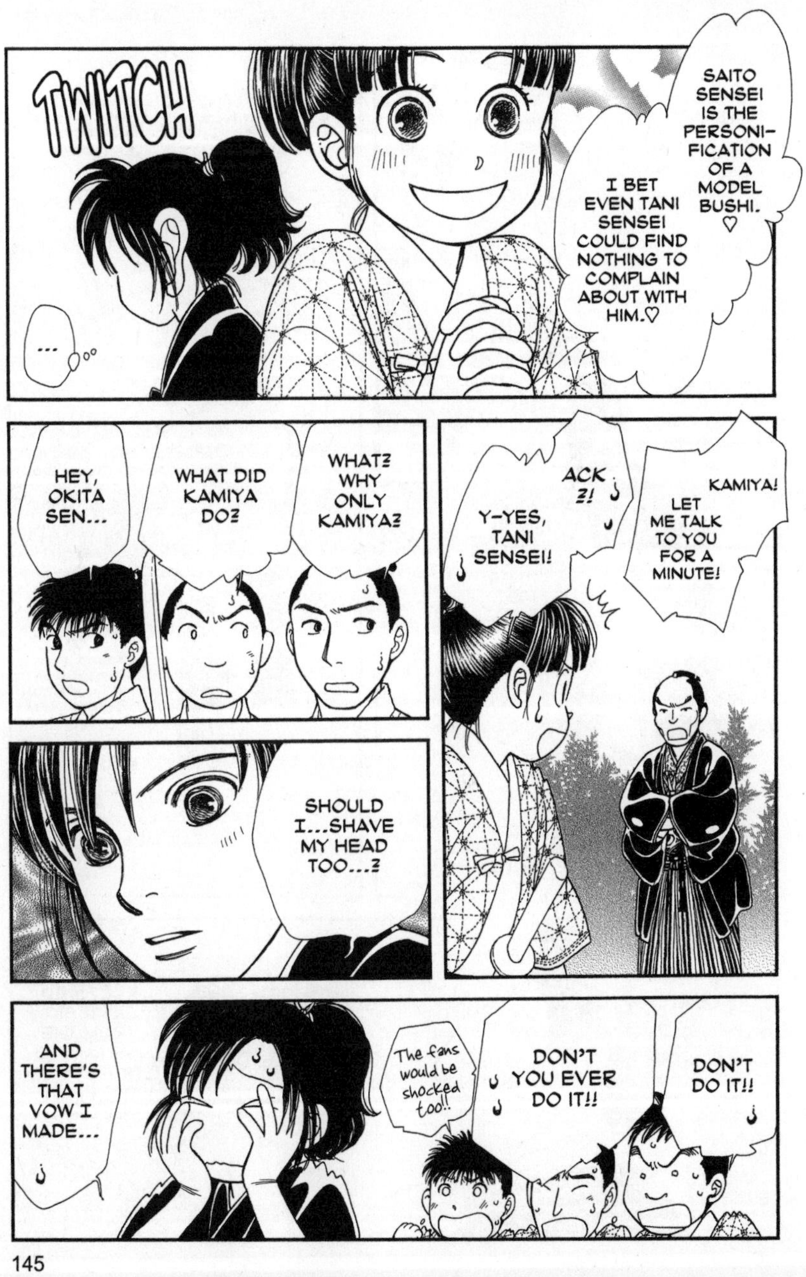
SAITO SENSEI IS THE PERSONIFICATION OF A MODEL BUSHI. ♡
I BET EVEN TANI SENSEI COULD FIND NOTHING TO COMPLAIN ABOUT WITH HIM. ♡
TWITCH
...
KAMIYA!
LET ME TALK TO YOU FOR A MINUTE!
ACK ?!
Y-YES, TANI SENSEI!
WHAT? WHY ONLY KAMIYA?
WHAT DID KAMIYA DO?
HEY, OKITA SEN...
SHOULD I...SHAVE MY HEAD TOO...?
DON'T DO IT!!
DON'T YOU EVER DO IT!!
The fans would be shocked too!!
AND THERE'S THAT VOW I MADE...

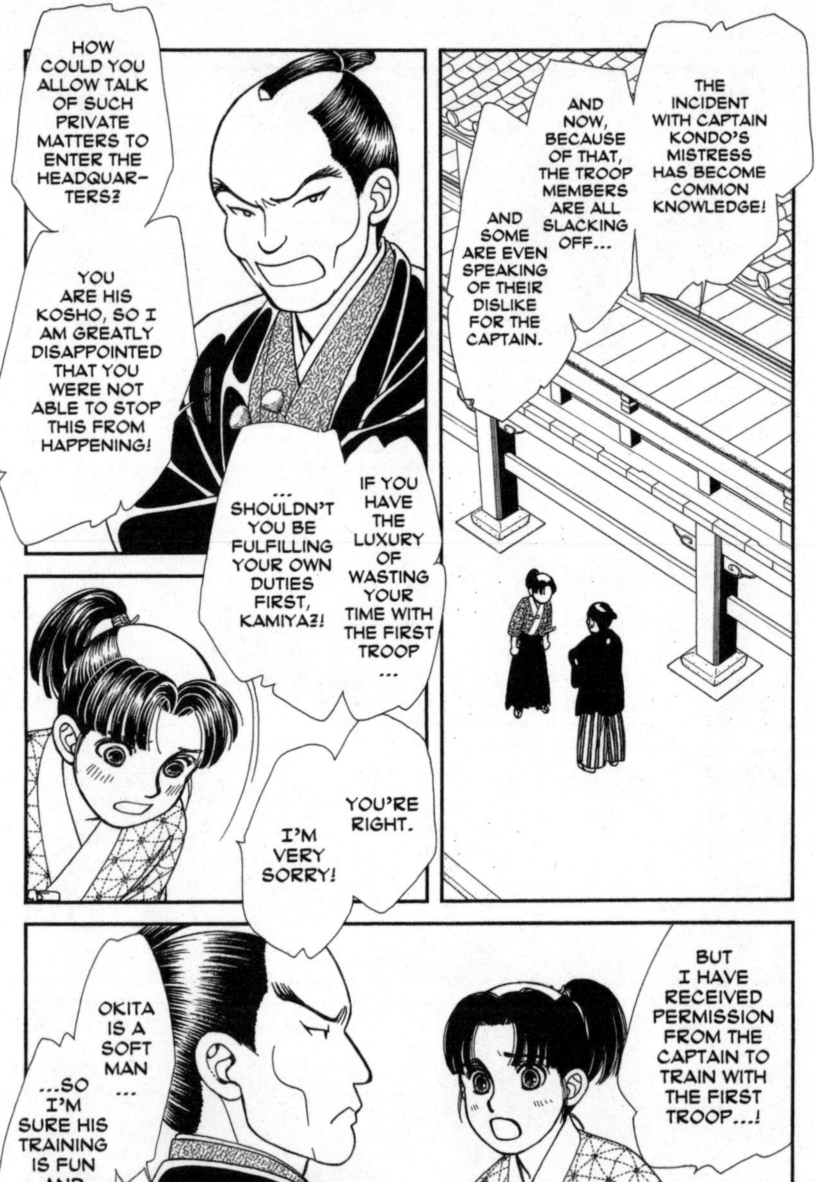
THE INCIDENT WITH CAPTAIN KONDO'S MISTRESS HAS BECOME COMMON KNOWLEDGE!
AND NOW, BECAUSE OF THAT, THE TROOP MEMBERS ARE ALL SLACKING OFF...
AND SOME ARE EVEN SPEAKING OF THEIR DISLIKE FOR THE CAPTAIN.
HOW COULD YOU ALLOW TALK OF SUCH PRIVATE MATTERS TO ENTER THE HEADQUARTERS?!
YOU ARE HIS KOSHO, SO I AM GREATLY DISAPPOINTED THAT YOU WERE NOT ABLE TO STOP THIS FROM HAPPENING!
IF YOU HAVE THE LUXURY OF WASTING YOUR TIME WITH THE FIRST TROOP ...
... SHOULDN'T YOU BE FULFILLING YOUR OWN DUTIES FIRST, KAMIYA?!
YOU'RE RIGHT.
I'M VERY SORRY!
BUT I HAVE RECEIVED PERMISSION FROM THE CAPTAIN TO TRAIN WITH THE FIRST TROOP...!
OKITA IS A SOFT MAN ...
...SO I'M SURE HIS TRAINING IS FUN AND EASY, TOO.

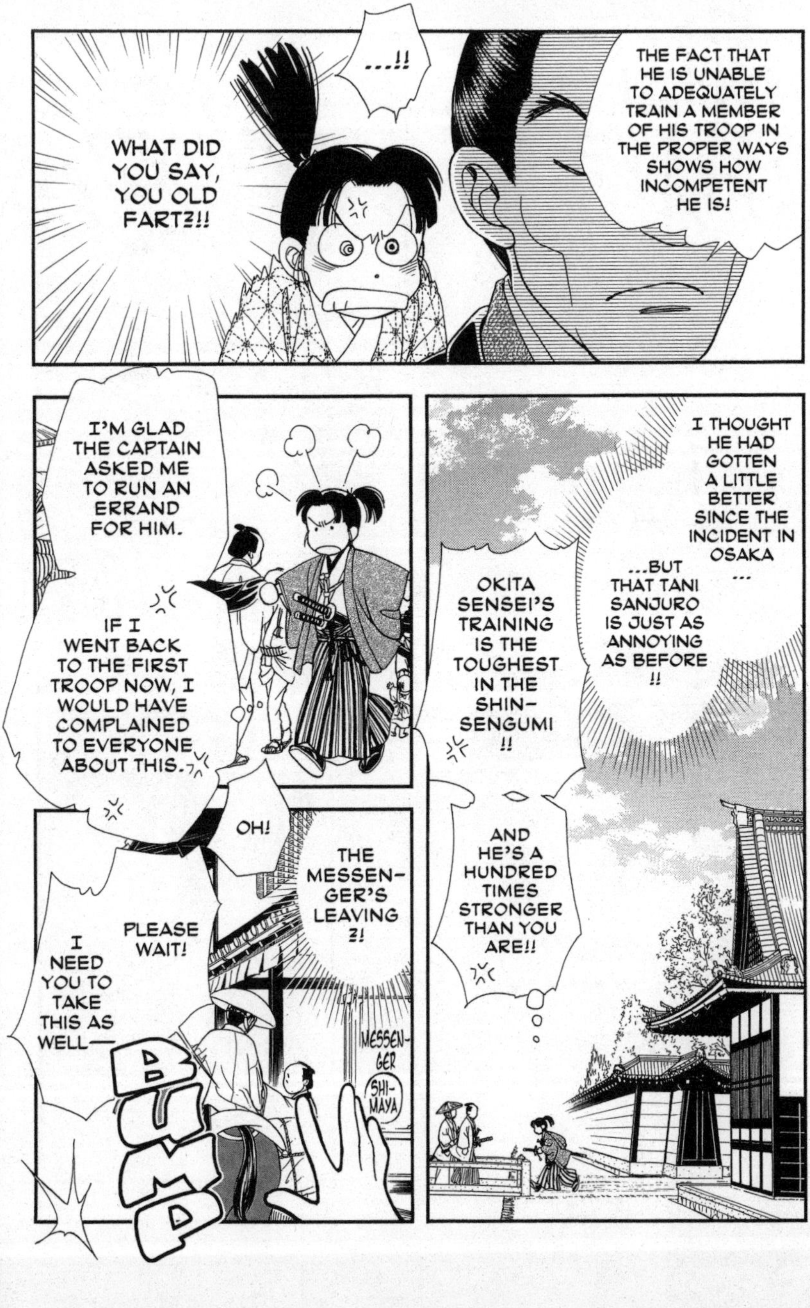
THE FACT THAT HE IS UNABLE TO ADEQUATELY TRAIN A MEMBER OF HIS TROOP IN THE PROPER WAYS SHOWS HOW INCOMPETENT HE IS!
...!!
WHAT DID YOU SAY, YOU OLD FART?!!
I THOUGHT HE HAD GOTTEN A LITTLE BETTER SINCE THE INCIDENT IN OSAKA...
...BUT THAT TANI SANJURO IS JUST AS ANNOYING AS BEFORE!!
OKITA SENSEI'S TRAINING IS THE TOUGHEST IN THE SHIN-SENGUMI!!
AND HE'S A HUNDRED TIMES STRONGER THAN YOU ARE!!
I'M GLAD THE CAPTAIN ASKED ME TO RUN AN ERRAND FOR HIM.
IF I WENT BACK TO THE FIRST TROOP NOW, I WOULD HAVE COMPLAINED TO EVERYONE ABOUT THIS.
OH!
THE MESSEN-GER'S LEAVING?!
PLEASE WAIT!
I NEED YOU TO TAKE THIS AS WELL—
MESSEN-GER SHI-MAYA
BUMP

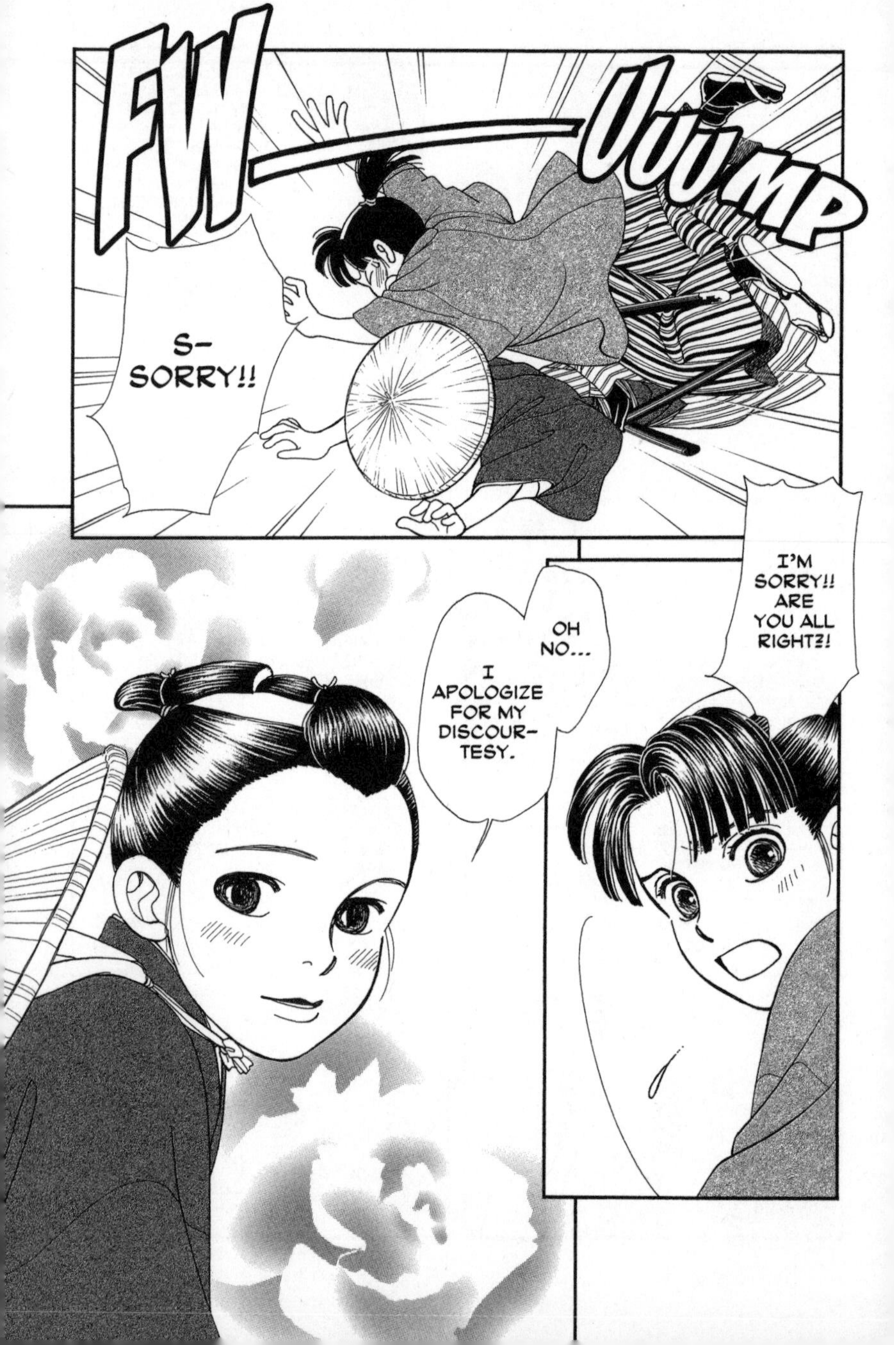
FW—UUUMP
S-SORRY!!
I'M SORRY!! ARE YOU ALL RIGHT?!
OH NO...
I APOLOGIZE FOR MY DISCOUR-TESY.

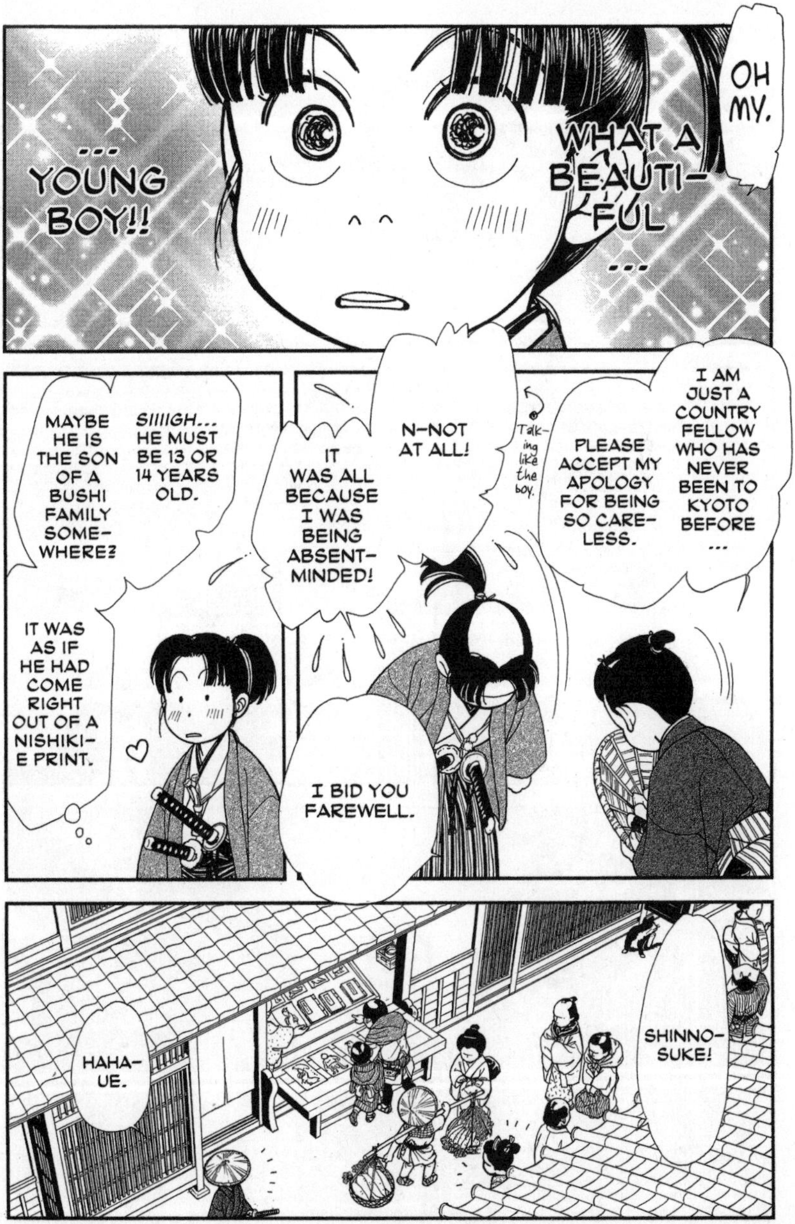
OH MY.
WHAT A BEAUTIFUL ...
... YOUNG BOY!!
I AM JUST A COUNTRY FELLOW WHO HAS NEVER BEEN TO KYOTO BEFORE ...
PLEASE ACCEPT MY APOLOGY FOR BEING SO CARELESS.
Talking like the boy.
N-NOT AT ALL!
IT WAS ALL BECAUSE I WAS BEING ABSENT-MINDED!
I BID YOU FAREWELL.
SIIIGH... HE MUST BE 13 OR 14 YEARS OLD.
MAYBE HE IS THE SON OF A BUSHI FAMILY SOMEWHERE?
IT WAS AS IF HE HAD COME RIGHT OUT OF A NISHIKI-E PRINT.
SHINNOSUKE!
HAHA-UE.

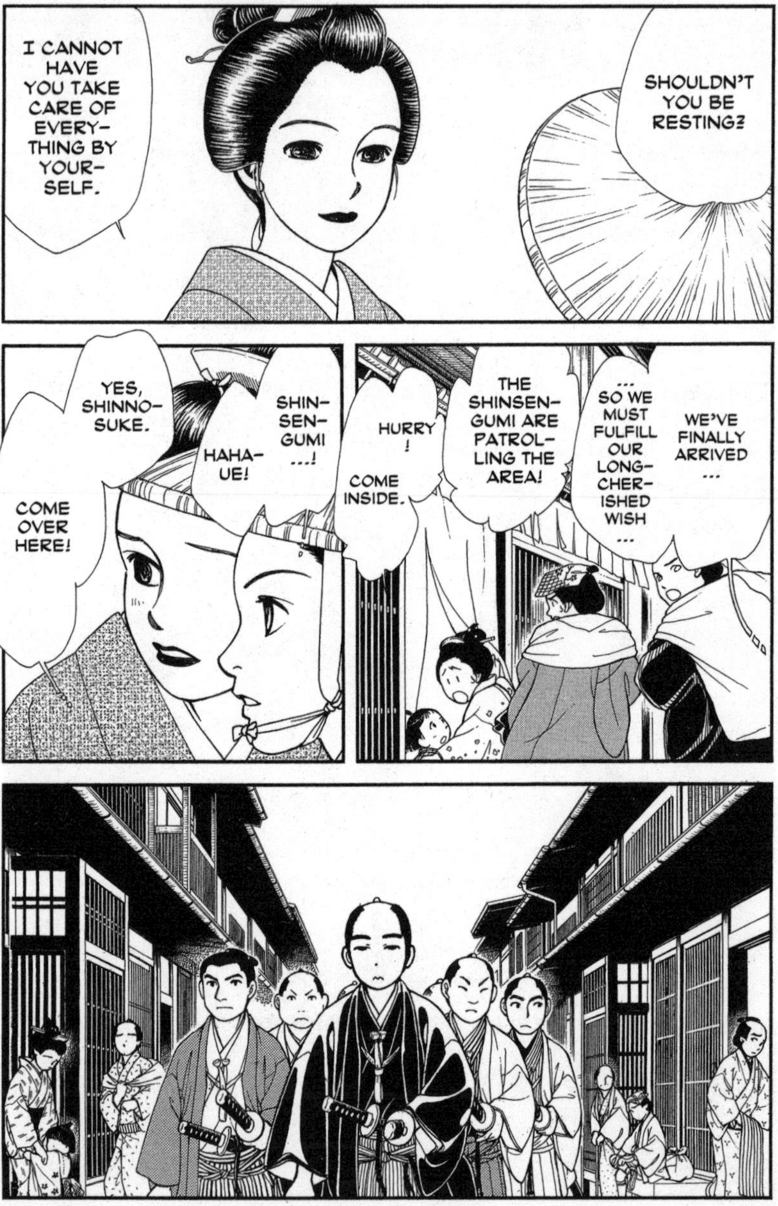
SHOULDN'T YOU BE RESTING?
I CANNOT HAVE YOU TAKE CARE OF EVERYTHING BY YOURSELF.
WE'VE FINALLY ARRIVED...
...SO WE MUST FULFILL OUR LONG-CHERISHED WISH...
THE SHINSENGUMI ARE PATROLLING THE AREA!
HURRY!
COME INSIDE.
SHINSENGUMI...!
HAHAUE!
YES, SHINNOSUKE.
COME OVER HERE!

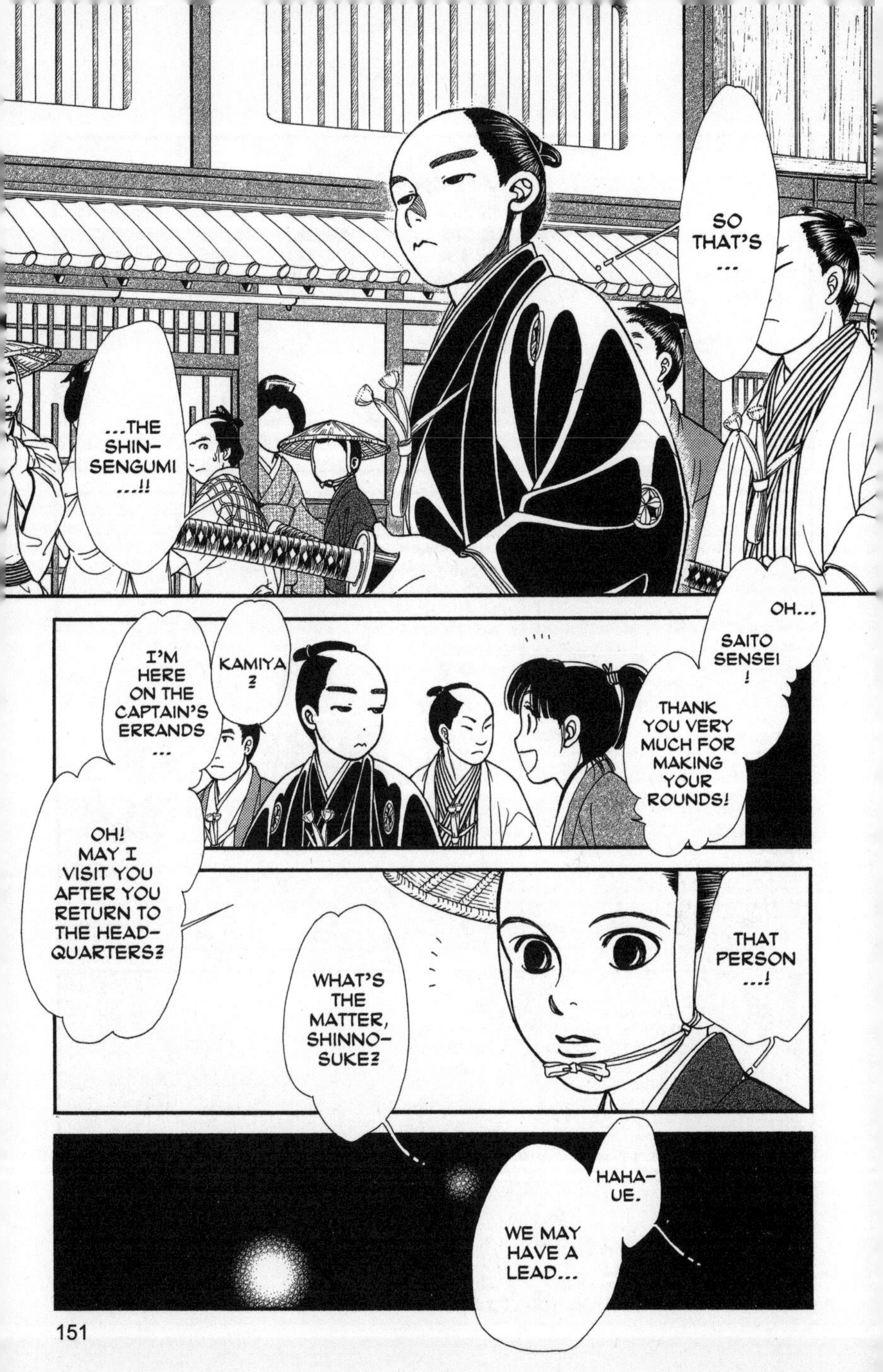
SO THAT'S ...
...THE SHIN-SENGUMI ...!!
OH... SAITO SENSEI!
THANK YOU VERY MUCH FOR MAKING YOUR ROUNDS!
KAMIYA?
I'M HERE ON THE CAPTAIN'S ERRANDS ...
OH! MAY I VISIT YOU AFTER YOU RETURN TO THE HEAD-QUARTERS?
THAT PERSON ...!
WHAT'S THE MATTER, SHINNO-SUKE?
HAHA-UE.
WE MAY HAVE A LEAD...

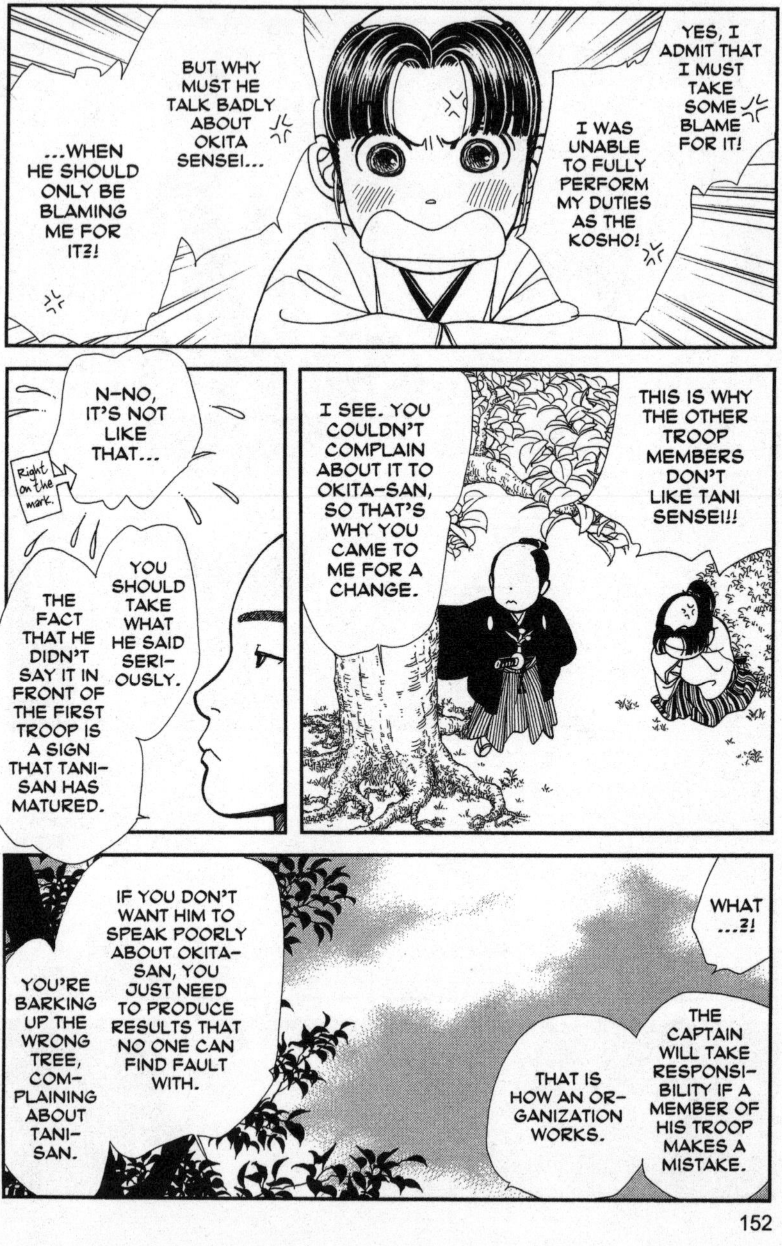
YES, I ADMIT THAT I MUST TAKE SOME BLAME FOR IT!
I WAS UNABLE TO FULLY PERFORM MY DUTIES AS THE KOSHO!
BUT WHY MUST HE TALK BADLY ABOUT OKITA SENSEI...
...WHEN HE SHOULD ONLY BE BLAMING ME FOR IT?!
THIS IS WHY THE OTHER TROOP MEMBERS DON'T LIKE TANI SENSEI!!
I SEE. YOU COULDN'T COMPLAIN ABOUT IT TO OKITA-SAN, SO THAT'S WHY YOU CAME TO ME FOR A CHANGE.
N-NO, IT'S NOT LIKE THAT...
Right on the mark.
YOU SHOULD TAKE WHAT HE SAID SERI-OUSLY.
THE FACT THAT HE DIDN'T SAY IT IN FRONT OF THE FIRST TROOP IS A SIGN THAT TANI-SAN HAS MATURED.
WHAT ...?!
THE CAPTAIN WILL TAKE RESPONSI-BILITY IF A MEMBER OF HIS TROOP MAKES A MISTAKE.
THAT IS HOW AN OR-GANIZATION WORKS.
IF YOU DON'T WANT HIM TO SPEAK POORLY ABOUT OKITA-SAN, YOU JUST NEED TO PRODUCE RESULTS THAT NO ONE CAN FIND FAULT WITH.
YOU'RE BARKING UP THE WRONG TREE, COM-PLAINING ABOUT TANI-SAN.

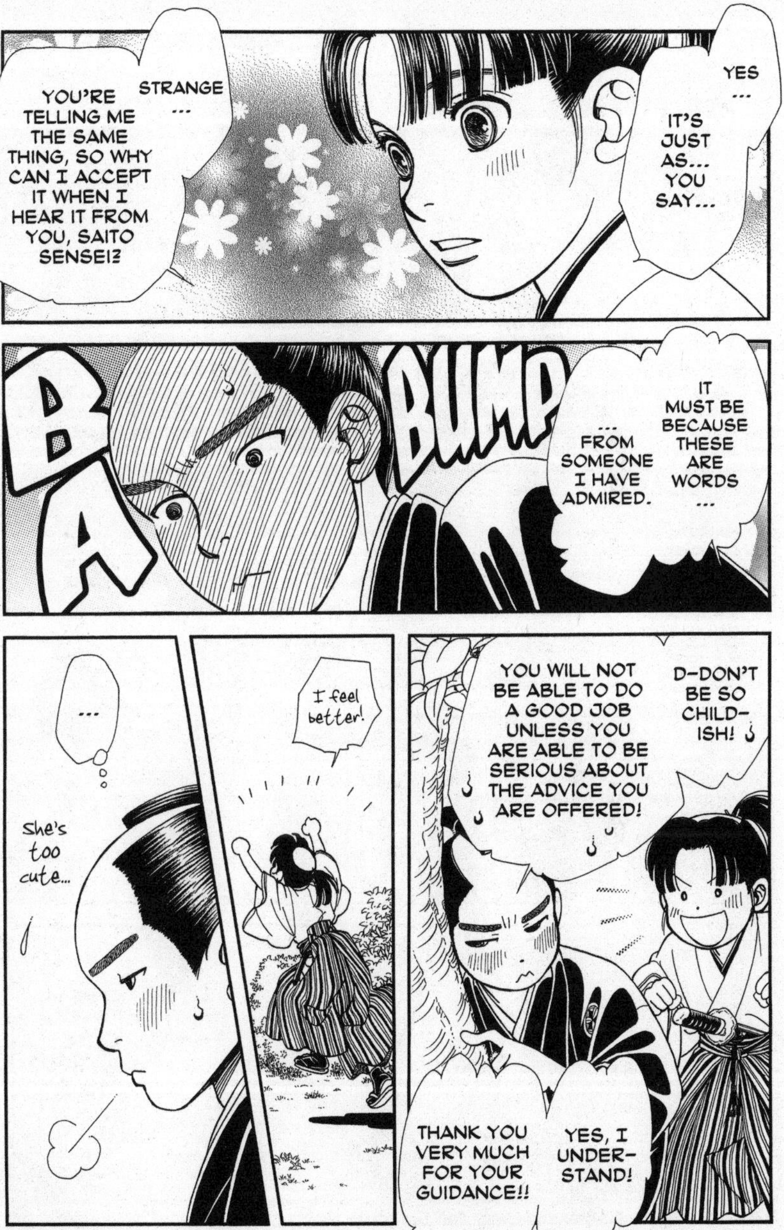
YES... IT'S JUST AS... YOU SAY...
STRANGE... YOU'RE TELLING ME THE SAME THING, SO WHY CAN I ACCEPT IT WHEN I HEAR IT FROM YOU, SAITO SENSEI!?
IT MUST BE BECAUSE THESE ARE WORDS...
...FROM SOMEONE I HAVE ADMIRED.
BUMP
BA
D-DON'T BE SO CHILD-ISH!
YOU WILL NOT BE ABLE TO DO A GOOD JOB UNLESS YOU ARE ABLE TO BE SERIOUS ABOUT THE ADVICE YOU ARE OFFERED!
YES, I UNDER-STAND!
THANK YOU VERY MUCH FOR YOUR GUIDANCE!!
I feel better!
...
She's too cute...

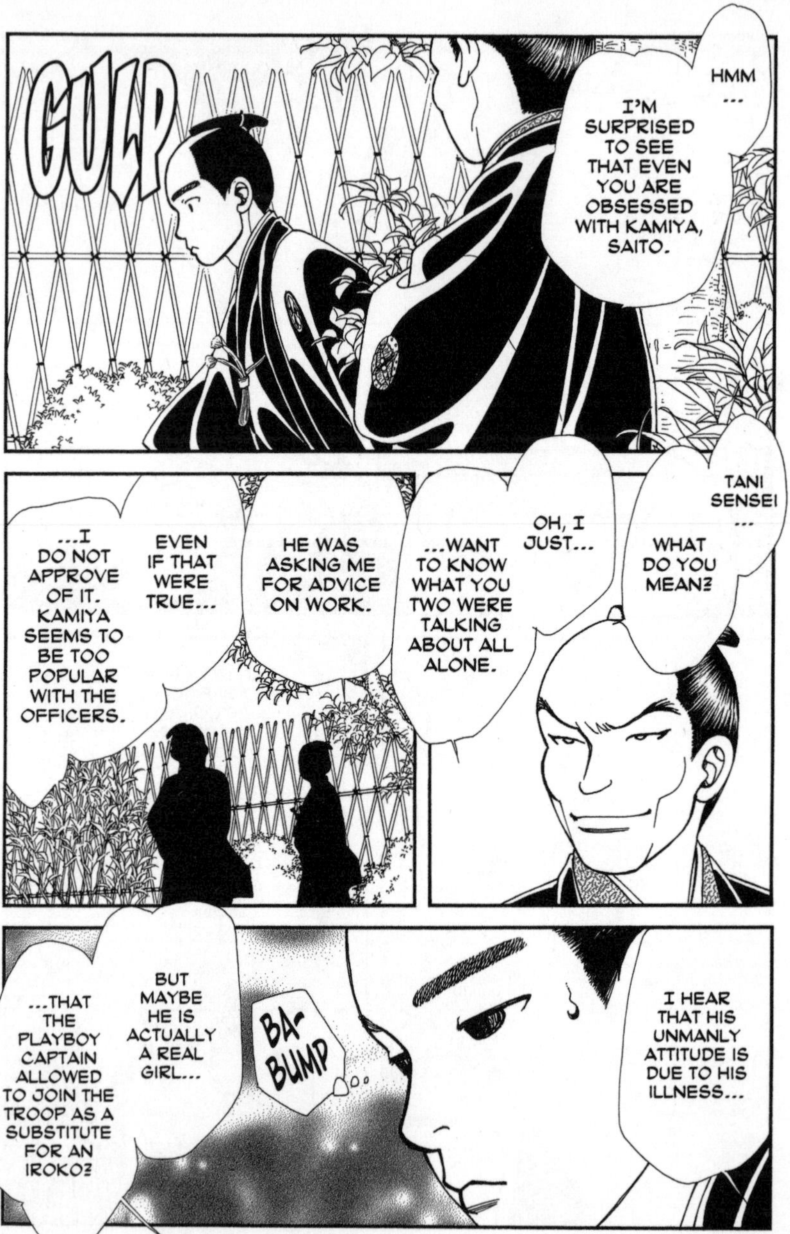
HMM... I'M SURPRISED TO SEE THAT EVEN YOU ARE OBSESSED WITH KAMIYA, SAITO.
GULP
TANI SENSEI... WHAT DO YOU MEAN?
OH, I JUST...
...WANT TO KNOW WHAT YOU TWO WERE TALKING ABOUT ALL ALONE.
HE WAS ASKING ME FOR ADVICE ON WORK.
EVEN IF THAT WERE TRUE...
...I DO NOT APPROVE OF IT. KAMIYA SEEMS TO BE TOO POPULAR WITH THE OFFICERS.
I HEAR THAT HIS UNMANLY ATTITUDE IS DUE TO HIS ILLNESS...
BA-BUMP
BUT MAYBE HE IS ACTUALLY A REAL GIRL...
...THAT THE PLAYBOY CAPTAIN ALLOWED TO JOIN THE TROOP AS A SUBSTITUTE FOR AN IROKO?

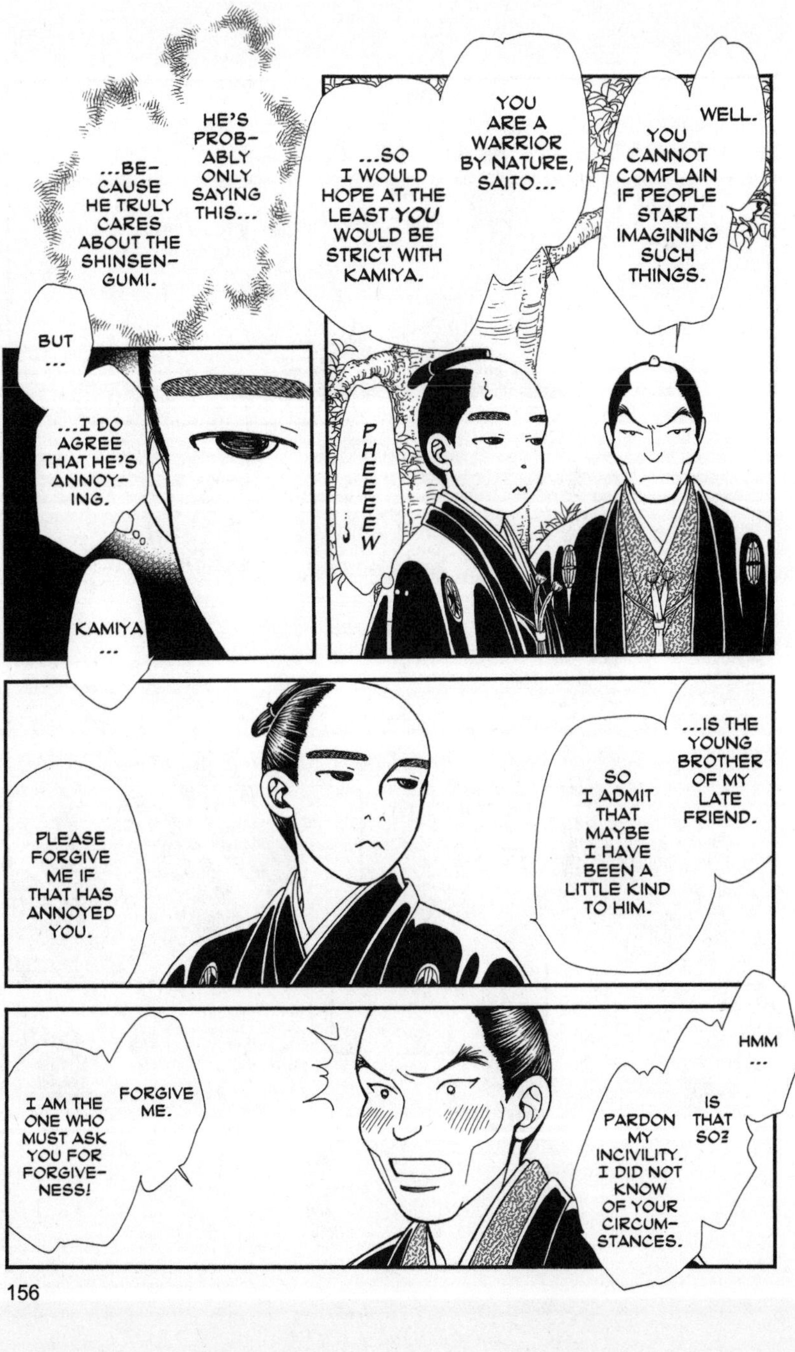
WELL.
YOU CANNOT COMPLAIN IF PEOPLE START IMAGINING SUCH THINGS.
YOU ARE A WARRIOR BY NATURE, SAITO...
...SO I WOULD HOPE AT THE LEAST *YOU* WOULD BE STRICT WITH KAMIYA.
PHEEEEW
HE'S PROBABLY ONLY SAYING THIS...
...BECAUSE HE TRULY CARES ABOUT THE SHINSENGUMI.
BUT...
...I DO AGREE THAT HE'S ANNOYING.
KAMIYA...
...IS THE YOUNG BROTHER OF MY LATE FRIEND.
SO I ADMIT THAT MAYBE I HAVE BEEN A LITTLE KIND TO HIM.
PLEASE FORGIVE ME IF THAT HAS ANNOYED YOU.
HMM...
IS THAT SO?
PARDON MY INCIVILITY. I DID NOT KNOW OF YOUR CIRCUMSTANCES.
FORGIVE ME.
I AM THE ONE WHO MUST ASK YOU FOR FORGIVENESS!

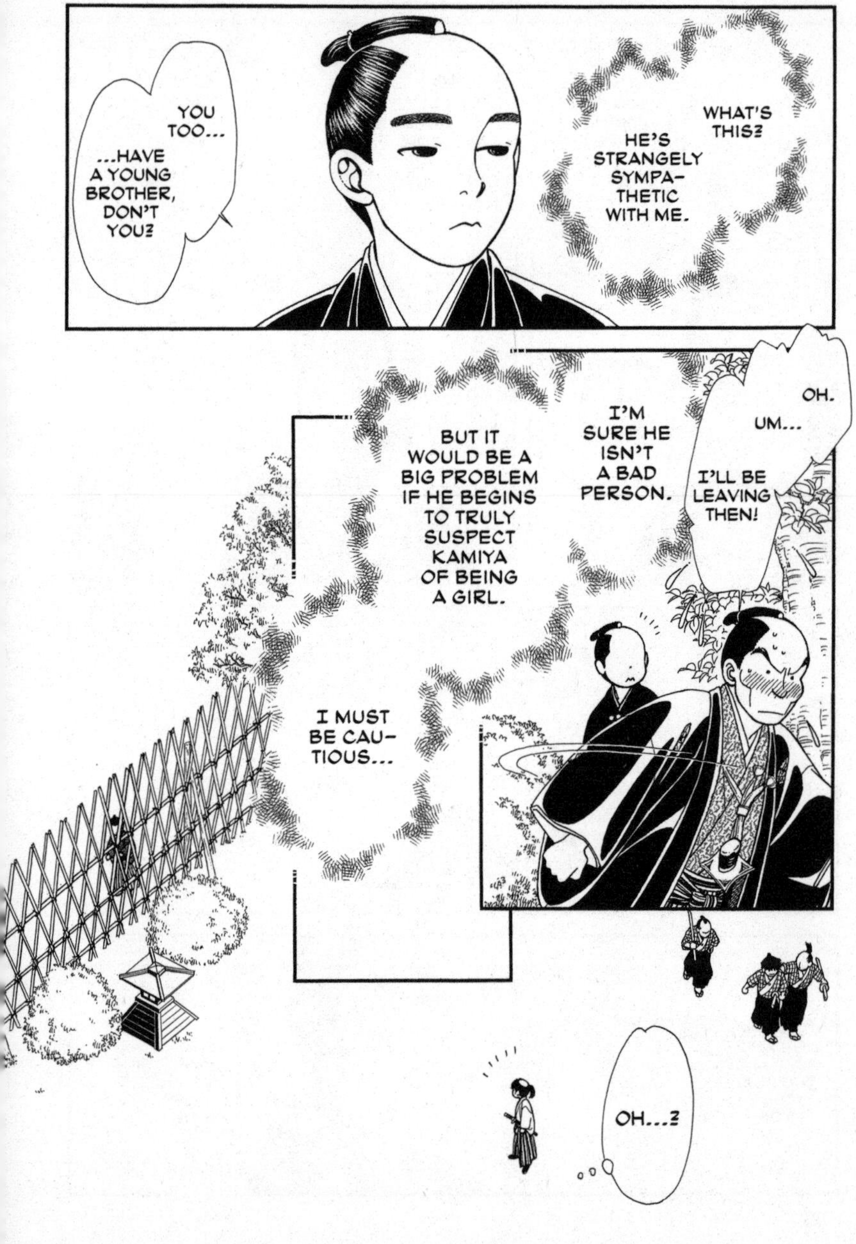
WHAT'S THIS?
HE'S STRANGELY SYMPA-THETIC WITH ME.
YOU TOO...
...HAVE A YOUNG BROTHER, DON'T YOU?
OH.
UM...
I'LL BE LEAVING THEN!
I'M SURE HE ISN'T A BAD PERSON.
BUT IT WOULD BE A BIG PROBLEM IF HE BEGINS TO TRULY SUSPECT KAMIYA OF BEING A GIRL.
I MUST BE CAU-TIOUS...
OH...?

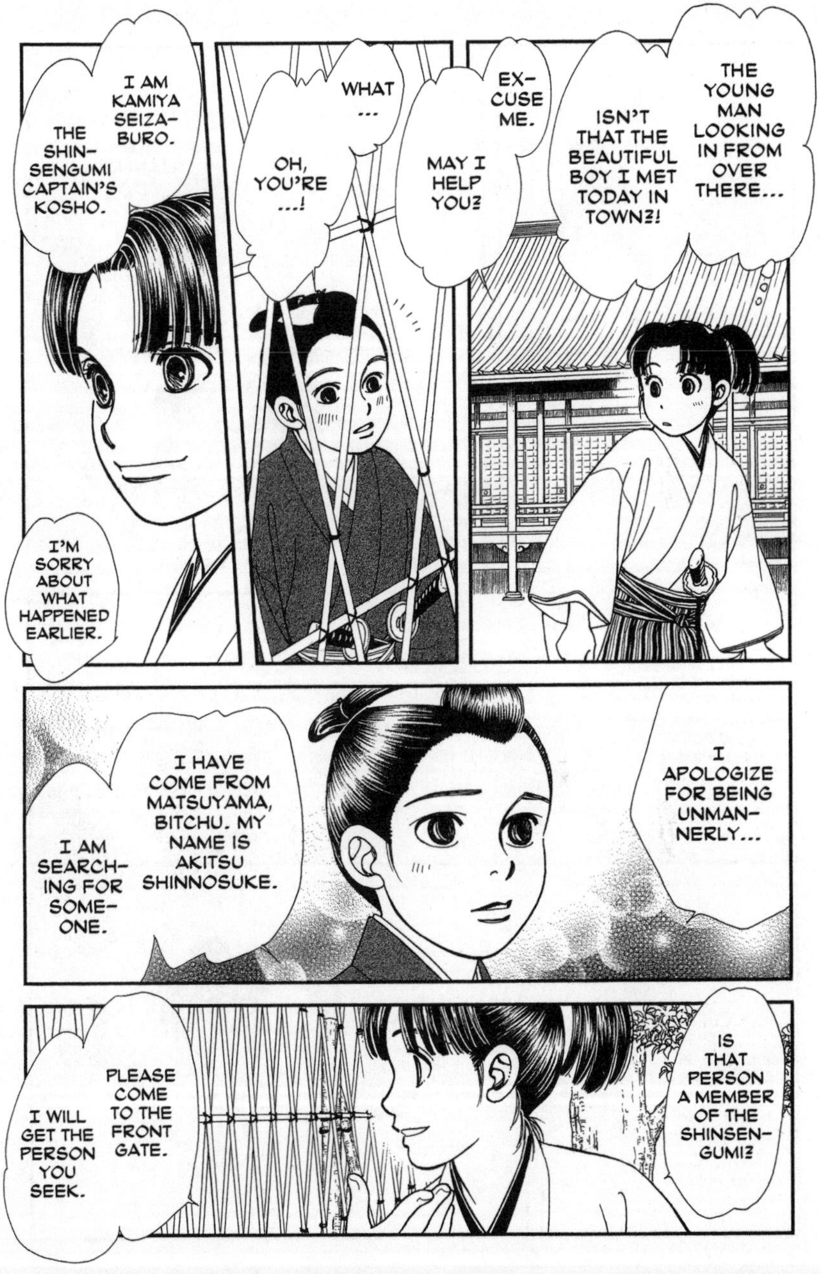
THE YOUNG MAN LOOKING IN FROM OVER THERE...
ISN'T THAT THE BEAUTIFUL BOY I MET TODAY IN TOWN?!
EX-CUSE ME.
MAY I HELP YOU?
WHAT...
OH, YOU'RE...!
I AM KAMIYA SEIZA-BURO.
THE SHIN-SENGUMI CAPTAIN'S KOSHO.
I'M SORRY ABOUT WHAT HAPPENED EARLIER.
I APOLOGIZE FOR BEING UNMAN-NERLY...
I HAVE COME FROM MATSUYAMA, BITCHU. MY NAME IS AKITSU SHINNOSUKE.
I AM SEARCH-ING FOR SOME-ONE.
IS THAT PERSON A MEMBER OF THE SHINSEN-GUMI?
PLEASE COME TO THE FRONT GATE.
I WILL GET THE PERSON YOU SEEK.

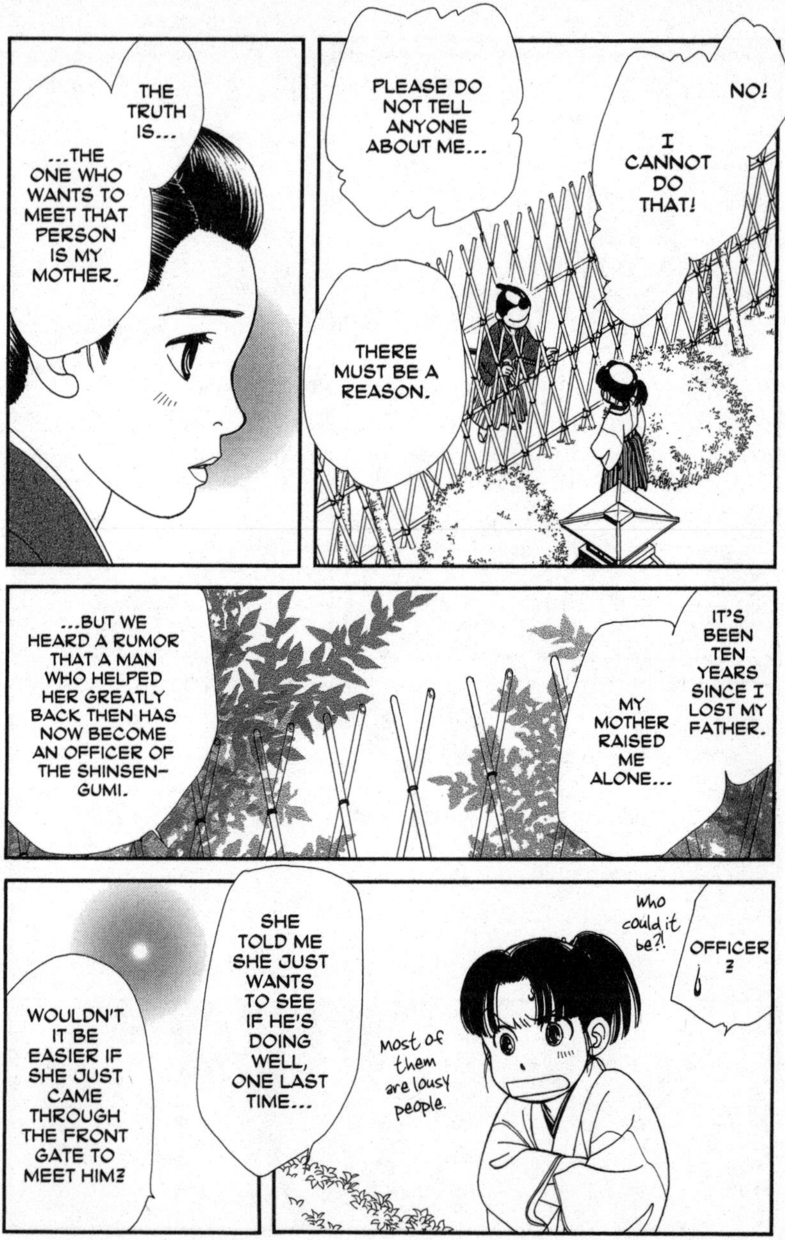
NO!
I CANNOT DO THAT!
PLEASE DO NOT TELL ANYONE ABOUT ME...
THERE MUST BE A REASON.
THE TRUTH IS...
...THE ONE WHO WANTS TO MEET THAT PERSON IS MY MOTHER.
IT'S BEEN TEN YEARS SINCE I LOST MY FATHER.
MY MOTHER RAISED ME ALONE...
...BUT WE HEARD A RUMOR THAT A MAN WHO HELPED HER GREATLY BACK THEN HAS NOW BECOME AN OFFICER OF THE SHINSEN-GUMI.
OFFICER?
Who could it be?!
Most of them are lousy people.
SHE TOLD ME SHE JUST WANTS TO SEE IF HE'S DOING WELL, ONE LAST TIME...
WOULDN'T IT BE EASIER IF SHE JUST CAME THROUGH THE FRONT GATE TO MEET HIM?

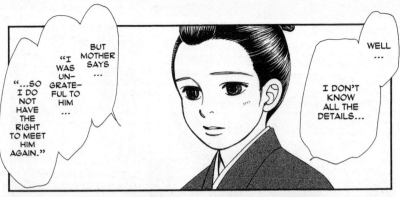

WELL ...
I DON'T KNOW ALL THE DETAILS...
BUT MOTHER SAYS ...
“I WAS UNGRATEFUL TO HIM ...
“...SO I DO NOT HAVE THE RIGHT TO MEET HIM AGAIN.”
HMM?!
A SYMPATHETIC MAN WHO HELPED HER.
WIDOW.
GROWING LOVE.
PROPOSAL.
BUT THE WIDOW
I SEE...
I UNDERSTAND YOUR SITUATION.
I think.
It's not something a mother can tell her child.
SO HOW MAY I HELP YOU?
AAH! THANK YOU VERY MUCH, KAMIYA-SAMA!
IF WE CAN FIND OUT WHEN HE COMES OUT TO TOWN...
...I WILL BE ABLE TO LET MY MOTHER SEE HIM FROM AFAR!
UH-HUH.
AND WHAT IS THAT MAN'S NAME?!

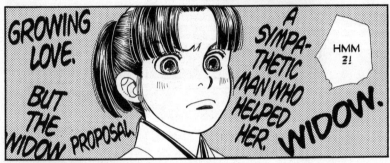

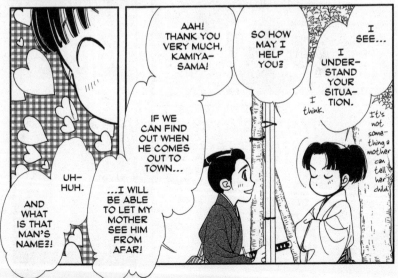

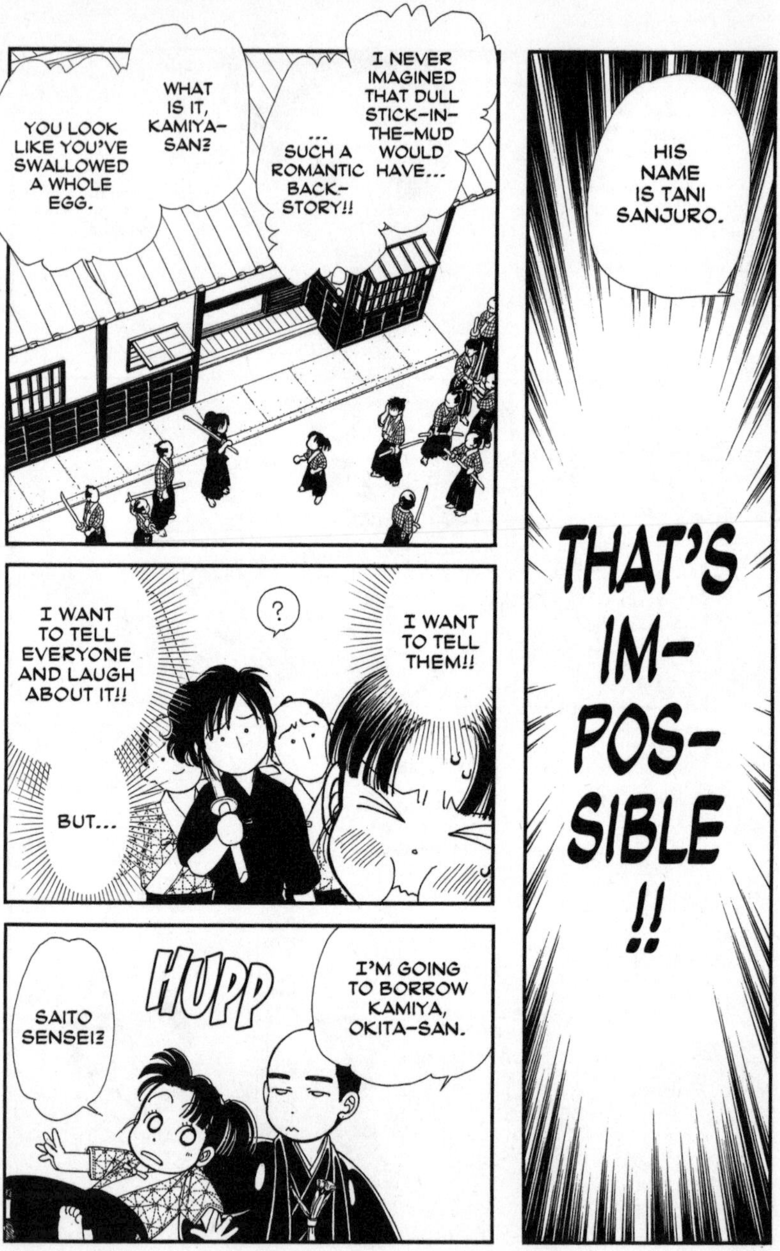
HIS NAME IS TANI SANJURO.
THAT'S IM-POS-SIBLE!!
I NEVER IMAGINED THAT DULL STICK-IN-THE-MUD WOULD HAVE...
...SUCH A ROMANTIC BACK-STORY!!
WHAT IS IT, KAMIYA-SAN?
YOU LOOK LIKE YOU'VE SWALLOWED A WHOLE EGG.
I WANT TO TELL THEM!!
?
I WANT TO TELL EVERYONE AND LAUGH ABOUT IT!!
BUT...
I'M GOING TO BORROW KAMIYA, OKITA-SAN.
HUPP
SAITO SENSEI?

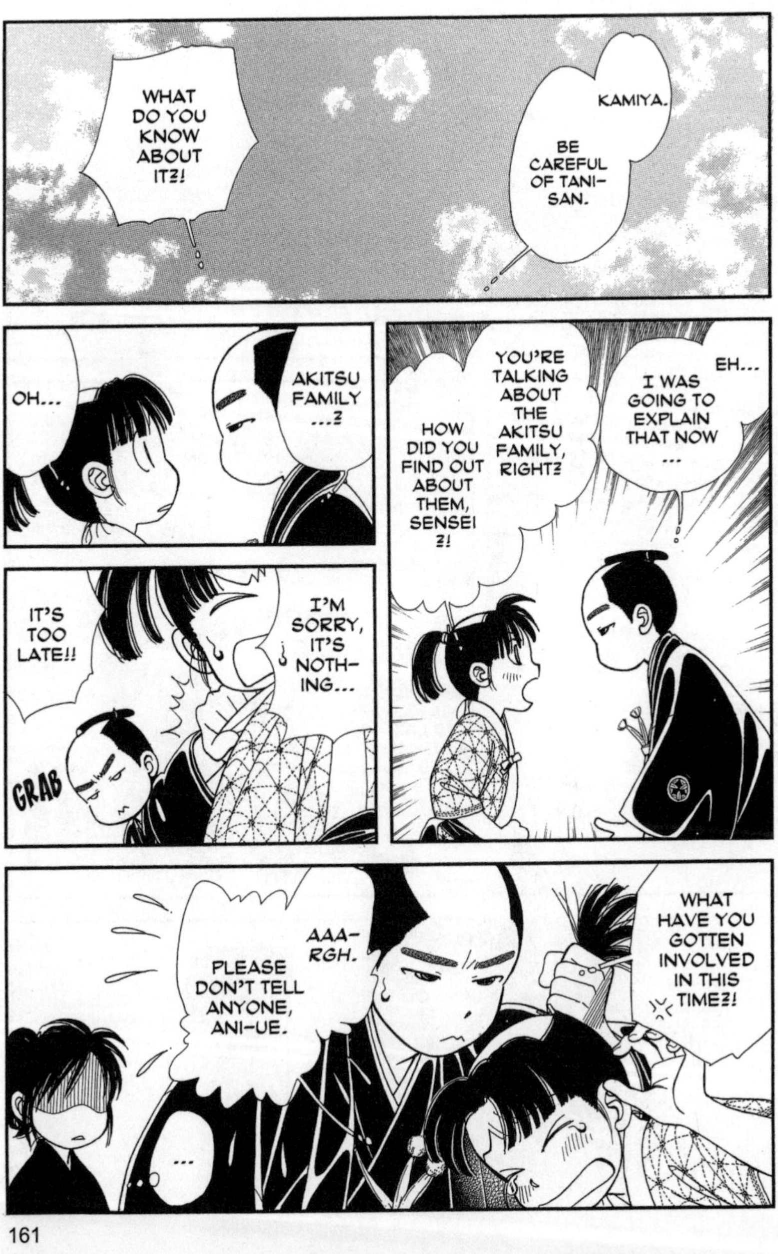
KAMIYA.
BE CAREFUL OF TANI-SAN.
WHAT DO YOU KNOW ABOUT IT?!
EH... I WAS GOING TO EXPLAIN THAT NOW ...
YOU'RE TALKING ABOUT THE AKITSU FAMILY, RIGHT?
HOW DID YOU FIND OUT ABOUT THEM, SENSEI?!
AKITSU FAMILY ...?
OH...
I'M SORRY, IT'S NOTHING...
IT'S TOO LATE!!
GRAB
WHAT HAVE YOU GOTTEN INVOLVED IN THIS TIME?!
AAA-RGH.
PLEASE DON'T TELL ANYONE, ANI-UE.
...

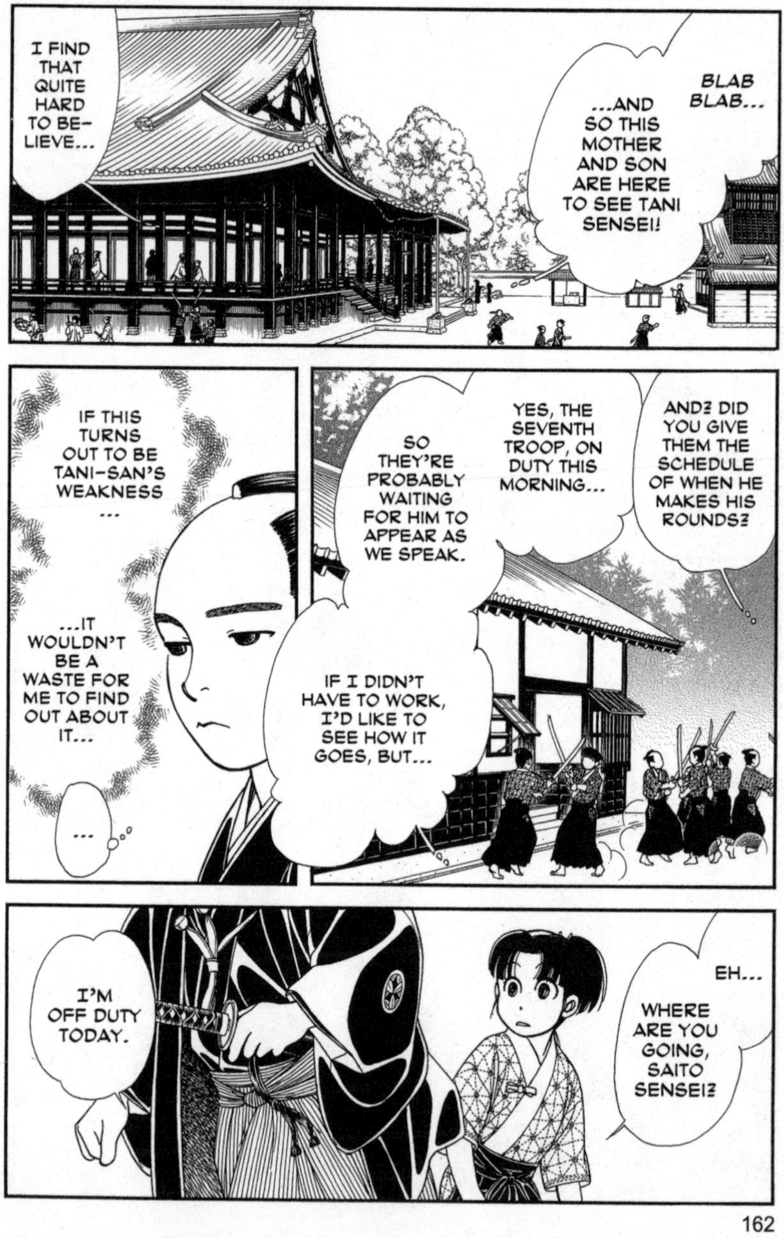
BLAB BLAB...
...AND SO THIS MOTHER AND SON ARE HERE TO SEE TANI SENSEI!
I FIND THAT QUITE HARD TO BE-LIEVE...
AND? DID YOU GIVE THEM THE SCHEDULE OF WHEN HE MAKES HIS ROUNDS?
YES, THE SEVENTH TROOP, ON DUTY THIS MORNING...
SO THEY'RE PROBABLY WAITING FOR HIM TO APPEAR AS WE SPEAK.
IF I DIDN'T HAVE TO WORK, I'D LIKE TO SEE HOW IT GOES, BUT...
IF THIS TURNS OUT TO BE TANI-SAN'S WEAKNESS ...
...IT WOULDN'T BE A WASTE FOR ME TO FIND OUT ABOUT IT...
...
EH...
WHERE ARE YOU GOING, SAITO SENSEI?
I'M OFF DUTY TODAY.

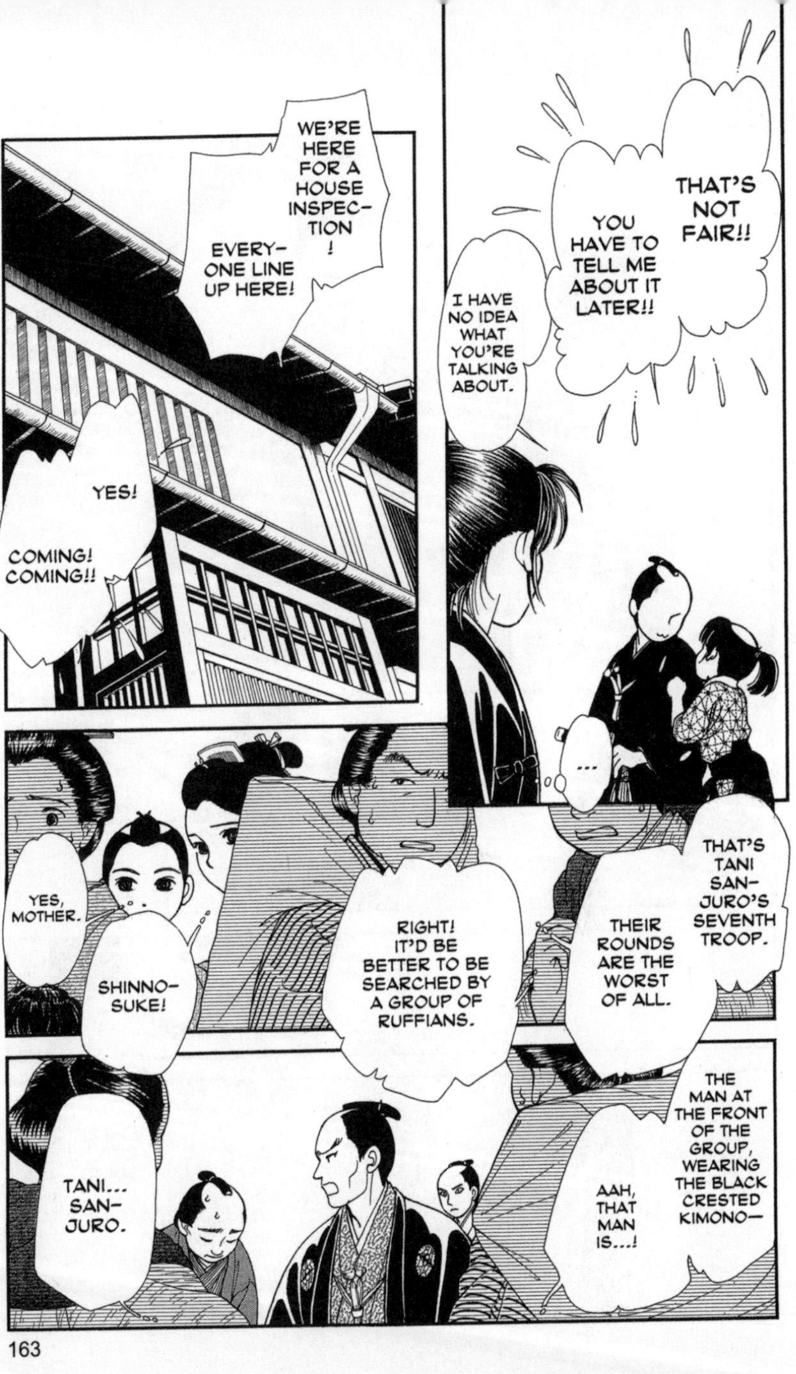
THAT'S NOT FAIR!!
YOU HAVE TO TELL ME ABOUT IT LATER!!
I HAVE NO IDEA WHAT YOU'RE TALKING ABOUT.
...
WE'RE HERE FOR A HOUSE INSPECTION!
EVERYONE LINE UP HERE!
YES!
COMING! COMING!!
THAT'S TANI SANJURO'S SEVENTH TROOP.
THEIR ROUNDS ARE THE WORST OF ALL.
RIGHT! IT'D BE BETTER TO BE SEARCHED BY A GROUP OF RUFFIANS.
SHINNOSUKE!
YES, MOTHER.
THE MAN AT THE FRONT OF THE GROUP, WEARING THE BLACK CRESTED KIMONO—
AAH, THAT MAN IS...!
TANI... SANJURO.

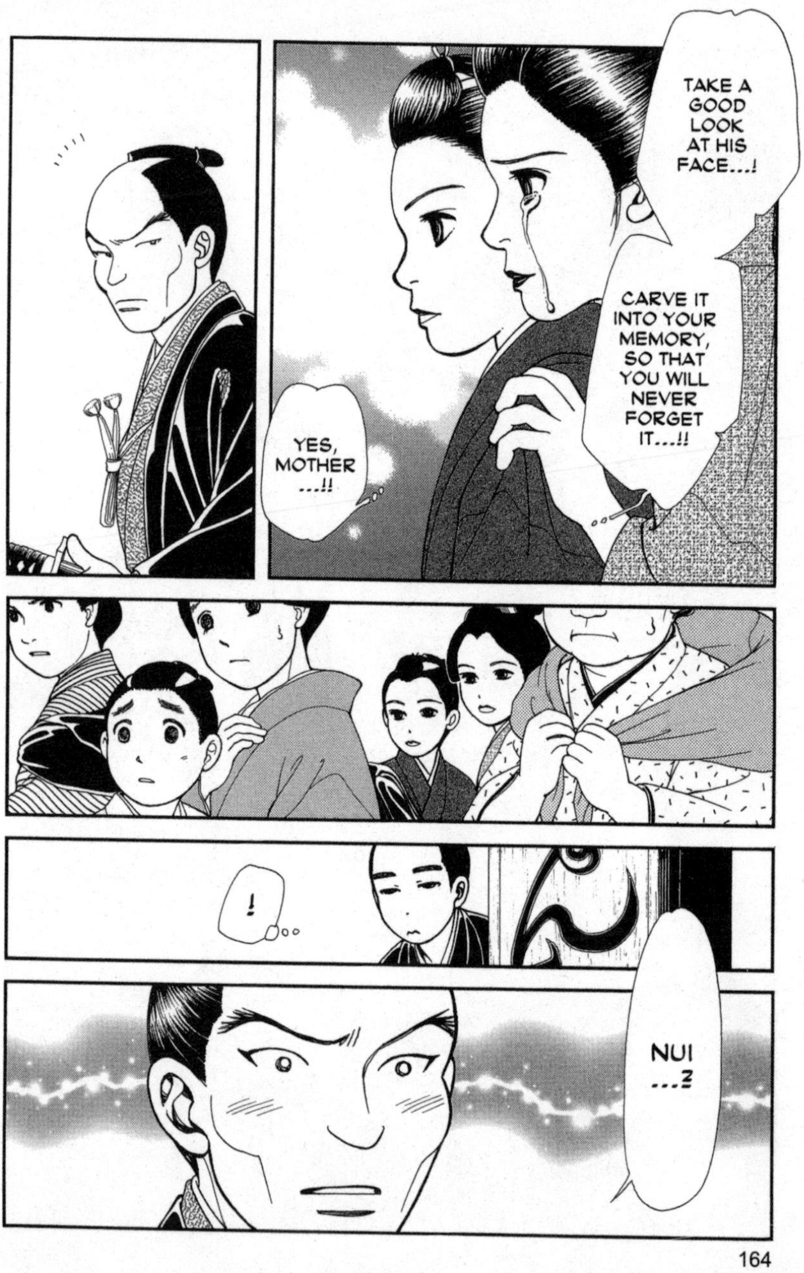
TAKE A GOOD LOOK AT HIS FACE...!
CARVE IT INTO YOUR MEMORY, SO THAT YOU WILL NEVER FORGET IT...!!
YES, MOTHER ...!!
!
NUI ...?

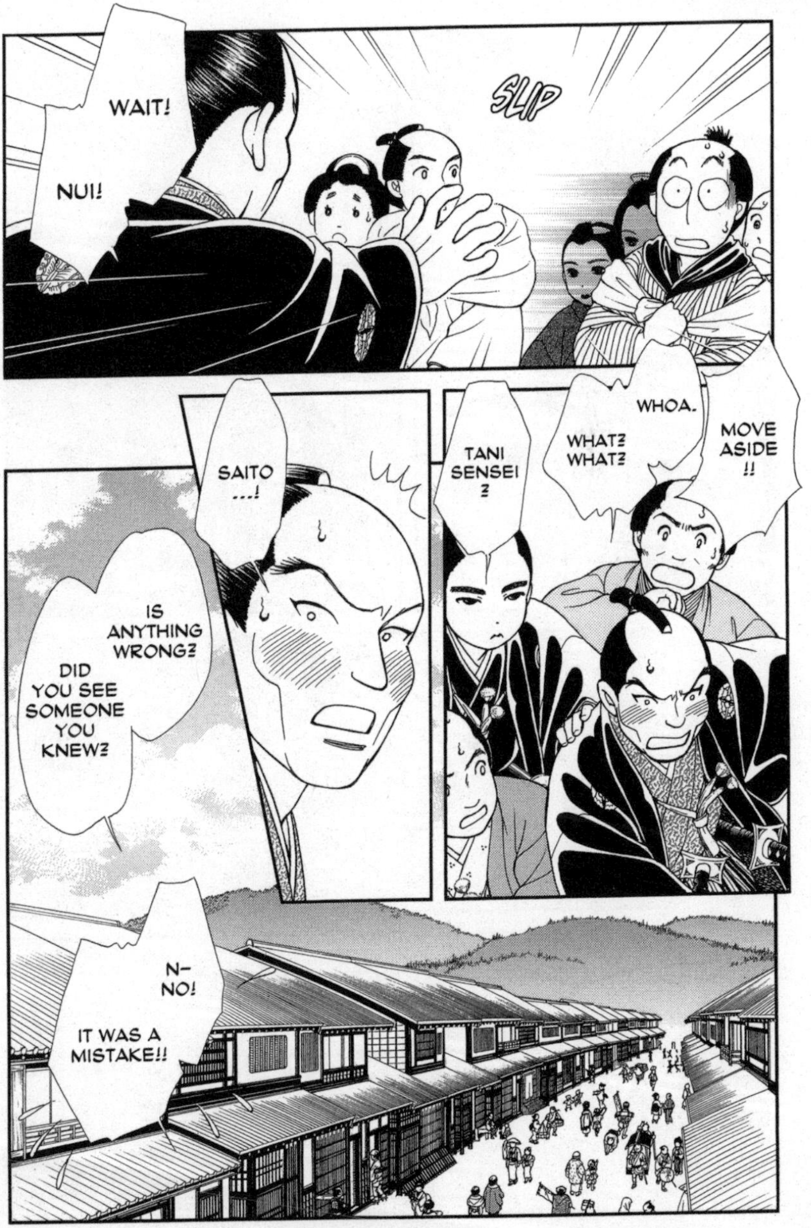
SLIP
WAIT!
NUI!
MOVE ASIDE!!
WHOA.
WHAT? WHAT?
TANI SENSEI?
SAITO...!
IS ANYTHING WRONG?
DID YOU SEE SOMEONE YOU KNEW?
N-NO!
IT WAS A MISTAKE!!

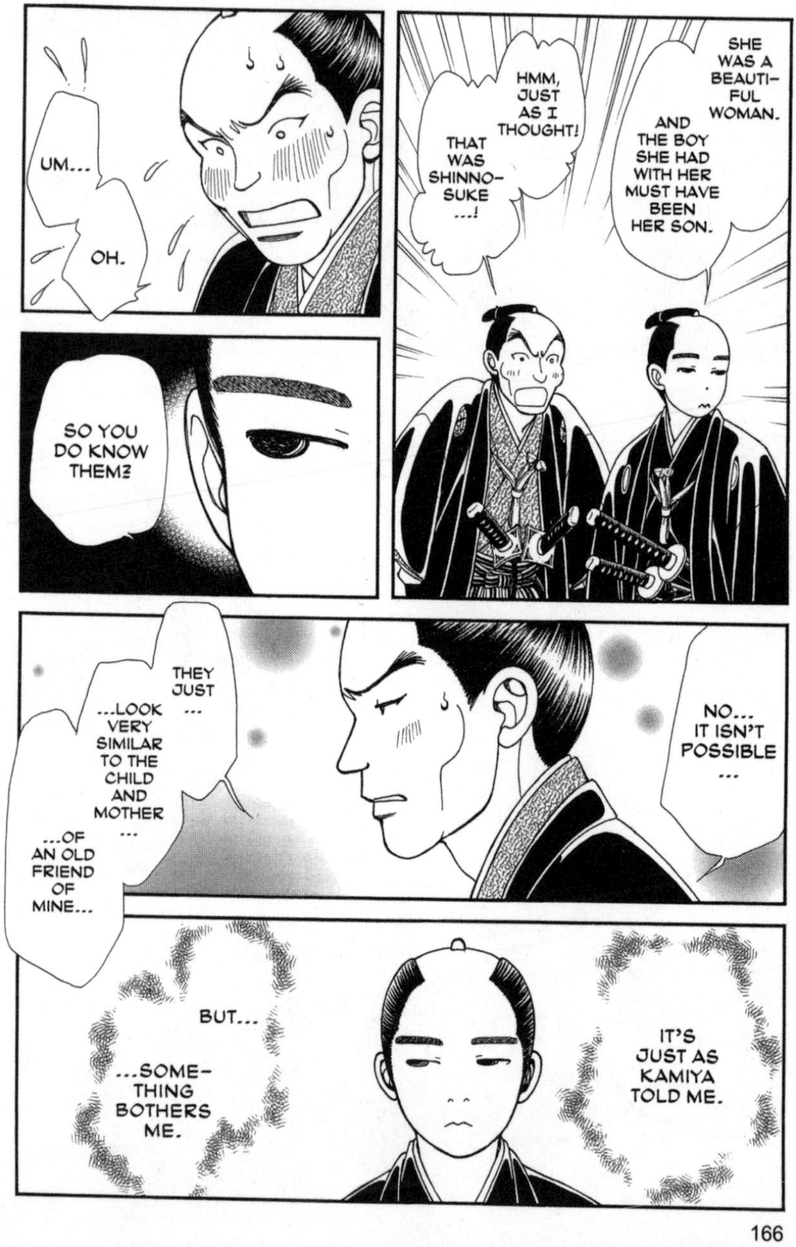
SHE WAS A BEAUTIFUL WOMAN.
AND THE BOY SHE HAD WITH HER MUST HAVE BEEN HER SON.
HMM, JUST AS I THOUGHT!
THAT WAS SHINNOSUKE...!
UM...
OH.
SO YOU DO KNOW THEM?
NO... IT ISN'T POSSIBLE...
THEY JUST...
...LOOK VERY SIMILAR TO THE CHILD AND MOTHER...
...OF AN OLD FRIEND OF MINE...
IT'S JUST AS KAMIYA TOLD ME.
BUT...
...SOMETHING BOTHERS ME.

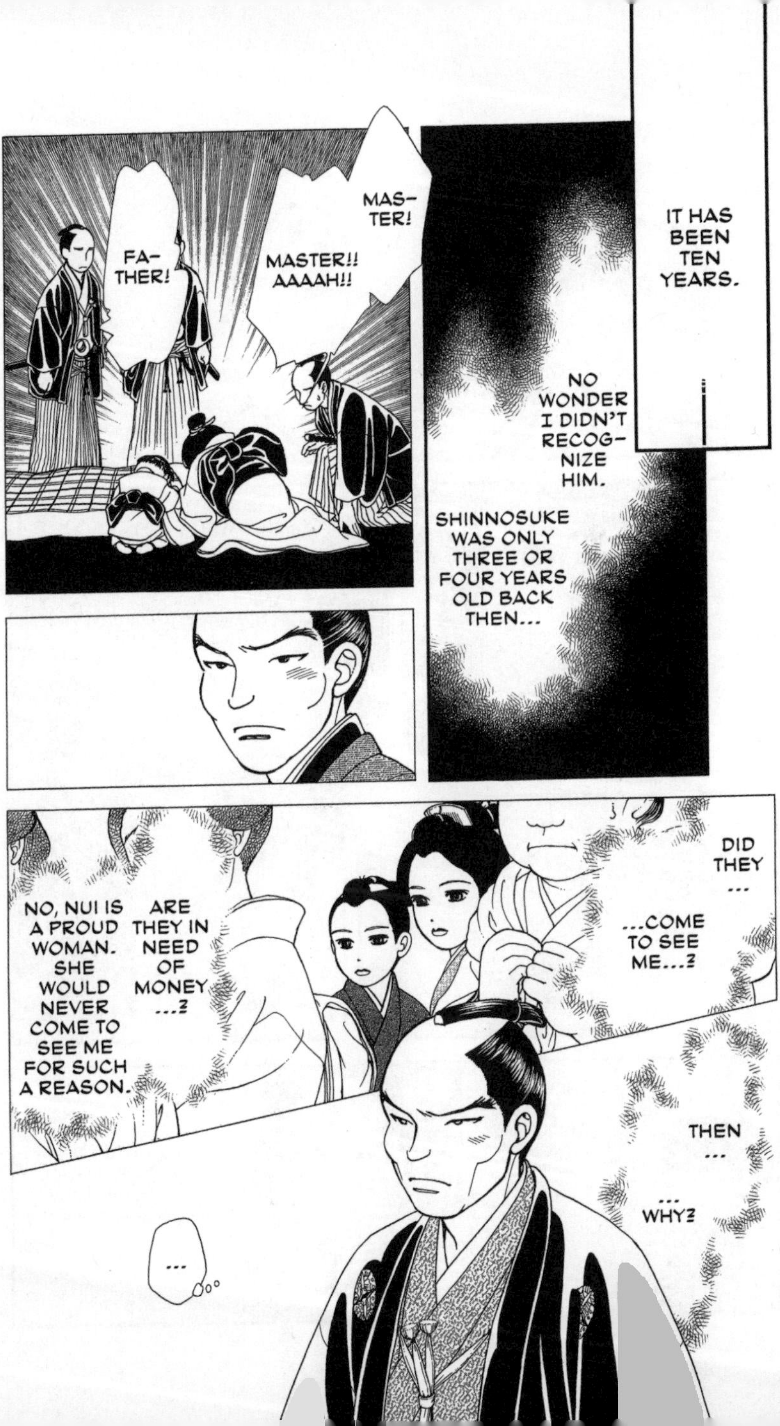
IT HAS BEEN TEN YEARS.
NO WONDER I DIDN'T RECOGNIZE HIM.
SHINNOSUKE WAS ONLY THREE OR FOUR YEARS OLD BACK THEN...
MASTER!
MASTER!! AAAAH!!
FATHER!
DID THEY ...
...COME TO SEE ME...?
ARE THEY IN NEED OF MONEY ...?
NO, NUI IS A PROUD WOMAN. SHE WOULD NEVER COME TO SEE ME FOR SUCH A REASON.
THEN ...
... WHY?
...

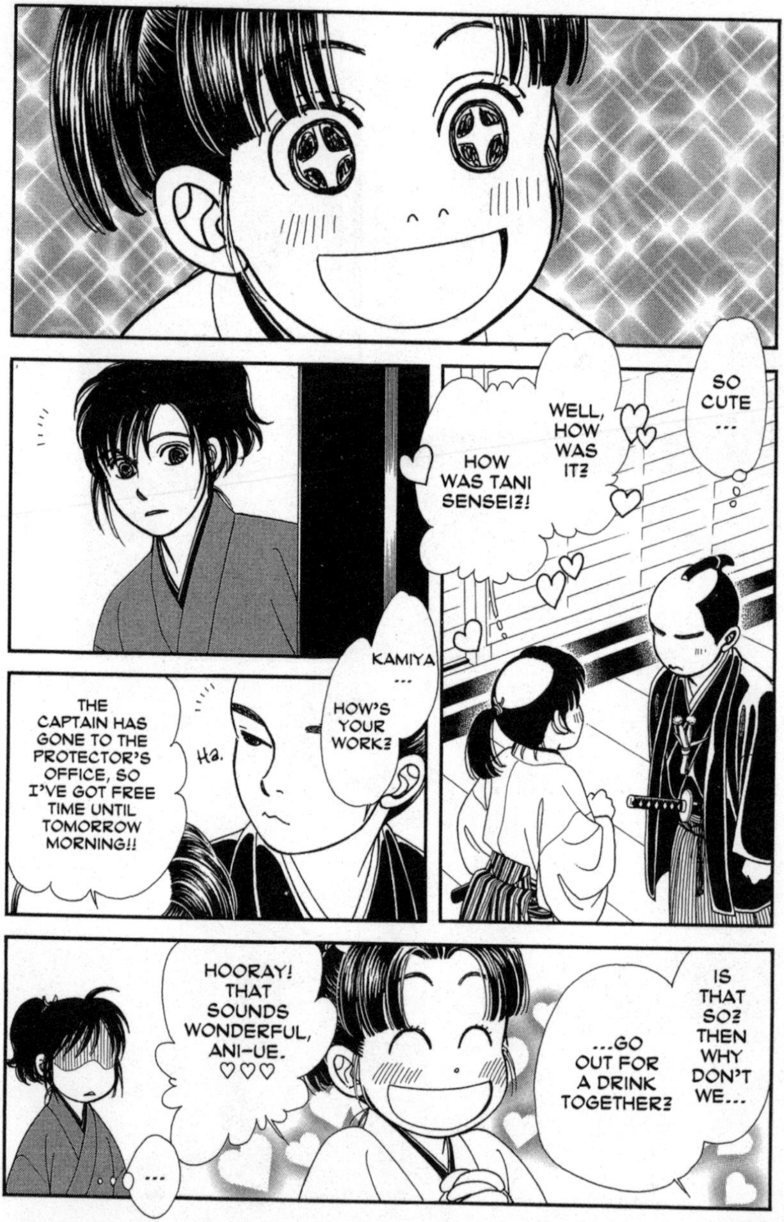
SO CUTE ...
WELL, HOW WAS IT?
HOW WAS TANI SENSEI?!
KAMIYA ... HOW'S YOUR WORK?
Ha.
THE CAPTAIN HAS GONE TO THE PROTECTOR'S OFFICE, SO I'VE GOT FREE TIME UNTIL TOMORROW MORNING!!
IS THAT SO? THEN WHY DON'T WE...
...GO OUT FOR A DRINK TOGETHER?
HOORAY! THAT SOUNDS WONDERFUL, ANI-UE. ♡♡♡
...

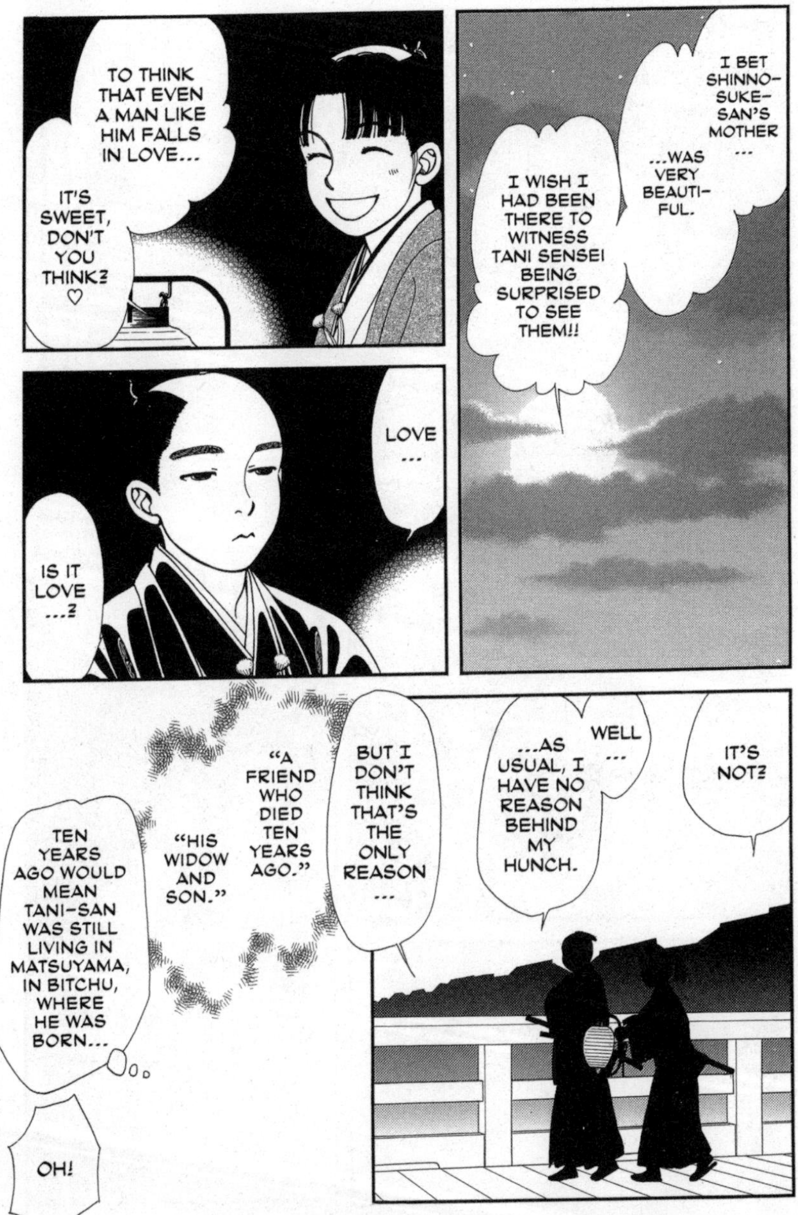
I BET SHINNOSUKE-SAN'S MOTHER ...
...WAS VERY BEAUTIFUL.
I WISH I HAD BEEN THERE TO WITNESS TANI SENSEI BEING SURPRISED TO SEE THEM!!
TO THINK THAT EVEN A MAN LIKE HIM FALLS IN LOVE...
IT'S SWEET, DON'T YOU THINK? ♡
LOVE ...
IS IT LOVE ...?
IT'S NOT?
WELL ...
...AS USUAL, I HAVE NO REASON BEHIND MY HUNCH.
BUT I DON'T THINK THAT'S THE ONLY REASON ...
"A FRIEND WHO DIED TEN YEARS AGO."
"HIS WIDOW AND SON."
TEN YEARS AGO WOULD MEAN TANI-SAN WAS STILL LIVING IN MATSUYAMA, IN BITCHU, WHERE HE WAS BORN...
OH!

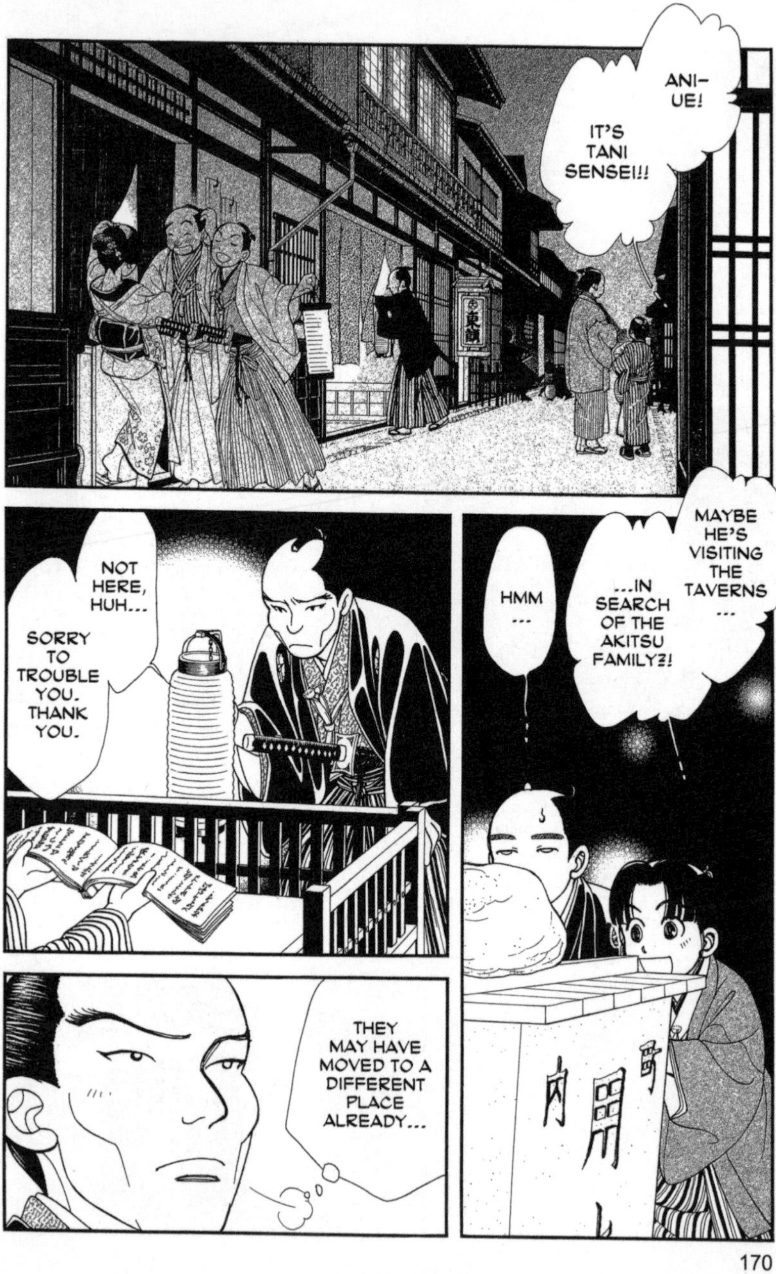
ANI-UE!
IT'S TANI SENSEI!!!
MAYBE HE'S VISITING THE TAVERNS ...
...IN SEARCH OF THE AKITSU FAMILY?!
HMM ...
NOT HERE, HUH...
SORRY TO TROUBLE YOU. THANK YOU.
THEY MAY HAVE MOVED TO A DIFFERENT PLACE ALREADY...

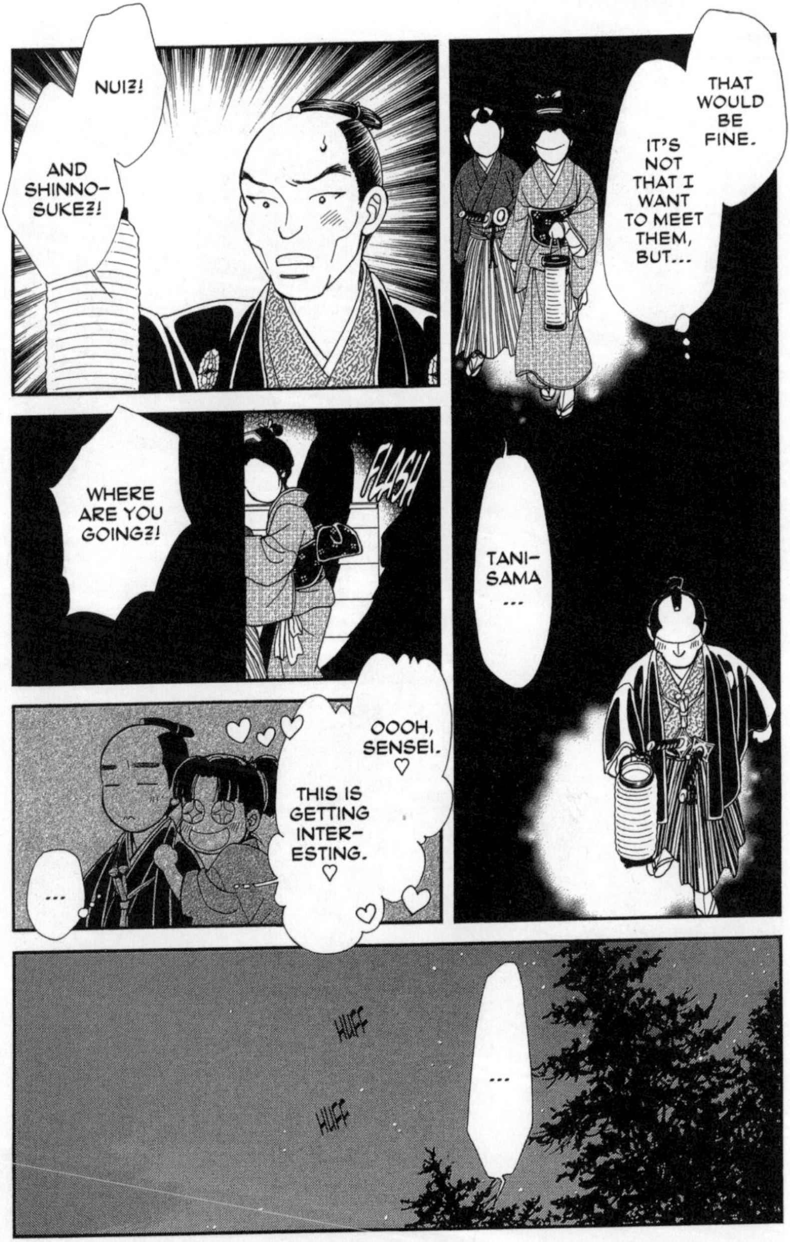
THAT WOULD BE FINE.
IT'S NOT THAT I WANT TO MEET THEM, BUT...
TANI-SAMA...
NUI?!
AND SHINNO-SUKE?!
FLASH
WHERE ARE YOU GOING?!
OOOH, SENSEI. ♡
THIS IS GETTING INTER-ESTING. ♡
...
HUFF
HUFF
...

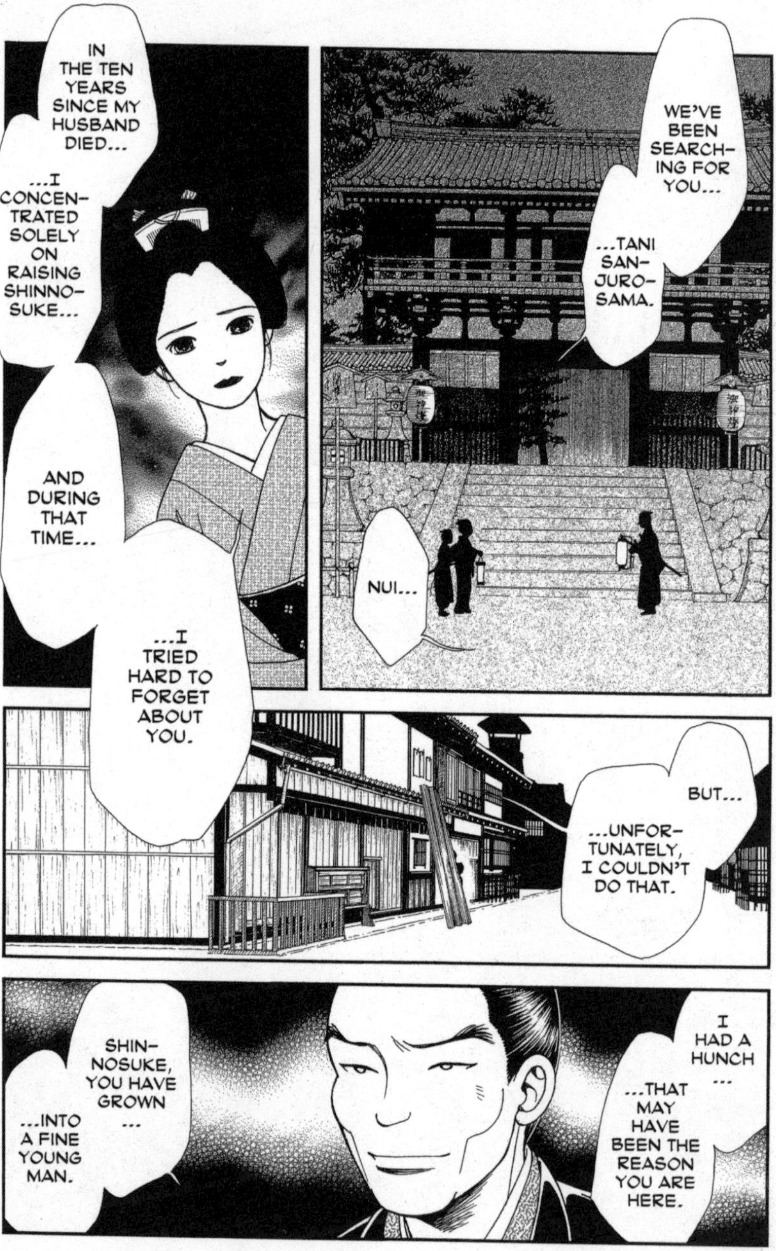
WE'VE BEEN SEARCHING FOR YOU...
...TANI SANJURO-SAMA.
NUI...
IN THE TEN YEARS SINCE MY HUSBAND DIED...
...I CONCENTRATED SOLELY ON RAISING SHINNOSUKE...
AND DURING THAT TIME...
...I TRIED HARD TO FORGET ABOUT YOU.
BUT...
...UNFORTUNATELY, I COULDN'T DO THAT.
I HAD A HUNCH...
...THAT MAY HAVE BEEN THE REASON YOU ARE HERE.
SHINNOSUKE, YOU HAVE GROWN...
...INTO A FINE YOUNG MAN.

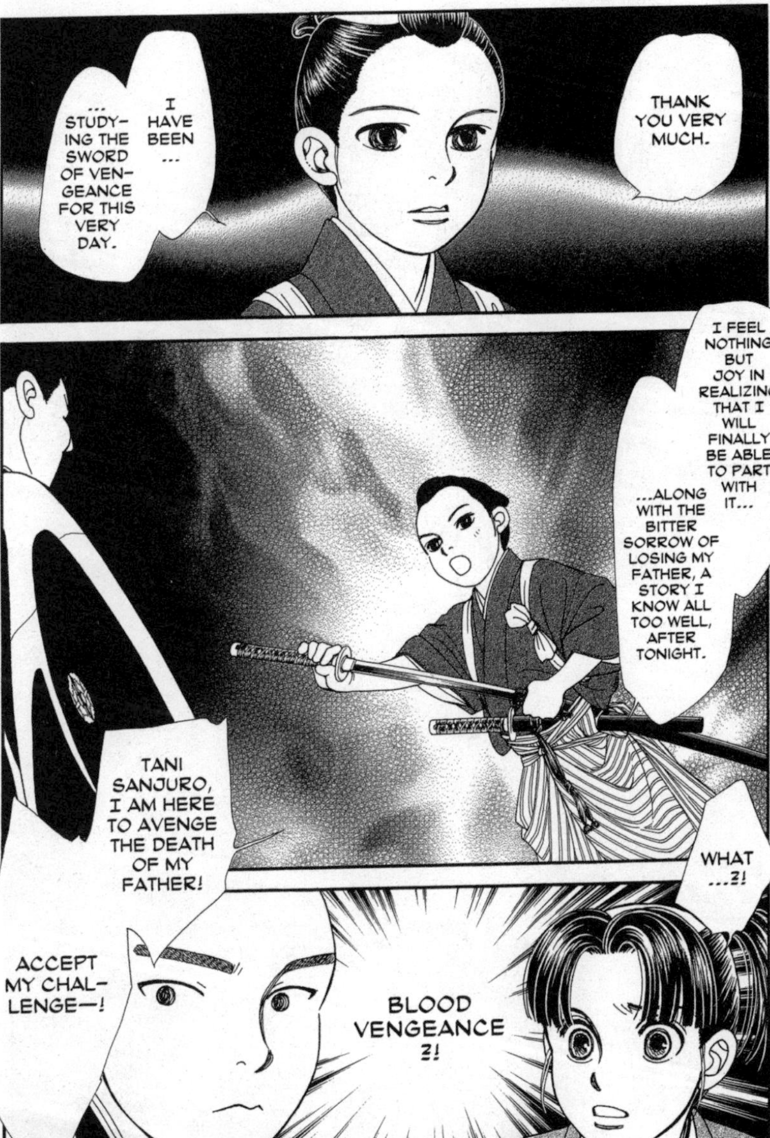
THANK YOU VERY MUCH.
I HAVE BEEN ...
... STUDYING THE SWORD OF VENGEANCE FOR THIS VERY DAY.
I FEEL NOTHING BUT JOY IN REALIZING THAT I WILL FINALLY BE ABLE TO PART WITH IT...
...ALONG WITH THE BITTER SORROW OF LOSING MY FATHER, A STORY I KNOW ALL TOO WELL, AFTER TONIGHT.
TANI SANJURO, I AM HERE TO AVENGE THE DEATH OF MY FATHER!
ACCEPT MY CHALLENGE—!
WHAT ...?!
BLOOD VENGEANCE ?!

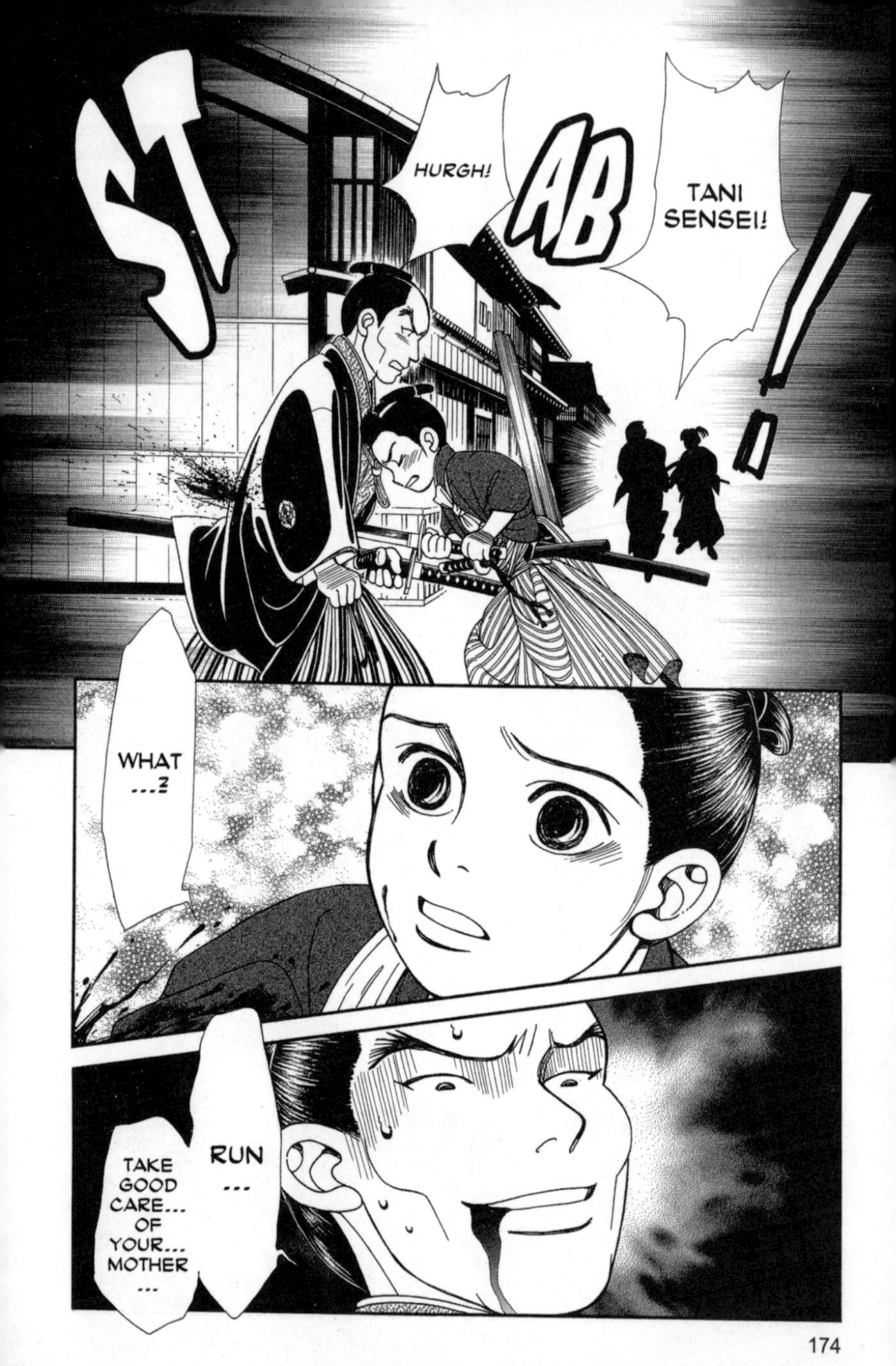
TANI SENSEI!
STAB
HURGH!
WHAT ...?
RUN ...
TAKE GOOD CARE... OF YOUR... MOTHER ...

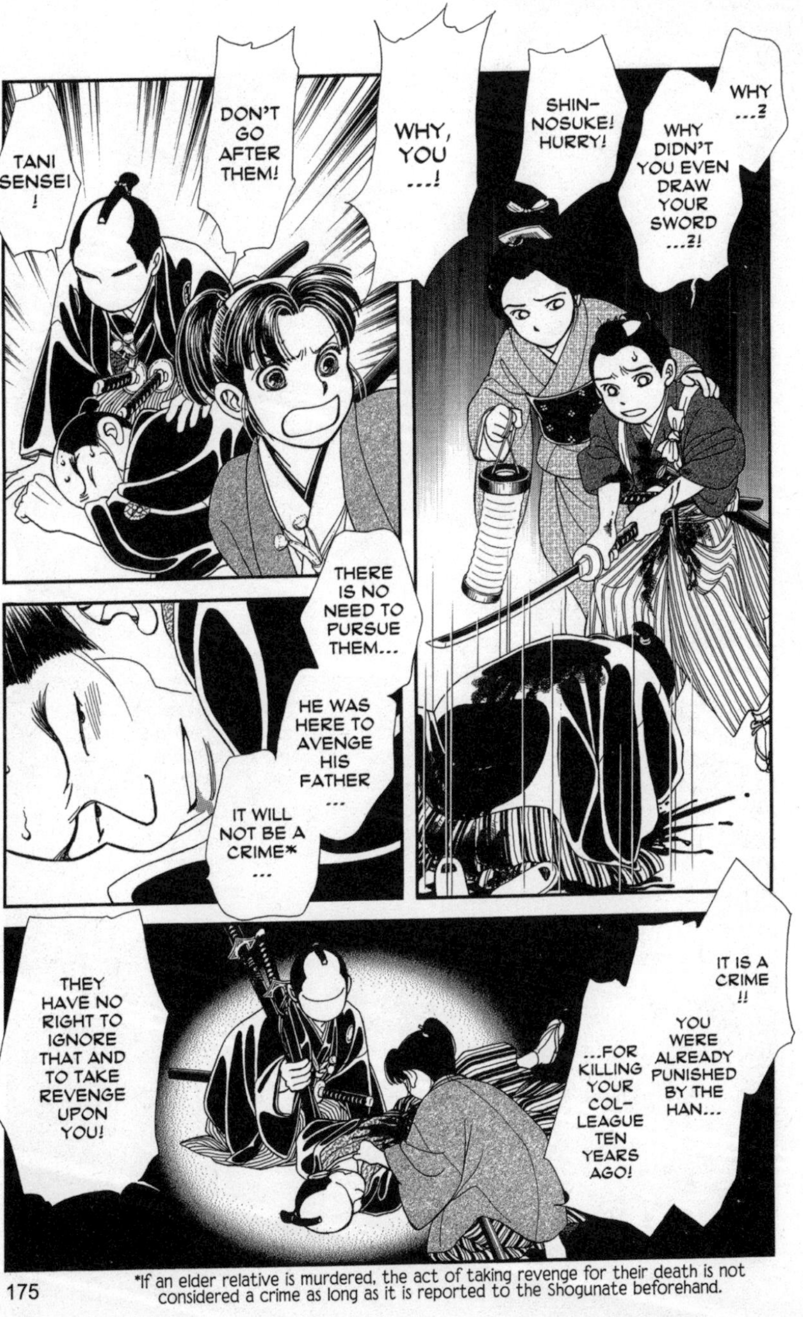
WHY...? WHY DIDN'T YOU EVEN DRAW YOUR SWORD...?!
SHIN-NOSUKE! HURRY!
WHY, YOU...!
DON'T GO AFTER THEM!
TANI SENSEI!
THERE IS NO NEED TO PURSUE THEM...
HE WAS HERE TO AVENGE HIS FATHER...
IT WILL NOT BE A CRIME*...
IT IS A CRIME!! YOU WERE ALREADY PUNISHED BY THE HAN...
...FOR KILLING YOUR COL-LEAGUE TEN YEARS AGO!
THEY HAVE NO RIGHT TO IGNORE THAT AND TO TAKE REVENGE UPON YOU!

*If an elder relative is murdered, the act of taking revenge for their death is not considered a crime as long as it is reported to the Shogunate beforehand.

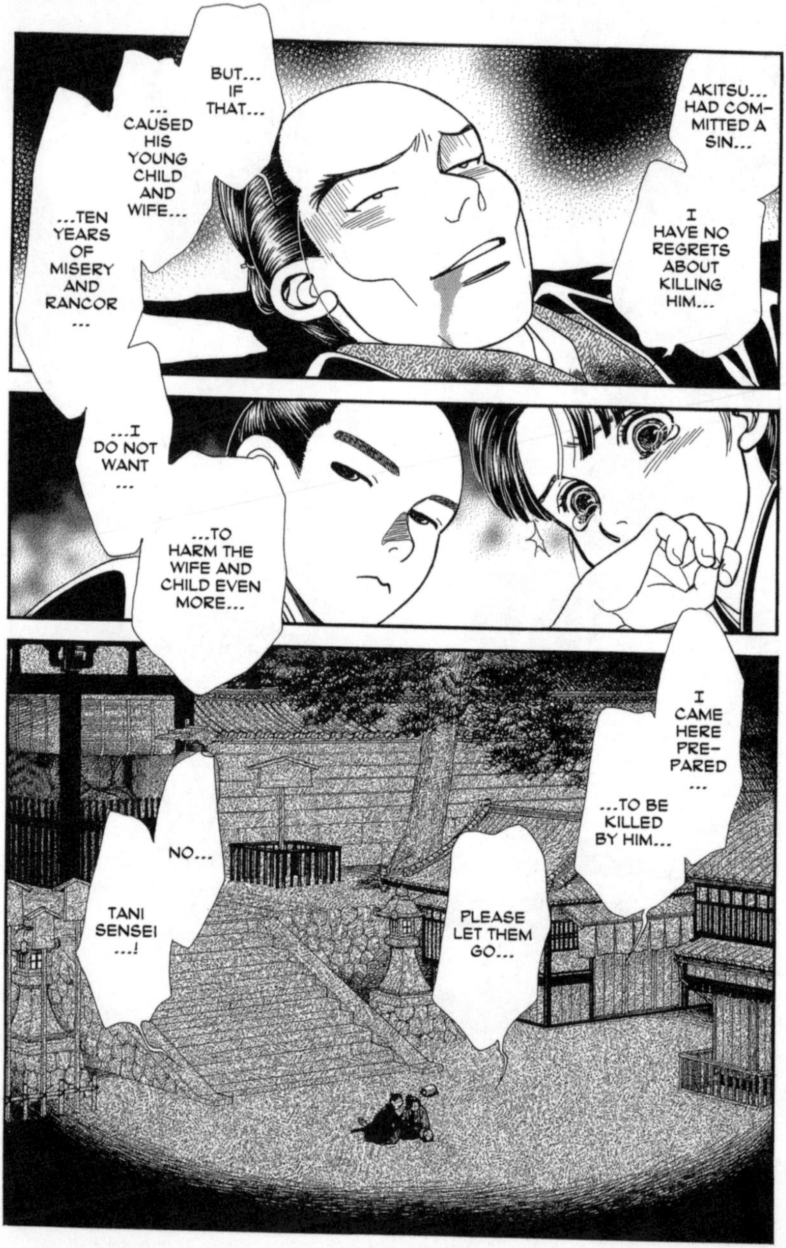
AKITSU... HAD COM-MITTED A SIN...
I HAVE NO REGRETS ABOUT KILLING HIM...
BUT... IF THAT...
... CAUSED HIS YOUNG CHILD AND WIFE...
...TEN YEARS OF MISERY AND RANCOR ...
...I DO NOT WANT ...
...TO HARM THE WIFE AND CHILD EVEN MORE...
I CAME HERE PRE-PARED ...
...TO BE KILLED BY HIM...
PLEASE LET THEM GO...
NO...
TANI SENSEI ...!

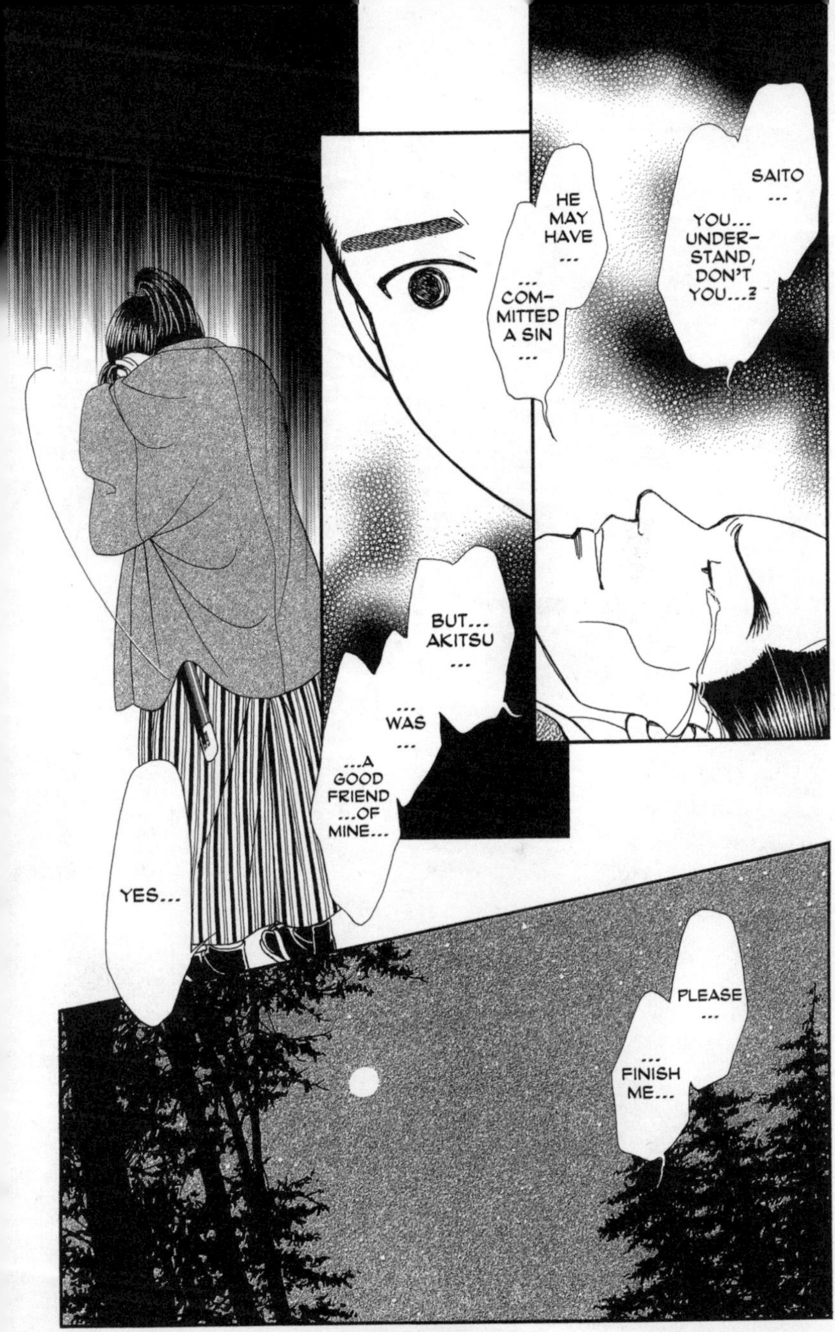
SAITO ...
YOU... UNDER-STAND, DON'T YOU...?
HE MAY HAVE ...
... COM-MITTED A SIN ...
BUT... AKITSU ...
... WAS ...
...A GOOD FRIEND ...OF MINE...
YES...
PLEASE ...
... FINISH ME...

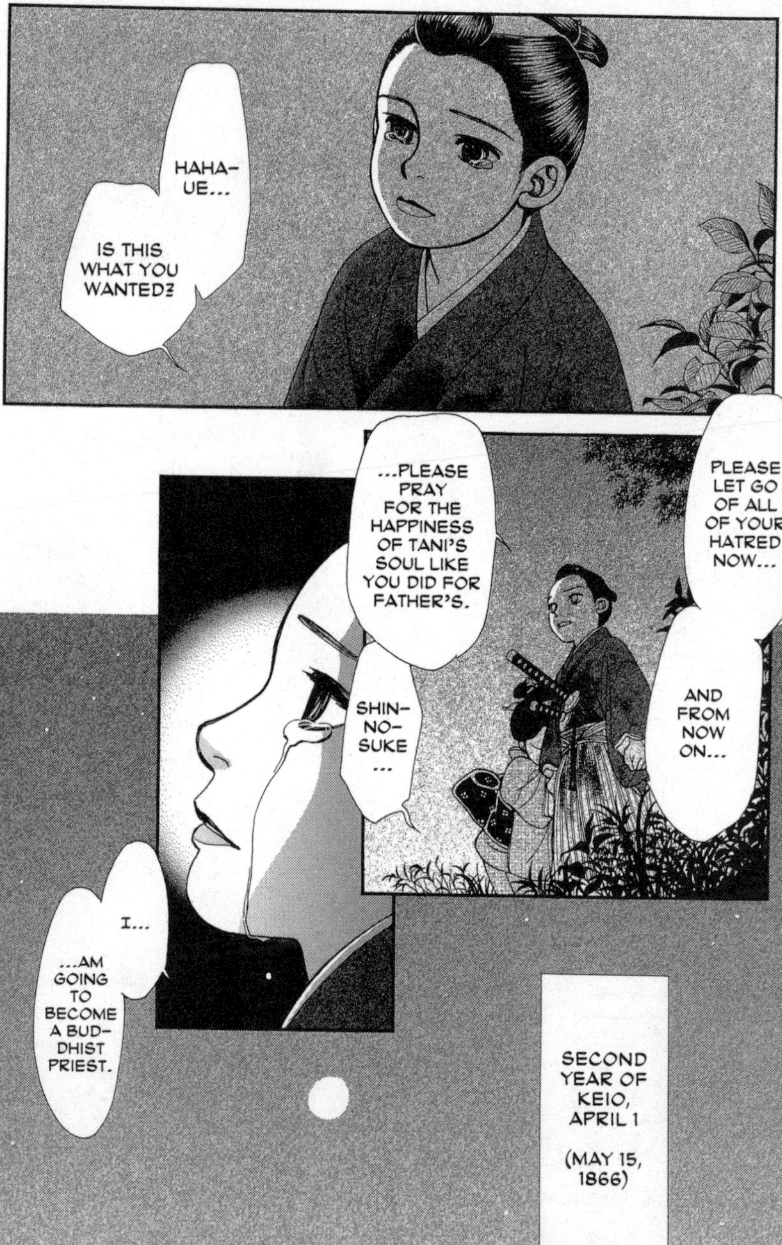
HAHAUE...
IS THIS WHAT YOU WANTED?
PLEASE LET GO OF ALL OF YOUR HATRED NOW...
AND FROM NOW ON...
...PLEASE PRAY FOR THE HAPPINESS OF TANI'S SOUL LIKE YOU DID FOR FATHER'S.
SHINNOSUKE...
I...
...AM GOING TO BECOME A BUDDHIST PRIEST.
SECOND YEAR OF KEIO, APRIL 1
(MAY 15, 1866)

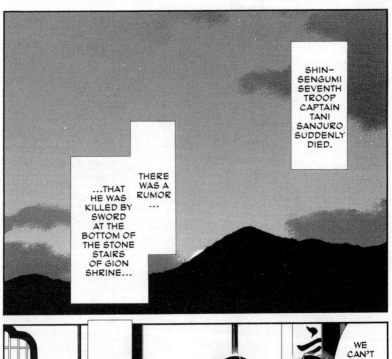

SHIN-SENGUMI SEVENTH TROOP CAPTAIN TANI SANJURO SUDDENLY DIED.
THERE WAS A RUMOR...
...THAT HE WAS KILLED BY SWORD AT THE BOTTOM OF THE STONE STAIRS OF GION SHRINE...
WE CAN'T RECORD HIS DEATH AS "KILLED IN RE-VENGE."
I SEE...
IT WAS A FINE DEATH, JUST LIKE TANI SENSEI HIMSELF.
BUT SAITO SHOWED RESPECT...
...AND HIS DEATH WAS ONLY RECORDED BY THE SHINSEN-GUMI AS "DEATH BY ILLNESS."
THIS REVENGE TOOK PLACE BECAUSE OF ME...
SNIFF

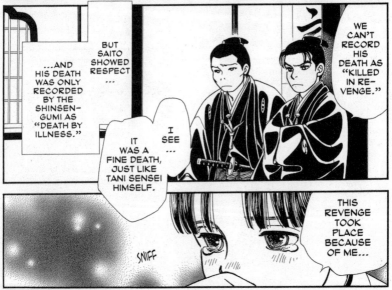

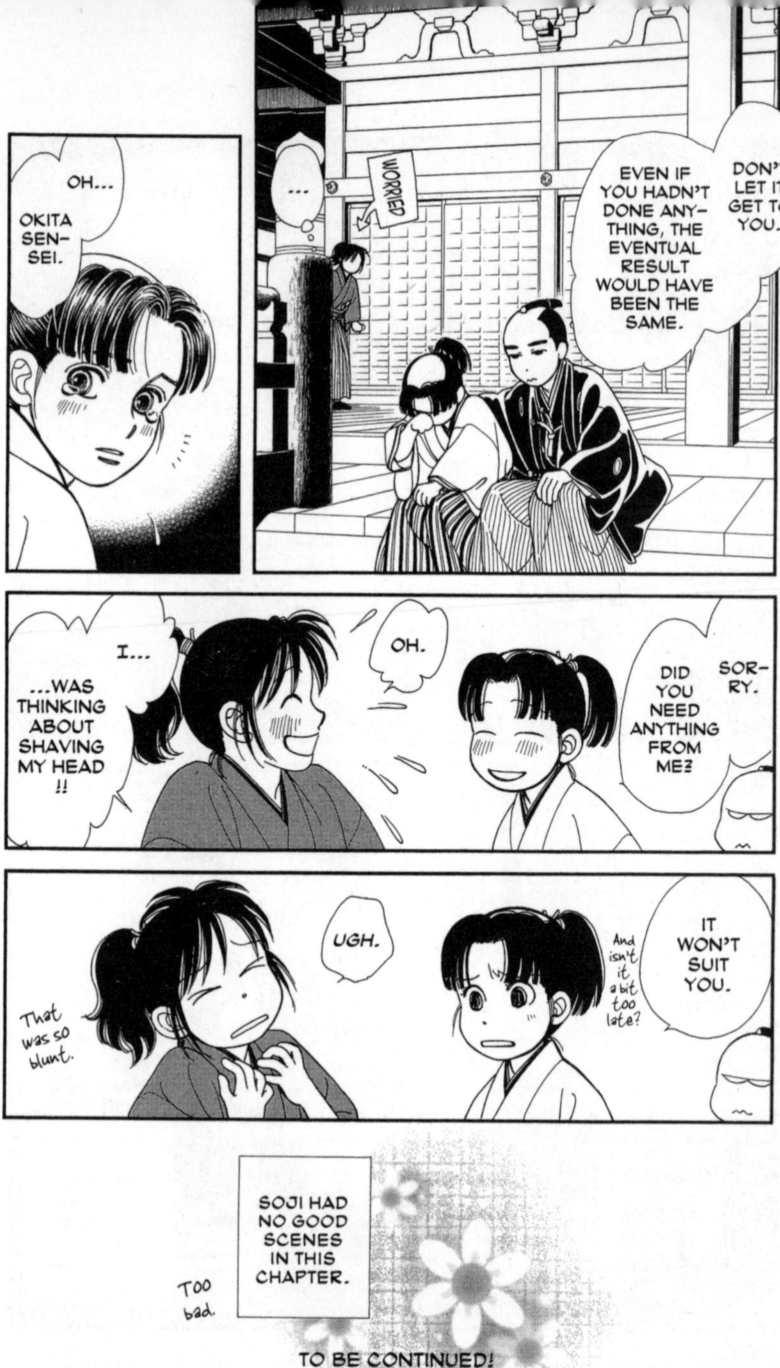
DON'T LET IT GET TO YOU.
EVEN IF YOU HADN'T DONE ANYTHING, THE EVENTUAL RESULT WOULD HAVE BEEN THE SAME.
...
WORRIED
OH...
OKITA SENSEI.
SORRY.
DID YOU NEED ANYTHING FROM ME?
OH.
I...
...WAS THINKING ABOUT SHAVING MY HEAD!!
IT WON'T SUIT YOU.
And isn't it a bit too late?
UGH.
That was so blunt.
SOJI HAD NO GOOD SCENES IN THIS CHAPTER.
Too bad.
TO BE CONTINUED!

TAEKO WATANABE PRESENTS

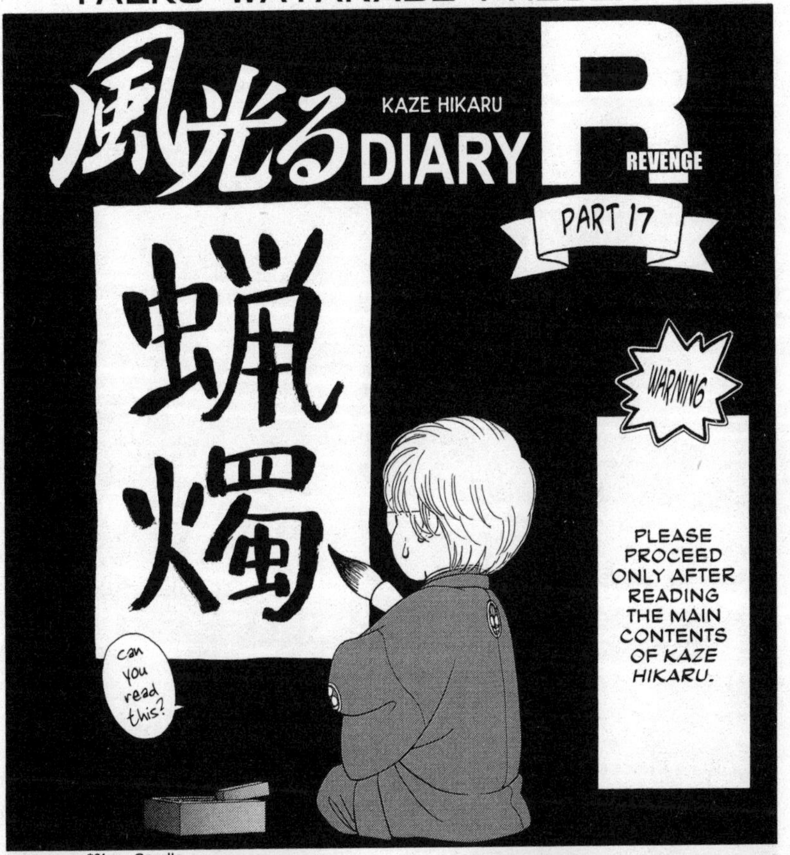
風光る KAZE HIKARU DIARY R REVENGE
PART 17
蝋燭
WARNING
PLEASE PROCEED ONLY AFTER READING THE MAIN CONTENTS OF KAZE HIKARU.
can you read this?

*Sign: Candle

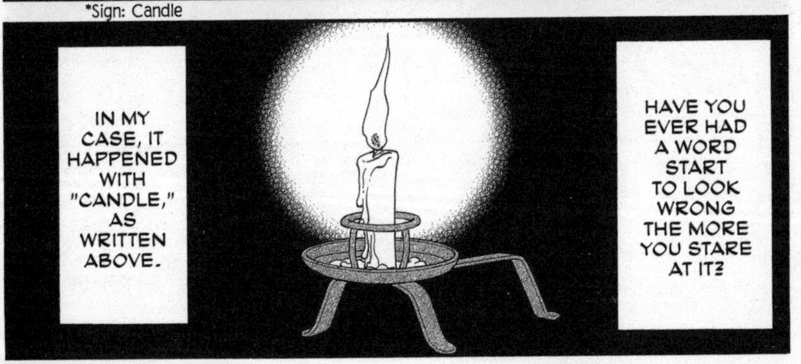
HAVE YOU EVER HAD A WORD START TO LOOK WRONG THE MORE YOU STARE AT IT?
IN MY CASE, IT HAPPENED WITH "CANDLE," AS WRITTEN ABOVE.

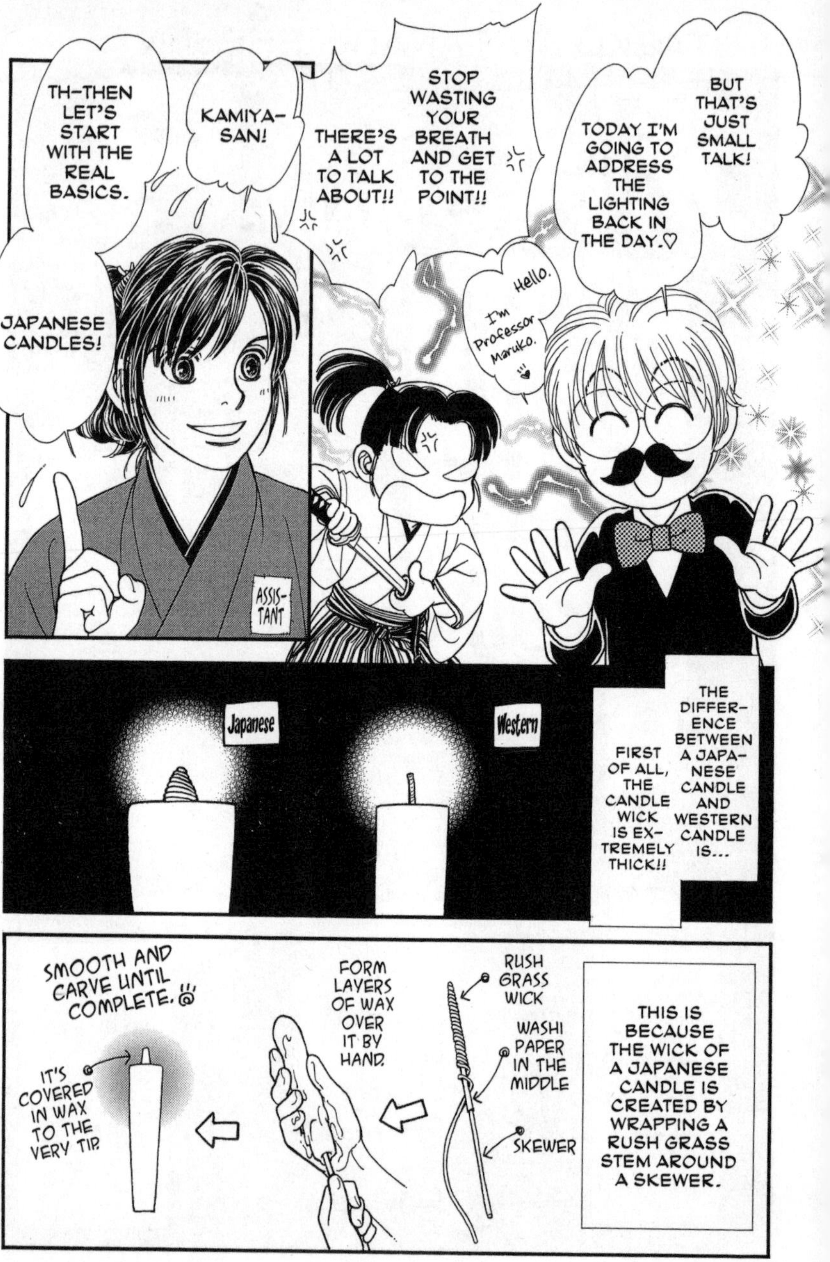
BUT THAT'S JUST SMALL TALK!
TODAY I'M GOING TO ADDRESS THE LIGHTING BACK IN THE DAY.♡
STOP WASTING YOUR BREATH AND GET TO THE POINT!!
THERE'S A LOT TO TALK ABOUT!!
Hello. I'm Professor Maruko.
KAMIYA-SAN!
TH-THEN LET'S START WITH THE REAL BASICS.
JAPANESE CANDLES!
ASSIS-TANT
THE DIFFER-ENCE BETWEEN A JAPA-NESE CANDLE AND WESTERN CANDLE IS...
FIRST OF ALL, THE CANDLE WICK IS EX-TREMELY THICK!!
Western
Japanese
THIS IS BECAUSE THE WICK OF A JAPANESE CANDLE IS CREATED BY WRAPPING A RUSH GRASS STEM AROUND A SKEWER.
RUSH GRASS WICK
WASHI PAPER IN THE MIDDLE
SKEWER
FORM LAYERS OF WAX OVER IT BY HAND.
SMOOTH AND CARVE UNTIL COMPLETE.
IT'S COVERED IN WAX TO THE VERY TIP.

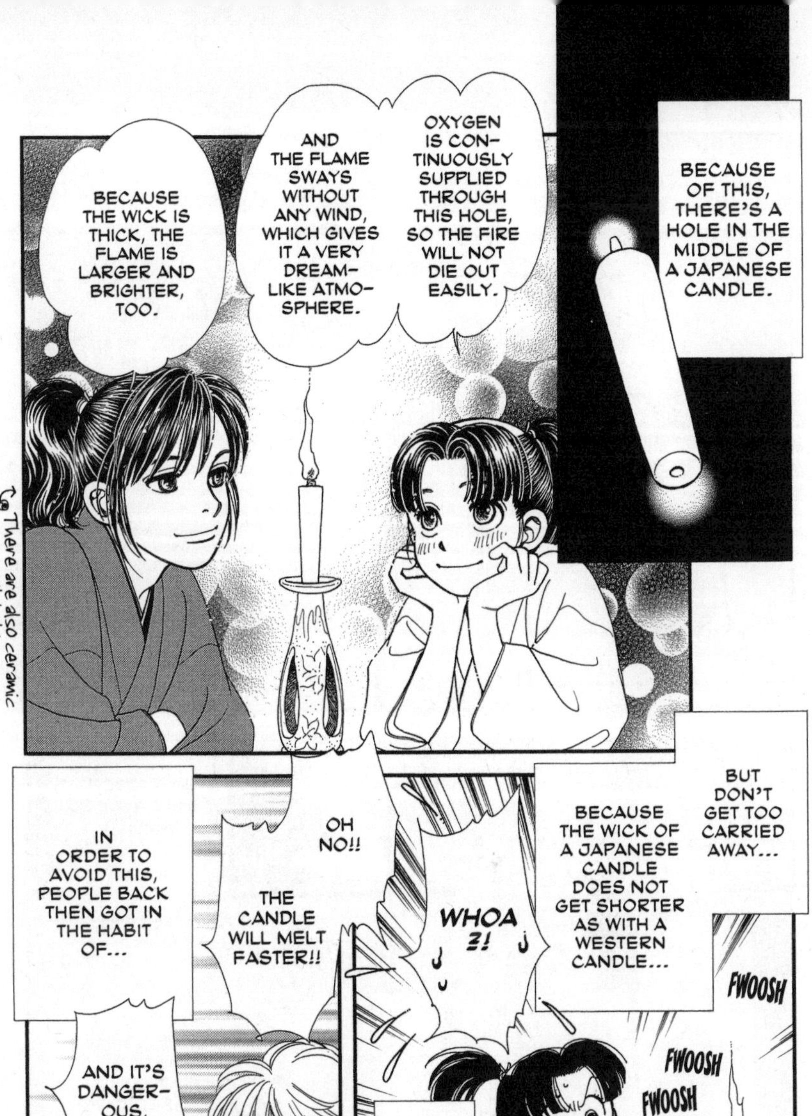
BECAUSE OF THIS, THERE'S A HOLE IN THE MIDDLE OF A JAPANESE CANDLE.
OXYGEN IS CONTINUOUSLY SUPPLIED THROUGH THIS HOLE, SO THE FIRE WILL NOT DIE OUT EASILY.
AND THE FLAME SWAYS WITHOUT ANY WIND, WHICH GIVES IT A VERY DREAMLIKE ATMOSPHERE.
BECAUSE THE WICK IS THICK, THE FLAME IS LARGER AND BRIGHTER, TOO.
There are also ceramic candleholders.
BUT DON'T GET TOO CARRIED AWAY...
BECAUSE THE WICK OF A JAPANESE CANDLE DOES NOT GET SHORTER AS WITH A WESTERN CANDLE...
WHOA ?!
FWOOSH
FWOOSH
FWOOSH
...THIS CAN HAPPEN QUITE OFTEN.
OH NO!!
THE CANDLE WILL MELT FASTER!!
IN ORDER TO AVOID THIS, PEOPLE BACK THEN GOT IN THE HABIT OF...
AND IT'S DANGEROUS, TOO!!
HURRY, SOJI!!

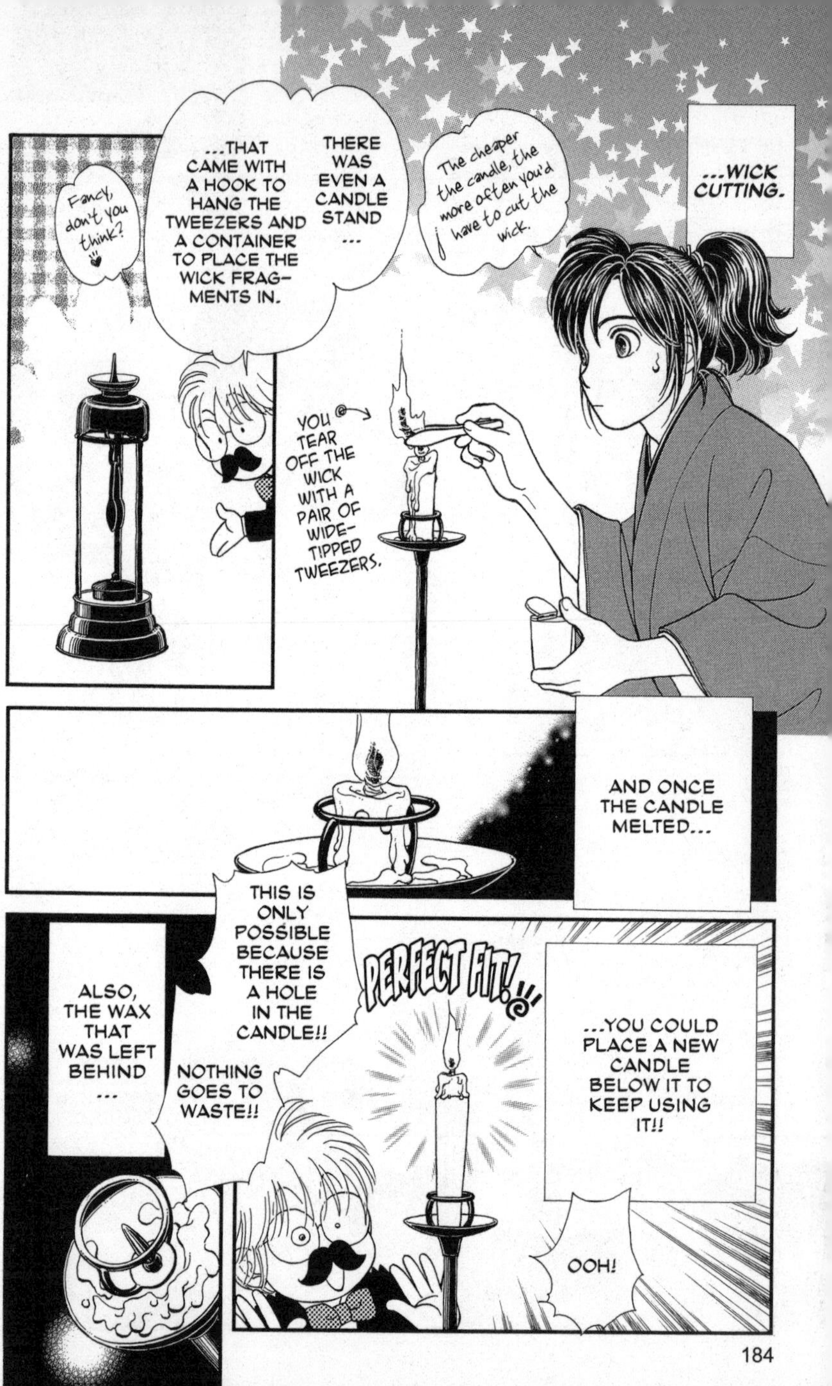
...WICK CUTTING.
YOU TEAR OFF THE WICK WITH A PAIR OF WIDE-TIPPED TWEEZERS.
The cheaper the candle, the more often you'd have to cut the wick.
THERE WAS EVEN A CANDLE STAND ...
...THAT CAME WITH A HOOK TO HANG THE TWEEZERS AND A CONTAINER TO PLACE THE WICK FRAGMENTS IN.
Fancy, don't you think?
AND ONCE THE CANDLE MELTED...
...YOU COULD PLACE A NEW CANDLE BELOW IT TO KEEP USING IT!!
PERFECT FIT!!!
OOH!
THIS IS ONLY POSSIBLE BECAUSE THERE IS A HOLE IN THE CANDLE!!
NOTHING GOES TO WASTE!!
ALSO, THE WAX THAT WAS LEFT BEHIND ...

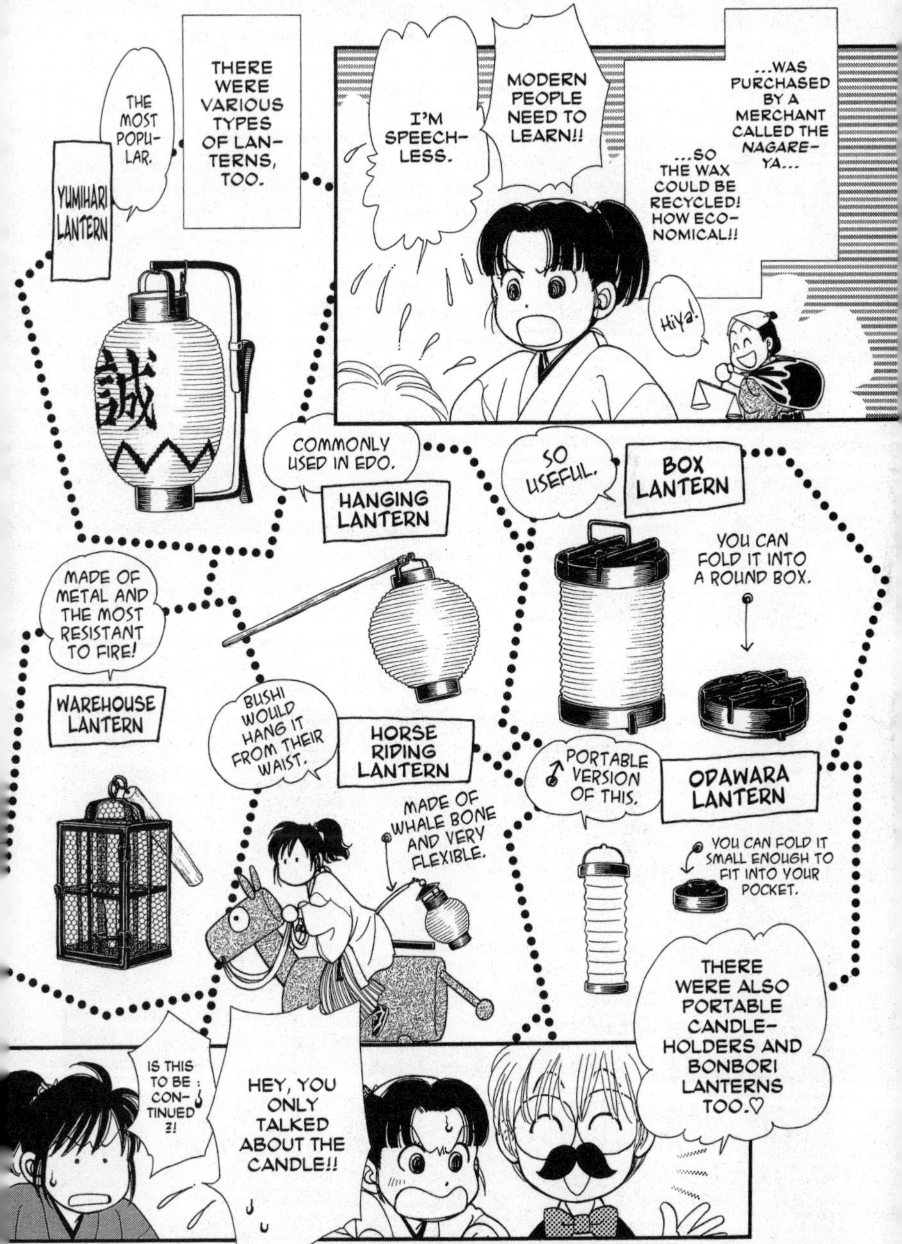
...WAS PURCHASED BY A MERCHANT CALLED THE NAGARE-YA...
...SO THE WAX COULD BE RECYCLED! HOW ECONOMICAL!!
Hiya!
MODERN PEOPLE NEED TO LEARN!!
I'M SPEECHLESS.
THERE WERE VARIOUS TYPES OF LANTERNS, TOO.
THE MOST POPULAR.
YUMIHARI LANTERN
BOX LANTERN
SO USEFUL.
YOU CAN FOLD IT INTO A ROUND BOX.
COMMONLY USED IN EDO.
HANGING LANTERN
MADE OF METAL AND THE MOST RESISTANT TO FIRE!
WAREHOUSE LANTERN
ODAWARA LANTERN
PORTABLE VERSION OF THIS.
YOU CAN FOLD IT SMALL ENOUGH TO FIT INTO YOUR POCKET.
HORSE RIDING LANTERN
BUSHI WOULD HANG IT FROM THEIR WAIST.
MADE OF WHALE BONE AND VERY FLEXIBLE.
THERE WERE ALSO PORTABLE CANDLE-HOLDERS AND BONBORI LANTERNS TOO.♡
HEY, YOU ONLY TALKED ABOUT THE CANDLE!!
IS THIS TO BE CONTINUED?!

Kaze Hikaru Diary R: The End

Decoding Kaze Hikaru

Kaze Hikaru is a historical drama based in 19th century Japan and thus contains some fairly mystifying terminology. In this glossary we'll break down archaic phrases, terms and other linguistic curiosities for you so that you can move through life with the smug assurance that you are indeed a know-it-all.

First and foremost, because *Kaze Hikaru* is a period story, we kept all character names in their traditional Japanese form—that is, family name followed by first name. For example, the character Okita Soji's family name is Okita and his personal name is Soji.

ANI-UE:
Formal term for an older brother.

BAKUFU:
Literally, "tent government." Shogunate; the feudal, military government that dominated Japan for more than 200 years.

BONBORI:
A Japanese paper lantern that often plays a role in traditional festivals.

BUSHI:
A samurai or warrior (part of the compound word *bushido*, which means "way of the warrior").

-CHAN:
A diminutive suffix that conveys endearment.

-DAYU:
An honorific suffix indicating the highest-ranking courtesan (*yujo*).

-DONO:
An honorific suffix that implies "Lord" or "Master."

GEIKO:
The term used in Kyoto for "geisha."

GENJI ERA:
The time period between March 1864 and April 1865.

HAHA-UE:
A term meaning "Mother."

HAN:

A feudal domain of Japan during the Edo period.

-HAN:

The same as the honorific *-san*, pronounced in the dialect of southern Japan.

HONGANJI:

A Buddhist temple.

IROKO:

A male prostitute.

KAISHAKU:

The official overseeing the beheading of one committing seppuku.

KIYOMIZU-DERA TEMPLE:

A famed Buddhist temple of Kyoto, founded in 778 and constructed without the use of nails.

KOSHO:

A Shinsengumi captain's personal assistant.

-KUN:

An honorific suffix that indicates a difference in rank and title. The use of *-kun* is also a way of indicating familiarity and friendliness between students or compatriots.

MIBU ROSHI or MIBURO:

A group of warriors that supports the Bakufu.

NEE-SAMA:

A respectful term for a sister or female relative.

NISHIKI-E:

A Japanese colored woodblock print of the era, often illustrating social scenes.

OBI:

Belt worn with a kimono.

OKAMI:

Female innkeeper.

OKIYA:

A lodging house for geisha in training.

ONI

Literally, "ogre."

RAKUGAN:

A traditional Japanese hard candy made of rice flour and powdered sugar.

RONIN:

Masterless samurai.

RYO:

At the time of this story, one and a half *ryo* was enough currency to support a family of five for an entire month.

-SAMA:

An honorific suffix used for one of higher rank; a more respectful version of *-san*.

-SAN:

An honorific suffix that carries the meaning of "Mr." or "Ms."

SENSEI:

A teacher, master or instructor.

SEPPUKU:

A ritualistic suicide that was considered a privilege of the nobility and samurai elite.

SHIMABARA:

Formerly the red-light district in Kyoto.

SHUDO:

A romantic relationship between a younger samurai and his older mentor.

SONJO-HA:

Those loyal to the emperor and dedicated to the expulsion of foreigners from the country.

TABI:

Traditional Japanese split-toe socks.

TEN'NEN RISHIN-RYU:

The form of martial art practiced by members of the Shinsengumi.

TOKUGAWA BAKUFU:

The last feudal military government of Japan's pre-modern period, directed by hereditary leaders—shoguns—of the Tokugawa clan.

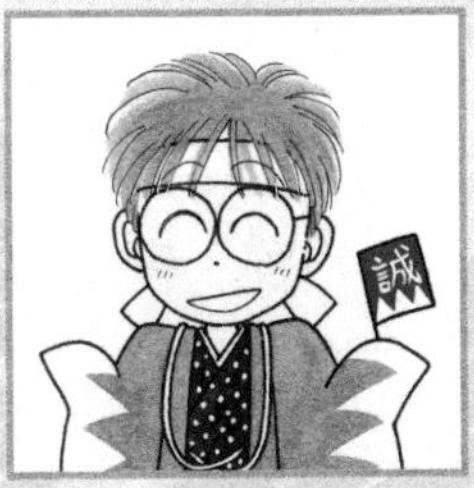
誠

Hello, it's me, the klutz. (Please read the previous volume, haha.) Thanks to everyone's support, I've now reached my 30th anniversary* as a manga artist. I often hear people say, "My mother and I both read your work!" So now I can't wait to hear people tell me, "My grandchild is a fan of yours too!" (haha). A resident of Edo (Edokko) was only recognized as being authentic when they had lived there for three generations, so don't you think a manga artist is only authentic if they have three generations of fans? (haha). Anyway, the seasonal word for this volume is *koshitayami*, or "shadow beneath the tree." The location where Soji is standing in the front cover illustration is exactly that. Ooh, the pleasure of taking off your hat here, after walking under the blazing sun for hours! And the expression on that dull guy's face as he watches Sei... Being able to imagine that is the essence of standing under the shadow beneath a tree, don't you think? ♡

*Original Japanese tankoban was published in 2009.

Taeko Watanabe debuted as a manga artist in 1979 with her story *Waka-chan no Netsuai Jidai* (Love Struck Days of Waka). *Kaze Hikaru* is her longest-running series, but she has created a number of other popular series. Watanabe is a two-time winner of the prestigious Shogakukan Manga Award in the girls' category—her manga *Hajime-chan ga Ichiban!* (Hajime-chan Is Number One!) claimed the award in 1991, and *Kaze Hikaru* took it in 2003.

Watanabe read hundreds of historical sources to create *Kaze Hikaru.* She is from Tokyo.

KAZE HIKARU
VOL. 26
Shojo Beat Edition

STORY AND ART BY
TAEKO WATANABE

KAZE HIKARU Vol. 26
by Taeko WATANABE
© 1997 Taeko WATANABE
All rights reserved.
Original Japanese edition published by SHOGAKUKAN.
English translation rights in the United States of America and Canada arranged with
SHOGAKUKAN.

Translation & English Adaptation/Tetsuichiro Miyaki
Touch-up Art & Lettering/Rina Mapa
Design/Veronica Casson
Editor/Megan Bates

Printed in the U.S.A.

Published by VIZ Media, LLC
P.O. Box 77010
San Francisco, CA 94107

10 9 8 7 6 5 4 3 2 1
First printing, August 2018

viz.com

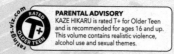

PARENTAL ADVISORY
KAZE HIKARU is rated T+ for Older Teen
and is recommended for ages 16 and up.
This volume contains realistic violence,
alcohol use and sexual themes.

shojobeat.com

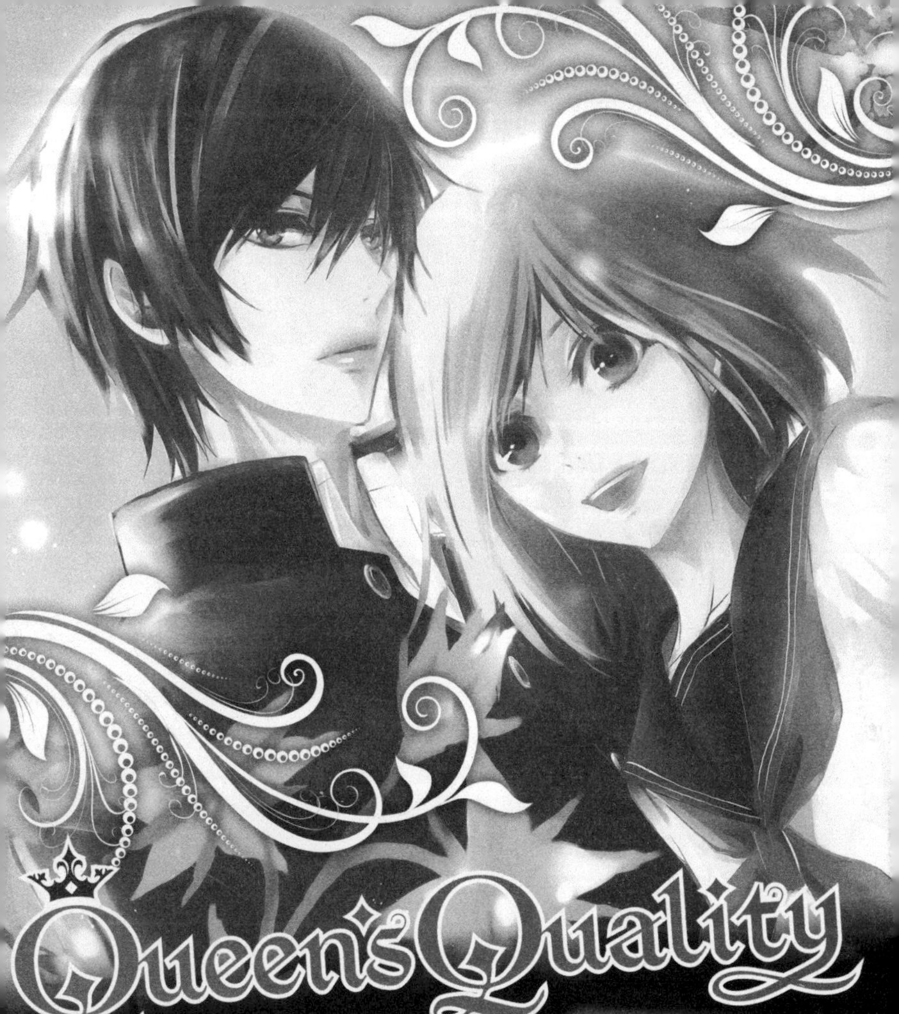
Queen's Quality

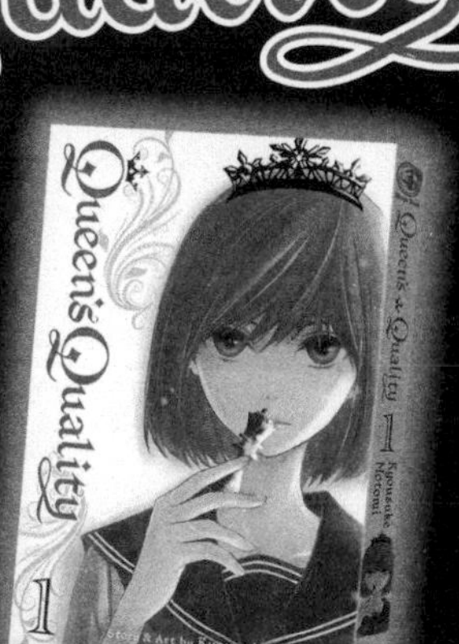
Queen's Quality
1
Queen's Quality 1 Kyousuke Motomi
Story & Art by Kyousuke Motomi

SURPRISE

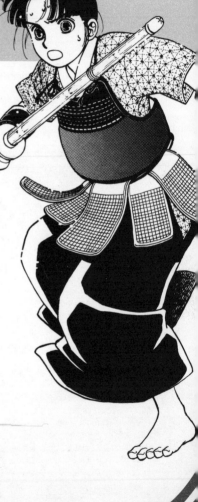

You may be reading the wrong way!

It's true: In keeping with the original Japanese comic format, this book reads from right to left—so action, sound effects, and word balloons are completely reversed. This preserves the orientation of the original artwork—plus, it's fun! Check out the diagram shown here to get the hang of things, and then turn to the other side of the book to get started!

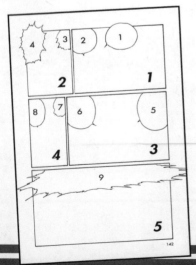